WEB WEAVING

DESIGNING AND MANAGING AN EFFECTIVE WEB SITE

Eric Tilton, Carl Steadman, and Tyler Jones

Addison-Wesley Developers Press

Reading, Massachusetts • Menlo Park, California • New York
Don Mills, Ontario • Wokingham, England • Amsterdam
Bonn • Sydney • Singapore • Tokyo • Madrid • San Juan
Paris • Seoul • Milan • Mexico City • Taipei

Copyright © 1996 by Eric Tilton, Carl Steadman, and Tyler Jones
ISBN 0-201-48959-7

Sponsoring Editor: Kim Fryer
Project Manager: Vicki L. Hochstedler
Cover design: Ann Gallager
Set in 11-point Palatino by the Clarinda Company

1 2 3 4 5 6 7 8 9 -MA- 9998979695
First printing, December 1995

A-W Developers Press is a division of Addison-Wesley Publishing Company.

Addison-Wesley books are available for bulk purchases by corporations, institutions, and other organizations. For more information please contact the Corporate, Government and Special Sales Department at (800) 238-9682.

Find us on the World-Wide Web at:
http://www.aw.com/devpress/

Contents

Preface

Introductory remarks to books on the World Wide Web tend to promise some on-line utopia of instant information, entertainment, and gratification. Perhaps this is just the nature of the writer who sets out to author a book on hypertext: for those of us who have waited decades for an on-line, linked repository of information, it's almost impossible to write about the World Wide Web except in the glowing words of a "hyper" text, with a hyper-enthusiasm that seems inexhaustible.

But newcomers to the Internet and the World Wide Web—drawn to the on-line "docuverse" so hyped in the popular press—often return tired and disappointed from their first trip through cyberspace, claiming there's no "there" there.

Although it's a common reaction to nod, mutter, and pass out a few URLs to more interesting lands, these first-time impressions shouldn't be so quickly dismissed: talk to users who haven't already managed their expectations based on many hours spent online (because that resource you're looking for always seems to be beyond the next link), and you'll find a set of expectations that simply aren't being met.

If we do take these initial reactions seriously, who's to blame? Readers, accustomed to their role as passive consumers, are often disappointed with the content of the on-line world, with resources that consume only a fraction of the bandwidth of a motion picture, TV program, or radio broadcast—and the proportionally fewer bells and whistles of an on-line "multimedia" environment such as the World Wide Web. Indeed, oftentimes, reading is a misnomer—"browsing" is commonly the on-line equivalent of channel surfing, with a rapid-fire assault of inlined images and blinking banners, with rare interludes of content that is useful and stimulating to the information grazer.

Certainly, content providers can do more, by providing content that is moving, involving, and relevant, and by organizing that information in such a way as to become both navigable and useful to users. This is the purpose of the book you hold in your hands, to offer content providers the information necessary to produce sites that will encourage people to involve themselves with the resources made available to them, while giving publishers the foresight necessary to build sites that are both maintainable and scaleable, so sites can become true information repositories, and grow in both breadth and depth over time.

But a burden remains on readers to continue to demand more—and not necessarily from those already providing content on the Web. The complaints of shallowness leveled at the Web by users disregard one of the Web's greatest strengths—the ease with which one can provide new resources. It's as if someone gives you a four-pack of Play-Doh,[1] and you open up each container, peer inside, and declare that it smells funny and doesn't do much.

You get out of anything exactly what you put into it. It's no different with the Web. If you seem to have difficulty finding appealing content, it may be because someone like you hasn't made the effort to put content you find appealing on-line yet. That's not to say

---

1. Or a recipe for a Play-Doh substitute:

Ingredients:

1 cup flour
1/2 cup salt
2 teaspoons cream of tartar
2 tablespoons vegetable oil
1 cup water

food coloring

Mix flour, salt, and cream of tartar. In a separate bowl, mix the oil and water (and you thought oil and water don't mix). Combine all ingredients. Add food coloring as desired. Stir over low heat until the mixture forms a ball. Remove from heat and knead. Lasts 4–6 weeks.

Of course, this isn't as good as the real thing, but Play-Doh's not the real thing, either. (And if pointing that out seems to do some harm to our metaphor, it's meant to. There is another world outside your computer screen, one infinitely more rich and earthy, if lacking a bit in neon shades. Never become so engrossed in the phosphorescent glow of your computer screen as to lose sight of the world that surrounds it.)

that there's not already appealing and compelling content on the Web; there is. But that's because someone had a story to tell, a product to sell, or a vision to share (and is there any real difference between these?), and to do so made himself or herself an active participant instead of a passive reader. There is a richness here that so far is untouchable by any other form of mass media; a breaking down of the dichotomy between the consumer and the producer, the reader and the writer, the broadcaster and the receiver.

Wherever you go, there you are. If there's no there there, it may be necessary to claim your own space, and contribute what you can—as an individual, as a collective, or as a representative of your organization—to the global, on-line community. As you do so, you bring the Web closer to the diversely rich cultural archive so often anticipated, yet still awaited. By all of us.

Audience

This book deals with creating content on the World Wide Web. If you're not already familiar with the Web, you'll want to become so before using this book—you might browse the section on clients and servers in Chapter 1, and find another text that can walk you through using a Web browser on the Internet.

This is not an introductory text to HTML (Hypertext Markup Language). However, Chapter 3 walks you through all the needed basics of HTML, and goes beyond the dynamics of a single HTML document by calling attention to issues that affect your Web as a whole. In addition, Chapter 13 provides a complete, detailed HTML reference. If you only plan on putting up a single, vanity homepage, though, and to go no further, there might be other books better suited to your needs. This is also not an introduction to programming, although Chapter 8 does provide an introduction to using the Common Gateway Interface (CGI) programming interface. Be warned that Chapter 8 expects familiarity with programming, especially in Perl.

What this book *is*, then, is a resource for those who wish to create Webs that are easily navigable for the user, and that are both scaleable and maintainable for the provider. If we've done our jobs, *Web Weaving* will save you time by helping you create a site that, if you're just starting out, is well-structured from the start; or, if you're now restructuring your site in order to grow or refocus it, by helping you avoid other common oversights that might cause you to go back and restructure your site yet another time.

And even if you're not in charge of an entire Web server, *Web Weaving* can help with the creation and maintenance of any large body of documents that you, your group, or your organization may want to put on-line via a Web server maintained by others.

So . . . Why Isn't This Book on the Web . . . on the Web?

With these words being written by such fans of hypertext, you might think that a more logical place for such a work would be on-line. Indeed, a portion of this book is available on the Web, since Eric maintains his style guide (Chapters 11 and 12) on-line, which predates this book. The on-line edition can be found at:

```
http://www.cs.cmu.edu/~tilt/cgh/
```

However, we think you will find this book useful in printed form. It's true that an on-line book could be kept updated (though whether it indeed would be is another question) as the Web continues spinning in different directions; but working with more immutable print as a destination for these words has kept us focused on those aspects of Web design and administration that will remain timeless and important whatever the newest HTML tags are. And it's these aspects, which we gather under the umbrella of managing an infostructure, that will probably be of greatest value to a Web designer.

A printed book can be more immediate than an on-line resource, as well, in that it's always available as a reference, whatever the status of your network or the amount of real estate you might have on your virtual desktop at any given moment. And even today, a printed book available at the local bookstore will reach an audience it might not otherwise find if it were only available as bits instead of atoms.

That said, the authors have all published extensively on the Web. See *About the Authors,* below, for locations of on-line resources we provide.

About the Authors

Eric Tilton is a Graduate Fellow at Carnegie Mellon University, which some suspect is because he doesn't know what he would do with himself if he weren't on a campus somewhere. He is co-author of the Internet textbook, *Every Student's Guide to the Internet,* and has been working with HTML, the World Wide Web, and the Internet since before they became household words. He has managed the Web servers for Willamette University, built the document management system for the Oregon Online state government information gopher (`gopher://gopher.state.or.us/`), and maintains Composing Good HTML (`http://www.cs.cmu.edu/~tilt/cgh/`), a popular on-line style guide. His next project is to move to Pittsburgh and learn how to "redd up some gumbands" (if you don't get that last joke, don't worry, neither does he).

Carl Steadman is the Production Director for HotWired (`http://www.hotwired.com/`), and the World Wide Web editor for CTHEORY (`http://english-www.hss.cmu.edu/`). During the writing of this book, he went through the (for him) arduous task of packing all his belongings, transporting them more than 2,000 miles, and unpacking them again, all the while reflecting on the amount of private possessions he's acquired in the last decade, especially as compared to his cat. A complete listing of the on-line resources he provides can be found at Bordeaux and Prague (`http://www.winternet.com/~carl/`).

Tyler Jones graduated from Willamette University in 1995 with a major in Computer Science. During his undergraduate years, he made a name for himself on the Web by organizing the Human-Languages Page (`http://www.willamette.edu/~tjones/`

Language-Page.html) and writing the popular WebChess chess server (http://www.willamette.edu/~tjones/ chessmain.html), both of which are internationally renowned sites. Tyler plans to attend graduate school to work toward a Ph.D. in Computer Science, while continuing and expanding his development on the Web.

Acknowledgments

Books, despite the illusion of the author, are never simply a production of one person (or three, in this case). Many people have helped guide and shape this work, and we are indebted to all of them.

Eric says: I would like to thank everyone at Willamette Integrated Technology Services and the Mark O. Hatfield Library, for providing a place to grow and learn about this wonderful Internet thing; Keiko Pitter, for leading me down the dark road to writing (and for that wonderful Author's Pen); Sara Amato, for asking the right questions and knowing the right answers; my family, who didn't know what they were doing when they brought home that Apple] [+ so many years ago; and, most important, I would like to thank Jeliza Patterson for *everything*, but especially for reading over every word here and making sure we still made sense after hours and hours of dazed writing.

Carl says: I'd like to thank everyone at the Star Tribune Online and the University of Minnesota's Center for the Development of Technological Leadership for understanding my time commitment to this project; HotWired Ventured LLC, for giving me a place to live; and all the people that make HotWired what it is, for the quick friendships, and allowing me to call dibs; Melissa Pauna and T. Jay Fowler, for help with my day-to-day activities while I was hard at work on my text; Benjamin Koo, for being a friend; Matt Lee, for asking the really basic questions over a beer; Barry Boone, Jim Hurley, and Andrew Williams, for looking at the book in it earliest stages; the Krokers, John Mowitt, Joe Austin, Liz McLemore, Geoff Sauer, and the members of the English Collective; and everyone who took the time to share a kind word for my Web pages. Special thanks to Jeff Curtis, for the Freedonia illustration, and to Joey Anuff, for his kind assistance with Chapter 4. I've thought of Andra a lot while I've been working on this project. While this isn't the book to dedicate to her, none of this would have been possible without her.

Tyler says: I'd like to thank Eric Tilton, for keeping me in line and guiding me through the rough spots; Jennifer Chambers, for being there and being my friend; Willamette University, for getting me on the Internet in the first place; Don Kirkwood at North Salem High School, for everything; Mindy Hart, Matt Hodson, and Aabra Jaggard, just because; everyone who took a look at our proposal and outline and showed us what we missed; Little Alex, for the world she will inherit; and of course, my parents, Alex and Linda, who were genuinely surprised when they heard about this.

We would also like to thank Vicki Hochstedler, who helped shepherd us through to the bitter end; Janice Borzendowski, who understood what we *meant,* which sometimes didn't correspond to what we *said;* and to Kim Fryer, who was more than just an editor.

1

Introduction

Infostructures and the Web

What is an Infostructure?

An *infra*structure, as we all know, refers to the physical substrate that must be laid down in order to provide a service. A notable example of an infrastructure is the U.S. national highway system, providing roads that make it possible to travel from nearly any point in the United States to nearly any other point. Similarly, there is the telephone infrastructure that makes it possible to speak from most points on the globe to most other points. Finally, the Internet is an infrastructure that provides global networking to millions of people. In all of these cases, the infrastructure refers solely to the wires, or the asphalt, and not to the things that ride on top.

An *info*structure is similar, except that it does not refer to anything physical. An infostructure is the layout of information in a manner such that it can be navigated—it's what is created any time an amount of information is organized in a useful fashion. A table of contents is an infostructure, as is a bibliography or an index. The World Wide Web as a whole is an infostructure. Each content provider, as he or she builds a Web, builds an infostructure.

As the Internet continues to grow in popularity and use, there will be more and more demand for the development of quality content to be transmitted over the wires. This content needs to be not only interesting and intelligent in and of itself, but it also needs to be well-organized and placed within the context of other information available on-line. There is an ever-increasing need for the construction of usable and intuitive infostructures.

Hypertext in particular has been claimed as a wonder technology that will change the way we organize information by mirroring the way we think. By providing tools for allowing us to structure information in an associative way—in the same way that our thought processes leap from topic to topic on the barest of connections—we are given the building blocks for building powerful structures of information. But hypertext has a vast potential for disorganization. Care must be taken to create structures that are flexible enough to allow exploration (anticipating connections that the reader may want to follow), while restrained enough so as not to overwhelm with too many choices.

What is Important in an Infostructure?

Take a look at existing examples—bibliographies or tables of contents, for instance. Traditional methods of making information available to readers—the editorial process—are being lost in the rush to make information available instantly, on-line. Much of what we've gained in speed on the way in is lost in time on the way out: there seems to be a trend to discard everything we've learned in the past millennia in favor of the "revolutionary new possibilities of the computer." What is often forgotten is that there is nothing new about what the computer does. This may seem a somewhat radical stance, but think about it for a moment—all computers do for us is simplify the task of moving data around. Computers make it easier for us to store, generate, and manipulate information, but they do not do anything that wasn't possible before—except, perhaps, in terms of sheer volume of information processed. Computer technology only speeds up and automates the things we've always done to process information.

For example, we could have called up text and graphic images from halfway around the world 20 years before the advent of hypertext browsers, using a system called Interlibrary Loan. In addition, it would have been possible to follow the hypertext links from those documents by looking at the footnotes and retrieving the documents in question.

Now, obviously, this example is exaggerated, but it is exaggerated to make a point. What the World Wide Web and the Internet have done is to further cheapen the effort involved in finding information. Instead of waiting a week for a document to arrive, we wait a minute. This changes our searching habits and the importance we place on expending energy in finding information. But at a deep and fundamental level, nothing has really changed. We're still interested in finding information as rapidly as possible, without having to slog through dozens of meaningless menus and side paths. In other words, browsing is fun, but it can quickly become tedious, especially in the data-rich environment of the Web. (Data-rich is a euphemism. We mean that there is much more irrelevant, irreverent, useless, and incorrect information available on-line than there is of any other kind. This doesn't mean that we don't enjoy wading through for entertainment's sake; it just means that we don't enjoy wading through it to find the relevant and correct information that we may *need* at a given time.)

There are two kinds of searching that are encouraged by the Web, and can be supported by a well-designed infostructure: the general and the specific. *General* searching is the kind of loosely directed searching done by individuals or agents who know what kind of information they are interested in, but don't know what specific information they seek. Examples of this include someone who is looking for information about euphoniums, for astronomical data, or for Web resources related to Latin. *Specific* searching is conducted by individuals or agents who knows exactly what information they seek: what the difference is between a euphonium and a baritone; the distance between the Earth and the Sun; or how a certain Latin sentence should be translated.

A good infostructure will support both. A well-designed infostructure should lead searchers to the information they desire in a short amount of time from initial contact; otherwise, the infostructure becomes relatively useless except for finding serendipitous information. If it took 10 minutes to follow ambiguous hyperlinks to find out from a library's on-line catalog whether the library held the *Principia Discordia,* the catalog would be considered useless by many.

A good infostructure benefits more than just readers, however; it leads to content that is easily maintained and updated through time. An ill-conceived infostructure can become a labyrinth in which documents can become lost; an ill-planned infostructure can suffer from enthusiastic authors who develop documents and never update them. Designing an infostructure is as much a question of developing the support structure for creation and maintenance as it is a question of creating and organizing the content itself.

These are ambitious goals, but important ones. Some of the issues involved are:

- **Organization of documents and document collections.** A Web server does not necessarily address only a single subject area, or provide a single service. Several collections of documents may coexist on a server, and each collection must be navigable and searchable. A related issue is the *maintenance* of documents, so that they remain accurate and current. Part I discusses ways to address organizing and maintaining at the document, collection, and service levels.

- **Server organization.** While each collection of information needs to be able to stand individually, the server as a whole must also be navigable and searchable. Readers must be able to find the information on a server easily, without having to stumble upon it. Conversely, related collections of documents should not be isolated, and ways should be provided to navigate within collections without having to search at a global level. Part II discusses the organization and maintenance of the infostructure at the server-wide level.

- **Content and style.** Organization and navigation are important, but they are subordinate to the real business at hand, which is providing usable content in usable form. Part III discusses the elements of style—which, if followed, can provide that usable form—from the document through the server level.

Servers and Clients

The Web divides its activities between *servers* and *clients.*

Servers make content available to the Web. Because the Web is "worldwide," servers are usually expected to be available 24 hours a day, 7 days a week, and require a dedicated, full-time connection to the Internet. The exception to this is servers that provide resources that are only intended for local use—such as an in-house documentation system. This book deals with the proper care and maintenance of servers and the content they provide. (See Chapter 6 for details on installing the actual server software.)

Clients, or browsers, make the content that servers provide available to users. Most often this is through an interactive display terminal of some type, but clients might also make this information available as hardcopy, as a voice readout, or as a summarized report—there's no restriction on how clients might make information provided by servers available to users, although the way that information is stored on the server—its infostructure—can make it less or more difficult for users to view information in the desired format. Unlike servers, clients don't require a full-time, dedicated connection.

The real power of the client/server abstraction is that it provides flexibility. A reader can use any number of clients, and a provider can use any number of servers, leaving the Web unbound to any specific hardware or software. A client can take advantage of the reader's local computing and display power, and a server can handle many more readers efficiently because it does not have the added overhead of interactively providing a user interface to each reader.

This division the Web makes between servers and clients can be likened to the difference between writers and readers. The server provides the information, the client uses it. Some of the early proponents of hypertext—of which the World Wide is a specific instance (see Chapter 2)—had hoped to see this division between writers and readers diminished, by envisioning a networked environment in which all readers had the ability to become authors by annotating text through the use of hypertext links. Although the current architecture of the Web, with its more or less strict division between servers and clients, tends to enforce the reader/writer dichotomy, content providers can allow readers to provide feedback, commentary, or to interactively revise documents through the creation of dynamic documents, as outlined in Chapter 8.

Organization of This Book (or, Where the Good Bits Are)

This book is one part philosophy and one part practical solutions. After reading it, you should be aware of the issues that you need to understand before creating and maintaining your Web server, and you should also be able to use the tools that will help you address these issues successfully.

You may not want to read this book straight through. Large chunks of most chapters (including 2, 4, 6, 8, and especially 13) are intended as reference material, covering similar topics and tools for Unix, Windows, and Macintosh platforms. Other parts are intended as stylistic and philosophical discussions, meant to give you food for thought on how to plant and tend your web; Chapters 3, 5, 11, and 12 are especially good in this area. Chapter 7—maintenance tools—falls somewhere between, providing practical solutions to the philosophical points raised elsewhere. Your best bet is to read the philosophical stuff first, check out the reference information for your platform, and then consider the various maintenance tools and tricks available to you.

On the other hand, reading from cover to cover might not be a bad idea. Such are the vagaries of the hypertext, even when it is in printed form, as it is here. But be warned: as you read, you'll find plenty of side trails referring you to other chapters, and staying on course may be quite a challenge!

Part I, *The Document,* introduces Web design at the document and service level.

- Chapter 2 is a discussion of the formats available for publishing documents, with an in-depth look at HTML, the Hypertext Markup Language.

- Chapter 3 provides a quickstart tutorial, going through, from the ground up, the design and implementation of a collection of documents that collectively provide a unified service.

- Chapter 4 describes the tools that can assist in the creation of documents, including in-depth looks at several HTML editors.

Part II, *The Web,* introduces Web design at the server level.

- Chapter 5 introduces the issues involved in content creation, organization, and maintenance.

- Chapter 6 describes several HTTP (Hypertext Transport Protocol) servers, including a close look at installation procedures for three of the most popular servers.

- Chapter 7 discusses tools that aid in automating maintenance of your Web server.

- Chapter 8 explains CGI scripts, a powerful tool for creating dynamic documents.

- Chapter 9 covers security: why it is useful, whether you need it, and how you can use it.

- Chapter 10 provides tips on publicizing your Web, so that you can attract the audience you desire.

Part III, *Style Guide,* revisits issues raised in Parts I and II. While Parts I and II are primarily concerned with technical issues involved in providing content on a Web server, Part III provides tips and techniques for making your documents—and your entire Web—a more effective infostructure for your audience and for you.

- Chapter 11 discusses elements of style for individual documents, from good practices in composing text and using images, to common errors to avoid in creating HTML code.

- Chapter 12 considers elements of style for the entire Web, including organization, usability, and content development.

Part IV, *HTML Reference,* provides a comprehensive reference to the Hypertext Markup Language, including HTML 2.0, 3.0, and the Netscape extensions.

Notation

We have used several notational conventions in this book in order to make it easier to understand what is what. New concepts are introduced in italic, and the names of programs are in initial capitals. When on-line resources are referred to, the URL (see Appendix A) is provided in fixed-width Courier. Because of their length, some of the URLs we list break across more than one line of text. If they break in the middle of a word, that word is hyphenated; however, this does not mean that the URL itself is hyphenated. If you have trouble with the URLs, try removing some or all of the hyphens. In addition, any long examples of HTML, C, and Perl code are set off in the text in:

```
fixed-width Courier
```

Any HTML, C, or Perl code that is referred to in the course of a sentence is also set in fixed-width.

Commands that you need to enter at the shell prompt appear in **boldface**.

In places, we have also included screen shots from browsers in order to give you an idea of what these infostructures will actually look like, under the same conditions that your audience will see them. Since different browsers render HTML differently, we have selected three that should give a good flavor of the diversity available:

- **Netscape Navigator 1.1N,** for MacOS, Microsoft Windows, and X Windows. Netscape is available via FTP from `ftp://ftp.netscape.com/netscape/`.

- **Arena 0.96,** the HTML 3.0 testbed browser, for X Windows. Arena is available from `ftp://ftp.w3.org/pub/www/arena/`.

- **Lynx,** the text-based browser, for Unix (version 2.3.7) and MS-DOS (version 0.8). Lynx is available from `ftp://ukanaix.cc.ukans.edu/pub/WWW/`.

Each figure is labeled so that you will know which browser has been used.

Because of the rapidly changing character of the Web, we have tried to address upcoming trends in Web design, as well as to cover the more standard and stable aspects. There are two potentially competing futures for HTML, which at the time of this writing may or may not converge back into a single stable path. These two directions are HTML 3.0 and the Netscape extensions (see Chapter 2). In order to give coverage to these, and to help you deal with the cutting edge without turning it into the bleeding edge, we have interspersed special sections through the HTML-related sections of the book that highlight issues specific to either.

Sections marked with this icon deal with a concept specific to the HTML 3.0 specification.

Sections marked with this icon deal with a concept specific to the Netscape extensions.

Part I

The Document

We begin our journey by considering the document itself as an infostructure. Like your web as a whole, your documents are entities that require careful organization and construction in order to be useful. And like your web as a whole, what you call a "document" may consist of several HTML, image, and sound files, interlinked into a cohesive whole. This section describes how to build the documents for your web.

We start in Chapter 2 by discussing the formats available to you for creating Web documents, especially concentrating on HTML, the Hypertext Markup Language. Chapter 3 dives in with a "quickstart" tutorial in HTML to get you started creating documents. Finally, Chapter 4 discusses some of the tools that are available for creating documents in HTML and other formats. Later, in Part III, Chapter 11 returns to the document, wrapping up our discussion with a document-level style guide.

2 Approaching Your Document as an Infostructure

The infostructure metaphor applies at many levels. You can think of your document as an infostructure, just as you can think of your Web as an infostructure. Although Chapter 3 will guide you through much of the thought that you should put into each document's design and how it might be incorporated into the rest of your infostructure, this chapter will cover some of the fundamental concepts of hypertext and the specific implementation of hypertext that is the World Wide Web. Also included are some guidelines on incorporating nontext data types (such as images, sound, and video), for creating true hypermedia documents.

Hypertext

Hypertext is text that is not constrained to be linear; that is, text with links. A link is an explicit connection from one text to another text. Links are common to most texts, and have existed in printed works for many years, as section and illustration references, footnotes, bibliographies, indexes, and notes in margins. Computers simply make the use of links immediate and transparent. The concept of hypertext is not new; Theodor Nelson first coined the term in the 1960s. The World Wide Web is a specific implementation of a networked hypertext system, first proposed at CERN, the European Laboratory for Particle Physics, in 1989.

Hypertext Bound

If hypertext, by making links between texts immediate and transparent, makes it possible to create a text without bounds—which could be seen, in the case of the World Wide Web, as the whole of the Web—it's the information provider's responsibility to group related text in a manner that makes this context easy to read and navigate. The fundamental unit for managing text after the paragraph and section levels is the *document.*

The word document is often used ambiguosly, depending upon its context. It is sometimes used to refer to a single "page" of hypertext, which might be a single screen or many screensful (which are "paged" or scrolled through) of information. Othertimes, it refers to a set of interrelated files that together form a document, the equivalent of a book or other reference work. This ambiguity points out one of the more powerful ways to organize information on the Web: by determining the organizational boundaries of a particular text—which obviously can be done many ways—you're making important decisions as to its readability and usefulness.

Some of the early theorists of hypertext claimed that all informational text could be divided into index-card size units. Indeed, organizing information in such a way can make for wonderfully complex collections of hypertext, with multiple paths to the same point, and multiple ways to traverse, or read, the document, which would be the collection taken as a whole, through the reader's eyes. The problem with arranging text in this way is that it's easy for a reader to become disoriented. Unless a browser manages a history of traversed links extremely well, readers may have to shuffle among these index card-sized containers repeatedly to find the information they need. This can prove a frustrating experience.

On the other extreme, you can flow all the text to a book-length work into a single file, creating a content listing at the beginning of the document, which links to sections within the document, delineated by the appropriate headings and divider bars. From the user's perspective, however, it's just as easy to get lost within the text as the prior example: instead of a maze of text, as before, we now have a crush of text, without the benefit of pagination to form physical, if not logical, breaks in the text, as we would if it were a printed work. However, if you see the document as primarily being printed and used as a paper resource—perish the thought—this way of organizing the text might be most appropriate.

Obviously, you need to find functional units that make sense within the logical structure of your document in order to decide how to divide it across a file system or database that stores your hypertext. Your goal should always be to allow readers to find the information they are seeking easily and quickly, while maintaining the context of that information within the larger whole of your hypertext.

HTML and Logical versus "Physical" Tags

The World Wide Web uses the Hypertext Markup Language, or HTML, both to define the structural characteristics of documents and to define links from one document to another. One of the original design goals of the World Wide Web project was to make information available across a wide variety of display hardware. Because of this, HTML was designed for a great degree of platform independence: one of its key attributes was, and is, to embed *markup tags* within plain, 7-bit (ASCII) text, making it available across a wide variety of systems.

Markup tags are generally used in pairs—an opening tag and a closing tag—as containers that describe the information within them. Tags are delimited from other text by angle brackets (⟨ and ⟩), and closing tags are labeled as such by a preceding slash (/), so that the common form can be abstracted as ⟨TAG⟩content⟨/TAG⟩. Something of this form—a start tag, some included content, and an end tag—constitutes an element. Elements such as EM, A, and LI are the building blocks by which authors describe the contents of their documents.

NOTE: The terms *element* and *tag* are often confused with each other. To keep them straight, remember this: a tag is what starts or ends an element, and is anything enclosed in angle brackets (⟨⟩). An element is everything, including the start tag, the end tag, and the content contained between them.

Not all elements contain content. Some elements, such as HR and IMG are *empty*, which means that they only have a start tag (e.g. ⟨HR⟩ or ⟨IMG⟩), contain no content, and have no end tag. And some tags that are empty in HTML 2.0 (P being the most notable example) are no longer empty in HTML 3.0. Chapter 13 describes the semantics of the various elements, as well as the difference between the various HTML specifications.

For example, the element EM describes emphasized text, so that

```
⟨EM⟩content that requires emphasis⟨/EM⟩
```

might be rendered as

content that requires emphasis

on a display that supports italic text. However, since EM is a *logical* element, a display that doesn't support italics can still display the contents of the tag to the user with emphasis—perhaps as underlined text. Figures 2.1 and 2.2 give real-world examples of this; the former shows how Netscape renders the text (in italics), and how Lynx renders it (underlined).

NOTE: Tags can either be upper- or lowercase; however, we'll represent them as all uppercase throughout this book. Using all uppercase tags allows us to more easily identify tags amongst other text in HTML documents.

For example, the element EM describes emphasized text, so that

<EM>content which requires emphasis</EM>

might be rendered as

content which requires emphasis

on a display which supports italic text. However, since EM is a logical element, a display which doesn't support italics can still display the contents of the tag to the user with emphasis -- perhaps as underlined

---

Figure 2.1
EM Rendering
(Netscape)

HTML also contains elements that describe the *physical* characteristics of text. For example, if we wished to simply specify italicized text in the preceding example, we could have used the I element, as in

```
⟨I⟩content that should be italicized⟨/I⟩
```

At first glance, the difference between logical and physical elements might seem minimal—after all, a browser that doesn't include italic support can just display all italicized text as underlined. However, logical elements store important information about content that is lost when physical elements are used instead. Take, for example, the book title *Web Weaving.* If we use the physi-

```
For example, the element EM describes emphasized text, so that

  <EM>content which requires emphasis</EM>

might be rendered as

  content which requires emphasis

on a display which supports italic text. However, since EM is a
logical element, a display which doesnt support italics can still
display the contents of the tag to the user with emphasis -- perhaps
as underlined text. (Tags can either be upper or lower case; however,
```

Figure 2.2
EM Rendering (Lynx)

cal I element to contain the text, the citation might still be displayed properly even in a browser that doesn't directly support italic text, but only if it has the intelligence to render text within tags that call for italics as underlined. However, what about the browser doing text-to-speech "display"? If the logical EM element were used, there's a good chance the software will be able to speak the text as a human reader would; if the physical I element were used, this is much less likely. And let's imagine a tool that attempts to build a list of primary resources from secondary sources on the Web: the success of such a tool is dependent upon being able to understand what the meaning of the text is, and is greatly diminished when content providers use physical, versus logical, elements.

Logical elements also allow browsers to further process information within a document, not just properly render text within tags. For example, HTML has six levels of header elements, from H1 to H6. It's always been strongly recommended that these tags be used in order, from H1 to H2, on down, but many people producing markup have instead used these tags for the relative sizing of text: for example, using an H3 or H4 tag instead of an H2 tag because it gives the best appearance in a particular browser. By misusing these tags in this way, the content provider misunderstands what elements actually represent; that is, a certain type of information rather than a certain way to display information.

The content provider who misuses these tags cannot achieve the desired goal: different browsers render headings in different type and sizes, making it relatively difficult to predict the results on all possible browsers. Further, this same person who chooses to use logical tags for physical rendering is limiting the usefulness of the document for the users. It's easy to imagine a browser that includes an outline capability similar to that in most popular word processors, in which a document that uses header tags for typographical versus logical reasons may not be able to collapse properly to an outline view, making the document less manageable for users.

Some, especially those involved in graphic design, have claimed that the predilection of HTML for logical markup only creates content for the lowest common denominator, content that does not take advantage of the capabilities of high-end (or even middle-of-the-road) workstations, so that most users don't benefit. That's clearly not the case—even as HTML 3 includes better facilities to control the presentation and layout of documents, it's always been true that design is limited by the medium it works within. The reason the Web is so popular is that, to a large extent, it delivers on its promise of a readily accessible, worldwide repository for information; this simply wouldn't be possible if the Web were to assume certain hardware and bandwidth capabilities. The modern four-color offset press itself has limitations, which designers have learned to work within, both physical and of cost; these limitations have simply become naturalized, as designers have become familiar with them. Those designing multimedia components for the Web need to be aware of the real benefits of structured documents to the users of those texts.

HTML Versions and Extensions

The first release of HTML is the original CERN specification. Although this is the base-level HTML reference, some of the elements present in version 0 have since become deprecated, largely because they contain functionality that other commonly used tags provide in a more robust fashion.

HTML 1.0 includes the original CERN tags, with some additional features, such as images, primarily introduced by the Mosaic development team. HTML 2.0 primarily contained revisions to HTML to make it an SGML-compliant language, and added support for forms. (SGML stands for Standard Generalized Markup Language.) It has been an attempt to capture current usage of

HTML, and to codify it, before moving on to the revisions planned in 3.0 and later versions.

Netscape introduced many tags that were particular to its browser, `BLINK` being the most notorious of them. Netscape has since joined the ranks of the standards committees, and has labeled the tags it introduces that are not within the official HTML specification as "experimental"; within this book, we've labeled Netscape-specific tags with a Netscape-specific icon.

HTML 3.0 includes work to include support for non-Western European writing systems, table, figure, and scientific notation support, client-side image maps and other interactive applications, and style sheets.

Beyond HTML

Web documents can also refer to formats other than HTML. In fact, Web documents can refer to *any* computer file format—it's just a matter of browsers supporting the file formats in question, or being able to hand the file to a program that can handle the format. With at least three major flavors of computers surfing the Web (Mac, Windows, and Unix), and a myriad of different system configurations and usable browsers, it's important to pick file formats that all of your audience can use. Several file formats for nontextual media have widespread (though not universal) cross-platform support, and are discussed in this section.

Bandwidth versus Impact Considerations

It's important, when adding media content other than text, to consider users' bandwidth—the speed at which they can download information—and the amount of time they might have to wait for a particular content piece. This is a particularly important consideration for inline images (see the next section), since most graphical browsers will be set to autoload these images. However, keep in mind that inline images aren't necessarily loaded when the page is; users with low bandwidth may have this option turned off, and only load images, inline or not, selectively—design your pages accordingly (see Table 2.1).

Table 2.1

Approximate Download
Times

	50K	250K	1MB
14.4K SLIP	40 to 60 seconds	3.5 to 5 minutes	14 to 20 minutes
28.8K SLIP	20 to 30 seconds	1.25 to 2.5 minutes	7 to 10 minutes
1.5Mb T1	3 to 10 seconds	15 to 50 seconds	1 to 3 1/4 minutes

Keep in mind that actual download times for users can vary considerably, depending upon the availability of network resources between your site and your users' sites. Approximate download times are very useful, however, whenever designing nontext media content; obviously, if a user waits four minutes for your page to load because of heavy use of inline images, the impact should be such that the user feels that it's worth the time involved.

Still Images

GIF (file extension: .gif MIME type: image/gif)

Almost all browsers that support graphical displays include support for the 8-bit, 256-color Compuserve GIF (Graphics Interchange Format) format, for both inline and linked images. Inline images are those that display in the same window as HTML-tagged text, either using the IMG tag and, in HTML 3.0 and above, the FIG tag. The backward-compatible GIF89a format, an extension to the original GIF specification, allows for such features as images with transparent backgrounds, in which one color in the image's color table is mapped to the browser's current background color when displayed, and interlaced images, which allow browsers to load and display images progressively.

It's important to note that on displays that only support 256 colors, multiple GIFs on the same page with different color tables will quickly use the 256 colors available (depending upon the number of colors used in each image), producing unpredictable color results and, with some browsers, longer rendering times. It's recommended that if you do plan on using multiple GIFs on the same Web page, they all use the same color table for best results across different browser environments.

See Chapter 4, *Document Creation Tools,* for a discussion of tools to help you create images with transparent backgrounds, create interlaced images, and render multiple images to the same color table.

JPEG (file extension: .jpeg or .jpg; MIME type: image/jpeg)

JPEG (Joint Photographic Expert Group) is a lossy compression algorithm for 24-bit, millions of colors images. When you save an image in JPEG format, you can choose whether to have more compression but greater loss of image quality, or greater fidelity to the original image, with less compression. JPEG files can both be better quality and realize greater compression than GIF images, especially for photo-real images—although this isn't always the case, because smaller, more basic images, such as Web page icons, are often smaller when saved in GIF format. Because of this "fudge factor" in compression, JPEG is much more suited to photographs than it is to diagrams and line drawings, where the lossyness of the compression will be more apparent. At the time of this writing, a small number of browsers (including Netscape Navigator and NCSA Mosaic) supported inline JPEG images.

The number of browsers supporting inline JPEG images will undoubtedly increase, due to a late 1994 announcement that browsers that render GIF images would require a license from UNISYS, which holds a patent on a portion of the GIF compression algorithm. Some browsers that support the display of inline JPEG images also support the display of external JPEG images directly within the browser; most users of browsers that don't include that capability have installed a helper application that will display JPEG images.

The ALT Attribute and Other Considerations for Inline Images

The ALT attribute, that displays alternative text for nondisplayed images, can be used with inline images for better support of text-only browsers; it's recommended you use ALT whenever practical, and it is especially important when you use inline images as links. The ALT attribute is placed inside an IMG tag; for example,

```
⟨IMG ALT="This alternative text is displayed when
the image isn't loaded." SRC="image.gif"⟩
```

 If you're using the FIG element defined in HTML 3, you can do the same thing through the use of figure description text, as well as using the CAPTION and CREDIT elements to display further information regarding the image on all browsers. For example,

```
⟨FIG SRC="image.gif"⟩
⟨CAPTION⟩This caption displays on all
browsers.⟨/CAPTION⟩
⟨P⟩This descriptive text displays when the image
isn't loaded.⟨/P⟩
⟨CREDIT⟩This credit text displays on all
browsers.⟨/CREDIT⟩
⟨/FIG⟩
```

Another important consideration for the use of inline images is that not all Web browsers that display images default to the same screen width and height, and users can always make these windows bigger or smaller. When making banners intended to run across the user's screen lengthwise, assume a reasonable value, such as 480 pixels horizontally, and design your graphic such that a windows opened wider or smaller than yours will still produce a reasonably good-looking display. Do the same for images that run vertically or are large in both directions; it's probably reasonable to assume a maximum size of 344 pixels vertically. The maximum number of pixels in both horizontal and vertical directions is based on a browser with its standard buttons and scroll bars occupying a 640 x 400 pixel screen.

It's also good to keep in mind that not all displays produce images at the same dpi (dots per inch); if you assume a 72-dpi screen, and a user is browsing with a screen set at 85 dpi, your images will be physically smaller on the screen, although the same size relative to other objects. However, icons or graphical elements might be hard to distinguish from other icons or graphical elements at higher resolutions, and should be designed accordingly. At the same time, not all displays are color displays, so don't make color the sole indicator of difference for important informational graphics.

Reediting Still Images

It's important to note that, if you plan on further editing any images you save in GIF or JPEG formats, you should also save them in a nonlossy 24-bit format; TIFF or the native format for your image editing application are good choices. Otherwise, you'll have difficulty getting good results from your reedited images.

Sounds

Not all users have equipment that supports the display of images, and even fewer have the hardware necessary to play sounds. Sound files can also become very large very quickly, and, for many users, unless they contain fairly compelling content, may not be worth the wait. There are three popular sound file formats:

- **Ulaw (file extension: .au; MIME type: audio/basic).**

Ulaw or μlaw (pronounced mu-law) is the standard NeXT and Sun sound format, and most other platforms have Ulaw players readily available. The sampling rate is 8kHz at 8-bit mono (international telephony format).

- **AIFF (file extension: .aiff or .aif; MIME type: audio/x-aiff).**

AIFF was developed by Apple, and is also supported by SGI platforms. AIFF players for other platforms are readily available. Several sample rates are possible using AIFF, but the most popular is 22.3kHz at 8-bit mono, the default sampling rate for most Apple Macintosh hardware. As a point of comparison, CD-quality audio is sampled at 44kHz at 16-bit stereo resolution. Of course, larger files are produced at higher sampling rates and numbers of bits. AIFC is an extension of AIFF that allows compression in 3:1 and 6:1 rates, but isn't supported by as many sound-playing applications as the AIFF format.

- **WAV (file extensions: .wav; MIME type: audio/x-wav).**

WAV is the standard Microsoft Windows sound format. Players for this format on other platforms are not readily available, so we recommend that you use either AIFF or Ulaw (which are more readily supported on multiple platforms).

Movies

Movie data can become extremely large very quickly, and requires that users not only have relatively high-speed connections to download the movie in a reasonable amount of time, but also the display hardware and processing power to decompress movies at reasonable display rates. You can keep file sizes smaller by reducing your sampling rates and by making your display window size as small as possible, but be careful not to over-compromise the value of your content by attempting to save too much in bandwidth. As with still images and audio, there are three popular formats to consider:

• **MPEG (file extension: .mpeg or .mpg; MIME type: video/mpeg).**

MPEG (Moving Pictures Expert Group) is a common file format across all platforms, and MPEG players are generally more widely available across platforms, especially Unix platforms, than Quick-Time players.

• **QuickTime (file extension: .mov; MIME type: video/quicktime).**

QuickTime was developed by Apple Computer for the Macintosh, and is now an ISO standard. Although QuickTime players are fairly common, only three QuickTime CODECs (compression/decompression algorithms) are widely supported: Apple Animation, Apple Video, and Apple CinePak. It's recommended you use one of these three CODECs when producing your movie file.

• **Video for Windows (file extension: .avi; MIME type: video/x-msvideo).**

Video for Windows is the standard video format for Microsoft's Windows operating system. Unfortunately, players for other platforms do not exist, so we recommend you use another format, such as QuickTime or MPEG, instead.

If a QuickTime movie is produced on a Macintosh, it's necessary to "flatten" the movie (make sure all the movie's data is stored in the file's data fork) in order for the movie to be played on non-Macintosh platforms. Chapter 4, *Document Creation Tools*, covers tools that can flatten QuickTime movies.

Platform-Independent Electronic Printing Formats

There are several platform-independent electronic printing formats, of which Adobe Acrobat's PDF format is the best example. Many of those within the graphic design community and the traditional publishing industry are attracted to Adobe's electronic printing technology, and we should soon see direct support by Web browsers of the PDF format.

The Acrobat system seems to address the needs of both those in the graphic design field—many of whom have had numerous complaints about HTML's emphasis on content structure versus presentation—and those in the traditional publishing industry, which, with an electronic printing format, can continue to use its current software and knowledge base to produce texts for both print-based and on-line works.

Indeed, Acrobat does seem to address these very issues: publishing in Acrobat format is as easy as printing from your authoring application of choice, by selecting the Acrobat software as the printing device, instead of an actual printer. Text can remain searchable and copyable for users, or can be "glued" to the page, to prevent the easy manipulation of copyrighted materials by users. And, with Adobe's Weblink plug-in to Acrobat, PDF files can be embedded with hypertext links that point to other resources anywhere on the Web.

There are drawbacks to PDF, however: PDF files are often much larger than the equivalent HTML files with inline images, which can lengthen the time users spend waiting for information. Users are no longer allowed to view only a portion of a document—an HTML page that displays as it's being interpreted—to determine if it's the resource being sought; rather, they must wait for the entire PDF file, which is usually a whole document, whether that be a book chapter or an entire newsletter (although this does result in much faster access and greater portability when the entire document does arrive). At the same time, users can no longer pass on links pointing to a specific section of a document, but must rather point to the entity as a whole.

Publishing in Acrobat format also limits the audience of a resource. Publishers who choose PDF to supplement or establish their Web presence want the vast audience of a "World Wide Web," but then choose to limit their readership to those who have access to the proper display hardware and platform. Additionally, one of the strengths of HTML is that it describes a document's structure, instead of its appearance; not only does this make it possible to create browsers that can render documents in Braille, text-to-speech, and other formats that can make the same information available to a wider audience, it also creates the possibility of Web clients that are intelligent agents, can search for information, and abstract, and summarize their findings for their users.

At the same time, the future direction of HTML has moved to address the concerns of those in graphic design and commercial publishing, with support for tables, figures with captions, and style sheets in HTML 3.

Although Adobe Acrobat might be geared to a specific need, publishers who choose to use an electronic printing format need to realize they're taking an enabling medium and disabling it, in order to make it conform to a publishing model—print—with which they're already familiar. Even on the author's 17-inch monitor, at 1280 x 1024 resolution, an Acrobat document is still a bit too large to be read comfortably on the screen, while HTML documents can be resized manageably. It's the interactivity that's the key—people are not coming on-line to find the same content that's available at their local bookstore, which they must now wait to download, then print. It's a good thing to keep in mind.

3

Quickstart Tutorial: Building a Document

This chapter walks you through the assemblage of a local web. By no means does it cover every HTML element; in fact, it uses only a few. But it should be enough for you to begin assembling documents, while giving you a good foundation in the basics of HTML.

(Not Quite) Getting Started

Believe it or not, we don't begin our quickstart section by putting together a document skeleton, and then arbitrarily filling it with content. Instead, we first take a look at the content we wish to present. After all, that's why you're putting your web together in the first place—in order to display content. Before the Web was available, you might have put together a pamphlet, a brochure, a packet, or a book—and, in most cases, the nature of the production process within the medium would have dictated some reflection about your content, and how it was organized. The Web can be much more immediate, but this can be a liability as well as an asset. On the Web, you are, as with more traditional media, a publisher of information, with the attendant responsibilities that being a publisher entails.

Remember, too, that content is not suddenly "free" (free from cost, and hence free from responsibility) via the Web, even if you're not charging for access to that content. As with everything, there is no free lunch: the Web simply distributes costs among you, the information provider, the access providers, and the information consumer—your reader. Cost, under this new distributed model, shouldn't just be factored as the price of net access and display hardware; it also involves time, both yours and the reader's. A resource costs you time to maintain, and costs your reader time to peruse. Content that is well-focused and well-structured will find a receptive and appreciative audience; content that is disorganized or duplicative will not.

That said, for the purposes of this chapter, we'll consider putting together a web that covers the history of Freedonia and its outlying regions. It's a good example because it can entail a large amount of information to be managed (although it will be quite limited in this example); and the obvious geographic aspect can be used to topologically organize our web, for both writers and readers.

Basic (Re)search

Now that we have a subject matter chosen—a history of Freedonia—it's a good idea to take advantage of the search mechanisms on the Web to check for duplicative content. If we search for Freedonia using Lycos at `http://lycos.cs.cmu.edu/` we get no matches, as shown in Figure 3.1.

If we had found content already available that was similar to what we had planned, we might have, upon browsing the established site:

- Decided that the site covers the information we would have covered at least as well as or better than we might have, and that no further effort is necessary. We can drop the project and find other ways to contribute to the community.

- Noted that although the site does cover much of the same information we would have, it can be strengthened in certain areas or aspects. We might send an e-mail to the maintainer of the site, offering our knowledge or services to improve upon the content being offered there.

- Concluded that we have a fundamentally different approach to the information being presented, or that overlap is minimal. Here, you might still send an e-mail to the maintainer of the

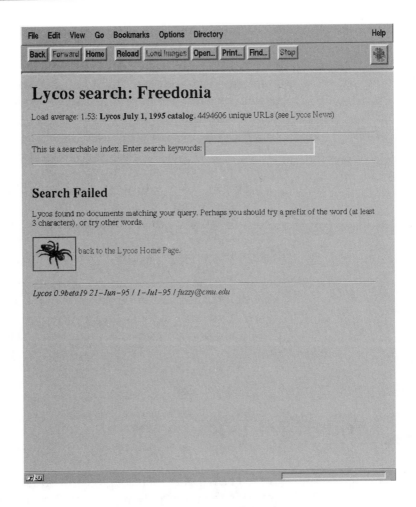

Figure 3.1
Lycos Results

site to explain your project, and perhaps discuss the different approaches.

Editing HTML

HTML documents are just plain text files. As such, they can be produced with any text editor or word processor—although a good HTML editor or HTML converter may give you a production environment that might address your needs better than a generic text editor, you certainly don't require anything beyond the most basic of editors in order to produce HTML. If you're producing HTML in a graphical windowing environment, a small, memory-resident editor in one window and a Web browser in another to preview your work in progress will usually suffice. In your text editor, you edit your HTML document and save it without quitting the editor when you'd like to preview your work; with your Web browser, you begin by opening the file using Open Local, or Open File, or the equivalent, and then reload after you've saved a new version from your text editor using the Reload command. HTML is so simple and straightforward, in fact, that this may be your preferred work environment—just remember to view your work in a browser other than your preferred one from time to time. Otherwise, you could very well begin producing documents for one browser, versus the whole Web.

That being said, remember to take a look at Chapter 4 for some ideas about editing tools, and at Chapter 11 for some ideas about producing nonbrowser-specific HTML. Also, if you have further questions about any HTML element discussed here, Chapter 13 provides an extensive HTML reference.

Your HTML Document

Every HTML document begins and ends with HTML tags. The document is then divided into a HEAD part and a BODY part. Within the document head, a TITLE element is required. The title of the document is usually displayed in graphical browsers as part of the window's title bar but it may also be returned as the identifying part of a document by a search mechanism; and when readers make bookmarks to your document, these are normally named according to your document title, so your title should not only be descriptive, but understandable outside of context.

The basic skeleton for an HTML document, then, is:

```
⟨HTML⟩

⟨HEAD⟩
```

```
⟨TITLE⟩ ⟨/TITLE⟩
⟨/HEAD⟩

⟨BODY⟩

⟨/BODY⟩

⟨/HTML⟩
```

So far, we have an empty body, so there's nothing to display within a browser window; we can now start adding that content.

We'll begin by adding several header entities, which will describe the basic structure of the document. There are six levels of headers, from H1 to H6; they should be used logically to describe different structural levels of your document, rather than to achieve any sizing effects.

```
⟨HTML⟩

⟨HEAD⟩
⟨TITLE⟩A History of Freedonia: Overview⟨/TITLE⟩
⟨/HEAD⟩

⟨BODY⟩
⟨H1⟩A History of Freedonia: Overview⟨/H1⟩

⟨H2⟩A History of Freedonia, the nation-state⟨/H2⟩

⟨H2⟩The Freedonian principalities⟨/H2⟩

⟨/BODY⟩

⟨/HTML⟩
```

We can then view this document as displayed by Lynx (see Figure 3.2).

Now that we have the basic structure of the document established, we can start filling in content. Paragraphs, the main building blocks of content, are denoted with the P element. (Closing P tags are usually implied by the next ⟨P⟩.)

```
⟨HTML⟩

⟨HEAD⟩
⟨TITLE⟩A History of Freedonia: Overview⟨/TITLE⟩
⟨/HEAD⟩
```

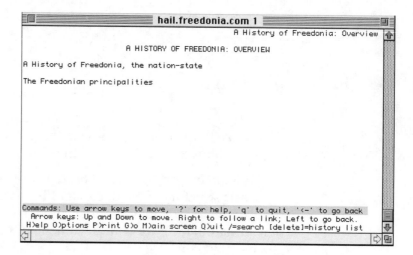

Figure 3.2

A Basic Document

⟨BODY⟩

⟨H1⟩A History of Freedonia: Overview⟨/H1⟩

⟨H2⟩A History of Freedonia, the nation-state⟨/H2⟩

⟨P⟩One of the last (if not only) colonies ruled by the Esperantinos, Freedonia consists of five small islands just off the coast of Chile. The primary exports of Freedonia are cane sugar and precious metals.

⟨H2⟩The Freedonian principalities⟨/H2⟩

⟨/BODY⟩

⟨/HTML⟩

NOTE: When using the Paragraph (P) element, you'll undoubtedly discover, if you haven't already assumed, that all white space within HTML is collapsed. Any series of spaces, tabs, line feeds, or carriage returns are always reduced down to a single space. If you need to preserve white space, you can use the BR element to introduce a line break; the nonbreaking space entity (&nobr;), or use the PRE element to block out a passage of preformatted text.

We can view the document again, in Netscape (see Figure 3.3).

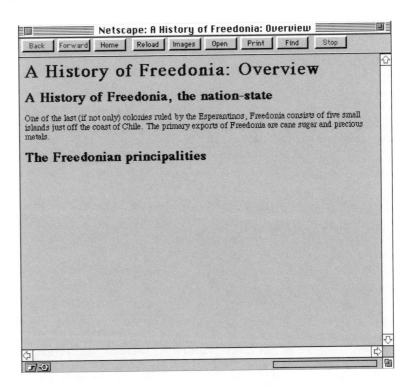

Figure 3.3

A Basic Document with
Paragraphs

Adding a List to Your Document

Under our second second-level heading, The Freedonian Principalities, we'd like to start out by providing a list of the principalities of Freedonia. Lists occur quite often within structured text; they're a good way to quickly organize and present small pieces of information that can be logically grouped and perhaps ordered. The OL element is used for Ordered Lists; the UL element is used for Unordered lists. For the Freedonian principalities, we'll use the UL element, since we don't want to make it appear as if we favor one region over another, which could cause regional strife and political infighting among the Freedonians:

```
⟨HTML⟩

⟨HEAD⟩
⟨TITLE⟩ A History of Freedonia: Overview⟨/TITLE⟩
⟨/HEAD⟩
```

```
⟨BODY⟩
⟨H1⟩A History of Freedonia: Overview⟨/H1⟩

⟨H2⟩A History of Freedonia, the nation-state⟨/H2⟩

⟨P⟩One of the last (if not only) colonies ruled by
the Esperantinos, Freedonia consists of five small
islands just off the coast of Chile. The primary
exports of Freedonia are cane sugar and precious
metals.

⟨H2⟩The Freedonian principalities⟨/H2⟩

⟨UL⟩
⟨LI⟩Doj
⟨LI⟩Mundungus
⟨LI⟩Rheingau
⟨/UL⟩

⟨/BODY⟩

⟨/HTML⟩
```

Looking at this list in Arena, it is rendered as illustrated by Figure 3.4.

You can also nest lists, like so:

```
⟨UL⟩
⟨LI⟩ Knit 1
⟨LI⟩ Perl 2
  ⟨UL⟩
  ⟨LI⟩ Perl 4.136
  ⟨LI⟩ Perl 5.0
  ⟨/UL⟩
⟨/UL⟩
```

The items in the list following "Perl 2" will appear as a subordinate list. (For more information on the list elements, see Chapter 13.)

Pulling It Together

There are still a lot of things we can do to improve our document. The two most obvious tasks are to add links, to make it a *hypertext* document, and to add images, to incorporate information that is more easily relayed via graphics than text.

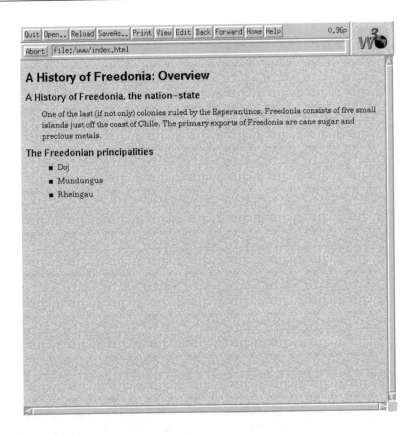

Figure 3.4
A Basic Document
with List

Before we do that, however, we should take a little time to sign our document; it will give readers an opportunity to contact us if they find any omissions or errors, or wish to provide other feedback. We'll place this signature at the bottom of our document, separated by a horizontal rule:

```
⟨HTML⟩

⟨HEAD⟩
⟨TITLE⟩A History of Freedonia: Overview⟨/TITLE⟩
⟨/HEAD⟩

⟨BODY⟩
⟨H1⟩A History of Freedonia: Overview⟨/H1⟩

⟨H2⟩A History of Freedonia, the nation-state⟨/H2⟩

⟨P⟩One of the last (if not only) colonies ruled by
the Esperantinos, Freedonia consists of five small
```

```
islands just off the coast of Chile. The primary
exports of Freedonia are cane sugar and precious
metals.

⟨H2⟩The Freedonian principalities⟨/H2⟩

⟨UL⟩
⟨LI⟩Doj
⟨LI⟩Mundungus
⟨LI⟩Rheingau
⟨/UL⟩

⟨HR⟩
⟨P⟩1 July 1995
⟨ADDRESS⟩
Carl Eadmanst / &lt;carl@freedonia.com&gt;
⟨/ADDRESS⟩

⟨/BODY⟩

⟨/HTML⟩
```

Note that we've dated the document, letting our readers know how up to date this information is, and placed a name and contact information inside the ADDRESS element, which was intended for just that purpose. We've also used the entity names for angular brackets around the e-mail address, since angular brackets in HTML normally denote the start or end of tags (see Appendix C for more information on character entities). Let's take another look at our document, again with Lynx (see Figure 3.5).

Adding Links

We've succeeded in placing a lot of text on the screen, but we could have done that with the most basic of text editors or word processors. We'll now add some hypertext links with the anchor element A, in conjunction with the HREF attribute:

```
⟨HTML⟩

⟨HEAD⟩
⟨TITLE⟩A History of Freedonia: Overview⟨/TITLE⟩
⟨/HEAD⟩

⟨BODY⟩
⟨H1⟩A History of Freedonia: Overview⟨/H1⟩
```

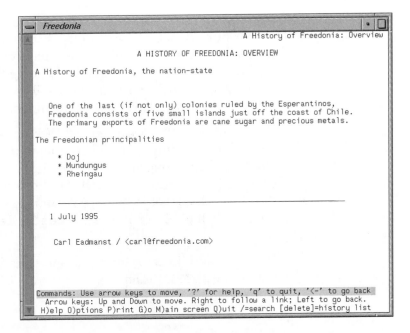

Figure 3.5
A Basic Document
with Signature

⟨H2⟩A History of Freedonia, the nation-state⟨/H2⟩

⟨P⟩One of the last (if not only) colonies ruled by the Esperantinos, Freedonia consists of five small islands just off the coast of Chile. The primary exports of Freedonia are cane sugar and precious metals.

⟨H2⟩The Freedonian principalities⟨/H2⟩

⟨UL⟩
⟨LI⟩⟨A HREF="doj/index.html"⟩Doj⟨/A⟩
⟨LI⟩⟨A HREF="mundungus/index.html"⟩Mundungus⟨/A⟩
⟨LI⟩⟨A HREF="rheingau/index.html"⟩Rheingau⟨/A⟩
⟨/UL⟩

⟨HR⟩
⟨P⟩1 July 1995
⟨ADDRESS⟩
Carl Eadmanst / <carl@freedonia.com>
⟨/ADDRESS⟩

⟨/BODY⟩

⟨/HTML⟩

Here, we're using *relative* links: we're pointing to a file "index.html" in a directory "doj" which is in the same directory as the current document. This makes our document and its associated files and directories *portable,* meaning they can live anywhere within a server's file structure and still have links that point to other documents relative to this document's location.

Why "index.html"? Because most Web servers will serve up a file "index.html" if only given a URL that indicates a directory; for example, a client requesting the URL `"http://www.freedonia. com/doj/"` would have the file "index.html" from the top-level directory "doj"; that is, `"http://www.freedonia.com/doj/"` is equivalent to `"http://www.freedonia.com/doj/index. html."`

We'll also add links for the name and e-mail address provided within the ADDRESS element:

```
⟨HTML⟩

⟨HEAD⟩
⟨TITLE⟩A History of Freedonia: Overview⟨/TITLE⟩
⟨/HEAD⟩

⟨BODY⟩
⟨H1⟩A History of Freedonia: Overview⟨/H1⟩

⟨H2⟩A History of Freedonia, the nation-state⟨/H2⟩

⟨P⟩One of the last (if not only) colonies ruled by
the Esperantinos, Freedonia consists of five small
islands just off the coast of Chile. The primary
exports of Freedonia are cane sugar and precious
metals.

⟨H2⟩The Freedonian principalities⟨/H2⟩

⟨UL⟩
⟨LI⟩⟨A HREF="doj/index.html"⟩Doj⟨/A⟩
⟨LI⟩⟨A HREF="mundungus/index.html"⟩Mundungus⟨/A⟩
⟨LI⟩⟨A HREF="rheingau/index.html"⟩Rheingau⟨/A⟩
⟨/UL⟩

⟨HR⟩
⟨P⟩1 July 1995
```

```
⟨ADDRESS⟩
⟨A HREF="http://www.freedonia.com/~carl/"⟩Carl
Eadmanst⟨/A⟩ /
⟨A HREF="mailto:carl@freedonia.com"⟩&lt;carl@free-
donia.com&gt;⟨/A⟩
⟨/ADDRESS⟩

⟨/BODY⟩

⟨/HTML⟩
```

We've used an absolute URL for the author's address because we don't want to rely on it being in the same position relative to the other documents we're working on. If we move this document within the server's file structure, it's doubtful we'd move the author's home page along with it. We've also used the `mailto:` URL, which, in most Web browsers, will allow the reader to send an e-mail message when selected. (See Appendix A for more information on URLs.)

Adding Images

Images are a large part of what made the Web as successful as it is today. Remember, though, that not everyone browsing the Web is using a client that displays images, or has a connection rapid enough to make loading images worthwhile. In addition, relying heavily on images means that Web robots like Lycos will not be able to index documents (since they can only index text), making the site that much harder to find by readers. On the other hand, images can be used tastefully and well to enhance your content.

There will always be tension between those who would convey information with text and those who would convey information with images (or sounds, or movies). Today, the Web is a flexible enough medium to provide elements of all these media types, but you should keep in mind those without access (for technical or physical reasons) to nontextual media types, and, if possible, provide the same information in a textual form as an alternative for these people. (See Chapter 11 for more thoughts on image use.)

That said, if we have a graphic saved in GIF format—today, the most widely supported format for inline images (images dis-

played directly within the browser window)—named
freedonia.gif, we can include it in our document by using the
Image element, IMG, in conjunction with the Source attribute, SRC:

```
⟨HTML⟩

⟨HEAD⟩
⟨TITLE⟩A History of Freedonia: Overview⟨/TITLE⟩
⟨/HEAD⟩

⟨BODY⟩
⟨H1⟩A History of Freedonia: Overview⟨/H1⟩

⟨IMG SRC="freedonia.gif"⟩

⟨H2⟩A History of Freedonia, the nation-state⟨/H2⟩

⟨P⟩One of the last (if not only) colonies ruled by
the Esperantinos, Freedonia consists of five small
islands just off the coast of Chile. The primary
exports of Freedonia are cane sugar and precious
metals.

⟨H2⟩The Freedonian principalities⟨/H2⟩

⟨UL⟩
⟨LI⟩⟨A HREF="doj/index.html"⟩Doj⟨/A⟩
⟨LI⟩⟨A HREF="mundungus/index.html"⟩Mundungus⟨/A⟩
⟨LI⟩⟨A HREF="rheingau/index.html"⟩Rheingau⟨/A⟩
⟨/UL⟩

⟨HR⟩
⟨P⟩1 July 1995
⟨ADDRESS⟩
⟨A HREF="http://www.freedonia.com/~carl/"⟩Carl
Eadmanst⟨/A⟩ /
⟨A HREF="mailto:carl@freedonia.com"⟩&lt;carl
@freedonia.com&gt;⟨/A⟩
⟨/ADDRESS⟩

⟨/BODY⟩

⟨/HTML⟩
```

The IMG element also supports an ALT attribute, which displays
an alternative text string in text-only browsers (or in a graphical
browser that has automatic image loading switched off), so that
the line that loads in our image would become:

```
⟨IMG SRC="freedonia.gif" ALT="a map of Freedonia"⟩
```

Figure 3.6 shows our page using Netscape.

In HTML 3, we can use the Figure element, `FIG`. Figure is much more flexible and powerful than Image; instead of using the `ALT` attribute, it allows you to embed any HTML you like as alternative text inside the element tags (and since browsers that do not understand a tag will ignore it, the alternative text will be displayed by default by any browser that does not understand `FIG`). It also supports embedded `CAPTION` and `CREDIT` elements, which are rendered in both graphical and nongraphical browsers. Using `FIG`, we get the following:

```
⟨FIG SRC="freedonia.gif"⟩
⟨CAPTION⟩Political Map of Freedonia,
1995.⟨/CAPTION⟩
⟨P⟩Freedonia is made up of three small islands:
Doj, Mundungus, and Rheingau.
⟨/FIG⟩
```

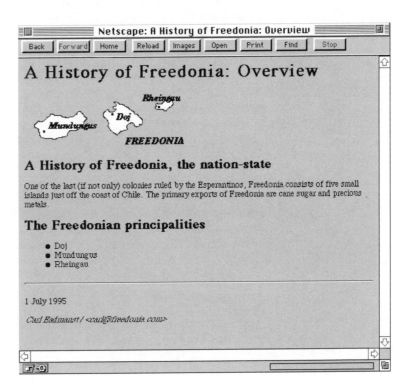

Figure 3.6
A Basic Document
with Image

A Second Document

Let's now create a document for one of the Freedonian principalities, Doj. Using the HTML elements we used in the last example, we can quickly put together the following page, shown in Figure 3.7, viewed in Arena.

```
⟨HTML⟩

⟨HEAD⟩
⟨TITLE⟩A History of Freedonia: Doj⟨/TITLE⟩
⟨/HEAD⟩

⟨BODY⟩
⟨H1⟩A History of Freedonia: Doj⟨/H1⟩

⟨P⟩In 1701, the Dojians decided by popular tyranny
to join the federal democratic government of
Freedonia. In 1702 the Freedonian popular vote
to dissolve the federal democratic union was lead
by the rallying calls of the (former) Dojian gen-
ral, Major Philo, whose historic words still ring
true today:

⟨BLOCKQUOTE⟩
⟨P⟩Ask not what you can do for your federal
democratic union, but whether you
⟨STRONG⟩like⟨/STRONG⟩ being a jelly donut.
⟨/BLOCKQUOTE⟩

⟨P⟩When a united Freedonia surfaced again in 1981,
it was largely due to a group of Dojian
revolutionaries, the ⟨EM⟩Jelly Donutarians⟨/EM⟩,
whose political agenda consisted of the demand to
freely elect aging movie stars to high offices. At
the time, the Donutarians argued that a united
Freedonia could more easily attract a larger, more
bloated aging movie star than any of the (what is
now) Freedonian principalities alone; at the time
of the writing, however, Freedonia is still
without a head of state, while Dojal Palace has
```

been occupied by such dignitaries as Ralph Eubanks
and Bill Matthews.

⟨HR⟩
⟨P⟩Return to ⟨A HREF="../index.html"⟩Freedonia⟨/A⟩ |
On to ⟨A HREF="../mundungus/index.html"⟩Mundungus⟨/A⟩

⟨P⟩1 July 1995
⟨ADDRESS⟩
⟨A HREF="http://www.freedonia.com/~carl/"⟩Carl
Eadmanst⟨/A⟩ /
⟨A HREF="mailto:carl@freedonia.com"⟩<carl@
freedonia.com>⟨/A⟩
⟨/ADDRESS⟩

⟨/BODY⟩

⟨/HTML⟩

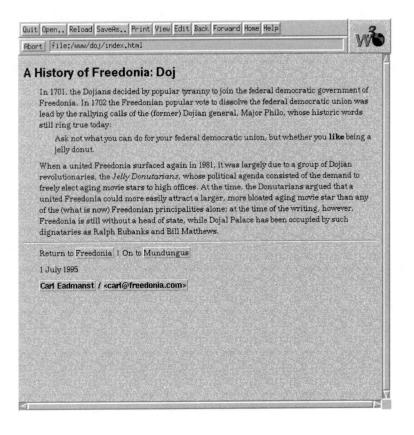

Figure 3.7
A Second Document

Well, it does seem as if we've added a few new HTML elements, three of them, actually: BLOCKQUOTE, STRONG, and EM.

- BLOCKQUOTE is fairly obvious from its name and context: the element contains quoted text, which is typically rendered slightly left indented.

- The EM element indicates emphasis, and its contents are typically rendered in italics.

- The STRONG element indicates strong emphasis, and its contents are typically rendered in bold text.

Others might have used the Italic element, I, and the Bold element, B, for EM and STRONG, respectively. These are *physical formatting* elements rather than *logical formatting* elements, and their use is discussed at greater length in Chapter 11. The truly religious, of course, would use ⟨!DOCTYPE HTML PUBLIC"-//IETF//DTD HTML 2.0//EN"⟩ as the first line of their document, describing the document to be an HTML 2.0 document for an SGML (Standard Generalized Markup Language) parser. (!DOCTYPE and a list of possible values surfaces again in Chapter 7, in the discussion of the HTML Check Toolkit). In the end, given your understanding of the issues involved, the audience you hope to reach, and whether you consider the longevity or appearance of your documents more important, you'll have to make informed decisions as to whether you use logical or physical tags, or elements or attributes—or entire programming languages—only supported in a particular browser.

Beyond the use of these additional elements, note that we added a text-only menu bar at the bottom, which allows the reader to return to the top-view document (the one we originally created), or to move on to the next Freedonian principality, Mundungus. This gives flexibility to readers that they would undoubtedly appreciate, if they didn't just expect it as a matter of course; for any Web, it should always be easy to move to the next logical topic, as well as return to a top, table-of-contents-like view.

Another Top View

Assuming we go on and create pages for the other Freedonian principalities, we might like to add an alternate method to reach that information: we can make the map of Freedonia we placed on the top page a clickable image map. A clickable image map is an image for which certain "hot" areas have been defined: when a user clicks on one, the click coordinates are mapped to a URL, to which the user is then sent. In HTML 2, the server performs the mapping of image coordinates to a URL; the Web browser passes the number of pixels down and over to the server, which consults a table—in most cases, located within a separate map file—to determine the appropriate URL. In HTML 3, the client does the mapping; embedded in the HTML are the coordinates and URLs, which is easier on servers, since clients now do the processing, and also allows browsers to do such things as displaying a different type of pointer for a hotspot. For server-processed maps, the content provider should be careful to produce images so that the areas in which a user should click are fairly obvious.

Our first step in making our GIF of Freedonia a clickable image map is to determine the coordinates for the boundaries between the principalities. The following numbers were generated by drawing boundaries on freedonia.gif with WebMap, and saving in NCSA format (a format compatible with the Web server developed at NCSA and many other servers), although any mapping utility would do (see Chapter 4 for more information on Web mapping utilities):

```
default index.html
poly mundungus/index.html 9,43 36,25 72,21 88,37 33,68 9,43
poly doj/index.html 102,30 124,10 160,37 123,58 102,30
poly rheingau/index.html 172,21 192,7 201,19 185,28 172,21
```

Note that this file contains a default, index.html, which is returned by the server if the client passes coordinates that don't match any of the hotspots. The default file can be anything appropriate, although it usually is the same page that contains the image map. The rest of the file defines polygon shapes, by providing the points of the polygons, and by providing the URL the shapes it should map to.

If we save these coordinates in a file, `freedonia.map`, we can then link the file to our GIF by modifying our image element:

```
⟨A HREF="/cgi-bin/users/imagemap/freedonia.map"⟩⟨IMG
SRC="freedonia.gif" ALT="a map of Freedonia" ISMAP⟩⟨/A⟩
```

`ISMAP` tells the client that this is a clickable image map, and to pass coordinates to the map-serving application listed in the Anchor (`A`) reference, `imagemap`, which then refers to the file `"freedonia.map"` to map the coordinates to a URL.

You'll also need to tell the `imagemap` program about your map file: by default, the imagemap configuration file (`imagemap.conf`) is located in the `conf` directory where your server's configuration files are stored. The format is straightforward: the name the map file will be referred to as in URLs, followed by a colon, followed by the full pathname of the imagemap file:

```
freedonia.map: /usr/local/etc/httpd/mapfiles/freedonia.map
```

The preceding Anchor reference works for the NCSA and Apache servers that have an application "imagemap" installed to process the client request; if you were using a Mac and the MapServe application, your Anchor and Image elements might look like

```
⟨A HREF="/map/MapServe.acgi$/freedonia.map"⟩⟨IMG SRC="freedo-
nia.gif" ALT="a map of Freedonia" ISMAP⟩⟨/A⟩
```

As you can see, the imagemap processing application, in this case `MapServer.acgi`, lives in a different place in the file structure in this example, and the location of the map file is passed in a slightly different way.

If all of the preceding seems a bit complicated—having clients pass coordinates to the server so the server can send back a URL that the client should then connect to—it is. Luckily, HTML 3 provides a simpler way to do the same thing. The equivalent HTML within an HTML 3 file would look like this:

```
⟨FIG SRC="freedonia.gif"⟩
⟨CAPTION⟩Political Map of Freedonia, 1995.⟨/CAPTION⟩
⟨P⟩Freedonia is made up of three small islands:
⟨A HREF="doj/index.html" SHAPE="polygon 102,30 124,10 160,37
123,58 102,30"⟩Doj⟨/A⟩,
⟨A HREF="mundungus/index.html" SHAPE="polygon 9,43 36,25
72,21 88,37 33,68 9,43"⟩Mundungus⟨/A⟩, and
⟨A HREF="rheingau/index.html" SHAPE="polygon 172,21 192,7
201,19 185,28 172,21"⟩Rheingau⟨/A⟩.
⟨/FIG⟩
```

The contents of the `FIG` element should look very similar to the NCSA-format imagemap file. You'll note, however, that the same information can be interpreted by both graphical and nongraphical browsers. Those browsers capable of showing graphics can use the `SHAPE` attributes to define hotspots for the figure source, while text-only browsers can display the formatted text instead. And in both cases, there are no parameters to pass to the server—the imagemap is handled entirely within the client-parsed HTML.

Additional Tricks and Formatting

At this point, you may have a very workable local Web, but it might not look or act exactly like that cool site that's in your hotlist. Never fear; you don't need to laboriously walk through more and more tutorials until you find out how to use the element that achieves the effect you're after. Instead, when browsing the site with your Web client, simply select its View Source command or equivalent. The browser should display (or save) the HTML source that it is using to render the page you're viewing. By studying this source—and comparing the usage found in the source to the HTML documentation in Chapter 13 of this book, or the official (or browser-specific) HTML specifications listed in the Bibliography—you can quickly increase your knowledge of

HTML in those areas that are most important to you. And by using the stylistic pointers in Chapter 11 and 12, you can identify the information you need to create Webs that are informative, attractive, and intelligently designed. And that, after all, is what it's all about.

4

Document Creation Tools

The World Wide Web supports a wide variety of media formats, and creating documents in these many media can be a tricky proposition. The dominant format of the Web is HTML, and the most common means of creating HTML remains mired in ASCII; a large number of hypertext documents placed on the Web are still created in text editors like Emacs, Notepad, or SimpleText.

This chapter takes a look at the tools that are available that can assist in the creation of documents. We survey HTML editors for Unix, Windows, and Macintosh, describe how to use them, and evaluate their usefulness. We also discuss the current state of HTML editors, and give some thoughts on what a *good* HTML editor *should* provide.

In addition, this chapter takes a look at tools for manipulating inline images for your hypertext documents. Many Web browsers support inlined images that have transparent backgrounds (allowing you to include images without worrying about the background color of a reader's browser), and display interlaced images as they are loaded (providing an illusion of faster loading by allowing the reader to see a rough version of the graphic quickly, and then filling in the details). We focus on tools that can create transparent and interlaced GIF images, although additional tools of interest have been included. We do not cover tools for drawing or painting images; creating illustrations and icons is a topic that merits a book by itself.

The Ideal Editor: Some Thoughts

Most modern word-processing programs (and, in general, most modern programs of any stripe) support the notion of WYSIWYG, or, "What You See Is What You Get" (the acronym is pronounced "wizzy-whig," and conjures up thoughts of over-eager toupees flying around the room . . .). This model promises that the screen will display your document in a way that is identical (within the bounds of your screen's display capabilities) to any other rendition of your document, be it on paper or on another screen.

An ideal HTML editor should be WYSIWYG, yet *not* WYSIWYG. What does this mean? Since HTML is not a page description language, a WYSIWYG editor is a terribly misleading thing. What is on your screen is probably *not* going to be an exact copy of what will show up on another screen, and any person (or program) who leads you to believe that is steering you horribly wrong. At the same time, formatting clues and page layout based on the HTML elements being used can greatly aid an author in creating documents. One way to approach this is that of HoTMetaL—providing formatting but also leaving HTML tags visible. Another approach might be an editor that provides two "views" of a document, one as rendered HTML, and one as "raw" HTML tags and text—thus allowing the author to edit in either view (ASHE, reviewed in the Unix section, provides exactly this). Many editors allow authors to preview documents via a browser, but authors cannot edit the rendered text. Also, an ideal editor will provide the ability to create tables, math, and forms in semi-WYSIWYG format; tables will be presented in tabular format and editable in tabular format. Equations will be editable with a graphical equation editor (à la Microsoft Word).

An ideal HTML editor should take advantage of the structural information provided by HTML. It should provide outlining tools based on the various levels of headers (Internet Assistant provides this, by dint of Microsoft Word's outlining features). It should recognize what is and what is not legal HTML, and not allow illegal HTML in invalid places. HoTMetaL is the only editor that even attempts to do this, but it is so unforgiving that it is almost impossible to import badly crafted HTML documents (created with anything but HoTMetaL) into HoTMetaL. An HTML editor should not allow authors to edit tags directly; or, if it does allow this, it should ensure that the altered tags are still syntactically correct after editing is complete. An HTML editor should recognize that an author is in the middle of an EM element, so that when the author selects EM again it *removes* the EM element from around the selected text instead of adding another EM element inside the original element.

An ideal HTML editor should recognize what the intuitive next step is. After an author enters a header and presses RETURN, for example, the editor should provide a paragraph element for the text that follows. It should not be necessary to make a trip to the mouse for inserting every element. This includes providing usable (and customizable) keystroke alternatives for inserting elements, but it also includes recognizing what sorts of elements follow other elements. When adding an element that has attributes that must be supplied, a dialog box should appear for entering these attributes. When adding an element that has attributes that are infrequently supplied, a dialog box should *not* appear (unless the author double-clicks on the tag). HoTMetaL comes close to this, but seems to arbitrarily choose which elements it will or will not automatically supply an attribute dialog box for.

An ideal HTML editor should allow the author and the reader to become the same person. It, in conjunction with the ideal HTTP server, supports collaborative authoring and editing, and is both a browser and an editor. When readers find a document they wish to edit or annotate, their browser becomes an editor, and allows them to modify and resubmit the edited document. As we write this, a browser/editor/server set (NaviPress and NaviServer) that does just this has been announced (too late for proper inclusion here, unfortunately)—look at http://www.navisoft.com/ for details.

We can only hope that as interest in the World Wide Web grows, there will be more interest in providing professional editing tools with truly intuitive and usable user interfaces. As you will see, several of the available HTML editors come close—and with work could become truly great—but none hit the mark directly.

Table 4.1

Explanation of HTML
Editor Features

HTML 2.0	This editor supports the HTML 2.0 elements.
Forms	This editor supports the HTML 2.0 form elements.
HTML 3.0	This editor supports the HTML 3.0 elements.
Tables	This editor supports the HTML 3.0 table elements.
Math	This editor supports the HTML 3.0 math elements.
Netscape Elements	This editor supports the Netscape extensions to HTML 2.0.
Validity Checking	This editor checks for, and only allows, legal HTML.
WYSIWYG	This editor provides quasi-WYSIWYG editing of HTML.
Special Requirements	Any special requirements of the software are listed here.
Additional Notes	Any additional notes are listed here.

Explanation of HTML Editor Features

In order to avoid repeating ourselves too much, the Features section for each HTML editor review consists of a table of features. These features are explained in Table 4.1. Most features are marked simply with a "✔" to indicate that the feature (as described in Table 4.1) is present; if there are any caveats to this, they will be mentioned in place of the "✔."

Unix Tools

HTML Editors

HoTMetaL Free 1.0

HoTMetaL Free is a freeware version of SoftQuad's HoTMetaL Pro 2.0 HTML editor, which provides HTML validation, and an X Windows-based environment.

Features

HTML 2.0	✔
Forms	✔
HTML 3.0	In HoTMetaL Pro 2.0
Tables	
Math	
Netscape Elements	In HoTMetaL Pro 2.0
Validity Checking	✔
WYSIWYG	In HoTMetaL Pro 2.0
Special Requirements	X11R4 or OpenWindows 3 (for Unix)
Additional Notes	HoTMetaL Free is also available for Microsoft Windows (Mac version to be available in late 1995). HoTMetaL Pro is also available for Macintosh and Microsoft Windows.

Use

First you'll need to get the HoTMetaL Free package from Soft-Quad, via the Web page `http://www.sq.com/products/hotmetal/hm-ftp.htm`, then uncompress and untar it. Installation of HoTMetaL is more complex than the other packages reviewed here, so we'll take some time to go over it.

Once the package has been unpacked and placed in an appropriate directory (such as `/usr/local/bin`), the following path information needs to be added to your `PATH` and `SQDIR` environment variables:

```
setenv SQDIR /usr/local/hotmetal
setenv PATH $SQDIR/bin:$PATH
```

Notice that this is for the C shell (`csh`). These lines may be added directly to your `.cshrc` file. If you are using the Bourne shell, you can use

```
SQDIR=/usr/local/hotmetal; export SQDIR
PATH=$SQDIR/bin:$PATH; export PATH
```

instead. These lines may be added directly to your `.profile` file.

Next, the file `Sqhm` (note the capitalization) must go into the `/usr/lib/X11/app-defaults` directory if you're using X Windows, X11R4 or later, or the `/usr/openwin/lib/` `app-defaults` directory if you're using OpenWindows, 3 or later. If HoTMetaL won't run after these steps, consult with the `README` file that came with the HoTMetaL package for further instructions.

The HoTMetaL binary resides in the `bin` directory of the distribution. If you are in the main distribution directory, you can invoke it with:

```
darwin% bin/sqhm
```

After an opening "Welcome" window, the editing screen will appear.

The editing screen (see Figure 4.1) in HoTMetaL is a text editor. HTML tags may be added by selecting them from the Insert Element window, which you open by selecting Insert Element from the Markup menu. If HTML Checking is on (this is set via the Markup menu), the elements you are allowed to insert depend on where the cursor is in relation to other elements. For example, begin a document by inserting the `HTML` element (note that the `HEAD` element is also added by default). Place the cursor between the start and end `HEAD` tags. If HTML Checking is on, only tags al-

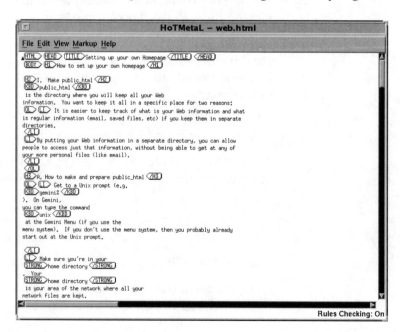

Figure 4.1
HoTMetaL

lowed in the HEAD of a document will be displayed (these include BASE, ISINDEX, and TITLE). Place the cursor past the end HEAD tag to insert the BODY element (which is the only option available). Place the cursor between the BODY tags and the list grows much longer, to include all the available elements that are legal in the BODY section of an HTML document. If you turn HTML Checking off, you are shown a complete list of HTML elements no matter where the cursor is.

HoTMetaL doesn't actually display tags (bits of text with 〈 and 〉 around them); it displays an icon with the element's name as the begin tag and one with a slash followed by the element's name as the end tag. By selecting "Hide Tags" from the View menu, you can optionally hide or show these icons on the page. HoTMetaL tries to do basic formatting on the screen as you're editing documents, such as indenting lists, so by hiding the tags you can get a basic idea of what your document will look like.

When you insert an element that has one or more attributes (such as the A element), in order to give values to the attributes, you must place the cursor between the start and end tags for that element and select "Edit Links and Attributes" from the Markup menu. This displays a pop-up window with fields for each possible attribute associated with that element—for the A element, this includes HREF, REL, REV, and NAME. To change the attributes of an element, again place the cursor between the start and end tags and choose "Edit Links and Attributes." The data that was previously entered will appear in the pop-up window for you to change. (The only exception is the IMG element, whose pop-up window appears when you first insert the element into the document.)

When you insert an element that has one or more attributes (such as the URL for an 〈IMG SRC=" "〉 tag), a pop-up window may appear requesting the additional information. For the IMG element, the box asks for the URL of the image, alternative text (ALT text), alignment (top, middle, bottom), and whether the image is an imagemap (by way of the ISMAP attribute). This information can be changed later by placing the cursor between the start and end tags of the element and selecting "Edit Links and Attributes" from the Markup menu. A pop-up window appears with fields for each of the element's attributes. (Unfortunately, for the A element, the initial pop-up window did not appear—the only way to enter the

URL of the link was to select the "Edit Links and Attributes" after placing the element in the document.)

Under the View menu are two unique and useful options. "Show Link and Context View" displays a new window that will always list the hierarchy of open elements terminating in the current cursor position. For example, if your document began with the HTML element, next had a BODY element, and then an OL element, placing the cursor before the ending OL element tag will cause the HTML, BODY, and OL elements to be displayed in the Context Window. By placing the cursor after the end of the OL list, only the HTML and BODY elements will be listed, because they are the only unterminated tags at the cursor position. This can be helpful to debug documents that may contain many nested lists, so you can keep track of which lists are embedded in each other. "Show Structure View" gives essentially an outline view of the current document in another window. By clicking on individual elements, the elements contained between their start and end tags are either shown or hidden. You can use this outline view to easily organize your document into sections, and to track nested elements such as lists. While you can't edit in the Structure View, by moving the cursor in the Structure View window, the cursor in the main document moves to the same area of the document so you can't get lost between the two windows.

HoTMetaL also includes a pop-up window for inserting ISO characters from ISO-8879 (Latin-1). This is available under the Markup menu as "Insert Character Entity".

To delete elements in your document, you must select both the start and end tags, and any text in between them and press the Backspace or Delete key. To change one element to another, place the cursor between the start and end tags, and select "Change" from the Markup menu. The Change Element window will appear and let you select an element to replace the current element with (subject to HTML Checking, if on). The text between the tags should be preserved with a change.

To preview your document, select "Preview" from the File menu. This will launch Mosaic and display your document. To change your document, you must go back to HoTMetaL, edit the document, then select "Preview" again (which invokes a new copy of Mosaic).

When you are done editing your document, the "Publish" option on the File menu will allow you to change any relative URLs to fully qualified URLs should you deem it necessary. In addition, from the File menu, you may open, save, or rename your document, as you might expect.

Evaluation

HoTMetaL Free is a very cumbersone package, from its installation to its use. Its useful features—inserting character elements, an outline view, and HTML checking—are overwhelmed by the difficulty of getting what you want. The HTML checking itself, which is a good idea, can be extremely frustrating at times, simply preventing rather than assisting the user to put the elements in the correct places. The "Preview" option, while accurate, is too slow for extended use. It's great to see your document actually being displayed by a Web browser (NCSA Mosaic), but a quick, internal preview would give much faster, if less accurate, results. The organization of the element icons in the editing window are often confusing, such that hiding the icons (by using the "Show/Hide Tags" item on the View menu) made the document much easier to look at (in editing mode). For all it tries to do, HoTMetaL Free misses the mark of being a really useful tool.

The HoTMetaL Pro 2.0 version of this package, which was not reviewed, has touted itself as being a much better tool for document creation. The Pro 2.0 version includes a WYSIWYG editing environment, forms, HTML 3.0, Netscape tags, macros, spell-checking, toolbars and more, but expect to pay for this increased functionality.

Availability

Product and ordering information for HoTMetaL Pro 2.0 can be found on the Web at

    http://www.sq.com/products/pst.htm

Download information for HoTMetaL Free can be found on the Web at

    http://www.sq.com/products/hotmetal/hm-ftp.htm

ASHE—A Simple HTML Editor 1.1

ASHE is an X Windows-based HTML editor from John Punin of the Department of Computer Science at Rensselaer Polytechnic Institute. It has the notable feature of providing both "raw" and formatted views of your HTML as you type it.

Features

HTML 2.0	✔
Forms	✔
HTML 3.0	Allows manual insertion of nonsup-
Tables	ported tags.
Math	
Netscape Elements	
Validity Checking	
WYSIWYG	Built-in Preview window
Special Requirements	X Windows
Additional Notes	

Use

ASHE uses a simple two-window system (see Figure 4.2) to display both HTML source code and a graphical preview of the document being edited. Text is entered into the upper window, using the pull-down menus (or keystroke shortcuts) to place HTML entities in or around the text. ASHE includes pull-down menus for generic HTML (document divisions, paragraph breaks, images, and anchor references, and so on), character attributes, list elements, and form elements. By selecting a menu, then an item from the menu, the HTML tags are deposited in the editing window at the cursor, such that the cursor is placed between the start and end tags. If the HTML tag requires one or more attributes (such as the URL for the SRC attribute of IMG), a pop-up window appears, requesting the additional information. For example, to add a form, select the "Forms" menu and select "Form... ." The pop-up menu has a selection list for METHOD (either GET or POST) and an input box for the ACTION URL. If you enter data into the pop-up box and select the OK button, the opening FORM tag is inserted at the cursor with that data already entered. If you select some text (us-

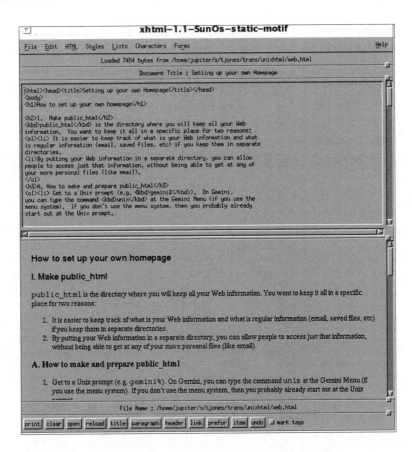

Figure 4.2
ASHE

ing the mouse) and select a menu item, the tag is placed so that it surrounds the selected text, instead of being placed at the cursor.

The bottom window displays the document, WYSIWYG-style, when the Reload button at the bottom of the screen is selected. Hypertext links are selectable, and cause the new page to be loaded in a new window (frame). Links to absolute URLs break—only logical URLs are followable. Images are not themselves displayed, but an icon is inserted to let you know that an image would be displayed there in the actual document.

Evaluation

ASHE isn't at the professional level of operation that some of the editors out there are. It isn't bug-free in operation nor does it have the most elegant look, but for quickly and easily editing HTML with a fast output display, ASHE works well. It has the look and feel of a simple text editor bundled with a Web viewer, which is much more integrated and flexible than HoTMetaL Free's implementation of both document viewing and editing. The ability to follow links in your documents and then edit those pages is an interesting and occasionally useful addition which isn't present in any of the other HTML editors reviewed here. If you can work around the occasional crashes and the requirement to navigate menus to insert elements, ASHE will work well for most general HTML editing work.

Availability

Information on ASHE, as well as links to the current source, can be found on the Web at

```
ftp://ftp.cs.rpi.edu/pub/puninj/ASHE/README.html
```

ASHE is free software.

HTML-Helper-Mode 2.0 for Emacs

HTML-Helper-Mode, from Nelson Minar at the Santa Fe Institute, is a Emacs major-mode for editing HTML.

Features

HTML 2.0	✔	
Forms	✔	
HTML 3.0	Allows manual insertion of nonsupported tags.	
Tables		
Math		
Netscape Elements		
Validity Checking		
WYSIWYG		
Special Requirements	Emacs text editor v. 19 or better.	
Additional Notes	Familiarity with the Emacs editor is helpful.	

Use

From the Web address listed here, download `tempo.el` and `html-helper-mode.el`. Put them in their own directory (such as, `"emacs-lisp"`), then add the following lines to the .emacs file in your home directory (if you don't have a .emacs file, create it first):

```
(setq load-path (cons (expand-file-name
"/home/tjones/emacs-lisp") load-path))
(autoload 'html-helper-mode "html-helper-mode"
"HTML helper mode." t)
(setq auto-mode-alist (cons '("\\.html$" .
 html-helper-mode) auto-mode-alist))
```

Be sure and change the path in the first line to match your system (the path should be the directory where the `html-helper-mode.el` and `tempo.el` files are located). Next, run Emacs with the name of an HTML file (if the file doesn't exist, it will be created):

```
emacs index.html
```

The main function of HTML-Helper-Mode is the use of keybindings (key sequences) to insert HTML tags into the text or around a text selection. The entire list of keybindings is too lengthy to include here, and may vary by version, but the current keybindings can always be had by hitting CONTROL-h,m once in Emacs with HTML-Helper-Mode mode active. The bindings are roughly broken down into categories, with a key sequence for the category and a final letter for a specific tag. For example, the key sequences for lists (and list-related tags), begin with CONTROL-c, CONTROL-l, and end with d for the ⟨dl⟩ tag, u for the ⟨ul⟩ tag, l for the ⟨li⟩ tag, and so on. Not all keybindings are this mnemonic, however. Be sure to check the keybindings list when you install HTML-Helper-Mode.

Using HTML-Helper-Mode involves regular text editing using Emacs (see Figure 4.3) while inserting tags with HTML-Helper-Mode. There are three methods by which a tag can be added. The first is the method just described, using a control-key sequence to insert a tag (both start and end tags are inserted at the cursor, and the cursor is moved to between the tags). The second method is to select a block of text in the editor and begin the key sequence with CONTROL-u. This will wrap the begin and end tags around the selected text, such that the selected text occurs between the tags. The third method is to type in enough of the tag to be uniquely identified (such as "⟨blo" which can only expand to "⟨block-quote⟩", but "⟨b⟩" could be "⟨base⟩", "⟨b⟩", "⟨blockquote⟩", and so on) and hit ESC-TAB to complete the tag (and place the cursor between the start and end tags). If a tag has attributes that must be filled in (such as the URL of the SRC attribute of IMG), the cursor will instead be placed at the point where text should be entered for the first attribute. If there is more than one attribute (that is, if the ALT attribute of IMG is also included in the tag), the key sequence ESC-CONTROL-f will move forward to the next attribute, and ESC-CONTROL-b will move back to the previous attribute (the cursor will be placed where text should be entered).

Evaluation

If your only (or preferred) system for editing HTML documents is a Unix server with an ASCII terminal, then HTML-Helper-Mode

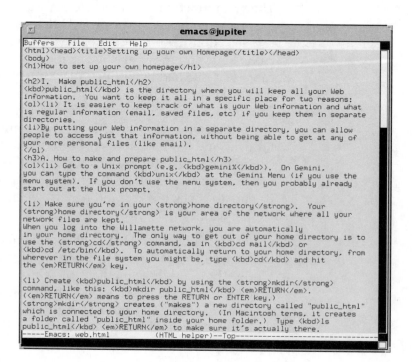

Figure 4.3
HTML-Helper-Mode
and Emacs

will significantly reduce your typing of HTML tags once you have all the keybindings memorized. Even if you don't memorize the bindings, you can still use the tag completion (ESC-TAB) to shorten the names of some of the longer tags. HTML-Helper-Mode has a steeper learning curve (compared to the other HTML editors), especially if you don't know how to use Emacs.

However, if you're already a big fan of Emacs, or if you prefer editing HTML without having to reach for the mouse every time you want to insert a new element, HTML-Helper-Mode can be extremely helpful. It's not WYSIWYG, it's not mouse-driven and blindingly intuitive, but it can be an extremely productive tool for the power user who's taken the time to learn how to use it.

Availability

Information on HTML-Helper-Mode, including links to the current sources, can be found on the Web at

```
http://www.santafe.edu/~nelson/tools/
```

HTML-Helper-Mode is free and is subject to the GNU General Public License version 2 or later.

Other Editors

Table 4.2 lists additional Unix HTML editors available.

Table 4.2
Other Unix HTML Editors

City University HTML Editor	
http://web.cs.city.ac.uk/homes/njw/ htmltext/htmltext.html	Freeware WYSIWYG HTML editor.
Phoenix	
http://www.bsd.uchicago.edu/ftp/pub/ phoenix/README.html	Freeware WYSIWYG HTML editor

Image Tools

WWWimagesize 1.6

Features

WWWimagesize, by Alex Knowles, adds WIDTH and HEIGHT attributes to all IMG elements in HTML documents. This information can then be used by Netscape, Arena, and other Web browsers to calculate the layout of a Web page before loading all the images (thereby speeding the display process).

Use

WWWimagesize is a Perl script that will automatically add WIDTH and HEIGHT attributes to all IMG elements that point to GIF, JPEG, or XBM image files, based on the actual width and height of the image. (Note: WWWimagesize 1.6 balked on some of our smaller XBM files.) Just download the Perl script from the site listed here, make sure you have Perl installed on your system, and invoke the script like so:

```
wwwimagesize document.html
```

WWWimagesize will look for IMG elements in document.html, determine the size of the image referenced by the SRC attribute, and insert the width and height into the IMG tag. A copy of the original document is saved as a backup document (usually document.html~, but this is configurable) in case WWWimagesize did something disastrously wrong. The converted document has a slightly changed group and/or user file attribute, which occurs as part of the WWWimagesize processing (but which shouldn't affect anything adversely).

WWWimagesize is configurable through a .wwwimagesizerc file located in your home directory. The options are:

- SearchURLS [YES|NO]—If YES, WWWimagesize will attempt to connect to other servers to grab images (such as if you have a reference to an image at another site). If NO, WWWimagesize will process image files located only on your site.

- BackupExtension text—Replace text with an extension to add to the filename when creating a backup copy of a document, such as .bak. Default is "~", such as the backup of document.html will be document.html~.

- OverwriteBackup [YES|NO|ASK]—If WWWimagesize finds a backup copy of a document, this option determines what it will do. If YES, the backup copy will be overwritten by the new backup copy. If NO, WWWimagesize will stop. If ASK,

WWWimagesize will ask you if it should overwrite the backup file (yes or no). The default is YES.

- ChangeIfThere [YES|NO|ASK|CLEVER]—If WWWimage-size comes across an IMG element that already has HEIGHT and WIDTH attributes, this option determines what it will do. If YES, WWWimagesize will recalculate the size of the image and replace the existing HEIGHT and WIDTH values. If NO, WWWimagesize will skip that particular IMG element without changing the values. If ASK, WWWimagesize will ask you if it should replace the existing values with new ones (yes or no). If CLEVER, WWWimagesize checks the size of the image and compares it to the existing values for WIDTH and HEIGHT. If they are some integer multiple of the image's actual size, the values are not changed; otherwise you are asked if WWWimagesize should replace the existing values with new ones (yes or no). This is provided because the Netscape browser has the ability to scale images, in which case the HEIGHT and WIDTH values are not the image's size but the display size.

- DoChmodChown [YES|NO]—On some systems, setting this to YES will stop WWWimagesize from changing the owner/ group attributes of the file it is working on.

A sample .wwwimagesizerc file (to be placed in your home directory):

```
SearchURLS YES
BackupExtension .bak
ChangeIfThere YES
```

Evaluation

WWWimagesize doesn't do much, but it does what it does well. The service it provides is especially useful for documents that use a lot of in-lined images, because the layout of the document can be determined (and the text displayed) before all the images have been loaded. This makes for a (seemingly) quicker loading page. If you're developing graphics-intensive documents, setting the HEIGHT and WIDTH attributes in IMG tags is highly recommended, and WWW-imagesize is the easiest tool out there to do it for you.

Availability

WWWimagesize is freeware. Documentation and source are available from

```
http://www.dcs.ed.ac.uk/home/ark/wwwimagesize/
```

GIFtool 1.0

GIFtool is a straightforward program from Home Pages Inc. that can create GIFs that are interlaced, and have transparent backgrounds.

Features

Transparent images	Specify a transparent color in a GIF file by RGB value, palette index, or name (such as white).
Interlaced images	Interlace or uninterlace GIF files.
Image comments	Add or remove GIF file comments.
Batch mode processing	Allows wildcard list of GIF files; saves modified image under same name.

Use

Download the appropriate package from the address here, and uncompress and unarchive it (if necessary). If you downloaded the correct version for your system, everything should be ready to go. To get information about your particular version of GIFtool, including available options and flags, run `giftool -help`. Table 4.3 lists the GIFtool 1.0 options.

To use GIFtool, run it with one or more of the previous options followed by a filename or wildcard list. For example, to turn all the GIF files in the current directory into interlaced GIFs:

```
giftool -B -i *.gif
```

To make white become transparent in a single image file:

```
giftool -B -rgb white image.gif
```

Table 4.3

GIFtool Command Line Options

-B	Run in batch mode, saving the modified image under the same name as the original image.
-i	Turn interlacing on for the image file(s). (+i turns interlacing off.)
-p	Print information (comments and color palette) for the image file(s).
-c	Print comment data from the image file(s).
+c "text"	Set comment data for the image file(s) to "*text*".
-C	Remove comment data from the image file(s).
-o filename	Save modified image as *filename*.
-rgb *name*	Sets *name* (i.e. white) as the transparent color for the image(s).
-rgb *num,num,num*	Sets the RGB color (specified as three decimal values between 0 and 255) of the transparent color for the image(s).
-*num*	Set the *num*-th color (starting at 1) in the palette to be the transparent color for the image.
-help	List GIFtool's options.
-info	List information about GIFtool, including registration information.

or

```
giftool -B -rgb 255,255,255 image.gif
```

To make the second color in the image's palette become transparent, save the transparent image as a new file (image2.gif in this case):

```
giftool -B -2 -o image2.gif image.gif
```

To show the palette for the image:

```
giftool -p image.gif
```

To add comments to an image:

```
giftool -B +c "This image was created by Tyler Jones" image.gif
```

The palette (which you can view by running `giftool -p on an image`) is a list of colors that are used by the image. Both the index and the RGB values are shown with the `-p` option.

Evaluation

GIFtool is an excellent tool for creating transparent and interlaced GIFs. The comments option is something you probably won't use very often, but it's nice to have if you need it (especially if you would like to add attribution or copyright information). Because GIFtool runs at the command line, and doesn't have a big graphical interface, it can be run more quickly and more often than a comparable graphics package without a command-line interface. Choosing the correct color to turn transparent can be a hit-or-miss operation until you get used to it, but the ability to specify a color name, an RGB value, or a palette index number lets you choose the best way to select the right color. This really is a useful tool for people who use a lot of transparent or interlaced images.

Availability

Various GIFtool binaries and limited documentation can be found at

```
http://www.homepages.com/tools/
```

GIFtool is shareware—if you find it useful, please send $10 to the authors (to get an address for the authors, run `giftool -info`). In addition to being available for Unix, it is also available for MS-DOS.

GDIT

Another pair of tools worth looking at (although we will not review it here) are GDIT and the GD library. GDIT (by David Harvey-George) is a front end to GD (by Thomas Boutell), and both are designed for on-the-fly manipulation of GIFs within CGI scripts. More information about GDIT is available at

```
http://www.demon.co.uk:80/3Wiz/gdit/
```

More information about GD is available at

```
http://siva.cshl.org/gd/gd.html
```

GDIT is also available for Windows.

MapEdit

MapEdit (see review in the next section, in Windows Tools), Thomas Boutell's map editor is also available for X Windows. See

```
http://sunsite.unc.edu/boutell/mapedit/mapedit.html
```

for details.

Windows Tools

HTML Editors

Internet Assistant 1.0

Internet Assistant, from Microsoft, is an add-on to Microsoft Word. It takes advantage of Word's interface to provide a quasi-WYSIWYG HTML editor and a Word-based Web browser.

Features

HTML 2.0	✔
Forms	✔
HTML 3.0	Unsupported HTML elements can be inserted as raw HTML.
Tables	
Math	
Netscape Elements	
Validity Checking	
WYSIWYG	✔
Special Requirements	Microsoft Word for Windows 6.0a or better
Additional Notes	

Use

Using Internet Assistant is just like using Word—literally. Internet Assistant is somewhere between a document template and a Word to HTML converter, with a Web browser thrown in (see Figure 4.4). To create an HTML document, you select New... from the File menu, and then select the HTML template. Then you start typing.

To create various HTML elements, you use the Style pop-up menu on the Word toolbar, and select the element you want to use. Character formatting commands, like bold and italic, work as they normally do—selecting bold once turns bold formatting on, and selecting it again turns it off.

To add anchors to your documents, you select the text to be linked and select HyperLink... from the Insert menu. Word allows anchors to be created to local documents (such as on your hard drive), URLs, or to "bookmarks." The third option, bookmarks, really allows links to be created within a document—the equivalent of making an anchor like

```
a link to ⟨A HREF="#foo")the Widdershins
Galaxy⟨/A⟩.
```

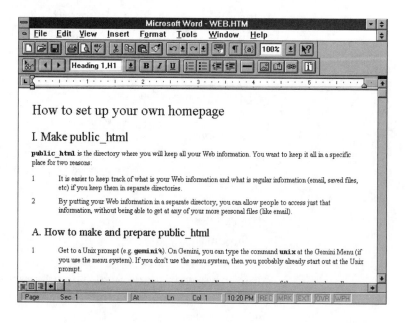

Figure 4.4
Internet Assistant

where "foo" is the name of a bookmark elsewhere in the same document.

Another useful feature is the integration of Word's outlining capability with HTML documents. If you break your documents into logical sections, and use headers to begin each section, you will find that Word's outline view can then be used to collapse and expand sections of text (to provide an overview of the document), as well as to quickly move whole chunks of text around. (Even more interesting, the outlining capacity works in Internet Assistant's browser mode, providing functionality that cannot be found currently in any other browser.)

To create forms, you select Form Field... from the Insert menu. The first time you insert a form field, a dialog box will inform you that you are creating a new form, and prompt you for information about the form (such as whether it should be posted via GET or POST, and what CGI script should handle the output of the form). After the form has been created, horizontal rules labeled "Top of Form" and "Bottom of Form" indicate the boundaries of the new form, and new form fields can be inserted between them.

To add HTML not directly supported by Internet Assistant, select HTML Markup... from the Insert menu.

NOTE: When you are done creating your document, you will need to use the Save As... option under the File menu in order to save it as HTML (Save will save it as a Word document). You will need to save your document as HTML in order to serve it via Web server, as well as to view the HTML source of your document (by saving it and reopening it in a text editor).

Evaluation

Internet Assistant applies the power of a mature, feature-rich word processor to the business of creating structured text, and comes out surprisingly well. The integration is a bit rough at times, especially when creating a definition list (it turns out that the definition term [DT] style is really composed of 〈DT〉...〈DD〉; there is no style for the definition [DD]. A definition is, apparently, anything that follows the Definition Term style, inside of the Definition List style. This took some rooting around in the on-line help to work out). In addition, there is a tendency to favor physical character emphasis (bold and italic) over logical emphasis (emphasized and strongly emphasized). Also, there is no easy way to see the actual HTML code that Internet Assistant is generating, short of saving your document as HTML and opening the HTML file in a text editor like Notepad. Using Internet Assistant means sacrificing precise control over your HTML.

On the other hand, Internet Assistant offers several features that distinguish it from other editors. First, it does provide WYSIWYG editing, and actually uses the HTML structure to influence how the document can be edited. This means that you are prevented, to a certain extent, from shooting yourself in the foot. Second, the outlining feature can be a truly powerful tool for writing lengthy HTML documents. Finally, you can employ all of the features of Word, including spellchecking and drag-and-drop editing, in creating HTML (and can more easily convert existing Word documents to HTML, via the Word to HTML converter).

If you're willing to give up fine control over your HTML, and if you have Microsoft Word for Windows, Internet Assistant is a good choice.

Availability

Internet Assistant is freely available, although you will have to purchase Microsoft Word for Windows (version 6.0a or later) in order to use it. Internet Assistant (and documentation about Internet Assistant) can be found on the Web at

```
http://www.microsoft.com/pages/deskapps/word/ia/de-
fault.htm
```

WebEdit 1.0c

WebEdit, from the Data Transfer Group, is a text-based HTML editor that supports HTML 3.0 elements.

Features

HTML 2.0	✔
Forms	✔
HTML 3.0	✔
Tables	✔
Math	(Math symbols, but no elements)
Netscape Elements	✔
Validity Checking	
WYSIWYG	Can use browser (such as Netscape or Mosaic) to preview document.
Special Requirements	
Additional Notes	Dialog boxes make element creation easier.

Use

WebEdit is a souped-up text editor (see Figure 4.5) that makes it easier to create HTML tags. To use it, you type in your text, using the toolbar to insert HTML tags as necessary. For example, to enter the line

```
This is some ⟨EM⟩emphasized⟨/EM⟩ text, and this
link goes to ⟨AHREF="http://www.cs.cmu.edu/~tilt/
principia/")subversive literature⟨/A⟩.
```

you would type "This is some, " then type Ctrl-E to add an emphasized text element (at which point your cursor is positioned between the ⟨EM⟩ and the ⟨/EM⟩). Then type "emphasized" and hit the End key (to get to the end of the line, after the ⟨/EM⟩). Then type " text, and this link goes to, " and click on the link button in the toolbar. In the dialog box that comes up, enter `http://www.cs.cmu.edu/~tilt/principia/` and press the Anchor button. Then enter "subversive literature" inside the anchor tags, and add the period to the end.

You can also select text and apply an element to it, either by selecting the element from a menu (or a toolbar), or by using the right mouse button to add character formatting information (like emphasized or bold) to the selection.

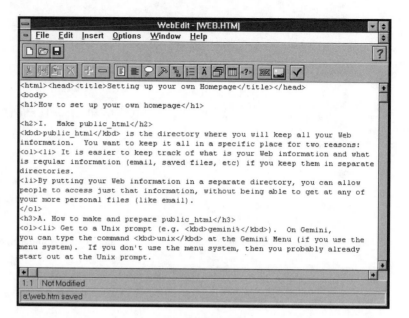

Figure 4.5
WebEdit

WebEdit also makes it easy to insert special characters that may not be on your keyboard. To do this, select Special Character... from the Insert menu, and select the character you want to insert.

Evaluation

WebEdit is representative of the bulk of Windows HTML editors—a toolbar or two is provided to make it easy to add tags, and dialog boxes are used to help define what will be in the tags, but once the tag has been inserted it's just plain old text. There is no provision for double-clicking on a tag to edit an element's attributes, or to represent the elements in any way that is similar to what the finished HTML might look like.

Among the problems with this class of editors (including Hot Dog, HTML Assistant, HTML Easy! Pro, HTML Writer, and Web-Spinner) is the lack of ability to validate your HTML. The editors will cheerfully insert HTML tags into your documents, but do not make use of the structure implied by these HTML tags to help you edit your document. You can insert a tag in the middle of another tag, or math elements in the middle of a table. While this is not terrible, it does mean that the editor cannot provide any sophisticated help in the creation of documents. The upshot is that you end up drifting a hand over to the mouse constantly in order to insert HTML tags, leaving you with the feeling that it would probably be faster just to type some of these elements in directly.

This being said, WebEdit is one of the better editors in this class, and does have some very nice features. Chief among these are the ability to insert HTML 3.0 and Netscape tags. Also nice is the proliferation of dialog boxes that clearly enumerate the attributes you can add to an element. And, since WebEdit displays the HTML source code, you have a fine control over what the HTML source of your document actually looks like.

(To give equal time to a competitor, Hot Dog is also one of the better editors in this particular class. It provides many of the same features of WebEdit, along with some additional ones like easy table creation. It suffers, however, from being overly baroque. However, if you like WebEdit, Hot Dog is also worth looking at.)

WebEdit is an editor designed for those who like to enter their HTML directly, or for those who want to mark up an existing ASCII-text document into HTML. If that sounds like what you want, give WebEdit a shot.

Availability

WebEdit (and additional documentation) is available via the Web from

```
http://wwwnt.thegroup.net/webedit/webedit.htm
```

WebEdit is *not* free—you can evaluate a fully functional copy for 30 days, and then register it for $99.95.

Live Markup (beta 6b)

Live Markup, from MediaTech, offers a quasi-WYSIWYG HTML editing environment.

Features

HTML 2.0	✔
Forms	(To be included in Professional version)
HTML 3.0	(To be included in Professional version)
Tables	(To be included in Professional version)
Math	(To be included in Professional version)
Netscape Elements	(To be included in Professional version)
Validity Checking	✔
WYSIWYG	✔
Special Requirements	
Additional Notes	ISO Latin virtual keyboard for easy insertion of symbols. Can add "raw" HTML not directly supported by editor (HTML 3.0, for example).

Use

Live Markup has a unique interface that combines a WYSIWYG editor with a mechanism for finely controlling the underlying HTML (see Figure 4.6). Live Markup uses "selectors" to visually represent HTML elements, and the relationships between them.

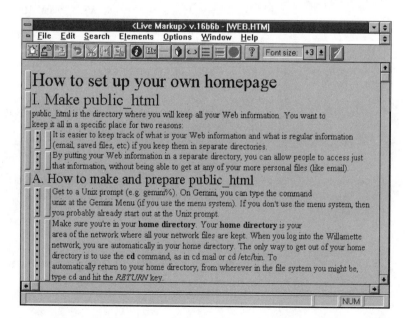

Figure 4.6

Live Markup

When creating a document in Live Markup, you use the toolbar to select the kind of element you want to insert. Once you have selected an element, a rectangle (the selector) will appear on the left margin to represent the element. The rectangle will appear to be depressed, indicating that this is the active selector, and the cursor will appear. Selectors can represent text blocks, headers, and lists, and other HTML elements are applied to text within a selector.

Selectors have attributes—a header, for example, might be of a certain level, or a text block might be a paragraph, a block quote, preformatted text, or something else. You can change the attributes of a selector with the right mouse button; right-clicking the selector brings up a pop-up list with attributes that can be modified. In addition, text that has been selected can also be modified (with physical and logical font styles, or font size information).

To start an average document, you begin by clicking the "Edit document information" button on the toolbar. This allows you to specify information about the document itself, such as the title. Next, you might add a level 1 header to start the document by selecting the Header button. Next, select the Text block button to begin entering text. You'll want to right-click the text block's selector in order to specify that this is a paragraph; by default, the text block is considered to be simply plain text.

Creating a list can be tricky. First you must create the list selector (with the New list button), then you must create each list item (with the New list item button). Then, you must create a block of text to go in the list item. Then you can type. Hitting ENTER isn't sufficient for creating a new list item—you select the list (the left-most) selector by left-clicking on it, and then again use the New list item button. Sound unpleasant? It is, but most operations are not this complicated.

A few caveats: when you first start a new document, you can't simply begin typing. You have to insert a text block or some other selector. Also, text blocks are not paragraphs by default; you'll need to right-click the selector to change that. Also, simply hitting Return in a text block will not create a new paragraph. Instead, it will insert a line break (⟨BR⟩) where you hit Return.

Evaluation

Live Markup's selectors are an innovative means of manipulating WYSIWYG HTML (love those acronyms . . .) while still being able to retain fine control. The features that enable you to nest selectors and to use the right mouse button to change the attributes are both very nice. You can add raw HTML to insert elements that are not supported directly by the program. And, the program's approach provides a measure of "sanity checking" to prevent you from composing bad HTML. In general, it is a program with a very promising air about it.

On the other hand, the version we evaluated was difficult to start using. The on-line help was able to point us in the right direction, but it was certainly not as intuitive as the authors claimed. Also problematic were the facts that a default text block is not supplied when you open a new document, or that text blocks are not automatically paragraphs, or that hitting ENTER in a text block does not create a new paragraph. Finally, the program was *slow*, noticeably slow on a 486/50, and slow on complicated documents on a Pentium 90. A lot of small interface problems combined to overwhelm the appeal of what is overall a very nice program.

Live Markup is a step in the right direction, but it is still very rough around the edges. To be fair, the version evaluated was a beta version. Hopefully by the time you read this, the authors of the program will have made some interface enhancements—at that point, it will be a program you will want to seriously consider trying.

Availability

Live Markup (and additional information) is available via the Web at

```
http://www.mediatec.com/mediatech/
```

Live Markup is not free, although a free 30-day evaluation copy is available. Live Markup costs $99 ($29 for educational users).

Other Editors

Table 4.4 lists additional Windows HTML editors available.

Table 4.4	Hot Dog	`http://www.sausage.com/`	
Other Windows HTML Editors	HoTMetaL	`http://www.sq.com/products/ hotmetal/hmp-org.htm`	Free and professional versions available. See review in Unix section.
	HTML Assistant	`ftp://ftp.cs.dal.ca/ htmlasst/htmlafaq.html`	
	HTML Easy! Pro	`http://www.trytel.com/ ~milkylin/`	
	HTML Writer WebSpinner	`http://lal.cs.byu.edu/ people/nosack/`	Free HTML editor. Supports Windows 95 long filenames.
	WP Internet Publisher	`http://wp.novell.com/ elecpub/intpub.htm`	Like Internet Assistant, but for WordPerfect for Windows 6.1.

Image Tools

GIF Construction Set

GIF Construction Set, from Alchemy Mindworks, is a GIF editor that allows you to create transparent backgrounds and interlaced GIFs (along with many other features).

Features

Transparent GIFs

GIF Construction Set allows you to create GIFs with transparent backgrounds. On most browsers, the browser's background color can then be seen through the transparent GIF background.

Interlaced GIFs

GIF Construction Set can create interlaced GIFs. Interlaced GIFs appear (but do not actually) load faster in some browsers, because the browser can display a rough version of the entire image faster, refining the image as more data is received.

Use

To create a GIF with a transparent background, open the image in GIF Construction Set. Select the entry immediately before the image, and select Insert from the Block menu. Select a Control block from the Insert Object dialog that appears. Once the control block is inserted, select Edit from the Block menu. Check the Transparent

Colour check box (this will cause the colored box containing a number to become undimmed). To select which color should be made transparent, select the colored box to the right of Transparent Colour (it will contain a number, most likely 0). This will bring up a palette of the colors, so you can decide which should be made transparent. Alternately, select the eyedropper to the right of the colored box, which will allow you to pick the color from the image itself. After you have selected a color to be made transparent, save the file.

To create an interlaced GIF, open the image in GIF Construction Set. Double-click on the IMAGE entry that you wish to interlace (in most GIFs, there will only be one IMAGE entry). A dialog will appear to allow you to edit the image. Check the Interlaced check box, and then select OK. Save the file.

Evaluation

GIF Construction Set is a useful tool for creating transparent and interlaced GIFs, but it can also do much more. It can insert multiple image and text blocks into your GIF, and allow you to add comments (such as copyright information or other information about the image). Because it can do so much, it might be slightly overwhelming. However, it does come with excellent documentation, and the price is right: GIF Construction Set is "bookware," which means that to register it, you must read a book (*The Order*, by Steven Rimmer). As authors ourselves, we fully appreciate such a strategy.

Availability

GIF Construction Set can be found via the Web at

```
http://uunorth.north.net:8000/alchemy/html/
gifcon.html
```

It is not free; as noted, it is "bookware."

MapEdit

Features

MapEdit, from Tom Boutell, is used to create map files, to turn existing images into imagemaps. The map files produced are usable with NCSA, CERN, and Windows httpd.

Use

To create an imagemap for a file, launch MapEdit and select Open/Create... from the File menu. Enter a GIF filename (either by typing it in, or with the Browse button), and then select a filename for the map file in the same fashion. If the filename you enter for the map file does not already exist, MapEdit will confirm that you wish to create a new map file. Select OK to create the file.

MapEdit will then load the image (be careful, it may not dither the image very well, so your colors may be off). You can then create one of three kinds of hyperlinked areas: circles, rectangles, and polygons. Each kind of area you describe can be linked to a URL, and a default URL can be specified for areas outside of any hyperlinked areas.

To create a region, you select the type of shape from the Tools menu. For a rectangle, you then click once with the left mouse button to indicate one corner, and again with the *right* mouse button to indicate the second corner. For a circle, you click once with the left mouse button to indicate the center, and again with the *right* mouse button to indicate the radius. For a polygon, you click once with the left mouse button for each point, and then click once with the *right* mouse button to select the final point (MapEdit will make the connection between the final point and the initial point). In all cases, it is the right mouse button, not the left mouse button, that indicates that the shape is correct and should be saved.

After clicking the right mouse button, the Object URL dialog box will appear, asking for the URL to which this region should point. You can also enter comments at this point. If you enter the URL and hit OK, the shape will remain, outlined in white, and you can continue adding additional shapes.

If you wish to edit or delete regions you have created, select Test + Edit from the Tools menu. Then, click inside any region you wish to edit or delete. After you have clicked on a region, the Object URL dialog box will reappear, offering you the opportunity to either edit the area's information or to delete the object entirely.

If you wish to set the default URL (for clicks that lay outside defined areas), use Edit Default URL... from the File menu.

To save the imagemap when you are done, use either Save or Save As... (in the File menu). Save As... will allow you to save the imagemap in either NCSA or CERN format—most servers support the NCSA format.

Evaluation

MapEdit is a straightforward program that does one thing—create imagemap files—and does it well. There are no fancy frills here, and there don't need to be. MapEdit makes the task of creating imagemaps much easier, and it is highly recommended.

Availability

MapEdit is available via the Web at

```
http://sunsite.unc.edu/boutell/mapedit/mapedit.html
```

MapEdit is not free software, except for educational or nonprofit institutions. Registration is $25. MapEdit is also available for X Windows.

Other Image Tools

Table 4.5 lists additional Windows image tools available.

Table 4.5 Other Windows Image Tools			
GIFtool	`http://www.homepages.com/tools/`	Reviewed in Unix section—also available for MS-DOS.
GDIT	`http://www.demon.co.uk:80/3Wiz/gdit/`	Described in Unix section—also available for MS-DOS.
Lview Pro	`ftp://oak.oakland.edu/SimTel/win3/graphics/lviewp1b.zip`	A full-featured graphics package; can create transparent and interlaced GIFs.

Mac Tools

HTML Editors

BBEdit (and HTML Extension Packages)

BBEdit is a quick, powerful and, most important, easily extendible text editor much beloved by programmers and serious HTML fiends.

Features

HTML 2.0	with BBEdit HTML Extensions or BBEdit HTML Tools v1.3
Forms	with BBEdit HTML extensions
HTML 3.0	Unsupported HTML elements can be inserted as raw HTML.
Tables	
Forms	
Netscape Elements	
Validity Checking	
WYSIWIG	with Preview extension
Special Requirements	
Additional Notes	

Use

BBEdit (see Figure 4.7), from Bare Bones Software, has earned its status as the Mac programmer's editing tool of choice due to its intuitive interface, speed, versatility, and extendibility. Getting started is easy—just click on the BBEdit icon, marvel at its launch speed, and open a new document.

BBEdit is designed as an all-purpose programmer's text editor, not as a special-purpose HTML tool. But you'll most likely learn to appreciate its general features, which include a nifty save status icon, document path info, and toggle menus for wrapping text and displaying line numbers, cursor position, and "invisibles"—paragraph marks, tab marks, and similar nonprinting characters.

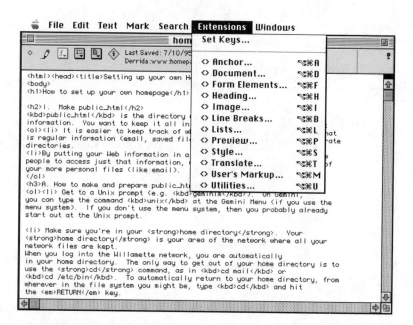

Figure 4.7
BBEdit

One of the first features you'll want to explore is BBEdit's Find & Replace capabilities. BBEdit will locate any character or word you designate and either display an annotated list of all occurrences or replace each one with any string or expression of your choosing. More impressive is its ability to search through folders and subdirectories, allowing you to change many files at once. This is a useful tool when you've got many files of unformatted text and you'd like to add anchor element information to all e-mail addresses and URLs, and similar batch processing tasks. Regular expressions are supported for truly sophisticated grep-like search and replaces. But whether your searches are simple or sophisticated, you can name and save each pattern for easy future access.

There are no cute HTML buttons in BBEdit and that's Okay—you wouldn't have used them anyway (would you really rather have to use a mouse to highlight text and then search for a button within a dialog box, or just type ⟨B⟩to get bold⟨/B⟩?).

Two sets of HTML-specific extensions are available: Carles Bellver's BBEdit HTML Extensions and Lindsay Davies's BBEdit HTML Tools v1.3. Lindsay Davies's extensions are a personal favorite and, while you may never put many of the extensions to use, a few are Gifts from Above. Take the translate extension.

From this dialog box, the process of translating Quark or Word files of a print magazine, brochure, or term paper is transformed from a major chore to a trivial task. This extension will take your clichés and turn them into clichès (è is the HTML entity for é, which is a non-ASCII character) or execute the same process in reverse. While you'll love the option to automatically place ⟨P⟩ tags before paragraphs, this'll also come in handy when you want to strip out all those HTML tags from your awesome e-zine and distribute beautiful paper copies to the unwired population of this world.

Since you'll probably be using the preview extension to view your docs with your Web browser, you can expect to develop a tight interplay between it and BBEdit. The Anchor extension is a clever helper that is nicely integrated within the whole environment. Not only are the last 10 URLs from your document available from a pop-up menu, but you can also insert any URL from any site of your Web browser's hotlist into your HTML document.

To make both Preview and Anchor fully functional, you should open the Utilities extension and click on the Preferences button. From here you can use the pull-down menu to first select your Web browser, and then select your browser's hotlist, which should be found either within the Preferences folder inside the System folder (or a subfolder in this directory belonging to your Web browser), or within your browser application's directory.

Beyond Preview and Anchor, you may want to take advantage of templates; and, conceivably, the forms and image extensions may prove useful to you when you're just starting to learn HTML. Probably you'll just go straight to this extension set's last great feature, Check Markup. Located in Utilities, this button quickly generates a new document with a detailed list of all possible HTML errors and shows you where they occur.

Evaluation

Unlike some of the other text editors to be reviewed, BBEdit lacks a front end designed specifically for HTML editing. But what it lacks in flash it more than makes up for in sheer utility. If you have a serious interest in doing professional HTML writing, or if you intend on committing a professional amount of time to your Web weaving, you'll be glad you started here. BBEdit will grow in its utility as you grow in your ability, a sure sign of a healthy application. Do give it and BBEdit HTML Tools v1.3 a try.

Availability

BBEdit is commercial software. BBEditLite is freeware. A demo of BBEdit and BBEditLite can be downloaded from

```
ftp://ftp.std.com/pub/bbedit/
```

Lindsay Davies's BBEdit HTML Tools v1.3 are freeware, and are available at

```
http://www.york.ac.uk/~ld11/BBEditTools.html
```

Carles Bellver's BBEdit HTML Extensions are available at

```
ftp://ftp.std.com/pub/bbedit/third-party-
extensions/HTML_extensions_r10.hqx
```

Webtor 0.9.1

Webtor, from Jochen Schales, is the closest thing to a WYSIWYG HTML editor that currently exists on the Mac, and it is designed to facilitate a rapid learning curve for the novice HTML writer.

Features

HTML 2.0	✔
Forms	
HTML 3.0	
Tables	
Forms	
Netscape Elements	
Validity Checking	✔
WYSIWIG	✔
Special Requirements	
Additional Notes	

Use

Webtor was, at the time of this writing, poorly documented, had several bugs that sometimes result in crashes, and had a couple of nonfunctioning major features. Still, a buzz about this app exists, and for a good reason: even in its primitive "pre-alpha" state, it still accomplishes some very respectable goals.

Webtor is designed as a WYSIWYG editor and, as such, looks more like a word processor such as Microsoft Word than a text editor (see Figure 4.8). All changes you make to the text, such as adding various spacings, italicizing or bolding text, or making headlines, are displayed as they will ultimately look on your reader's browser. The HTML is written for you as you arrange the text and graphics on the page.

After launching Webtor, your first task will be to link it to your browser and a text editor. This is easily accomplished by setting the preferences under the Edit menu. From here, Webtor acts as in intermediary between the two applications. To see either the raw HTML or the final display, View Source and Test Document (under the Extras menu) will open either the editor or the browser, respectively.

All sorts of HTML text formatting is made simple by Webtor. The preset hotkeys are intuitive—command-I italicizes, command-1

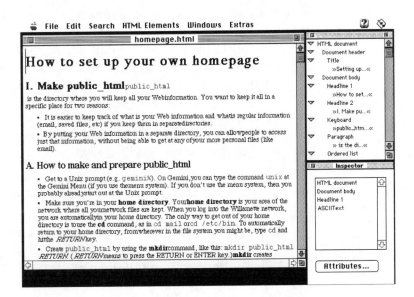

Figure 4.8
Webtor

through command-6 turn yield H1 through H6, and so on—and you'll immediately know not only whether a tag will display according to your preferences, but whether it's even possible.

Creating anchors and placing images is a bit more problematic. Once these elements are created, an Inspector box opens that presents you with a menu of link types, each of which can open into a more detailed dialog box. These dialog boxes, while allowing you to type any path, give no added features for minimizing repetitive entries. You can, however, cut and paste images and anchors within and between documents, if this is appropriate for your project.

The search and replace tool has the potential to be almost as useful as that of BBEdit (it appears to be crafted in its likeness) but it lacks the power to do multifile searches, use regular expressions, and, most of all, to save useful searches.

One last interesting feature is a document structure window. This provides you with a hierarchical (and collapsible) outline of your HTML, which could prove very useful when creating large documents.

Evaluation

Some envision a future in which all casual Web users may easily create their own content, not as an occupation but simply for the sake of scribbling their initials and/or a few hastily conceived witticisms (read: home page) on the bathroom wall. The key to this particular utopia will depend both on the growth of people connected to the Internet and the available of easy-to-use authoring tools. What this means is that ultimately somebody will release the perfect WYSIWYG HTML editor, something that might look like an ultra-simplified Quark Xpress.

While Webtor, at present, may not be the fulfillment of such a dream, it does take several steps in the right direction and may, over time, develop into a killer app. If you're only interested in putting up a small home site and find yourself struggling with other net applications and various graphics packages, you may not be enthusiastic about the sort of commitment needed to take advantage of an editor like BBEdit—in which case, Webtor could be just what you're looking for.

Availability

Webtor 0.9.1 pre-Alpha 2 is freeware, and is available at

```
http://www.igd.fhg.de/~neuss/webtor/webtor.html
```

HTML.edit 1.7

HTML.edit, by Murray Altheim, is a special-purpose HTML text editor that features an impressively robust set of icons and menus for inserting and formatting all 2.0 and 3.0 tags.

Features

HTML 2.0	✔
Forms	✔
HTML 3.0	✔
Tables	✔
Forms	✔
Netscape Elements	
Validity Checking	
WYSIWIG	
Special Requirements	
Additional Notes	

Use

Because of its many options and capabilities, approaching HTML.edit may be daunting, but you may find the familiarization process well worth your time. The immediate presence of an authoritative set of tutorials is a nice start (Murray Altheim, the app's author, was a part of the HTML 3.0 working group, and it shows), and does a nice job of taking the user from beginner status to a reasonable level of competence in as short a time as possible.

The display of this set of tutorials immediately highlights one of HTML.edit's strongest assets, which is its ability to handle a large amount (100+) of separate documents simultaneously. Navigating through your set of files is easy—you may either use the VCR-like controls for advancing and reversing through the stack or use the quick menu function.

A floating list of icons can be placed anywhere on your display, which you will find convenient, and provides quick and intuitive access to just about any HTML tag outside of those that are Netscape-specific. The tool icon conceals a useful pop-up menu with a few key functions such as remove HTML, convert ¶'s to 〈P〉's, table conversion, and customizable entity lists. (See Figure 4.9 for a screen shot of HTML.edit.)

This is the sort of package that invites in-depth usage and, thankfully, excellent on-line help is provided that graphically and textually describes every function. Clicking on the question mark in the button bar gives you the same bar located statically within a larger explanatory help box. From here you may continue clicking on the various icons in order to view their corresponding uses. The name of the game here is obsessive comprehensiveness.

Evaluation

While it may seem that HTML.edit is the most sophisticated HTML authoring tool for the Mac, there are drawbacks. Obviously, this package is written exclusively for the construction of

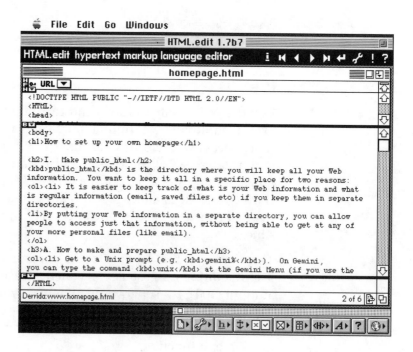

Figure 4.9
HTML.edit

HTML pages. One disadvantage is the restrictive framework imposed upon your HTML writing process. Though many functions are included with the package, building your own specialized operations may range from difficult to impossible, and third-party extensions à la BBEdit's are unlikely.

The interface is pretty but a price is paid in speed (same as it ever was!). Even running the PowerPC version gives you an only-adequate performance, which can be a drag when you really want to crank out those pages.

Still, for those who need a serious editor, yet are intimidated by the depth of BBEdit, HTML.edit is probably the best all-around compromise. Users can expect to expand their knowledge about HTML through the use of this package and, hopefully at the same time, expand their contribution to the Web.

Availability

HTML.edit 1.7beta4 is freeware (license required for commercial use), and is available at

```
http://www.metrics.nttc.edu/tools/htmledit/
HTML Edit.html
```

Image Tools

Transparency

Transparency, by Aaron Giles, is a simple utility that allows you to set the transparency index for GIFs, for display of graphics on nonwhite backgrounds.

Availability

Transparency 1.0 is freeware, and can be found at

```
ftp://ftp.freedonia.com/utilities/
```

WebMap

WebMap, by Rowland Smith, generates imagemap files in NCSA or CERN format by allowing you to outline areas in GIF or PICT files to define hotspots.

Availability

WebMap 1.0.1 is shareware. WebMap 2.0.x is commercial software. Both are available from

```
http://www.city.net/cnx/software/webmap.html
```

Other Image Tools

Table 4.6 lists additional Macintosh image tools available.

Multimedia Tools

Ulaw (Rod Kennedy)

Ulaw converts Macintosh `snd' resources into Sun µ-law format.

Availability

Ulaw 1.4b is freeware, and available at

```
ftp://ftp.freedonia.com/utilities/
```

FlattenMOOV (Robert Hennessy)

FlattenMOOV is a simple utility that flattens QuickTime movies—it moves information from the resource fork to the data fork of the movie file, for use on non-Macintosh platforms. This is an *essential* tool, if you want to use QuickTime movies in your infostructure.

Availability

FlattenMOOV is freeware, and can be found at

```
ftp://ftp.freedonia.com/utilities/
```

Shutterbug (Cannibal Island)

Shutterbug is an application for use with the QuickCam, the very affordable 4-bit, 320 × 240 pixel greyscale camera from Connectix. It snaps a JPEG image at regular intervals, and writes the resultant file to disk, which can then be served by your Web server.

Table 4.6 Other Macintosh Image Tools	GIFConverter	`ftp://ftp.freedonia.` `com/utilities/`	GIFConverter can convert a number of file formats to the GIF format, and supports GIF interlacing. It also conveniently displays the height and width of a GIF when it's displayed, making it easier to take advantage of the HEIGHT and WIDTH attributes of the IMG element. (Shareware)
	clip2gif	`ftp://ftp.freedonia.` `com/utilities/`	clip2gif converts PICT or GIF images to PICT, GIF, or JPEG format. It is also scriptable, and can be used to generate images on the fly for your Web documents. (Freeware)
	Photoshop	`http://www.adobe.com/` `Apps/Photoshop.html`	Photoshop is everyone's favorite all-purpose image editing tool. It can be used to create original images, to correct and retouch scanned images, to scale existing artwork, and to convert images between graphics formats. (Commercial)

Availability

Shutterbug 1.2 is shareware. More information can be found at

```
http://goldfish.physics.utoronto.ca/ShutterBug/
Sbug.html
```

Part II

The Web

We continue our journey by considering your web as an infostructure. From the hardware and software that actually do the serving, to the individuals and groups who will create and maintain your documents, there are many issues to consider. This section describes how to build your web as an integrated whole.

Chapter 5 begins by discussing the issues involved in content creation and maintenance. Chapter 6 looks at the HTTP servers you will be choosing between—the software engines upon which your infostructure will rest. Chapter 7 tackles the question of automated maintenance tools, and is perhaps the most important of all of the chapters in this section; consider the tools discussed here as indispensable. Chapter 8 discusses the Common Gateway Interface (CGI), a powerful tool for creating dynamic documents. Chapter 9 covers security, including access control and authentication. Finally, Chapter 10 discusses ways to advertise your web to potential readers. Later, in Part III, Chapter 12 finishes the discussion of the web with a web-level style guide.

5
Approaching Your Web as an Infostructure

This chapter provides an overview of the issues and questions that will confront you as you set up your web server. You will save much time and energy by thinking about these issues now, before dealing with the technical issues of setting up a server, and the creative issues of developing and deploying content.

The organization of your web is probably not what your readers are most interested in. They are interested in the information contained within your web, instead—the documents and services. And yet, if your web as a whole is not well-conceived, this is what your readers will notice most. If they cannot effectively use and navigate your infostructure, they will not be able to use the information provided within it.

As we cover the major issues involved in planning your web, we will consider three (fictional) groups, and watch how they resolve their problems. The three groups are diverse in background, and in their goals for setting up an infostructure:

Metanoia Bookworks has decided to place a server on the Web in order to promote its wide range of self-help computing books.

Springfield University a four-year liberal arts college, is investigating creating an online presence in order to provide information about the University, and to share research done by faculty.

The Upper Valley Historical Society has spent many years researching and archiving the regional development of the Upper Valley. It has an impressive collection including a rich set of oral histories from area residents. It has recently received a grant to place this information online in order to make it more widely accessible.

Planning your Web

Purpose

The first question you must ask yourself is, "Why am I placing a Web server online?" The answer to this question will define the sorts of services you provide, and will also help to define maintenance strategies for documents. Is this Web server providing a service (free or commercial) to the online community, or is it only providing internal services to your local organization? Is it acting as a source to the Internet for information about your organization? Will it only provide information supplied by a centralized source, or will it provide any information that your organization's members choose to publish?

Metanoia Bookworks

Metanoia Bookworks is primarily concerned with placing information about its company on-line, thereby creating an Internet presence for itself. It would like to provide a catalog of books that it publishes, as well as distribution information for potential buyers. In addition, it would like to experiment with on-line distribution, allowing readers to read portions of books before deciding to buy, in an electronic analogue of real-life browsing in bookstores.

Because it is primarily interested in providing company-related information, it is not providing content that is not specifically company-related. However, since some employees have expressed interest in providing personal Web pages and projects, the company has established a second server that is clearly distinguished as an "unofficial" server, and established policies for the sort of information that can be provided on this server.

Springfield University

Springfield University is interested in providing a Web server for many complementary reasons. The University itself wishes to place information on-line for prospective students, in the form of a hypertext viewbook and course catalog. Several departments also wish to provide departmental information, including information about faculty, facilities, ongoing projects, and repositories of journal papers. Finally, a sizeable proportion of the undergraduate student body would like to be able to publish information on-line, ranging from personal information to personal projects.

The University has decided to place all of these services on a single server, although some departments (including the Computer Science department) have opted to provide their own server on their own machine. The University is concerned about the appropriateness of some information that may be placed on the Web by members of the campus community, but feels that it is part of the mission of the University to provide this service to all of the campus. It has, however, developed guidelines for appropriate use of the Web server.

The Upper Valley Historical Society

The Historical Society is mainly concerned with making the information it has available. It is a more informal group, and has limited resources to spend on acquiring machines to act as servers, and for people to create and organize the information available. It is concentrating on making as much information as it can available, but not expending server resources to provide personal information for society members.

Audience

An issue related to purpose is audience. The sort of information you will provide will be influenced by the kind of readers you wish to attract. Attempting to serve every possible reader may turn out to be an impossible task, and specializing can save you time and effort in the long run.

For example, one trend among energetic Web publishers is to collect and provide a listing of Web resources on a specific topic. This is a fine and noble goal, but many of these authors quickly lose enthusiasm for the project, leaving an unfinished and out-of-date listing for readers to find. By focusing energy on projects directly related to your mission and your audience, you can avoid creating these sorts of on-line wastelands.

One thing to be aware of is that many readers will regard your Web site as a first source of information about your organization. If you are a company, they will expect to be able to find out information about your services; if you are an educational institution, they will expect to be able to find information about various departments, projects and individuals associated with your institution. Part of designing your infostructure (especially the main entry point) is being aware of the kinds of services that your readership expects and will use most often.

Metanoia Bookworks

MB is interested in potential customers. It serves this goal directly by making information available about the books that it publishes, as well as information about how to purchase books. It also serves this goal in a more indirect fashion in providing a "browse before you buy" service. By emulating the browsing model, it participates in the on-line culture of providing services and information back to the community, while still using the Web as a tool for selling books.

Springfield University

The University has a diverse range of services, because it serves a diverse audience. The information that the University is most interested in targeting to specific readership include the viewbook, course catalog, and general campus informational services. The University is interested both in providing information to potential students and providing campus information to the university community. The University has decided to coordinate this at an institutional level, and to leave responsibility for departmental and personal information in the hands of the departments and individuals.

However, in anticipation of the wide range of potential readers, the University has decided to also coordinate the overarching organization for the infostructure at an institutional level, so that readers can find the infostructures for departments quickly and easily from the University's homepage.

The Upper Valley Historical Society

The Historical Society is serving a very specific readership—those who have an interest in the history and development of the Upper Valley area. As such, the Society's infostructure will have a server deep in content, rather than wide in topics. The Society does not want to provide pointers to tools for finding other information on the Web, or for personal information about Society members; just information about the collection and about other on-line collections, all of which will be of interest to the Society's intended audience.

Organization

Organization flows naturally from purpose and readership. The information you will provide, and the audience to which you are providing it, influence heavily how you will present that information so that your readers can use it. There are any number of ways in which a body of information can be organized—by subject, by newness, or by department, to name a few—but only a few of these ways will actually be useful in terms of readership and maintenance. Your organization should reflect the areas of major importance in your server. Identify the major services you will be providing, and make these services easily reachable.

Organization not only assists readers, but aids maintenance. By placing related documents into subdirectories with each other, you create small collections of documents that can be easily tracked and that can (with the appropriate use of relative links) be moved around within and between servers with relative ease.

Remember that the organization of your infostructure really takes place on two levels. At one level, the organization of the server will be very clearly reflected in the organization of hierarchical subdirectories on the file system of your server. Subdirectories can, and should, be used to reflect the major areas and subdivisions of your organization. You may have a directory containing information about the organization, with subdirectories for each collection of documents that relate to a specific topic; you may have a directory for institution-wide icons, so that there is a unique and consistent style to your site.

To the reader's perspective, on the other hand, your organization need not have a direct correlation with this tree-like organization. Hypertext links can map a virtual structure over the top of your subdirectory structure easily and transparently. This can enhance your infostructure's organization, providing links across collections of documents that are interrelated in ways other than the main organizational divisions of your server. Another technique is to provide multiple views of your infostructure, with each view presenting the same information, but laid out along different organizational lines.

Too many views can be detrimental, however. Documents that are too richly interconnected can become like electronic spaghetti, with paths that wander around and around, but never lead readers to the information they seek.

Metanoia Bookworks

MB has ordered its content in several ways. The primary ordering it has chosen is to present the reader with three ways to find information: by browsing "bookshelves" arranged by subject, by searching a database by author and title, and by browsing through new books and offerings.

The information itself falls into three major categories. The first category is the publications catalog, which is what the bookshelves and search engine are interfaces to. The second category includes sets of sample chapters for many of the books, for patrons to browse through. The third category is information about Metanoia itself, including some company history.

Springfield University

The University organizes its information into three general categories: official University information, departmental information, and personal information. The homepage for the University provides an entry point to these categories, listing the University-wide information resources first, then providing a link to a list of departments, then providing a link to personal home pages.

The University has decided not to point to departmental and personal information directly from its home page, largely in order to prevent the page from becoming unwieldy. However, it has decided to subdivide University information sources, including a viewbook, course catalog, and an electronic "phone book," at the top level. This is based on the assumption that readers will most likely be arriving directly at an institutional home page to find out information about the institution itself; therefore, it should be made easier to retrieve.

The Upper Valley Historical Society

The Society has decided to organize its information into "virtual exhibits," with each exhibit as a largely self-contained entity. Each exhibit is organized in three ways: a general overview of the documents in the exhibit; a guided tour that leads through the pages in the exhibit; and a relatively dense set of hyperlinks which connect related documents in the exhibit with each other, with footnotes, and with scholarly annotations.

The Society's home page is a listing of all of the exhibitions, followed by links to information about the Society itself. There is also a bibliography of other relevant on-line historical resources, including a pointer to a well-maintained historical subject index at another site.

Creation

The creation of the content for your infostructure is the real task at hand. The kind of content you create will be a direct result of the purpose and audience of your web, and in turn will exercise great control over the way you organize your web. The most important issue here is *who* will create the content and have responsibility for populating your server with information.

There are several strategies for this. At one end of the spectrum, you can create all documents for your web from scratch. At the other end, you can populate it entirely with legacy documents that were originally created in other formats for other purposes (such as internal documentation, public relations material, and other publications produced by your organization). Many organizations adopt a strategy somewhere in the middle, using the Web as another means for distributing previously created content, as well as for publishing exclusively on-line materials.

You will probably meet with the most success if specific people within your organization are responsible for the creation of content, whether that entails them to be actively involved in creating it, or just in overseeing the creation of it. It is often easy to set up the skeleton of a server in an initial rush of enthusiasm, but as that enthusiasm wanes, the quality of the server may wane (as the information becomes dusty, and the structure is never finished).

Metanoia Bookworks

MB has created a working group within the company to develop content for its server. Most of the content on the server is in the form of legacy documents, either the text from book jackets, or selected chapters. Since these are already in electronic form, a small working group has been formed to convert them to HTML and adapt them as necessary. Existing public relations information has also been converted to HTML. One person has been designated as being in charge of content creation, and she ensures that all of the documents that are not already available as legacy documents are supplied, whether by her or from others.

Springfield University

The academic computing center at Springfield has been at the forefront of the infostructure effort, and they have taken responsibility for coordinating the development of content. In cooperation with the University's publications department, the computing center manages the organization and technical details of the server, while the publications department supplies content for University information. The computing center performs any necessary conversions, and places that information on-line.

Individual departments are left to their own devices to provide content, although the computing center offers help to interested faculty members. The computing center has developed a style guide, which it asks that all departments adhere to in putting together their documents, so that the entire server is consistent in structure.

Personal information is provided by individuals and is their own responsibility. The University has formulated an acceptable use policy, especially with regard to students publishing illegal or copyrighted material on-line, but strongly supports academic freedom in community members' ability to publish information.

The Upper Valley Historical Society

The Historical Society has several volunteers who work on scanning in historical documents so that they can be distributed on the Web. Also, under the terms of the grant, they have hired a full-time systems administrator whose job it is to keep the server running, and to also oversee the creation of content. One of the historians of the society also spends part of his time writing the text for the guided tours, and curating the on-line collections.

Maintenance Strategies

Many organizations have a false perception of Web publishing as "free," because the software neccessary for distributing the information is usually freely available. They fail to take into account the human resources necessary to populate the server with information; again, because they may have an individual or individuals who set up the server in the first place as a labor of love. Because of this, Web servers that may be set up very well (and cheaply) will often fall by the wayside, because the organization never allocates resources to maintain the infostructure.

Maintenance is probably the most important of all the issues involved in providing an infostructure. A server that is full of out-of-date information, full of "Under Construction" signs that never come down, is the Sargasso Sea of the information superhighway. And even a server that is actively updated with new information must still be checked periodically to ensure that links to documents both within the server and elsewhere on the Web have not become stale (or that the documents being pointed to have not changed dramatically).

Maintenance is a subject probably best tackled by means of automation. Chapter 7, in fact, is exclusively devoted to the topic of tools you can use to keep your infostructure in trim condition. However, maintenance tools cannot fix your infostructure by themselves; maintenance requires people to oversee it, to ensure that the necessary steps occur to prevent infostructure decay.

Becoming a Publisher

Responsible Publishing

The Internet can seem an awfully casual place. Throw up a machine, grab some server software, throw together some documents, and yow! you're a publisher. A good percentage of on-line "resources" announced on the newsgroup `comp.infosystems.www.announce` are still personal home pages, and the bulk of information that has been put on the Web has been put up by individuals who are providing a service as a labor of love.

This, of course, is a fabulous thing, and speaks volumes about the the power of the media. But it raises some problematic issues for readers:

- Is this resource authoritative? Has it been put together by someone or some organization that is qualified to maintain such a resource?

- It this resource timely? Even if this information was all true when it was put on-line, has it been maintained since then?

- Is this resource persistent? Yes, it's available now, but will it still be available in a month, or a year?

The problem with individual labors of love is that they tend to be eclipsed by other personal projects. To be a responsible publisher on the Web, you must bear in mind these questions of authoritativeness and availability. Are you or your organization qualified to maintain the on-line resource you are planning to provide? Will you keep them up to date, and persistent?

Another question is, if you will be providing space for others (such as your user base) to provide personal information, how much control do you have over the information they will provide? It is still an open question whether your organization will take responsibility for information "published" by employees or clients.

Setting down policies before you open up public space on your server would be a wise move, by giving guidelines for what is and is not acceptable content.

Netiquette

In order to coexist peacefully in the same spaces, there are certain rules of etiquette that should be followed in all areas of life. This is as true on-line as anywhere else. Because the Internet is fairly anarchic in structure and design, we must pay attention to how we deal with our neighbors, or else they might deal the same way with us.

In Web publishing, there are some general rules to follow that can help keep you and your organization happier:

- Do not mirror the Web resources that others have provided without first gaining permission from the authors. They undoubtedly would like to keep control over making sure the latest versions of documents are available to all, and would also like to know about who is using their documents.

- At the same time, do not place undue burdens on the resources provided by others. For example, if you are building an infostructure for a local user base, get permission to mirror off-site documents and indexes that are heavily used by your community.

In general, treat the resources and work of others with the same respect that you would have them treat yours.

Copyright

We are not lawyers, so please don't take anything in this section as authoritative. Rather, treat it as a set of observations from listening to other people who know more about copyright than we do.

The consensus on copyright seems to be that any work published after 1989 generally will qualify for copyright protection (whether or not there is a specific copyright notice). This means two important things to you: first, that any document you create and place on a Web server qualifies for copyright; and second, that any document you find elsewhere on the Internet (whether it be by FTP,

Web, Usenet, e-mail, or whatever) probably also qualifies for copyright. Therefore, if you want to copy and redistribute (that is, make a copy of the document on your own server), you'll need to get permission from the author. On the other hand, making a hyperlink to a document that someone else provides is more like providing a bibliographic reference to a document than it is to making a copy of it. Making links to other resources will not, in general, be a problem, unless the provider of the document has specifically asked that links to his or her document be made only under certain well-defined circumstances.

To get more information about copyright, you can refer to the Copyright FAQ, available via FTP at `ftp://rtfm.mit.edu/pub/usenet/news.answers/law/Copyright-FAQ/`. However, the best thing to do is to talk to a lawyer if you have any questions or concerns.

6

HTTP Servers

This chapter provides an overview of available HTTP servers on three major platforms: Unix, Microsoft Windows, and the Macintosh. Several HTTP servers are reviewed, and detailed installation information is provided for three of the most popular: NCSA httpd (version 1.4), Windows httpd (version 1.4d), and MacHTTP (version 2.2).

At this point, we will begin to deal with technical issues that are important to server administrators, such as server configuration. If you are not a server administrator, you may want to skip to Chapter 7, *Maintenance and Reporting Tools.*

HTTP Servers

Choosing a Server

The HTTP server is the cornerstone of your Web site, providing the mechanism by which the documents in your infostructure are served to clients like Arena and Netscape. A server is vitally important; without a server of some sort, you will have no infostructure at all.

The server you pick can have a dramatic effect on the kinds of content you can provide. Different servers provide different levels of functionality, from simply serving static documents, to serving dynamic documents and imagemaps via CGI, to providing multiple "virtual servers" (accessed with different domain names) on a single machine. Performance also varies from server to server; many of the commercial servers provide substantially better per-

The HTTP Protocol

HTTP, the Hypertext Transport Protocol, defines a simple mechanism for retrieving and interacting with hypermedia "objects," whether they be HTML documents, GIF or JPEG images, CGI scripts, or any other sort of document. It is independent of (although often associated with) HTML; HTTP simply defines a means of transportation, not a means of representing information.

HTTP is a stateless protocol. This means that, while a client and a server may interact several times, the server does not try to remember anything about what the client has done in the past. This in contrast to FTP, where a client maintains a connection for the duration of an FTP session, and information like the current working directory and the user's ID is remembered between file transfers. One advantage of HTTP is that a connection does not need to be maintained between the client and the server for the duration of the session; once a document has been downloaded, the user can read or use the document without also maintaining a costly connection to the server. The drawback to this is that each time the client wants another document from the server, a connection must be reinitiated (a process that can sometimes take longer than downloading the document itself, especially in the case of small colored list bullets).

Another feature that distinguishes HTTP from FTP is the ability to do content negotiatiation. With content negotiation, the client can send a list to the server of which *Internet Media Types* (see Appendix B) it can accept, and the server can compare this to the various formats it may have a particular document in. The server can then send whichever

format best suits the client's needs. While this feature is not yet widely implemented, clients and servers that support it (such as the emacs-w3 client and the Apache server) are starting to appear.

HTTP supports several methods of interaction between clients and servers, including GET, POST, HEAD, PUT, LINK, and UNLINK. GET, POST, and HEAD are the only commonly supported methods. GET is the most common, and is used to retrieve documents. POST is for submitting information to be dealt with by an object (such as a program); it is predominantly used for the transmission of form data to a CGI script (see Chapter 8, *CGI*). HEAD is used to get the HTTP header for a document, which includes information such as when the document was last modified (which is useful for making sure that caches of documents are current without retrieving entire documents). The additional methods are part of the proposed HTTP 1.0 specification, and anticipate browsers that will eventually also become editors, allowing authors to annotate and edit documents with the same tool that they navigate them with.

The current version of HTTP is 1.0, and it is in the process of becoming a formal specification as we write this. Future directions of HTTP include support for encryption (such as S-HTTP, described in Chapter 9, *Security*), and for allowing multiple requests with a single connection (HTTP-NG). For more information about HTTP, take a look at

```
http://www.w3.org/hypertext/WWW/
Protocols/Overview.html
```

formance than their free counterparts. Encryption—important if you want to transmit or receive sensitive information (such as credit card numbers)—is still only rarely available in servers, with the Netscape Commerce Server being the most notable.

One important consideration is the platform on which you run your server. Traditionally, Unix has been the platform of choice for Internet servers, and most Web servers available are available on this platform. Several of the Unix servers are free, and a few—the Webmaster Starter Kit (which is free), and the Netscape servers (which are not)—are remarkably easy to install and maintain (via forms-driven interfaces). In addition, the Unix operating system can provide exceptional performance for your server, especially if you invest in a powerful Unix machine.

The flip side to choosing the Unix platform is that most Unix workstations are expensive, and equivalent performance can often be found more cheaply by investing in high-end personal computers. PowerPC-based Macintoshes and Pentium-class Windows machines are becoming increasingly affordable and increasingly powerful, and several servers have become available for these platforms. In addition to the cheapness of the hardware, there is the extra benefit of a more genial operating environment than Unix, which can make installation and support easier. One such server—WebSite—stands out with sophisticated graphical Web analysis and development tools, and an interface that takes advantage of the user-friendly nature of Microsoft Windows. Unfortunately, no reliable free servers are available on the Mac or Windows platforms (although Windows httpd is free for personal and educational use), but the costs of the servers are more than made up for in the savings on hardware. Also, most of the more sophisticated servers require a more sophisticated operating system, such as Windows NT or Windows 95.

The cheapest option may be to invest in one of the "free" Unixes, such as Linux or FreeBSD, that are available for Intel-based machines. Any of the free servers will run on these machines, allowing you to turn a Pentium-class (or even a 486-class) machine into a powerful, cheap workstation. The major advantage is that this allows the use of some of the more sophisticated servers which are available on the Unix platform, especially as the free options for both Windows and Mac are not impressive. The major caveat with this solution is that you lose in technical support what you gain in savings—and while Linux and FreeBSD are remarkably stable, they are not guaranteed to be reliable. Using a free Unix is a viable option for the technically savvy (and adventurous), but it is probably not a wise idea for an organization that can afford a commercial solution.

In summary:

- When deciding between a free or a commercial server, remember that most free servers offer almost the same set of features as their commercial counterparts. However, commercial offerings often provide better performance, and offer features like encryption. Also, don't undervalue technical support.

- When choosing a platform, remember that Unix is often able to provide superior performance to Windows 3.1, or the Macintosh. In addition, several good free servers are available for Unix. On the other hand, Unix is expensive in terms of hardware and support costs.

Evaluate your needs before choosing a server, and find one that provides the features you require, plus some room to grow. And remember that you can always start out with a free server and upgrade to a commercial one at a later point with a minimum of effort, should it turn out to be necessary.

We will review several servers in the next few sections, but this is by no means an exhaustive list. We have tried to pick out the most notable servers for each platform, and to give an overview of their features (and their flaws), and to provide useful criteria by which to pick a server. Since we were not able to adequately review all available servers, each section ends with a list of other available servers, with pointers to on-line information for each.

Unix

In this section we discuss a few of the popular servers available on Unix platforms. Unix can refer to many different operating systems, including those supplied by vendors (such as SunOS and Solaris), and freely available clones (such as Linux and FreeBSD). In general, these servers should work on any Unix platform, especially if source code is supplied.

NCSA httpd 1.4

The NCSA (National Center for Supercomputing Applications, at the University of Illinois at Urbana-Champaign) httpd was developed in conjuction with the popular Mosaic browser. (httpd is an acronym for Hypertext Transport Protocol Daemon. Daemon is a term often used to describe Unix processes that run constantly in the background, and perform tasks that are not directly controlled by a user, such as serving Web documents. The word is not capitalized because it is the name of the actual server executable—which, like most Unix executables, is not capitalized.) While it was not the first server available, it quickly became popular along with Mosaic as the back end for Web applications, and it has maintained this popularity. Many of the other offerings we describe here are based on this server, and one of the primary developers of the Netscape Servers cut his teeth developing this server.

Features

NCSA httpd provides a rich set of features, including a flexible definition of your server's "virtual document tree," dynamic documents, access control, Common Log Format access logs, and a fast "preforking" architecture.

Virtual document tree: httpd provides a set of configuration options for mapping your disk's filesystem into a virtual document tree, so that you can provide to the world only those documents you wish to provide, rather than all files on your machine. This includes the ability to specify a directory in your filesystem which will serve as the root of your server. For example, if your server root directory is `/usr/local/web/documents`, then when a client tries to retrieve `http://www.freedonia.com/people.html`, this request is mapped on to the physical file `/usr/local/web/documents/people.html` instead of onto `/people.html`. The standard scheme used by Web servers is to make available only (and all) of the files in this server root directory and in all subdirectories of the server root directory.

To add flexibility to this scheme, you can include directories that are not subdirectories of the server root. httpd provides configuration options for mapping directories in your filesystem (such as making the Unix manual pages available via your server, by mapping /usr/man onto a virtual /manuals directory for your Web server). In addition, httpd provides an option for easily providing users with virtual directories in your Web server's document tree. You can specify that if a user (such as jsmith) has a certain subdirectory in his or her home directory (such as public_html) that it should be mapped on to a virtual directory of the form ~*user* (in this example, ~jsmith).

Dynamic documents: NCSA httpd also provides CGI (Common Gateway Interface) scripting, for providing dynamic documents. This capability allows for quite a bit of flexibility in the sorts of services you provide; in fact, most of the features provided in other servers can be implemented (at the cost of efficiency) as CGI scripts. For example, imagemapping support and user authentication are provided in the NCSA server by means of supplied CGI scripts. CGI is discussed in depth in Chapter 8.

Another feature provided that relates to dynamic documents is the ability of the server to modify a static document with special commands for the server embedded in the HTML document. These embedded commands (called server-side includes) can be used to include other documents (such as headers or footers), to insert information about the file (such as when it was last modified), or to insert the output of a CGI script.

Access Control: In order to provide finer control over how documents are served from the virtual document tree, NCSA httpd provides mechanisms for access control. Access to documents and directories can be limited to only certain hosts (or denied access to certain hosts) or explicitly not served to any host. Similarly, access can be allowed (or denied) only to certains users or groups of users. This allows you to provide subscription-based services or to provide services limited only to your local user base (without requiring that your local user base be using the service from local machines).

The access control mechanism is not limited to allowing and denying users and hosts. It is also possible to reconfigure some of the global configuration options on a per-directory basis (such as changing the default file type from text/html to text/plain in a directory full of plain ASCII documents, instead of giving each document the suffix .txt).

It is also possible to enable the serving of CGI scripts in arbitrary directories. The default behavior for CGI scripts is to provide certain "script" directories in which all documents are assumed to be CGI scripts, and are executed upon retrieval. This makes sense from a security standpoint, especially if you have numerous people providing information through your Web server, because each CGI script is executed with the same user permissions as your Web server is executed. However, it may be desirable (especially if you have a small and trusted user base) to allow CGI scripts to reside in directories alongside static documents. The access control mechanism allows you to enable or disable this on a per-directory basis.

Logging: NCSA httpd supports the NCSA/CERN Common Logfile Format, a standard format for access logs that the majority of servers now support. This means that most log analysis tools will work with the logs produced by this server (and any derivitive servers). Since most servers support this format, this means the bulk of log analysis tools will work with the bulk of servers.

Fast preforking architecture: In versions prior to 1.4, when httpd received a request for a document from a client, it would create another httpd process to service the request. Unfortunately, this requires a `fork()` Unix system call, which is a relatively costly process in terms of performance. This becomes readily apparent when a browser such as Netscape requests several documents from the server in parallel (such as a document's inlined images), and the server must spawn four simultaneous copies of itself in order to service the request.

The 1.4 version of httpd addresses this problem by preforking a set number of servers when it is first run. The master httpd program uses this pool of available servers to service requests. Upon receiving a request, instead of forking a new process to handle it, it finds an existing idle process and hands the request off to it. This technique dramatically speeds up handling of requests, and is most effective for sites that expect a large number of requests (over 100,000 a day, for example).

Limitations: Two features that are absent are built-in searching capabilities (such as the ability to full-text or keyword index the server) and any maintenance tools. On the other hand, it is possible to use other tools, such as a WAIS server, to provide an index to your server; and maintenance tools from other sources are readily available (see Chapter 7).

Evaluation

NCSA httpd is the standard Web server, and it provides a good benchmark against which other servers can be evaluated. It provides a rich set of features, and is a solid choice for almost any application. While the server does not provide some advanced features (such as built-in maintenance tools, full-text indexing, or encryption), many of these features can be implemented via the CGI interface or with programs available from other sources (some of which we will discuss in later chapters). Also, importantly, the most recent release has addressed problems with earlier releases, and has become competitive with commercially available servers in terms of speed.

Overall, this is a solid and usable server. It should fulfill the needs of most organizations, and has the added benefit of being freely available from NCSA. Precompiled executables are available for several platforms, and the source code is also available and should compile for most Unix platforms for which executables are not available. Especially if you already have a Unix platform available, this server deserves a serious look.

> **NOTE:** Versions prior to 1.4 have two significant flaws. The first is the performance flaw addressed by the preforking architecture (see the previous Features section). The second flaw is security-related: it is possible for a client request to overrun the space that the server uses to store text information, which in certain situations can allow outside intruders to run programs on your machine with the same user privileges that your Web server has. Fortunately, version 1.4 addresses both of these problems.

Availability

NCSA httpd is available via FTP at

```
ftp://ftp.ncsa.uiuc.edu/Web/httpd/Unix/ncsa_httpd
```

and on-line documentation is available at

```
http://hoohoo.ncsa.uiuc.edu/
```

NCSA httpd source code is in the public domain (at least, through version 1.4), and the server can be freely used for any purpose. It is possible that NCSA may change these terms for future releases, in which case Apache (discussed later in the chapter) may become a more viable alternative.

EIT's Webmaster's Starter Kit

The Webmaster's Starter Kit is based on the NCSA httpd (version 1.3), with a few enhancements (as detailed in Features, next). The biggest difference is that administration of the server is through a form-based interface—the administrator uses a browser such as Mosaic to change configuration options and to enable and disable options. EIT (Enterprise Integration Technologies) has developed this server as an experiment in providing easier ways to get started as an infostructure provider.

Features

The Webmaster's Starter Kit, being based on NCSA httpd, shares many of the same features. In addition, it includes some enhancements, such as form-based administration, additional configuration options, and additional maintenance and design tools.

Based on NCSA httpd: The Starter Kit is based on the source code for version 1.3 of the NCSA httpd. This means that it shares almost all of the features as were described in the previous NCSA httpd section, except for those introduced in 1.4 release.

Forms-based administration: The Starter Kit is most impressive because of the ease of installation and administration that is provided by its form-based interface. Installation is a matter of pointing a Web browser at the Starter Kit installation page, and following the instructions. Administration is similarly performed, through a password-protected set of forms on your own server.

Additional configuration options: The Starter Kit includes several additional configuration options. These include the ability to set additional environment variables to pass to CGI scripts, the ability to prevent the Web server from accessing any files outside of a particular directory and its subdirectories (in order to prevent compromised servers from being used to retrieve other documents from your hard drive—see Chapter 9), and the ability to automatically restart the server when it crashes without human intervention. The Starter Kit also extends the NCSA access control mechanism so that certain domains (or users) can be prioritized, so that they can get better (or worse) response times relative to other domains/users. Finally, there is a provision for "polite" downtime, so that the server can turn away users with an informative message when you are performing maintenance work.

Additional maintenance and design tools: The Starter Kit includes some helpful tools for getting started. These include a Web construction kit (which, at present, consists of a form-based interface for generating a homepage); a C library for CGI scripts; a Web maintenance tool for verifying links; a CGI script that represents e-mail as hypertext; and logfile reporting tools.

These are all useful tools, and many variants on them are available in many locations (see Chapter 7). However, it is very handy to have them packaged with the server itself, rather than having to hunt them down.

Evaluation

The Starter Kit is a nice package, largely because it provides all of the functionality of the NCSA server, and can be configured, installed, and maintained via any Web browser that supports forms. This can make this a much easier Web server to maintain than standard NCSA httpd, which is a big advantage if you do not want to devote your Unix support staff to the care and feeding of your server.

On the other hand, the Starter Kit is, as the name implies, a "starter kit." It is more of a proof-of-concept than a product, and it is not undergoing as much development as many of the other servers listed. The current Starter Kit (as of this writing) is still based on the 1.3 NCSA code, which means that it shares the performance bottleneck described in the NCSA httpd section. However, the security problem with version 1.3 (also described previously) has been addressed in the current release.

If you were considering using NCSA httpd, but are put off by the task of installation and configuration, this server is a good alternative. However, if you are interested in the extra performance gain in the latest version of NCSA, you'll want to wait until the Webmaster's Starter Kit has been updated to reflect the 1.4 revision (which may well happen by publication time).

NOTE: If you are planning on using your server for commercial purposes, you will not be able to use the Starter Kit. EIT allows you to use their server for "academic, research, or internal business purposes only."

A final thought: the optional extensions *are* helpful tools, and can be used independently of the server itself. You may want to consider getting them, even if you do not use the Starter Kit, especially if you are using an NCSA-variant server. One of them, the Link Verifier, is discussed in detail as a separate package in Chapter 7.

Availability

The Webmaster's Starter Kit is available at

```
http://wsk.eit.com/wsk/doc/
```

Installation requires an account on a Unix machine connected to the Internet, and a browser that supports forms.

The server is available, as just noted, for "academic, research, or internal business purposes" only, but (within those restrictions) is freely available.

Apache 0.6.5

Apache (version 0.6.5) is a play on **A PAtCH**y Server, and that is what it is, a series of patches to the NCSA server. These patches add some powerful functionality to the NCSA server, including the ability to provide several virtual hosts, and to use content negotiation to provide different documents to different clients (so that a user using a text-based browser can receive a text-based document, and so a user using a browser that supports inlined JPEGs can receive inlined JPEGs). In addition, it features enhancements to efficiency that can provide even better performance than the NCSA httpd.

Features

Apache shares many of the same features as the NCSA httpd, along with several enhancements. These include virtual hosts, content negotiation, faster user authentication, "send as is" file types, speed enhancements, and some additional configuration options.

Based on NCSA httpd: Apache is based on the source code for version 1.3 of the NCSA httpd. This means that it shares almost all of the features described in the NCSA httpd section, except for those introduced in 1.4 release. However, it addresses many of the same problems in NCSA 1.3 that NCSA 1.4 does, including the security and performance issues mentioned in the *NCSA httpd* section, as well providing other improvements.

Virtual hosts: If you are interested in providing servers for companies or organizations that want an on-line presence, but aren't interested in maintaining their own machines on the Internet, Apache can emulate multiple "virtual" servers. That is, if the addresses `www.freedonia.com` and `techno.nomi.com` both point to the same machine, Apache allows `http://www.freedonia.com/` and `http://techno.nomi.com/` to return different homepages (and different document trees). In this way, you can serve distinct infostructures with distinct names with the same physical hardware.

Content negotiation: This is a clever feature that provides a mechanism for catering to the wide range of capabilities in browser software. Most browsers will send information to the server about the kind of content they are willing to accept (such as whether they can accept GIF or JPEG images). Apache can use this information to return the best format for a browser. Thus, instead of creating two different versions of a document—one that has inlined GIFs, and one with inlined JPEGs—you can create one version of a document and allow Apache to negotiate with the browser to find the correct image format to retrieve.

Faster user authentication: Apache includes a faster mechanism for user authentication than is supplied by "vanilla" NCSA 1.3. This is used extensively by sites such as HotWired, that have extensive user databases which are constantly accessed.

"Send as is" file types: Apache supports certain files that should be sent "as is," including HTTP headers. This allows for extreme fine-tuning of server behavior, without having to run a CGI script.

Speed enhancements: Apache is an optimized version of NCSA httpd 1.3, offering a significant boost over the unoptimized version. It does not yet include the preforking architecture of 1.4 (at the time of this writing), but it is in the works and will probably be available by the time you read this.

Additional configuration options: Apache also supports custom error responses, the ability to define multiple defaults for directory index files (such as `"index.html"` or `"home.html"`), and several other enhancements for CGI scripting and server configuration.

Evaluation

Apache is billed by its developers as a plug-in replacement for NCSA 1.3, and by the time you read this, it should also be a plug-in replacement for NCSA 1.4. It provides the same feature set, as well as several additional modficiations. The speed enhancements and the support for content negotiation make this server an extemely attractive option; and the possibility that the terms of the NCSA license may change (which may mean that anything after 1.4 will no longer be freely available, at least for commercial use) may make this an even more attractive server in the future.

On the other hand, this server is an independent development effort, and is (at this writing) still in beta testing. Since it is based on a stable server, most features should work as expected, but there is no technical support and some features may be buggy or still in development at any time. Still, if you require the sort of enhancements provided by this server, and have the systems support staff to provide proper care and feeding, it is a compelling choice. Especially since, as with most of the freely available software available on-line, it does work extremely well, and failures are the exception rather than the rule.

Availability

Apache is available via FTP at

```
ftp://ftp.apache.org/apache/dist/
```

The documentation for the Apache server project, as well as a list of mirror sites from which the server can be retrieved by FTP is at

```
http://www.apache.org/apache/
```

The server is freely available and usable.

WN 1.04

WN (version 1.04), written by John Franks of Northwestern University, is designed to provide useful tools as part of the server package, such as indexing, searching, and authentication. Unlike previously discussed servers, these tools are an integral part of the philosophy of the server itself, rather than as add-on components from other sources.

Features

The most interesting feature of WN is the built-in searching capabilities. In addition, it provides dynamic documents (through several mechanisms, not limited to CGI), content negotiation, and security (including access control and authentication).

Searching capabilities: Several kinds of searches are supported by WN. These include title searches, keyword searches (with keywords deduced from the headers in HTML documents), user-supplied field searches, and various permutations of full-text searching across single and multiple documents.

Dynamic documents: WN supports the standard mechanism for dynamic documents, CGI. It also supports server preprocessing of HTML documents, so that different parts of a document can be served based on different conditions (see *Content Negotiation,* next).

Another form of dynamic document generation is through *filters* which can be attached to individual documents: a filter is a program which takes the requested file as input, and serves the output of the program to the browser. Finally, WN allows for ranges of documents to be requested, if the whole document is not required.

Content negotiation: Content negotiation is supported through the preprocessing mechanism. For example, if WN processed the following HTML fragment:

```
⟨!-- #if accept ~ "image/jpeg" --!⟩
    ⟨IMG SRC="tyler.jpg" ALT="[Tyler's Mug Shot]"⟩
⟨!-- #else --⟩
    ⟨IMG SRC="tyler.gif" ALT="[Tyler's Mug Shot]"⟩
⟨!-- #endif --!⟩
```

Then if the browser would accept JPEG images, the HTML which the browser would see would be:

```
⟨IMG SRC="tyler.jpg" ALT="[Tyler's Mug Shot]"⟩
```

and otherwise, the browser would see:

```
⟨IMG SRC="tyler.gif" ALT="[Tyler's Mug Shot]"⟩
```

NOTE: Why bother with an ALT attribute if the browser can accept JPEGs? Because the latest crop of graphical browsers (including Netscape and Mosaic) will display the text in the ALT attribute when image loading is turned off!

Security (access control and authentication): WN supports access control. By default, WN assumes that no file has permission to be served—permission must be explicitly given through an index. cache file in each directory. Tools are provided for maintaining these access control files. WN can, like most other servers, allow or deny access to files on a user, group of users, or host basis. In addition, WN supports an experimental mechanism for authentication via digest authentication, so that user passwords are transmitted across the network in an encrypted fashion (although, at the time of this writing, no "publicly available clients support this method," according to the WN documentation).

Logging: WN does not directly support the CERN/NCSA Common Log Format, but includes a utility (v2c) that can be used to convert its "verbose" logs into the common format, allowing the majority of log analysis programs to work with the log.

Evaluation

If you are looking for a server that supports indexing in a robust way, WN is the server for you. The WN indexing features are unmatched in any other Unix-based server, and the other features make this overall a well-rounded server.

Availability

WN source code is available via FTP at

```
ftp://ftp.acns.nwu.edu/pub/wn/
```

and on-line documentation is available at

```
http://hopf.math.nwu.edu/
```

The server (and source code) is freely available under the GNU Public License.

Netscape Communications/Commerce Server

Netscape Communications was one of the first companies formed to produce a set of commerical tools for using the World Wide Web, and its Netsite server was one of the first commercial HTTP servers available. Although the server has since been renamed (as the Communications or Commerce Server, depending on whether you purchase the secure version), it still remains the high-priced powerhouse of Web servers.

Features

The Netscape servers provide the same functionality as the NCSA httpd server, with the addition of the NSAPI interface for extending server functionality, a clever forms-based administration interface, virtual hosts, a different implementation of the preforking architecture, and Secure Sockets Layer-based encryption and authentication.

NCSA httpd feature set: In addition to the features described here, the Netscape servers implement the feature set of NCSA httpd.

Dynamic documents: In addition to CGI, the Netscape servers offer a proprietary interface called NSAPI, which allows the maintainer to extend the functionality of the server itself.

Forms-based administration: If the Starter Kit is impressive because of the ease of installation and administration that is provided by its form-based interface, the Netscape servers are incredible. Everything, from installation to administration to creating your own authentication key (see Chapter 9), is accomplished through forms and CGI scripts. A particularly useful innovation is an "open book/closed book" metaphor that allows you to administer with either verbose or minimalist documentation (depending on your tastes).

Virtual hosts: Like Apache, the Netscape servers provide the ability to serve different infostructures for different "virtual hosts."

Security: The Netscape Commerce Server provides encryption via the Secure Sockets Layer (SSL), as explained in Chapter 9, *Security*.

Additional configuration options: The Netscape servers provide additional configuration options not found in NCSA httpd, including the ability to define multiple index filenames (for example, allowing any of `home.html`, `index.html`, and `default.html` to serve as the index for a user's home directory). In addition, you can identify a specific unique filename for the server's main homepage.

Another intriguing feature is the ability to create *configuration templates*—which let you provide specific configuration options for a number of directories by creating the configuration once and then applying it multiple times.

Fast preforking architecture: The Netscape servers include a preforking architecture similar to that in NCSA httpd 1.4 (in fact, it predates the 1.4 implementation; until NCSA 1.4, the Netscape servers were the fastest servers, bar none).

Evaluation

Netscape Communications first burst onto the scene with the Netscape Navigator, an extremely popular Web browser. But its real product is its line of servers, which provide raw performance and robust encryption. And provide it they do; Netscape's server line does not fall short on its promises. The forms-based administration is slick, and the installation process is painless.

Where it does begin to show its wear and tear is in the pricing structure: the Netscape servers (especially the secure ones) are priced thousands of dollars more than some of the recently announced competition on cheaper Macintosh and Windows platforms. When WebSite 1.1 is available, and if it indeed does support SSL and S-HTTP encryption, it will provide all of the power and punch of Netscape's servers for a fraction of the price (but only for Windows 95 and NT). Perhaps in response to this, Netscape has priced the NT versions of these servers at greatly reduced prices.

It is entirely possible that competition will cause the cost of a Netscape server to fall by the time you read this; it certainly seems to be no coincidence that Netscape went from a policy of "no free evaluation copies" to offering a 60-day test drive very soon after WebSite was announced (with a similar 60-day test drive offer). And while NCSA httpd now provides similar performance, the Netscape servers are very attractive in the situation where you have a very fast Unix machine and you want to utilize the SSL-based encryption and authentication. Don't count Netscape out yet.

Availability

Further information about the Netscape line of products can be found at

```
http://home.netscape.com/
```

Installation requires a superuser account on a Unix machine connected to the Internet, and a browser that supports forms.

The Communications server (which does not provide SSL-based encryption and authentication) costs $1495, while the Commerce server (which *does* provide SSL) runs $5000. In addition, you are required to purchase a service contract. A 60-day free test drive of the software is available; look at

```
http://home.netscape.com/comprod/server_central/
```

for details.

Other Options

Table 6.1 provides a list of other Web servers available on the Unix platform.

Table 6.1
Other Web Servers for Unix

CERN httpd	http://www.w3.org/hypertext/WWW/Daemon/Status.html	The standard (free) reference implementation. Most useful as a proxy or cache server (see Box 6.2) but not a good choice fora a main document server because of slow performance.
OpenMarket WebServer (and Secure Server)	http://www.openmarket.com/	Another commercial offering, also providing encryption (via S-HTTP, see Chapter 9)
GN	http://hopf.math.nwu.edu:70/	An earlier server by the author of WN (discussed earlier), which can function as both a Gopher and a Web server.
Plexus	http://www.bsdi.com/server/doc/plexus.html	A Web server written in Perl.

Windows

In this section we discuss the two most popular servers available for Microsoft's popular Windows line of operating systems software. This line includes Windows 3.1 (and Windows for Workgroups 3.11), Windows NT, and Windows 95. Because of differences in these systems, neither of these servers runs on all three platforms. The platform on which each server runs is indicated in their descriptions.

Windows httpd 1.4d (for Windows 3.1/Windows for Workgroups 3.11)

Windows httpd is probably the most commonly used Windows server, providing the functionality of NCSA httpd for a personal computer. It provides roughly the same feature set as NCSA httpd, within the more familiar operating environment of Windows 3.1. It was written by Robert Denny, who has gone on to create Web-Site (which is covered in the next section).

Proxy Servers

The most interesting feature of the CERN server is its ability to act as a caching proxy server. This means that, rather than just serving your own information, the CERN httpd can also serve information to your local browsers by proxy. Your browser (such as Netscape) can be configured to point to your local CERN httpd for retrieving files, and then the httpd will in turn check to see if the requested file is in its cache; if so, it will quickly return the cached copy, and if not, it will retrieve the document for the browser. This is most useful to sites running behind firewalls, but it is also useful if you want to run a site-wide cache in order to speed up the fetching of frequently requested documents.

Features

Windows httpd features include a virtual document tree, dynamic documents, access control, Common Log Format, and configuration that is similar overall to NCSA httpd.

Virtual document tree: Windows httpd offers the same ability to map your filesystem onto a virtual document tree as is described earlier in *NCSA httpd*.

Dynamic documents: Windows httpd supports dynamic documents via CGI. This is supported in one of two ways: a DOS CGI interface, which passes the CGI environment to a program running in a DOS virtual machine; and a Windows CGI interface, which passes the CGI environment to a Windows program. See Chapter 8 for more details on Windows-based CGI scripting. In addition, support for imagemaps is built in.

Access control: Windows httpd provides access control to documents on a user, group of users, or host basis, via the same mechanisms as is described in *NCSA httpd*.

Performance: Because Windows 3.1 (and 3.11) is a cooperative multitasking system, applications that run under Windows must explicitly allow for sharing of the processor between them. If this does not happen, performance can suffer, especially with programs running in the background (such as Windows httpd). To its credit, Windows httpd has been built with these limitations in mind, with a design goal of trying to take up as little processor time as necessary, yielding time back to other applications when it is waiting on input or output from the network. The server also features multithreaded operation, allowing it to service 16 simultaneous requests at once. This allows it to take advantage of idle time during network communication on one request to service another request.

NCSA-like: Windows httpd implements a subset of the NCSA features, making setup very similar between the two (with the added bonus of not having to deal with Unix system administration).

Logging: Windows httpd supports NCSA/CERN Common Logfile Format access logging.

Limitations: The major limitation of this software is that it will only run under Windows 3.1 (or 3.11), because of "low-level CPU control and stack-switching used to get fast/true multithreading in the server" (according to the author), and there are no plans to make it run under Windows 95 or Windows NT (see WebSite, next, for these platforms). Also, server-side includes are not supported.

Evaluation

Upon setting up Windows httpd, it becomes clear very fast that this server is either modeled after, or based on a version of the NCSA httpd code. The configuration files are almost identical (to the point that pathnames are given Unix-style, with forward slashes (/), rather than DOS-style backward slashes, (\). If this is a port, it's a very good port—the server runs out of the box with few changes to configuration files. The only place where Windows httpd shows its heritage is in the included documentation, where default values occasionally incorrectly reflect the Unix roots (like listing a default ServerRoot directory of /usr/local/etc/ httpd, instead of the actual default, C:\HTTPD).

The advantage to such a port is that there are no Unix details to worry about, like multiple users or process ID numbers (as a testament to this, the upcoming NCSA setup section is three times longer than the following Windows setup section). On the other hand, some of the options in the latest NCSA httpd (such as additional encoding types or the ability to send back user-defined error messages) are lacking. The DOS and Windows CGI interfaces are also very nicely done, and it is possible to use the same Perl CGI programs here as you would for Unix or Macintosh servers (see Chapter 8, *CGI*).

Overall, this is a very nice server. It's not designed for heavy production use, if for no other reason than that Windows 3.1 is not designed for heavy production use. (If you're interested in a more robust server and platform, you'll want to consider WebSite under Windows NT, described next.) The $99 fee (free for personal and educational use) makes this the best bargain for your buck, especially if you're not anticipating a huge amount of traffic on your infostructure.

Availability

Windows httpd is available from

```
http://www.city.net/win-httpd/
```

Documentation comes with the package.

Windows httpd is free for personal and educational use, but it is not in the public domain. There is a $99 fee for a commercial use license.

WebSite 1.0 (for Windows NT/Windows 95)

WebSite is a commercial package developed by Robert Denny (developer of Windows httpd) and O'Reilly and Associates for the Windows NT and Windows 95 operating systems. It provides a full range of features—including a user interface for administration that is a joy to work with—for a reasonable price.

Features

WebSite's features include a virtual document tree, dynamic documents, support for virtual hosts, built-in indexing and searching, security (including access control, and a planned upgrade for SSL and S-HTTP encryption), Common Log Format access logging, a Windows user interface, and a full complement of maintenance tools.

Virtual document tree: WebSite provides the same ability to map your filesystem onto a virtual document tree as is described in the *NCSA httpd* section, although it offers a Windows-based interface for configuration.

Dynamic documents: WebSite offers CGI scripting for the creation of dynamic documents. Along with offering the DOS and Windows CGI interfaces (as described in the *Windows httpd* section), WebSite offers a standard CGI interface through the Windows NT Posix shell. This allows you to use CGI scripts developed for use with Unix servers with WebSite—O'Reilly has even made a version of Perl for standard CGI available that works under both Windows 95 and NT. In addition, WebSite offers built-in support for imagemaps (including an imagemap editor). WebSite does not offer server-side includes.

Virtual hosts: WebSite offers support for multiple virtual hosts (as described in Apache).

Searching: WebSite provides two programs—WebIndex and WebFind—for creating a full-text index of your site. Using Web-Index is simple: a list of directories in your site are displayed, and you can select which should be indexed and which should not. Unlike WN, you may not create more than one index for your site.

Security (access control and encryption): WebSite provides access control to documents on a user, group of users, or host basis. In addition, the 1.1 version of WebSite (to be released in the fall of 1995) will support the SSL and S-HTTP encryption methods for secure transmission of information (see Chapter 9, *Security*).

Logging: The WebView application provides log information on a document-by-document basis, including error messages and access logs. The global access log is in the CERN/NCSA Common Log Format, so you can use commonly available analysis tools.

Performance: WebSite uses a threaded model of execution; in short, this means that instead of creating a new process to handle each request, it creates a new "thread" that is much less costly to start than a traditional process would be. This can provide performance comparable (or perhaps better, depending on the circumstances) to the preforking architectures in NCSA 1.4 and the Netscape servers. In addition, a fast personal computer (of

Pentium-class or higher) is cheap compared to a comparable Unix workstation.

User interface: Unlike the bulk of servers, WebSite sports an excellent user interface for administration. Instead of editing configuration files, WebSite is configured through the Server Admin tool, much like you would set preferences or options in any Windows application.

Maintenance tools: WebSite includes several maintenance and administration tools, including Server Admin, WebIndex, and an enhanced version of Mosaic. The primary maintenance tool is called WebView, which provides a graphical map of your server. You can use this map to find broken links, check statistics on individual documents, to configure access control on individual documents, and to see error messages and diagnostics that have been generated for individual documents.

Evaluation

WebSite provides the best bang for the buck. It is remarkably easy to install and use, performs extremely well, and provides excellent software tools for administering your Web. It provides as full a range of features as most other servers, and leaps ahead by also offering a sophisticated user interface and a well thought-out design (the WebView application alone is worth the purchase price). The only major lack is encryption via either SSL or S-HTTP, but O'Reilly pledges that both of these security standards will be available in the 1.1 release in the fall of 1995 (so they should be available by the time you read this). This server is comparable to the Netscape servers, but is a thousand dollars cheaper than even the nonsecure version of the Netscape Communications server. To top it off, it runs on (relatively) inexpensive Windows machines.

Availability

WebSite information can be found at

```
http://website.ora.com/
```

While WebSite is not free (the list price is $499), you can "test-drive" a full copy for free for 60 days. See the WebSite site for more information.

Other Options

Table 6.2 provides a list of other Web servers available for the Windows platforms.

Table 6.2
Other Web Servers
for Windows

HTTPS	http://emwac.ed.ac.uk/ html/internet_toolchest/ https/contents.htm	A free Web server for NT from the European Microsoft Windows NT Academic Centre (EMWAC)
NetMagic WebServer	http://www.aristosoft.com/ netmagic/company.html	Commercial server from NetMagic for NT/95
NetPublisher	http://netpub.notis.com/	A commercial server handling Web, Gopher, and Z39.50 protocols from Ameritech Library Services for NT. Aimed at libraries, and based around a catalog model.
Netscape Commerce/ Communications Servers	http://www.netscape.com/	See the review in the Unix section
Purveyor	http://www.process.com/ prodinfo/purvdata.htm	Commercial server from Process Software for NT/95

Macintosh

MacHTTP 2.2

MacHTTP, by Chuck Shotton of BIAP Systems, was one of the earliest and most popular Macintosh HTTP servers available, providing a Web server without requiring a Unix machine. While it offers a somewhat smaller feature set than others, it provides a good set of baseline server features.

Features

MacHTTP's features include dynamic documents and access control.

Virtual document tree: MacHTTP does *not* allow the creation of a virtual document tree. That is, all folders out of which your Web server can serve documents must be contained within your server's root folder (which is the same as the directory in which the MacHTTP software itself resides). However, you can use Macintosh aliases to achieve the same effect.

Dynamic documents: MacHTTP provides CGI scripting for the creation of dynamic documents. CGI scripts can be written in AppleScript, MacPerl, and various other languages (see Chapter 8, *CGI*, for more information).

Access control: MacHTTP provides access control to documents on a user, group of users, or host basis.

Remote administration: MacHTTP can be remotely administered via AppleEvents.

Logging: MacHTTP does *not* provide NCSA/CERN Common Log Format. Instead, the access log is provided in a tab-delimited format, for importing into spreadsheet or database programs.

Evaluation

MacHTTP is easy to set up and easy to use, and provides a decent set of features, including CGI scripting and access control. The ability to remotely administer MacHTTP via AppleEvents is also interesting, but it is better exploited in WebSTAR (described next) which includes an administration application that takes advantage of this feature.

On the other hand, there are some features noticeably missing, like the ability to redirect URLs to other servers, or a user interface that takes advantage of the Macintosh environment. In addition, the server is not really designed for handling large amounts of traffic.

What this all boils down to is that MacHTTP is a good choice for a starter server if you are a Macintosh shop, but if you don't already have a Macintosh, or you are anticipating a high amount of traffic on your server, you'll want to try another server. MacHTTP's most attractive feature is its price, which puts it within reach of individuals and organizations that do not want to invest too much in server software. Another Mac-based option, the WebSTAR server, is discussed next. It is an enhanced version of MacHTTP that addresses many of MacHTTP's shortcomings (including performance).

Availability

MacHTTP documentation and information (as well as an evaluation copy) can be found at

`http://www.biap.com/` or

`http://www.starnine.com/`

MacHTTP is not free: prices are $65 for educational use, and $95 otherwise.

NOTE: By the time you read this, MacHTTP may be supplanted by a low-cost version of WebStar (described next) called WebSTAR SW. This will be a shareware version of Web-STAR, and should be in the same price range as Mac-HTTP. It will be distributed via the StarNine Web site, not the BIAP site.

WebSTAR

WebSTAR, from Chuck Shotton and StarNine, is an enhanced version of MacHTTP. It addresses many of the problems with Mac-HTTP, including enhanced performance, and is a user interface that takes advantage of the Macintosh environment.

Features

WebSTAR descends directly from MacHTTP, and inherits Mac-HTTP's features, such as access control and dynamic documents. However, it also expands upon these features with better support for virtual document trees and content negotiation, improved performance, and a server administration application (instead of a text-based configuration file).

Virtual document tree: WebSTAR supports a virtual document tree via MacOS aliases. In addition to its ability to create aliases to files (provided in MacHTTP), it also allows aliases to be made to folders, disks, and other volumes. In addition, CGI scripts can be invoked for the preprocessing of URLs, limiting the ability to map URLs only by your programming skills. Finally, WebSTAR supports "user-defined actions," which allow you to map all URLs ending with a specific suffix (such as "map," for imagemap files) onto a specific CGI script (such as an imagemap handler program).

Content negotiation: While WebSTAR does not support content negotiation *per se,* the ability to preprocess URLs via CGI scripts provides the potential to create scripts that can perform content negotiation (although no such scripts are provided with the distribution).

Performance: WebSTAR uses the MacOS threading package for greater performance.

User interface: WebSTAR includes WebSTAR Admin, a GUI-based administration application that can be used to configure one or multiple servers.

Additional features: WebSTAR is AppleScript scriptable and recordable.

Logging: WebSTAR's logging format is user-configurable, and can be configured to follow Common Logfile Format.

Additional tools: Two additional toolkits are available (at additional cost): the Security Toolkit, which provides Secure Socket Layers (SSL) encryption and authentication; and the Commerce Toolkit, which is an on-line payment support system.

Evaluation

WebSTAR is a definite improvement over MacHTTP, and provides some very interesting features (such as URL pre- and post-processing and user-defined actions). It is easy to set up, and easy to administer, and provides much better performance than MacHTTP. In addition, if you already have MacHTTP, StarNine offers an upgrade program.

It is likely by the time you read this that WebSTAR (and WebSTAR SW, a recently announced but not yet released low-cost version of the server) will have supplanted MacHTTP.

Availability

WebSTAR documentation and information (as well as an evaluation copy) can be found at

```
http://www.starnine.com/
```

WebSTAR is not free: the costs is $795 ($295 for education use).

Other Options

Table 6.3 provides a list of other Web servers available for the Macintosh.

Table 6.3 Other Web Servers for Macintosh	NetWings	http://netwings.com/	A commercial integrated Web and mail (SMTP/POP3) server for the Macintosh.
	Netscape Servers	http://www.netscape.com/	At the time of this writing, Netscape Communications has announced that they are porting their servers to the Macintosh platform. See the review of the Netscape servers in the *Unix* section.
	CL-HTTP (Common Lisp)	http://www.ai.mit.edu/projects/iiip/doc/cl-http/home-page.html	A freely available Web server based on the Common Lisp language, developed at MIT.
	httpd4mac	http://130.246.18.52/	A minimal, but freely available, Web server.

Server Configuration

Picking a Server Name

One general consideration before even starting to configure your server is to pick a domain name for your machine. Even though the machine that will be hosting your server might already have a name (`jupiter.willamette.edu`, for example), you might provide an alias with the machine name www (such as www. willamette.edu). The www machine name is a fairly standard convention, and makes it easier for you to later move your Web server to a different machine simply by changing which machine the alias points to.

Evaluation Criteria

For space reasons, we cannot describe how to configure each and every server. Instead, now that we've reviewed the available servers, we've picked the three most representative servers for each platform. In the sections that follow, we give an in-depth look at how to retrieve, install, and configure NCSA httpd, Windows httpd, and MacHTTP (and WebSTAR).

We chose these servers because they are fairly common, and have had a great deal of influence on the other servers available. In addition, they are all robust and fully featured. These are good servers to begin using, and if you ever need to upgrade to a more powerful server, you will find that the transition will not be difficult once you are familiar with these servers.

NOTE: For the sections that follow on setting up servers on Unix, Windows, and Macintosh computers, we assume that your machine is already TCP/IP ready. This should already be true for most Unix machines. For Windows-based computers, you will need a Winsock package of some sort; and for Macintosh-based computers, you will need MacTCP. See the Bibliography for information on obtaining these packages.

Unix: How to Configure NCSA's httpd 1.4

NCSA httpd 1.4 is easily the most representative of the Unix servers, with two other Unix (and one Windows) servers based directly on it. This section covers how to install and configure NCSA httpd 1.4, as well as how to configure some of the Apache-specific extensions to NCSA httpd.

NCSA Features

NOTE: In order to install NCSA httpd, you should have super-user privileges on your Unix system or the help of someone who does. While it is not mandatory, you will not be able to run the server on port 80 (the standard HTTP port) unless you have superuser privileges. In addition, it is usually a good idea to get the help (and approval) of the system administrator before installing something like a Web server. The following discussion assumes that you have superuser privileges.

Getting the Software

The first thing you must do is to get the server software itself. It is available via the FTP server `ftp.ncsa.uiuc.edu`, in the directory `/Web/httpd/Unix/ncsa_httpd/current`. The files in the `current` directory are distributions for the current version of NCSA httpd (which at the time of this writing is 1.4.1). Several precompiled binaries are available, for platforms including AIX, HPUX, Irix, Linux, OSF, Solaris, and SunOS. If you have one of these platforms, you can retrieve the appropriate file. If you do not have any of these Unix platforms, you must retrieve the file `httpd_1.4.1_source.tar.Z` (taking into account possibly changed version numbers), and compile the source code on your system.

You should notice that there are two files for each platform: one that ends in " `.tar.Z` " and one that ends in " `.Z` ". The difference between these two is that the first contains the entire distribution (including sample configuration files and CGI scripts), and the second is just the server program itself. The latter is provided for upgrade purposes—if you already have installed an earlier version, you can simply drop in the new server executable (without re-retrieving all of the supporting material you already have).

For now, we'll assume you need to get the source code itself. (If you do have a supported system, go ahead and retrieve the appropriate `.tar.Z` file, follow through the rest of this section, and then skip the section that discusses compiling.)

Once you have this file, you will need to find a place to put it on your machine. The default location for this is `/usr/local/etc/httpd`, but it can be placed anywhere. The main thing to consider is that whichever hard drive or hard drive partition you place the server on should have enough space to allow growth—this directory (and its subdirectories) will contain a good deal of the documents and CGI scripts that make up your infostructure.

Now you'll need to uncompress and untar the distribution. Because the distribution will untar into a directory named `httpd_1.4.1`, you'll want to move the distribution file into the directory a level above where the distribution will eventually rest (for example, `/usr/local/etc`). Then, uncompress and untar the file.

At this point, the directory contains the httpd files. You can delete the file `httpd_1.4.1_source.tar` or archive it at your discretion (it can be handy to keep around, especially if you accidentally delete an important file—but you'll probably want to recompress it using `compress`).

You'll also probably want to create a symbolic link named `httpd` to the directory `httpd_1.4.1`, making (in this example) the full pathname of the httpd directory `/usr/local/etc/httpd` (the default value). Alternately, you can move `httpd_1.4.1` to `httpd`:

```
darwin% cd /usr/local/etc
darwin% ln -s httpd_1.4.1 httpd        (to create a
                                        symbolic link) or
darwin% mv httpd_1.4.1 httpd           (to rename the
                                        directory)
```

If you retrieved a package the contains a precompiled server for your platform, you're ready to move on to *Editing Configuration Files*, next. If you've got the source code, you'll need to compile it.

Compiling the Server Software

In an ideal world, you should be able to use make and the Makefile in the main directory of the server distribution to compile the
server. This will build the server itself, the sample CGI scripts included, and the support programs provided. When you type
make, you'll be provided with a list of supported systems:

```
darwin% cd /usr/local/etc/httpd
darwin% make
Please choose a system type.
Valid types are ibm, sunos, sgi, decmips, decaxp,
hp-cc,
hp-gcc, solaris, netbsd, svr4, linux, aux
If you do not have one of these systems, you must
edit
src/Makefile, cgi-src/Makefile, and support/Makefile
darwin% make svr4     (if you have a system based on
                              AT&T System V, Release 4)
```

At this point, you should see several screensful of messages, indicating that the server is being compiled.

If you do not have a directly supported system, you should be
able to use either svr4 or netbsd to compile the code (depending
on whether your system is based on System V, Release 4; or BSD
4.x). If necessary, you may need to edit the make files in src/
Makefile, cgi-src/Makefile, and support/Makefile. Such
editing is beyond the scope of this book, unfortunately.

Editing Configuration Files

By this point, you should have a compiled server that is ready to
run. The only step remaining before you have a usable Web server
is to set up the configuration files. There are four configuration
files: httpd.conf, srm.conf, access.conf, and mime.types.
We will only cover the first two here—access.conf will be covered in Chapter 9, *Security;* and mime.types should not need to
be modified.

The configuration files are in the subdirectory conf. Three of the
four are supplied as samples that should be modified: httpd.
conf-dist, srm.conf-dist, and access.conf-dist. You

should make *copies* of these files with the correct names (leaving the originals as references):

```
darwin% cp httpd.conf-dist httpd.conf
darwin% cp srm.conf-dist srm.conf
darwin% cp access.conf-dist access.conf
```

Next, you'll need to modify httpd.conf. This file contains information about technical aspects of httpd's operation: which directory the server is located in, where the other configuration files are, where the server logs should be kept, and so forth. httpd. conf consists of several directives to the server, one directive on each line. Lines that begin with "#" are comments. (See Figure 6.1)

Figure 6.1
Example httpd.conf

```
# This is the main server configuration file. It is best to
# leave the directives in this file in the order they are in, or
# things may not go the way you'd like. See URL http://hoohoo.ncsa.uiuc.edu/
# for instructions.

# Do NOT simply read the instructions in here without understanding
# what they do, if you are unsure consult the online docs. You have been
# warned.

# NCSA httpd (comments, questions to httpd@ncsa.uiuc.edu)

# ServerType is either inetd, or standalone.

ServerType standalone

# If you are running from inetd, go to "ServerAdmin".

# Port: The port the standalone listens to. For ports < 1023, you will
# need httpd to be run as root initially.

Port 80
```

The sample httpd.conf-dist that is included can be used with almost no changes. The only change you will have to make is to the line:

```
ServerAdmin you@your.address
```

which should be changed to reflect the e-mail address to which administrative e-mail about the server should be addressed. This might be your address, or you might create a user "web" (or "www," or "webmaster") for receiving administrative e-mail. For example, you might change this to:

```
ServerAdmin web@www.freedonia.com
```

The remainder of the configuration directives (described in Table 6.4) can be used as is, unless you need to customize the default behavior of the server.

Next, you'll need to edit `srm.conf`, the "server resource map." This file describes where your server will find documents, and how it should interpret them. Again, the default configuration file should serve most needs, but the wealth of options ensure that you can customize the server to meet anything out of the ordinary.

The first thing you may need to change is the `DocumentRoot` directive, which describes where the start of your virtual document tree is. This directory is the top of your Web server. If you were to retrieve the file `"http://www.freedonia.com/flugblogs.html"`, the Freedonia server would return the file `"flugblogs.html"` from its DocumentRoot. The default is:

```
DocumentRoot /usr/local/etc/httpd/htdocs
```

If you installed your server in `"/usr/local/etc/httpd,"` this does not need to be changed. You will need to create the directory `"htdocs"` in order to start populating your server with documents.

The next important line is

```
DirectoryIndex index.html
```

This is the name of the file that serves as the index for a directory. For example, when you retrieve `"http://www.freedonia.com/,"` the Web server attempts to serve the index for the directory "/." If Freedonia's DirectoryIndex is set to `"index.html"`, then this translates to the file `"/usr/local/etc/httpd/htdocs/index.html."` If the directory does *not* have a directory index file, an automatically generated list of files in the directory is returned instead. This directive does not need to be changed—`"index.html"` is a good setting. It's fairly standard, and easy to remember.

Finally, you may want to change the default file type. Web servers typically identify the type of file based on the file extensions (such as files that end in `.html`, `.txt`, `.gif`, or `.jpg`). However, if you have a large number of documents that do not have such an

Table 6.4 httpd.conf Options	**ServerType [inetd | standalone]**
Port *num*	See *Starting the server,* following. *num* is the port the server runs on. The default is 80 This number will have to be >1023 if the server is not run initially by root.
User *userid*	*userid* is the name (or number, if prefixed with "#") of the user the server is run as. Default is #-1. See *Starting the server.*
Group *groupid*	*groupid* is the name (or number, if prefixed with "#") of the group the server is run under. Default is #-1 See *Starting the server.*
ServerAdmin *email*	*email* is the e-mail address to which administrative e-mail for the server should be sent.
ServerRoot *directory*	*directory* is the directory that the httpd program is in. Other directories can be relative to this directory. De- fault is /usr/local/etc/httpd.
ServerName *name*	*name* is a Fully Qualified Domain Name (such as www.freedonia.com). This is used if the host goes by multiple DNS names, and one name is preferred.
StartServers *num*	See *Preforking versus forking* later.
MaxServers *num*	See *Preforking versus forking.*
TimeOut *time*	*time* is the number of seconds the server will wait before aborting the request. The default is 1200 (20 minutes.)
ErrorLog *filename*	*filename* is the location of the error log file. Default is logs/error_log (this is relative to ServerRoot).
TransferLog *filename*	*filename* is the location of the transfer log file. De- fault is logs/access_log.
AgentLog *filename*	*filename* is the location of the agent log file. This file tracks which software is used to connect to your server, for statistical purposes. Default is logs/ agent_log.
RefererLog *filename*	*filename* is the location of the referer log file. A ref- erer is the object (typically an HTML document) that contained the link to the document on your server that was requested. Useful for determining where your documents are being referenced from (and to track down broken links others have to your server). Default is logs/referer_log.

Continued.

Table 6.4 continued	RefererIgnore *string*	If *string* is found in the URL of the document that refers to your document, it is not logged. For example, if string was `www.freedonia.com` (and this was also your server's name), no references from documents on your server to your server would be logged. Multiple RefererIgnore lines can be used in the `httpd.conf` file. No default.
	PidFile *filename*	*filename* is the location of the file that contains httpd's process ID. This is useful for killing/restarting the daemon. Only used if ServerType is standalone. Default is `logs/httpd.pid`.
	AccessConfig *filename*	*filename* is the location of the global access configuration file. See Chapter 9, *Security.* Default is `conf/access.conf`.
	ResourceConfig *filename*	*filename* is the location of the resource configuration file (see later). Default is `conf/srm.conf`.
	TypesConfig *filename*	*filename* is the location of the typing configuration file. Default is `conf/mime.types`.
	IdentityCheck [on|off]	Enables logging of the remote user name. Only worthwhile for basic usage tracking (best to leave it off, as it generates more network traffic). Default is `off`.

extension, you might want to set a default type. The default setting for this is

```
DefaultType text/plain
```

which can be useful if you have a large number of plain text (ASCII) documents that do not have the extensions ".txt" or ".text." On the other hand, if you have a large number of HTML files without the extension .html, you might change this to

```
DefaultType text/html
```

There actually are situations where this can be useful. A real world situation that we encountered was a conversion job for a library that had a large number of documents in another hypertext format, which needed to be converted to HTML. It was not feasible to simply add ".html" to the end of each filename, so the default type was changed to text/html instead.

Table 6.5 describes the directives in srm.conf, the Resource Configuration file. We do not have space to adequately cover the

Table 6.5 srm.conf Directives Enumerated	DocumentRoot *directory*	*directory* is the absolute pathname of the directory which httpd will serve files from. See *Virtual Directory Tree.* Default is `/usr/local/etc/httpd/htdocs`.
	UserDir *directory*	*directory* is the name of the subdirectory in a user's home directory which httpd will look for to serve that user's documents. See *Virtual Document Tree.* Default is `public_html`.
	DirectoryIndex *filename*	If *filename* exists in a directory, it is returned as the index for that directory. Default is `index.html`.
	AccessFileName *filename*	*filename* used for per-directory access control. See Chapter 9, *Security.* Default is `.htaccess`
	AddType *type/subtype extension*	Allows definitions of additional types not in mime.types. Files ending in *extension* are assumed to be of type *type/subtype.* See Appendix B, *Internet Media Types.*
	AddEncoding *type extension*	Allows definitions of encoding types (such as compression methods). Files ending in *extension* are assumed to be encoded with *type.*
	DefaultType *type/subtype*	Defines the default type that documents will be returned as, if their type cannot be determined from the file extension. See Appendix B, *Internet Media Types.*
	Redirect *virtual URL*	Allows redirection of URLs to other servers. See *Virtual Document Tree.*
	Alias *virtual path*	Allows inclusion of virtual directories. See *Virtual Document Tree.*
	ScriptAlias *virtual path*	Allows inclusion of virtual directories containing CGI scripts. See *CGI.*
	OldScriptAlias *virtual path*	Allows inclusion of virtual directories containing old-style NCSA scripts. Not recommended for use.
	FancyIndexing [on|off]	Turns on or off fancy indexing. When there is no index file in a directory, httpd creates an index. With fancy indexing on, this index includes icons and file sizes. Default is off.
	IconsAreLinks [on|off]	If set to `on` (and if FancyIndexing is on), the icons displayed next to filenames are part of the link to the file, along with the filename itself. When set to `off`, only the filename is a link. Default is on.

Continued.

Table 6.5 continued	DefaultIcon *virtual*	Defines the default icon for unknown file types when FancyIndexing is on. *virtual* is the virtual path to the icon on the server (i.e. relative to document root). No default.
	ReadmeName *filename*	Defines name of file in directory to use as a footer for an automatically generated index (when FancyIndexing is on).
	HeaderName *filename*	Defines name of file in directory to use as a header for an automatically generated index (when FancyIndexing is on).
	AddDescription *description string*	Defines descriptions for files (when Fancy-Indexing is on). If *string* matches the file (fully, or partially, if a wildcard is supplied), *description* is given.
	AddIcon *filename [string]**	Defines an icon to associate with files. Files matching the supplied *strings* are represented with the icon defined by the virtual path *path*.
	AddIconByType *filename [type/subtype]**	Defines an icon to associate with the given *types*.
	AddIconByEncoding *filename [type]**	Defines an icon to associate with the given encoding *types*.
	IndexIgnore *[pattern]**	Defines files (either full filenames, extensions, or wildcard patterns) that should not be listed in automatically that generated indexes.
	IndexOptions *options*	*options* can include: FancyIndexing (turns FancyIndexing on), IconsAreLinks (includes icons as part of anchor), ScanHTMLTitles (uses HTML document titles for file descriptions), SuppressLastModified (supresses display of last modified date), SuppressSize (suppresses display of files size), and SuppressDescriptions (suppresses display of file descriptions). Default is no options.
	ErrorDocument *type filename*	Causes httpd to return *filename* as an error message for an error of type *type*.

*Wildcard character to match 0 or more characters

FancyIndexing directives, but the example `srm.conf` that comes with httpd provides useful default values for them.

One comment on FancyIndexing directives: those that match filenames (for adding icons, ignoring in indexes, and so on.) can either match the supplied strings exactly, or match a wildcard.

When building wildcard expressions, * matches 0 or more characters, and ? matches exactly one character. Thus, cat* would match cat and cataract, but not ducat; and eri? would match eric and erik, but not eri or erick.

Starting the Server

Before we go further in describing how the configuration files can be modified to meet specific needs, let's take a side trip and start the server in order to demonstrate how easy it is to get up and running.

First, you must decide whether to run the server from inetd, or as a standalone program. Inetd is a meta-server—it listens for connections for other servers, such as Telnet or FTP. Whenever it receives such a request, it creates a new process of the appropriate type to handle it. This is useful if you do not anticipate a large volume of requests on a server—for example, telnet and FTP are programs that are started by inetd at the beginning of a session, and remain active until the user is done. However, the Web does not maintain a connection for longer than it takes to load a document, which can make using inetd an expensive way of handling requests.

On the other hand, you can also run the server standalone. This means that the server will run constantly—so, if it is not heavily used, it will be constantly using system resources without performing any service. But if it is used to any great extent, it is worth constantly running the server. This also gives you some less obvious extra benefits, like not having to reload the server code or reparse the server configuration files every time a request comes in. And if you use the preforking mechanism described shortly, which keeps extra copies of the server around after they have been launched (on the assumption they will be used again in the very near future), you'll need to run the server standalone.

We will describe here how to run the server in standalone mode, because in nearly all situations it is preferable to running it via inetd. Since standalone is the default mode, the appropriate line in httpd.conf should already read:

```
ServerType standalone
```

Next, you'll want to decide which user and group the server should run as. In Unix, every process runs with the permission of some user, which means that that program is able to do the same things that that user would be able to do. For this reason, it is a good idea to *not* run httpd as the user "root." However, in order to run on port 80 (the default port for http), the server must be started by the user "root." In order to avoid disaster, httpd is able to change which user it is running as (if it has been started as "root"). The two directives in question are in httpd.conf:

```
User nobody
Group #-1
```

These defaults effectively mean that the server runs without the ability to read or write to any files except those that are publicly readable and writable. An alternate strategy to these defaults is to create a new user and a new group for Web-related work (these are Unix users and groups, not users and groups for the server itself. How to do the former is covered in any good Unix system administration manual, and how to do the latter is covered in Chapter 9, *Security*). The user can be called "web," and the group can be called "webmgr" (for "web manager"). You can then make the document tree owned by the user "web," and by the group "webmgr." You can use the group mechanism to limit who can edit institution-wide documents by placing individuals in the "webmgr" group, or by creating new groups for different collaborative authoring projects. An additional advantage to this is that you can make the home directory of "web" to be the same as ServerRoot, which means that instead of typing:

```
darwin% cd /usr/local/etc/httpd
```

you can type

```
darwin% cd ~web
```

which is easy to remember, and easy on the fingers.

If you choose to adopt this strategy, you'll need to create the appropriate user and group, and then change the configuration lines in httpd.conf to read:

```
User web
Group webmgr
```

At this point, you're ready to run your server. As root, change to the ServerRoot directory, and run the executable:

```
darwin% cd /usr/local/etc/httpd  (change to ServerRoot,
                                        where the executable is)
darwin% ./httpd  (invoke the executable)
```

NOTE: If you have selected a different server root than /usr/
local/etc/httpd, you'll need to invoke httpd with
the -d option (which specifies httpd's ServerRoot, so it
can find configuration files). For example, if your Server-
Root is /home/web, you'll invoke httpd with:

```
darwin% ./httpd -d /home/web
```

That's it. The server is now running. However, before you test it,
you should probably put a sample home page in. Change to the
DocumentRoot directory, and use an editor to enter the following
document:

```
darwin% cd /usr/local/etc/httpd/htdocs
darwin% pico index.html        (replace pico with your fa-
                                    vorite text editor)
```
(Enter the following text:)
```
⟨HTML⟩⟨HEAD⟩⟨TITLE⟩Welcome to Freedonia!</TITLE⟩
⟨/HEAD⟩⟨BODY⟩
⟨H1⟩Welcome to the Freedonia Web Server⟨/H1⟩

⟨P⟩ Welcome to the Freedonia Web Server. The Free-
donia Web Server currently contains absolutely no
content, but soon it will be serving information
to the world. Please excuse the mess—our Web sup-
port staff is about to re-read Chapter 3 of the
book ⟨CITE⟩Web Weaving⟨/CITE⟩ in order to put some
sample information in this infostructure.

⟨HR⟩

Last modified: (put today's date here)
⟨ADDRESS⟩Freedonia Web Manager, web@mysite.com
⟨/ADDRESS⟩
⟨/BODY⟩
⟨/HTML⟩
```

In order for the Web server to be able to read this document, it will need to be readable by it. The easiest way to do this is to make the document world-readable:

```
darwin% chmod a1r index.html
```

(Alternately, you can use the "chgrp" and "chown" commands to, respectively, change which user or which group owns this file so that it is in the same group as httpd, or owned by it. You can use this if you have documents that you do not want to be readable by everyone on your system—which makes sense if they are also protected by httpd's security facilities.)

Now your server should be ready to go. Fire up a Web browser, and point it at http://www.yourserver.com/ (where "www.yourserver.com" is the name of your machine). You should see something similar to Figure 6.2.

Now that you've verified your server has been started correctly, you'll want to make sure it is started automatically every time you restart your Unix machine (which, while it doesn't happen often, does happen occasionally). The appropriate place to do this is in the "rc.local" file, although this will vary from sys-

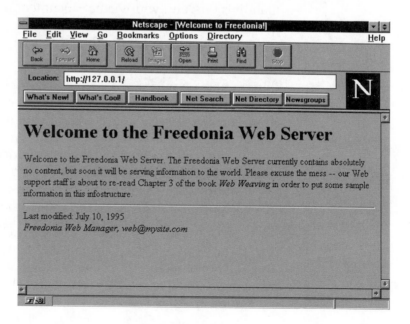

Figure 6.2
Your Homepage

tem to system. Consult your system manuals for more information.

Let's take a look at some of the important points here. First, the server is easy to get going. While we've covered a lot of things in the last few pages, most of them have been optional modifications. By and large, you can just put the server in the right place, and start it up. This leaves you to the business of developing content, which is what we're interested in here.

Second, the DirectoryIndex directive that we mentioned earlier— which was set to "index.html", and that we recommended should be left as is—came into play in the example here. The home page for your server is the document "index.html" in the Document-Root directory. Similarly, whenever you construct a URL that points to a directory (but not to a file within a directory) the "index.html" file will be returned for that directory.

Virtual Document Tree

As your server stands now, you can begin building your infostructure without another thought to configuration. You can create subdirectories of DocumentRoot for separating files into logical subdivisions, and your virtual document tree will match the part of your filesystem that starts with DocumentRoot. However, if you need more flexibility than this, you can do something about it.

First, a note on what a the virtual document tree is. As Figure 6.3a demonstrates, your filesystem is structured in the form of a tree. The Web server exports a portion of this tree (Figure 6.3b). URLs that refer to a document on your Web server do so relative to this virtual document tree that is exported by the Web server. In Figure 6.3b, the document tree exported by the Web server is straightforward—DocumentRoot and everything contained with it are exported, and URLs are relative to DocumentRoot.

However, you can also include directories that are not in Docu-mentRoot as part of your virtual document tree. For example, you might want to include the contents of your gopher server, but keep your Web documents in a distinct filespace. You can do this by adding an Alias directive to `srm.conf`. For instance, if your

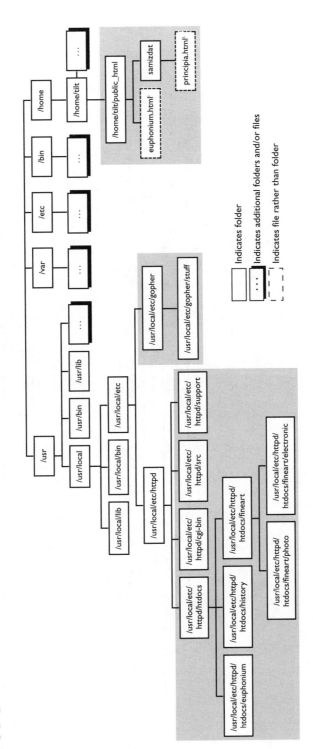

Figure 6.3a

Your Filesystem versus
the Virtual Document Tree

Indicates folder

Indicates additional folders and/or files

Indicates file rather than folder

153

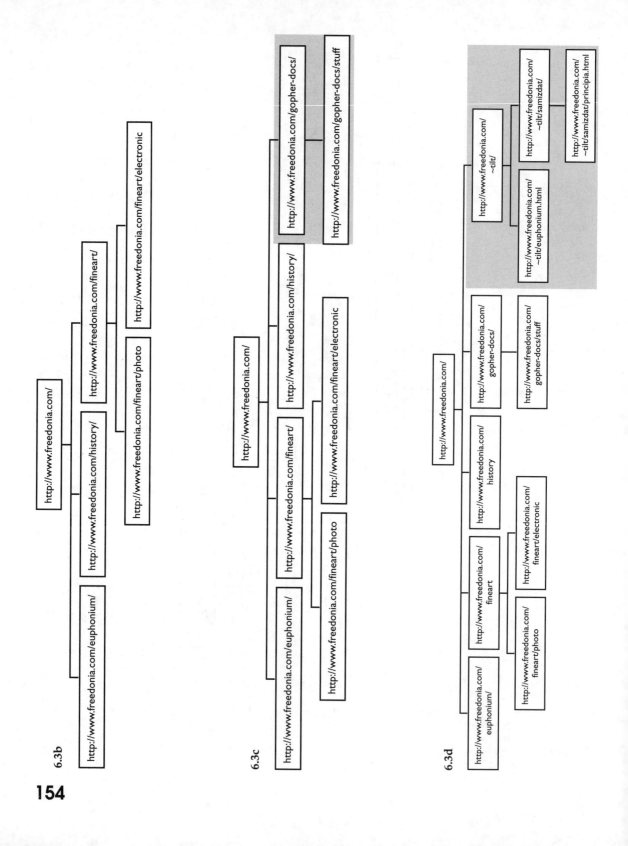

6.3b

http://www.freedonia.com/

http://www.freedonia.com/euphonium/

http://www.freedonia.com/history/

http://www.freedonia.com/fineart/

http://www.freedonia.com/fineart/photo

http://www.freedonia.com/fineart/electronic

6.3c

http://www.freedonia.com/

http://www.freedonia.com/euphonium/

http://www.freedonia.com/fineart/

http://www.freedonia.com/fineart/photo

http://www.freedonia.com/fineart/electronic

http://www.freedonia.com/history/

http://www.freedonia.com/gopher-docs/

http://www.freedonia.com/gopher-docs/stuff

6.3d

http://www.freedonia.com/

http://www.freedonia.com/euphonium/

http://www.freedonia.com/fineart

http://www.freedonia.com/fineart/photo

http://www.freedonia.com/fineart/electronic

http://www.freedonia.com/history

http://www.freedonia.com/gopher-docs/

http://www.freedonia.com/gopher-docs/stuff

http://www.freedonia.com/~tilt/

http://www.freedonia.com/~tilt/euphonium.html

http://www.freedonia.com/~tilt/samizdat/

http://www.freedonia.com/~tilt/samizdat/principia.html

gopher is in /usr/local/etc/gopher, you might add the following alias directive:

```
Alias /gopher-docs /usr/local/etc/gopher
```

which would result in a virtual document tree like that in Figure 6.3c.

The Alias directive takes the form

```
Alias virtual real
```

where *real* is the name of the actual pathname in your filesystem (/usr/local/etc/gopher), and *virtual* is the translated pathname used by the Web server. An alternate form is used to indicate where server scripts are located. This is covered in the section titled *CGI*.

Another powerful mechanism for building a virtual document tree is individual user Web directories. This mechanism allows users to supply HTML via subdirectories of their own home directories. If you want to allow users to provide information via your Web server, but don't want to give them permission to write to your main document tree, this feature is ideal. (In fact, it is probably this functionality—allowing users to publish on the Web easily—that has contributed most to the overwhelming popularity of the Web.)

This feature is controlled by the UserDir directive in srm.conf. The default value for this is

```
UserDir public_html
```

This means that if any user has a subdirectory (from their home directory) named "public_html," those documents can be served by the Web server.

The server translates a URL into something that should come from a user's public directory by looking for virtual directories starting with /~user/. For example,

```
http://www.freedonia.com/~tilt/euphonium.html
```

represents the virtual document /~tilt/euphonium.html on the server www.freedonia.com. The /~tilt/ at the *beginning* of this virtual path means that this virtual document is in user `tilt`'s public Web space. On `www.freedonia.com`, this might be translated to

```
/home/tilt/public_html/euphonium.html
```

(assuming that `tilt`'s home directory is `/home/tilt/public_html`, and UserDir has been set to `public_html`.)

To further illustrate this point,

```
http://www.freedonia.com/~tilt/samizdat/
principia.html
```

would be translated to

```
/home/tilt/public_html/samizdat/principia.html
```

(See Figure 6.3d.)

NOTE: In order for the Web server to be able to serve a user's documents, the server program must be able to read the files. This means that any publicly available Web document should be readable by any user. This can be accomplished with the chmod command:

darwin% **chmod a+r file.html**   (Where file.html is the name of the file to be made available)

The default configuration is to assume that user-supplied HTML is allowed, and that it will be in the user's public_html directory. If you wish to disable user-supplied HTML, set UserDir to

```
UserDir DISABLED
```

A final means of extending your virtual document tree is through redirection. This is useful when you move a document from your server onto another server. The Redirect directive in srm.conf allows you to do this. For example, if you were hosting a virtual museum on your main server, and decided to move it to a dedicated server (because it's so popular, and has many large images), you might use

```
Redirect /virtual-museum http://virtual-museum.freedonia.com/
```

which would translate any references to virtual directory "/virtual-museum" into references to the new server described by the URL.

Archiving Log Files

Something to think about, now that you have a Web server running, is that it will make a log entry every time a document is requested from it. If you have a Web server of any popularity, this will reach sizes of several megabytes over months, weeks, or even days.

This log can be a source of valuable statistical (and debugging) information (see Chapter 7 for more details), but it is not usually necessary to keep the entire log around from when you first started your server. You should decide on a strategy for archiving your log files. You might want to archive your log files once a week, and you might want to keep the last month's worth of logs (or you just might want to keep last week's logs— copying this week's logs onto files named "error_log-lastweek" and "access_log-lastweek").

However you decide to go about archiving log files, you should be warned that if you are running your server standalone, it must be restarted *after the log files have been moved.* This is so that the server can start a new log file, instead of continuing to output log entries to the old file. The easiest way to do this is to send the signal SIGHUP (-1) to the server process. You can do this by changing into your ServerRoot directory and issuing the commmand

```
darwin% kill -1 'logs/httpd.pid'
```

(This example assumes you have left the PidFile directive in httpd.conf unchanged.)

If you examine your error log, you should see the line

```
httpd: successful restart
```

at the end of it. This means you have successfully restarted httpd.

NOTE: You must also restart the daemon whenever you change your configuration files. Unless the standalone daemon is restarted, it will never reread the configuration files.

Preforking Versus Forking

The major difference between NCSA httpd 1.3 and 1.4 is the inclusion of a new architecture for streamlining performance. Under the old scheme, httpd would launch a new copy of the server to service each request. When running in standalone mode, the impact of this was minimized because the program did not need to be reloaded from disk; but when the server is servicing many simultaneous requests per second, the performance impact of starting up multiple programs can be dramatic.

To address this, httpd 1.4 uses a new method, which is based on the assumption that server processes, once started, can be reused. Instead of launching a new server for each request, a certain number of servers are launched when the server is first run. These servers are used to satisfy requests as they come in. If a request comes in and there is no server to service it, a new server is launched. After that request has been serviced, the newly launched server also remains. In this manner, enough servers can be launched to handle peak times.

NOTE: NCSA's preforking does not work on Linux. There is a patch which fixes this problem. It is available at

```
http://sunsite.unc.edu/pub/Linux/system/Network/
info-systems/httpd_1.4-linux-difts2.gz
```

Two directives in httpd.conf control how preforking works. They are StartServers, which controls the number of servers launched when httpd is first run, and MaxServers, which controls the maximum number of servers to "expand" to. For example, if StartServers is 5 and MaxServers is 20 (the values in the example configuration files that come with httpd), the server will launch five servers when first run. If, at some time, the server needs to service eight simultaneous requests, three more servers will be launched to handle the extra requests.

If there are more simultaneous connections than the number defined in MaxServers, additional servers are started to handle the additional load. For this reason, if you are expecting a large number of requests, it may behoove you to experiment with the setting of MaxServers. If it turns out that during your busy hours you are using the maximum number of servers, you are probably still launching (and then killing) extra servers to handle additional requests—which can cause a decrease in performance. On the other hand, you do not want to have a huge number of idle servers running, for the simple reason that they take up system resources.

If you wish to turn off preforking, and have the server act as httpd 1.3 does, use these settings:

```
StartServers 1
MaxServers 1
```

CGI

Setting up CGI scripting is fairly straightforward. There are two methods of enabling CGI: through specific CGI directories, and through the per-directory access control mechanism. Creating specific CGI directories is the recommended method. To do this, you create virtual directories (through the ScriptAlias directive in srm.conf). Whenever a file is retrieved from one of these directories, it is run as a program. The output of this program is returned as the document (Chapter 8, *CGI*, covers this mechanism in more detail). In order to create such a directory, you add the following line to `srm.conf`:

```
ScriptAlias /cgi-bin/ /usr/local/etc/httpd/cgi-bin/
```

(This line already is in the example `srm.conf` file which comes with httpd.) It maps the virtual directory `"cgi-bin"` onto the physical directory `"/usr/local/etc/httpd/cgi-bin/."` So, if you were to retrieve the URL

```
http://www.freedonia.com/cgi-bin/tic-tac-toe.pl
```

httpd would then map this onto the file `"/usr/local/etc/httpd/cgi-bin/tic-tac-toe.pl,"` and attempt to run the program.

NOTE: The `cgi-bin` directory comes with the NCSA distribution, and includes several sample CGI scripts (including one program that provides imagemap support). If you install httpd anywhere except `/usr/local/etc/httpd`, you will need to modify the default ScriptAlias line in `srm.conf` to reflect the new location.

An alternative to having specific directories with scripts is to allow CGI scripts in standard directories. This can be done by adding the line

```
Options ExecCGI
```

to a directory's .htaccess (access control) file. Creating access control files is covered in greater detail in Chapter 9, *Security*.

The only real reason to enable CGI scripts in directories is to allow users to create CGI scripts without having access to a global CGI directory. However, since CGI scripts run with the same permissions as the Web server, this can be a very big security hole. You should only allow this if you trust your users, and believe that they will not inadvertantly (or intentionally) introduce security holes. A program called CGI-wrap addresses this issue by allowing users' CGI scripts to be run as that user. It is available at

```
http://www/umr.edu/~cgiwrap/
```

Security

Configuring security for NCSA httpd is detailed in Chapter 9, *Security*.

Apache-specific Features

Apache is a free replacement to NCSA httpd. Because it is based on NCSA httpd 1.3, it provides the same feature set, in addition to several extra enhancements. The configuration files are identical, meaning that you can drop in the Apache server over the NCSA httpd executable without changing anything else.

This section discusses how to use two of the interesting features of Apache—content negotiation and virtual hosts. We will not discuss how to retrieve and compile Apache here, although the process is similar to that described for NCSA httpd. The source code can be found at ftp://ftp.apache.org/apache/dist/. No precompiled binaries are available; you will have to compile the code yourself. You will need to edit the file "Makefile," in the "src" directory, and uncomment the appropriate lines for your system. A wide range of systems are supported, and compilation should go smoothly.

Content Negotiation

Content negotiation is the process by which servers can provide documents in formats that browsers can accept and display. The browser, when making the HTTP request, can provide information about what sorts of formats it can accept, how desirable those formats are, and the quality with which it can display each format. The server, in turn, can use this information to select a "best-fit" format from multiple formats that a document might be available in.

In order for this even to occur, there must be some way in which the same document can be made available in different formats. At present, there are no automatic tools for this; rather, it is the author's responsibility to provide multiple formats. Furthermore, the server and client must both support content negotiation, in order for any benefit to be derived. While most clients and servers do *not* yet support content negotiation, it is likely that more and more will in the next few years; already, browsers such as emacs-w3 and Arena provide support.

Two obvious uses for content negotiation are for providing HTML 2.0 and HTML 3.0 versions of the same document; and for providing GIF and JPEG versions of the same image. Content negotiation is a way of providing content for all users, without resorting to links that read "Click here for JPEGs" and "Click here for GIFs."

There are two ways in which content negotiation is supported under Apache. The first is through a type map file, which explicitly describes multiple available versions of documents, along with quality ratings. In order to activate support for type maps, you'll need to add the line

```
AddType application/x-type-map .var
```

to your `srm.conf` file. With this line, files ending in `".var"` will be considered to be type maps for meta-files. For example, to server JPEG, GIF, and plain text versions of a map to get to Freedonia, you would create a file called `"freedonia-map.var,"` containing:

```
URI: freedonia-map; vary="type,language"

URI: freedonia-map.jpg
Content-type: image/jpeg; qs=0.8
```

```
URI: freedonia-map.gif
Content-type: image/gif; qs=0.5

URI: freedonia-map.txt
Content-type: text/plain; qs=0.01
```

Notice that this type map consists of four entries, with each entry separated by a blank line. Each entry begins with a URI: entry, which gives the Uniform Resource Identifier (a superset of URLs—see Appendix A) for an alternate version of this document. The first entry describes the document itself— "freedonia-map," which might be available in different types or languages. This first entry can remain unmodified in other type maps, with the exception that "freedonia-map" should be replaced with the name of the file.

After this is the entry describing the JPEG version of the document. This file—freedonia-map.jpg—should be in the same directory as freedonia-map.var. The Content type is described as image/jpeg, and the quality factor (as given by the server: the qs factor) is relatively high. This is the server's recommended format—if the browser can take it, it will.

Each additional entry describes an alternate format, in order of decreasing quality (qs). It is possible to add other information, such as Content-language:, Content-encoding:, and Content-length:.

In order to *retrieve* the document described by the type map, you construct a URL that refers to the document by name *but without an extension* (as extensions imply specific formats, and we are constructing a document theoretically available in more than one format). In the preceding example, you would use the URL

```
http://www.freedonia.com/freedonia-map
```

instead of

```
http://www.freedonia.com/freedonia-map.gif or
http://www.freedonia.com/freedonia-map.jpg
etc.
```

The server recognizes that "freedonia-map.var" exists, and uses it as a type map for content negotiation. It then returns the file listed in the type map that is the closest fit to what the browser wants (which, if the browser can accept it, will be a JPEG. If the browser cannot accept that, then it will be a GIF. If the browser cannot accept that, then the server will return the plain text version).

An alternate method is to use the MultiViews option. You can turn the MultiViews option on via the access control mechanism, on a per-directory basis. In order to enable MultiViews for a directory, you'll need to add MultiViews to the options. You can do this by adding the line

```
Options MultiViews
```

to the .htaccess file for the directory (see Chapter 9, *Security*, for more details on the .htaccess file). If you do not add this line, MultiViews will not work.

MultiViews works by creating a fake type map for a document. With a real type map, the author explicitly assigns content types and quality ratings to each version of a document. With Multi-Views, the server finds all documents that match the requested URL (without the extension), and assigns each a quality of 1. The first document the browser is willing to accept is returned. If the browser is willing to accept multiple types, the file with the smallest size is returned. This is useful for having JPEG and GIF versions of the same document, since the JPEG version is usually smaller; if the browser is willing to take it, it gets the inline JPEG, otherwise, it gets an inline GIF (unfortunately, the beta version of Apache we tested did not implement this correctly, so your mileage may vary).

This is also useful is in serving HTML 2.0 and HTML 3.0. If you add the following line to your srm.conf:

```
AddType text/html;level53 .html3
```

you can then supply documents that take advantage of HTML 3.0 as well as versions of the same document that do not. Simply name the HTML 2.0 version of the document "foo.html" as you normally would (assuming, of course, that the document would be named "foo"), and name the HTML 3.0 version of the document "foo.html3." Then request the document with the URL

```
http://www.freedonia.com/foo
```

Apache will return the appropriate version of the document.

NOTE: Current versions of Arena, the HTML 3.0 browser, do not correctly recognize HTML 3.0 served in this manner. If this problem is not fixed by the time you read this, you can address it by compiling the Apache server with the `"-DARENA_BUG_WORKAROUND"` option. Add this to the `CFLAGS` line in the Makefile in the src directory. The switch removes the `";level= 3"` parameter from the content type, which Arena does not handle properly.

NOTE: Remember that whenever you modify configuration files, you must restart the server. See *Starting the server,* earlier in the chapter.

Virtual Hosts

Virtual hosts is a mechanism by which one server can provide different virtual document trees, depending on the host name it is accessed by. This can be useful if:

- You are providing an internal Web server for local use and an external server for public use.

- You are providing Web services for other organizations that do not have direct access to the Internet.

NOTE: In order to use virtual hosts, each host name must have a different IP address associated with it. This means that each virtual host must either have a different physical connection to the network, or that the version of Unix you are running supports a virtual interface (which will probably require modifying the system's kernel—a task well outside the range of this book). Check `http://www.apache.org/docs/vif.info` for more details.

There are two ways to set up virtual hosts: either by running multiple daemons (binding each to a different address) or by running a single daemon. The multiple daemon method requires more overhead, but may be necessary if each virtual host needs a different srm.conf file. In order to use multiple daemons, create a separate set of configuration files for each, and use the BindAddress directive in the httpd.conf for each daemon to select which virtual host that daemon services:

```
BindAddress www.felix.com
```

Each daemon will then answer requests addressed to different network interfaces on the machine. The alternate method—and a preferable method, if you don't require different resource map configurations for each daemon—is to run a single daemon, using the VirtualHost directive to define a different document tree for each virtual server. Although the same server will fulfill each request, it will use the information in the VirtualHost directive to resolve URLs into filenames (and to use the correct log) depending on which IP address is used. For example, to create two virtual hosts, you would add the following to your srm.conf:

```
⟨VirtualHost www.freedonia.com⟩
ServerAdmin www@freedonia.com
DocumentRoot /usr/local/etc/httpd/docs
ServerName www.freedonia.com
ErrorLog /usr/local/etc/httpd/logs/www-error_log
TransferLog /usr/local/etc/httpd/logs/www-access_log
⟨/VirtualHost⟩

⟨VirtualHost localwww.freedonia.com⟩
ServerAdmin www@freedonia.com
DocumentRoot /usr/local/etc/httpd/local-docs
ServerName localwww.freedonia.com
ErrorLog /usr/local/etc/httpd/logs/local-error_log
TransferLog /usr/local/etc/httpd/logs/local-access_log
⟨/VirtualHost⟩
```

This will create a virtual document tree.

Windows: How to Configure Windows httpd

Windows httpd 1.4, by Robert Denny, is the most popular server for the Windows platform, and is very similar to NCSA httpd (covered earlier in the Unix server installation section). This section covers how to install and configure Windows httpd.

NOTE: This server does *not* run under Windows 95 or Windows NT (only under Windows 3.1 or 3.11), although WebSite

(by the same author) does. See the section on Windows
Web server evaluation for more details about WebSite.

Getting the Software

The first thing you must do is to get the server software itself. You
can do this via the Web:

```
http://www.city.net/win-httpd/
```

The link to download the file is at the end of the document—Mr.
Denny wants you to take at least a cursory look at the information
he has provided before you download the software (and taking an
in-depth look at the page is highly recommended).

Next, you'll want to uncompress the file. Because it is compressed
in ZIP format, you'll need PKUNZIP 2.04g (or later). The ZIP file
contains information about the directory structure, so you'll need
to use the -D option in order to correctly unzip it. It is recommended that you create a directory named C:\HTTPD, and unzip
the file here, because the default configuration files assume that
the server will be running from this location. So, in order to unzip
the file, do the following from a DOS prompt:

```
C:\> mkdir HTTPD
C:\> mv WHTTPD14.ZIP C:\HTTPD
C:\> cd HTTPD
C:\HTTPD> pkunzip -D WHTTPD14.ZIP
```

(If you would like to put httpd elsewhere, see *Editing Configuration
Files*, next).

You will also need VBRUN300.DLL, the Visual Basic runtime
library, in order to run some of the accompanying scripts. If
you are not sure whether you already have it, check for the file
VBRUN300.DLL in either your C:\WINDOWS or C:\WINDOWS\
SYSTEM directories. If you do not have the file, you can retrieve it
from the Microsoft FTP site, ftp.microsoft.com, in the directory /Softib/MSLFILES (there are a lot of of files in this directory—you are looking for the specific file named VBRUN300.DLL).

Editing Configuration Files

The server is almost ready to go. After you edit a few configurations files, you'll be ready to start serving documents on the Web.

The first step is to set the appropriate time zone information. This is necessary because the NCSA/CERN Common Log Format requires that each log entry provide a timestamp in Greenwich Mean Time (GMT). In order to set up time zone information, you'll need to add the TZ environment variable to your AUTO-EXEC.BAT file. This environment variable takes the form *sssnddd,* where sss is the three-letter abbreviation for your standard time zone; *ddd* is the three-letter abbreviation for your daylight time zone (if you have one); and *n* is your offset (in hours) from GMT. For example, a server in Oregon would have the line

```
SET TZ=PST8PDT
```

in the AUTOEXEC.BAT file. Table 6.6 lists TZ values for the U.S. time zones.

Table 6.6

TZ Values for U.S. Time Zones

Hawaii (no daylight savings)	HST10
Pacific	PST8PDT
Mountain	MST7MDT
Mountain (Arizona/no daylight savings)	MST8
Central	CST6CDT
Eastern	EST5EDT

You will also need to add some additional environment space for DOS shells run from Windows, so that your CGI scripts (and the demonstration scripts included with httpd) will be able to run. In order to do this, you will need to edit the file SYSTEM.INI (in your Windows directory, typically C:\WINDOWS). Find the line [NonWindowsApp] in SYSTEM.INI, and the following line immediately after it:

```
CommandEnvSize=8192
```

If there is already a line that begins with CommandEnvSize= after [NonWindowsApp], modify that line instead of adding a new line.

There are four configuration files for httpd proper: httpd.cnf, srm.cnf, access.cnf, and mime.typ. We will only cover the first two here—access.cnf will be covered in Chapter 9, *Security;* and mime.typ should not need to be modified. The configuration files are in the subdirectory `conf` of the distribution, and you'll probably want to make backup copies of them before modifying them.

Next, you'll need to modify `httpd.cnf`. This file contains information about technical aspects of httpd's operation: which directory the server is located in, where the other configuration files are, where the server logs should be kept, and so forth. (You will probably want to make a backup copy of this file before modifying it.)

`httpd.cnf` consists of several directives to the server, one directive on each line. Lines which begin with "#" are comments. Also, all file references are given Unix-style, with forward slashes separating directories (/) instead of DOS-style backward slashes (\). For example, C:\HTTPD would be given as "C:/HTTPD" (see Figure 6.4).

Most of these items can be left unchanged (especially if you have installed httpd in `C:\HTTPD`). The only change you will have to make is to the line:

```
# ServerAdmin www-admin
```

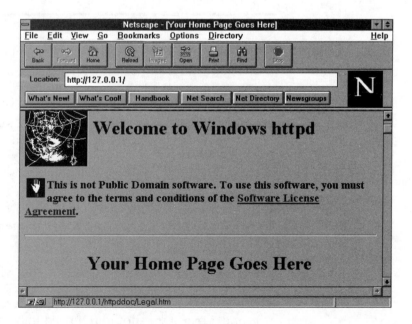

Figure 6.4
Example
Configuration File

which should be changed to reflect the e-mail address to which administrative e-mail about the server should be addressed (it should also be uncommented, by removing the "# " at the beginning of the line). This might be changed to your e-mail address, or you might create a user "web" (or "www," or "webmaster") for receiving administrative e-mail. For example, you might change this to:

```
ServerAdmin web@www.freedonia.com
```

The remainder of the configuration directives (described in Table 6.7) can be used as is, unless you need to customize the default behavior of the server.

Next, you'll need to edit `srm.cnf`, the server resource map. This file describes where your server will find documents and how it

Table 6.7 httpd.conf Options		
Port *num*	*num* is the port the server runs on. The default is 80. Servers not run on port 80 should be run on port 1024 or greater.
ServerAdmin *email*	*email* is the e-mail address to which administrative e-mail for the server should be sent.
ServerRoot *directory*	*directory* is the directory that the httpd program is in Other directories can be relative to this directory Default is `C:/HTTPD/`.
ServerName *name*	*name* is a Fully Qualified Domain Name (such as www.freedonia.com). This is used if the host goes by multiple DNS names, and one name is preferred.
TimeOut *time*	*time* is the number of seconds the server will wait before aborting the request. The default is 30.
ErrorLog *filename*	*filename* is the location of the error log file. Default is `logs/error.log` (this is relative to ServerRoot).
TransferLog *filename*	*filename* is the location of the transfer log file. Default is `logs/access.log`.
AccessConfig *filename*	*filename* is the location of the global access configuration file. See Chapter 9, *Security*. Default is `conf/access.cnf`.
ResourceConfig *filename*	*filename* is the location of the resource configuration file. Default is `conf/srm.cnf`.
TypesConfig *filename*	*filename* is the location of the typing configuration file. Default is `conf/mime.typ`.

should interpret them. Again, the default configuration file should serve most needs, but the wealth of options ensure that you can customize the server to meet anything out of the ordinary.

The first thing you may need to change is the `DocumentRoot` directive, which describes where the start of your virtual document tree is. This directory is the top of your Web server. If you were to retrieve the file `"http://www.freedonia.com/flugblogs.html,"` the Freedonia server would return the file `"fluglogs.html"` from its own DocumentRoot. The default is:

```
DocumentRoot c:/httpd/htdocs
```

If you installed your server in `C:\HTTPD`, this does not need to be changed. You will find the directory `htdocs` has already been provided, and even includes some sample documentation.

The next important line is

```
DirectoryIndex index.htm
```

This is the name of the file that serves as the index for a directory. For example, when you retrieve the document `"http://www.freedonia.com/,"` the Web server attempts to serve the index for the directory `"/."` If Freedonia's DirectoryIndex is set to `"index.htm"`, then this translates to the file `"c:\httpd\htdocs\index.htm."` If the directory does *not* have a directory index file, an automatically generated list of files in the directory is returned, instead. This directive does not need to be changed—`"index.htm"` is a good setting. It's fairly standard, and easy to remember.

Finally, you may want to change the default file type. Web servers typically identify the file type based on the file extensions (such as `.htm`, `.txt`, `.gif`, or `.jpg`). However, if you have a large number of documents that do not have such an extension, you might want to set a default type. The default setting for this is

```
DefaultType text/plain
```

which can be useful if you have a large number of plain text (ASCII) documents that do not have the extensions ".txt." On the other hand, if you have a large number of HTML files without the extension .htm, you might change this to

```
DefaultType text/html
```

There are situations where this can be useful. A real world situation that we encountered was a conversion job for a library that had a large number of documents in another hypertext format, which needed to be converted to HTML. It was not feasible to simply add ".htm" to the end of each file name, so the default type was changed to text/html instead.

Table 6.8 describes the directives in `srm.cnf`, the Resource Configuration file. We do not have space to adequately cover the FancyIndexing directives, but the example `srm.cnf` that comes with httpd provides useful default values for them.

One comment on FancyIndexing directives: those that match filenames (for adding icons, ignoring in indexes, and so on) can either match the names of files exactly or match file extensions. Full pathnames can also be supplied.

Starting the Server

Before we go further in describing how the configuration files can be modified to meet specific needs, let's take a side trip and start the server in order to demonstrate how easy it is to get up and running.

Using the File Manager, go into `C:\HTTPD` and run `HTTPD.EXE`. The server will briefly display a "splash" screen, and then minimize itself. (Before you do this, make sure you have a Winsock package, such as Trumpet Winsock, running.) That's it. The server is now running. A sample document tree has been included with the distribution, so you can just fire up a Web browser, and point it at `http://www.yourserver.com/` (replacing "www.your server.com" with the name of your machine). You should see something similar to Figure 6.5.

Now that you've verified your server has been started correctly, you'll want to make sure it starts automatically every time you restart your Windows machine. You can do this by adding httpd to your Windows `StartUp` group in the Program Manager.

DocumentRoot *directory*	*directory* is the absolute pathname of the directory from which httpd will serve files.See *Virtual Directory Tree*. Default is C:/HTTPD/ HTDOCS.
DirectoryIndex *filename*	If *filename* exists in a directory, it is returned as the index for that directory. Default is index.htm.
AccessFileName *filename*	*filename* used for per-directory access control. See Chapter 9, *Security*. Default is #htaccess.ctl.
AddType *type/subtype extension*	Allows definitions of additional types not in mime.types. Files ending in *extension* are assumed to be of type *type/subtype*. See Appendix B, *Internet Media Types*.
DefaultType *type/subtype*	Defines the default type that documents will be returned as, if their type cannot be determined from the file extension. See Appendix B, *Internet Media Types*.
Redirect *virtual URL*	Allows redirection of URLs to other servers. See *Virtual Document Tree*.
Alias *virtual path*	Allows inclusion of virtual directories. See *Virtual Document Tree*.
ScriptAlias *virtual path*	Allows inclusion of virtual directories containing DOS CGI scripts. See *CGI*.
WinScriptAlias *virtual path*	Allows inclusion of virtual directories containing Windows CGI scripts. See *CGI*.
FancyIndexing [on|off]	Turns on or off fancy indexing. When there is no index file in a directory, httpd creates an index. With fancy indexing on, this index includes icons and file sizes. Default is off.
IconsAreLinks [on|off]	If set to on (and if FancyIndexing is on), the icons displayed next to filenames are part of the link to the file, along with the filename itself. When set to off, only the filename is a link. Default is on.
DefaultIcon *virtual*	Defines the default icon for unknown file types when FancyIndexing is on. *virtual* is the virtual path to the icon on the server (i.e. relative to document root). No default.
ReadmeName *filename*	Defines name of file in directory to use as a footer for an automatically generated index (when FancyIndexing is on).

Continued.

Table 6.8 continued	AddDescription *description string*	Defines descriptions for files (when Fancy-Indexing is on). If *string* matches the file (either by name or extensions), *description* is given.
	AddIcon *filename [string]**	Defines an icon to associate with files. Files matching the supplied *strings* are represented with the icon defined by the virtual path *path*.
	IndexIgnore *[pattern]**	Defines files that should not be listed in automatically generated indexes. *Pattern* is matched against the right-hand side of filenames (i.e. `htm` would match `file.htm`, but not `bhtm.txt`).

While we've covered a lot of things in the last few pages, most of them have been optional modifications. By and large, you can just put the server in the right place and start it up. This leaves you to the business of developing content, which is what we're interested in here.

NOTE: An alternate, and useful, method of invoking httpd is with the -l (as in "ell," not "one") option:

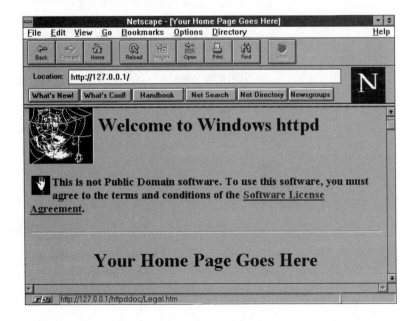

Figure 6.5
Your Homepage

```
httpd -1 vbrun300.dll
```

NOTE: This command line option tells httpd to load the "vbrun300.dll" library when it starts, and to keep it loaded until it exits. If you do not use this option, the library may be loaded every time a CGI script based on Visual Basic is run, and then unloaded every time such a CGI script completes.

Virtual Document Tree

As your server stands now, you can begin building your infostructure without another thought to configuration. You can create subdirectories of DocumentRoot for separating files into logical subdivisions, and your virtual document tree will match the part of your filesystem that starts with DocumentRoot. However, if you need more flexibility than this, you can do something about it.

First, a note on what a virtual document tree is. As Figure 6.6a demonstrates, your filesystem is structured in the form of a tree. The Web server exports a portion of this tree (Figure 6.6b). URLs that refer to a document on your Web server do so relative to this virtual document tree, which is exported by the Web server. In Figure 6.6b, the document tree exported by the Web server is straightforward—DocumentRoot and everything contained with it are exported, and URLs are relative to DocumentRoot.

However, you can also include directories that are not in DocumentRoot as part of your virtual document tree. For example, you might want to include the contents of your gopher server, but keep your Web documents in a distinct filespace. You can do this by adding an Alias directive to srm.conf. For instance, if your gopher is in `C:\GOPHER`, you might add the following alias directive:

```
Alias /gopher-docs C:/GOPHER
```

which would result in a virtual document tree like that in Figure 6.6c.

The Alias directive takes the form

```
Alias virtual real
```

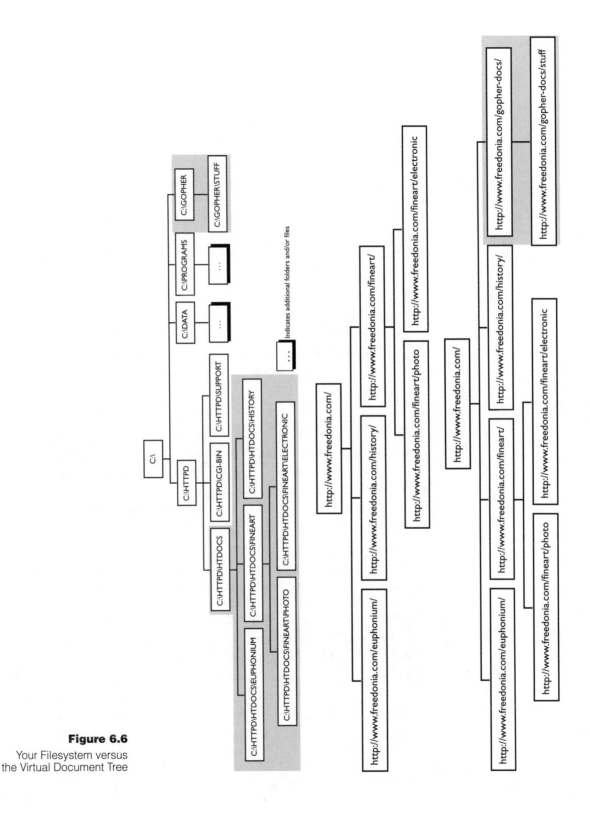

Figure 6.6

Your Filesystem versus the Virtual Document Tree

where *real* is the name of the actual pathname in your filesystem (C:/GOPHER), and *virtual* is the translated pathname used by the Web server. An alternate form of the Alias directive is used to indicate where server scripts are located. This is covered in the *CGI* section.

An additional means of extending your virtual document tree is through redirection. This is useful when you move a document from your server onto another server. The Redirect directive in srm.conf allows you to do this. For example, if you were hosting a virtual museum on your main server, and decided to move it to a dedicated server (because its so popular, and has many large images), you might use

```
Redirect /virtual-museum http://virtual-museum.
freedonia.com/
```

which would translate any references to virtual directory "/virtual-museum" into references to the new server described by the URL.

Archiving Log Files

Something to think about, now that you have a Web server running, is that it will make a log entry every time a document is requested from it. If you have a Web server of any popularity, this log will reach sizes of several megabytes over months, weeks, or even days.

This log can be a source of valuable statistical (and debugging) information (see Chapter 7 for more details), but it is not usually necessary to keep the entire log around from when you first started your server. You should decide on a strategy for archiving your log files. You might want to archive your log files once a week, and you might want to keep the last month's worth of logs. Or, you might want to archive your logs daily.

Httpd comes with a program called logcycle.exe (you'll find it in C:\HTTPD\SUPPORT). When you run it, it renames the current access log to include an extension of .001 (for example, access.log becomes access.001), and any previously archived logs are renumbered (.001 becomes .002, and so on). If you supply the "-e" option, logcycle.exe will cycle the error log. If you supply the "-ae" option, both the access and error logs will be cycled. (There is a third log, the console log, which is in C:\HTTPD\HTTPD.LOG, and which is cleared each time the server is restarted.)

CGI

Setting up CGI scripting is fairly straightforward. To do so, you create virtual directories (through the ScriptAlias directive in srm.conf). Whenever a file is retrieved from one of these directories, it is run as a program. The output of this program is returned as the document.

Windows httpd has two mechanisms for CGI scripts, a DOS interface and a Windows interface. The DOS interface runs CGI scripts in a virtual DOS machine, while the Windows interface runs Windows applications. (Chapter 8, *CGI*, covers these mechanisms in more detail).

NOTE: Remember that you must supply a large enough environment for DOS CGI scripts to run in. See *Editing configuration files*, previously, for more details.

In order to create a virtual directory for DOS-based CGI scripts, you add the following lines to srm.cnf:

```
ScriptAlias /cgi-dos/ c:/httpd/cgi-dos/
ScriptAlias /cgi-bin/ c:/httpd/cgi-dos/
```

(These lines are already in the example srm.cnf file that come with httpd.) This line maps the virtual directories "cgi-dos" and "cgi-bin" onto the physical directory c:\httpd\cgi-dos (cgi-bin is the defacto standard directory for CGI scripts, which is why it is included in addition to cgi-dos. The name cgi-dos refers to the fact that this directory contains DOS-based CGI scripts). So, if you were to retrieve the URL

```
http://www.freedonia.com/cgi-bin/tictacto.pl
```

httpd would then map this onto the file c:\httpd\cgi-dos\tictacto.pl, and attempt to run the program. Similarly, in order to create a virtual directory for Windows CGI, add this line to srm.cnf:

```
WinScriptAlias /cgi-win/ c:/httpd/cgi-win/
```

> **NOTE:**   The `cgi-dos` and `cgi-win` directories come with the
> Windows httpd distribution, and include several sample
> CGI scripts (including one program that provides im-
> agemap support). If you install httpd anywhere except
> `c:/httpd`, you will need to modify the default ScriptAl-
> ias and WinScriptAlias lines in `srm.cnf` to reflect the
> new location.

Security

Configuring security for Windows httpd is detailed in Chapter 9,
Security.

Macintosh: How to Configure MacHTTP

This section covers how to install and configure MacHTTP. It also
covers how to install and configure WebSTAR, the successor to
MacHTTP. Differences between MacHTTP and WebSTAR are
noted in the text.

> **NOTE:**   MacHTTP may soon be supplanted by WebSTAR SW, a
> low-cost version of MacHTTP. These instructions should
> still be valid for WebSTAR SW.

Getting the Software

The first thing you must do is to get the server software itself. You
can do this via the Web, using

```
http://www.biap.com/machttp/machttp_software.html
```

for MacHTTP, or

```
http://www.starnine.com/
```

for WebSTAR. (If the MacHTTP page does not work, try the Web-
STAR page—MacHTTP may have been replaced by WebSTAR
SW). These Web pages will provide links to the latest versions of
the software.

Once you have retrieved the file, you'll want to uncompress it.
MacHTTP is in BinHex and StuffIt formats, so you'll need StuffIt

or StuffIt Expander to uncompress it. WebSTAR is a BinHexed self-extracting archive; again, StuffIt Expander can decode and uncompress it.

After the file has been uncompressed, you will see a folder named "MacHTTP 2.2." This folder can be placed anywhere on your hard drive. It contains two folders: "MacHTTP Software & Docs" (which contains the server software itself) and "Apple's Scripting System" (which contains AppleScript).

At this point, you will need to install AppleScript, if you have not already done so. Open the folder "Apple's Scripting System"; you will find two folders: "For all Extensions folders" and "For Power Mac Extensions folder." You will need to open the "For all Extensions folders" folder, and copy the contents of this folder into your Extensions folder (located in the System folder). *Do not* simply copy the folder itself. If you have a Power Mac, you'll need to repeat this process with the folder "For Power Mac Extensions folder." You'll need to reboot the computer, and then MacHTTP will be ready to go!

(WebSTAR comes with an Installer script that will automatically install WebSTAR and AppleScript on your systsem, and then reboot your machine. Make sure you have quit all other applications, and then double-click the Installer icon.)

Starting the Server

Before we go further in describing how the configuration files can be modified to meet specific needs, let's take a side trip and start the server in order to demonstrate how easy it is to get up and running. To start the server, double-click on the MacHTTP (or WebSTAR) icon.

NOTE: Before you start the server, you should have installed MacTCP (which you can get from Apple).

That's it. The server is now running. A sample document tree has been included with the distribution, so you can just fire up a Web browser, and point it at `http://www.yourserver.com/` (replacing `"www.yourserver.com"` with the name of your machine). You should see something similar to Figure 6.7.

Figure 6.7
Your Homepage

Now that you've verified that your server has been started correctly, you'll want to make sure it is started automatically every time you restart your Macintosh. You can do this by adding an alias to MacHTTP to the `Startup` folder in your `System Folder`.

We'll cover a lot of things in the next few pages, but most of them will be optional modifications. By and large, you can just put the server in the right place and start it up. This leaves you to the business of developing content, which is what we're interested in here.

Editing Configuration Files

There are two configuration files that accompany MacHTTP: `MacHTTP Settings` and `MacHTTP.config`. `MacHTTP Settings` is created by MacHTTP, and you cannot edit it directly—it contains information like usernames and passwords, as well as options that can be set from within the program.

MacHTTP.config is a text file containing configuration directives. These configuration directives include information about how the server should run, how suffixes should be mapped onto *Internet Media Types* (see Appendix B), and information about security (the security options are covered in Chapter 9, *Security*). This file consists of multiple directives to the server, with one directive on each line; blank lines and lines beginning with "#" (indicating comments) are ignored (see Figure 6.8).

Table 6.9 describes the configuration directives. One important thing to note is that MacHTTP uses "Default.html" as the index file instead of "index.html," and that MacHTTP will not automatically create an index file for a directory if one does not already exist (in order to provide better security).

The values given to configuration directives can be full or partial pathnames. If you give a pathname beginning with a colon (for example, supplying ":Error.html" for the ERROR directive), the file is assumed to be in the same folder as the MacHTTP program. The INDEX directive should *not* be a partial pathname, it should just be a simple filename (such as "Default.html" or "index.html").

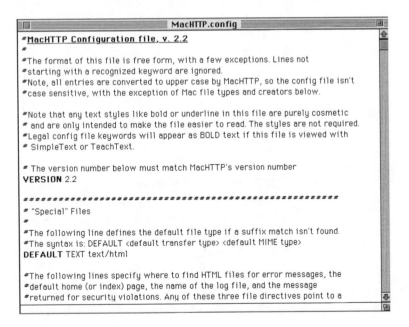

Figure 6.8
Example MacHTTP.config file

Table 6.9

MacHTTP.config
Configuration Directives

INDEX *filename*	*filename* is the name of the file that is returned when a directory index is requested. Default is `Default.html`.
ERROR *filename*	*filename* is the name of the file that is returned when an error is encountered. Default is `:Error.html`.
LOG *filename*	*filename* is the name of the file used for logging. If omitted, logging is disabled.
NOACCESS *filename*	*filename* is the name of the file returned when a user or host does not have permission to retrieve a document.
TIMEOUT *seconds*	*seconds* is the number of seconds the server will wait for an inactive connection. Default is 90 seconds.
MAXUSERS *num*	*num* is the maximum number of simultaneous connections allowed to MacHTTP. The larger this number is, the more resources MacHTTP will need. Default is 8.
MAXLISTENS *num*	*num* is number of simultaneous "listens" for incoming connections. Default is 5.
PORT *num*	*num* is the port on which MacHTTP listens for connections. The default is 80. If you wish to use a number other than 80 (for running a second server), you must use the number 1024 or greater.
PIG_DELAY *ticks*	*ticks* is the number of ticks that MacHTTP will use from other processes in order to process connections. A tick is a sixtieth of a second. Default is 30 (0.5 seconds).
DUMP_BUF_SIZE *bytes*	*bytes* is the number of bytes that MacHTTP will send at a time on a given connection. The higher this is, the longer MacHTTP will spend, on one connection before being able to service another connection. Default is 4096.
NO_DNS	If this directive is included, MacHTTP will not use DNS to look up the names of hosts that connect to the server (for logging purposes). Including this directive will improve MacHTTP's efficiency, if local DNS servers are slow.

In WebSTAR, the `MacHTTP.config` options are not in a text file; instead, they can be changed with the WebSTAR Admin program, via the Configure menu. WebSTAR also adds a few additional directives, including user-definable actions (which define CGI "handlers" for any documents with a particular suffix, such as an imagemap handler for .map files); and URL pre- and post-processing, which allow CGI scripts to handle URLs before and after WebSTAR is done with them.

The `MacHTTP.config` file also contains suffix mapping information. This information tells MacHTTP how to map Macintosh files onto various Internet Media Types (see Appendix B). The format of a suffix mapping directive is:

```
transfer-type suffix Mac-filetype Mac-creator Type/
Subtype
```

transfer-type can be one of the seven types listed in Table 6.10; *suffix* is a file suffix, such as `".txt"`; `Mac-filetype` and `Mac-creator` correspond to the MacOS file typing information scheme, which employs a four-character filetype and a four-character creator code. If a file matches the values given for `suffix`, `Mac-filetype`, and `Mac-creator`, it is typed as the Internet Media Type `Type/Subtype`. A value of `"*"` can be supplied for any `suffix`, `Mac-filetype`, or `Mac-creator` values that are unknown or undefined.

Table 6.10 MacHTTP.config Suffix Mapping Transfer Types	
TEXT	Matching files will be sent as text-only files to the client.
BINARY	Matching files will be sent as is (data fork only) to the client.
SCRIPT	Matching files will be invoked as AppleScript files; output will be returned as type TEXT.
CGI	Matching files will be launched as an application, with arguments passed to the files via the "Search Doc" AppleEvent.
ACGI	Matching files will be launched as an application, with arguments passed to the files via the "Search Doc" AppleEvent. These applications are executed asynchronously; after invocation, MacHTTP will continue to process other requests.
DEFAULT *transfer-type Type/Subtype*	Defines default transfer type and Internet Media Types. If a file is not matched by any other suffix mapping directives, it is considered to be of transfer type *transfer-type* and Internet Media Type *Type/Subtype*.

For example, you might define HTML and text files with the following directives:

```
TEXT .HTML TEXT * text/html
TEXT .TEXT TEXT * text/plain
TEXT .TXT  TEXT * text/plain
```

These and many more default suffix mappings are already defined in the supplied MacHTTP.config file.

Virtual Document Tree

MacHTTP

MacHTTP does *not* support a virtual document tree. The only documents that may be served are those that are in folders contained in MacHTTP's main directory. The only exception to this is that MacHTTP can follow aliases to files (such as those created with the Finder). It *cannot* interpret aliases to directories or disks (although WebSTAR addresses this, as noted in the next section).

WebSTAR

WebSTAR does not support a virtual document tree in the sense that the NCSA family of servers does. Instead WebSTAR extends support of aliases so that they can refer to directories and to disks. This means that you can create a virtual subdirectory by creating an alias for it in one of your existing infostructure directories (using the Finder). For example, if you have a directory of historical documents that you wish to serve, which already exists in another place on your Macintosh (and which you do not wish to move, because you like the way your Mac is organized, gosh darn it . . .), you can create an alias for that directory in your main WebSTAR document directory.

In addition, WebSTAR supports URL pre- and post-processing, which can be used to implement virtual directories and redirection (see WebSTAR URL processing, next).

WebSTAR URL Processing

WebSTAR allows you to use CGI scripts to preprocess and post-process URLs. If a URL preprocessor program is designated, it is handed each URL that is requested from WebSTAR as input. If the program returns output to WebSTAR, WebSTAR uses that output to the client that requested the URL (that is, the preprocessor is responsible for either returning the proper file as output, or for returning some alternate message). If the program does *not* return any output, WebSTAR goes ahead and processes the URL itself. The CGI script gets all CGI information, such as the CGI environment variables.

Potential applications of this include redirection of certain URLs to other servers (for documents that have moved, for example), alternate authentication schemes, or for adding headers or footers to documents returned by the server.

If a URL post-processor is specified, WebSTAR will send the file retrieved for the request both to the client that requested the file and to the post-processor. The contents of the file that were sent to the client are sent as input to the CGI script, which can then perform customized logging or accounting tasks. The CGI script gets all CGI information, such as the CGI environment variables.

To configure a URL pre- or post-processor, select Misc. Settings... under the Configure menu (in WebSTAR Admin), and enter the name of the pre- or post-processor in PreProcess or PostProcess, respectively. The processors should be standard CGI scripts (see Chapter 8 for further details on CGI scripting).

Archiving Log Files

A method for archiving and analyzing log files is described in Chapter 7, in the *WebStat* section (under *Analyzing Logs*).

CGI

Beyond installing AppleScript and using the default suffix mapping of applications that end with ".cgi" onto CGI scripts, no additional configuration needs to be done. Be aware that applications with filenames ending in ".cgi" will be executed as CGI scripts, and applications with filenames ending in ".acgi" will be executed as ACGI (asynchronous CGI) scripts. Additional CGI information for MacHTTP is detailed in Chapter 8, *CGI*.

Security

Configuring security for MacHTTP is detailed in Chapter 9, *Security*.

Web Robots and `robots.txt`

A Web robot is a client that is not controlled directly by a human, traversing webs automatically in order to extract information from or about them. Two common kinds of robots are those that index webs (such as Lycos or the WWWWorm) and those that check the integrity of webs (such as MOMspider, which is discussed in Chapter 7).

When human-controlled clients (browsers, such as Netscape or Lynx) rummage through your infostructure, they tend to do it politely. The human reader tends to take anywhere from a few seconds to several minutes looking over the document that the client has requested from your server, giving the server some breathing space (relatively speaking) between requests. On the other hand, a robot, operating at much faster speeds, can quickly find new links in the retrieved document, and then immediately retrieve them—effectively saturating your server. In addition, robots may not be able to recognize things like CGI scripts which contain a potentially infinite number of virtual URLs, such as CGI scripts that use additional path information to pass information back to the script. Such a script might generate a new, unique URL each time it is invoked, but that new URL will probably reinvoke the CGI script. A robot blindly following such URLs may become trapped in an endless loop.

To alleviate the potential problems of badly written robots, a group of Web robot authors have created an ad hoc standard for robot authors to follow. This standard, among other things, defines a mechanism enabling server maintainers to exclude robots from parts or from all of a site. The robot exclusion policy is described in detail on the Web at:

`http://web.nexor.co.uk/mak/doc/robots/norobots.html`

The exclusion policy defines the format of a file called `"robots`
`.txt,"` which describes those URLs robots should not retrieve,
on a client-by-client basis. It consists of one or more records, with
each record separated by one or more blanks lines. Each record
has one or more `User-agent` lines, with these lines followed by
one or more `Disallow` lines.

Each `User-agent` line gives the name of a robot that is affected
by this record. There can be more than one `User-agent` line in a
record, and a separate `User-agent` line should be provided for
each agent to which this record applies. Most robots should recognize case-insensitive substrings of their own names. The value "*"
in this line means that this record applies to *all* robots, unless they
find another record that specifically refers to them (this is useful
for providing a default access policy, and then providing a more
liberal policy for locally run robots).

Each `Disallow` line specifies a partial, local URL that is not to be
retrieved. This can be either a full or partial URL; any URL that begins with the specified value will not be retrieved. The `Disallow`
lines should follow the `User-agent` lines.

Also, comments can be included in the file—any line beginning
with "#" is considered to be a comment. For example, to prevent
all robots from accessing your CGI directory, and potentially becoming trapped, you might use:

```
# robots.txt for http://www.freedonia.com/

User-agent: *
Disallow: /cgi-bin/
```

To disallow robots from accessing a particularly volatile collection
of documents (if, for example, you didn't want a Web indexer indexing documents that might only exist for a few days at a time),
but to allow your own local link analyzer to analyze that collection, you might use:

```
# robots.txt for http://www.freedonia.com/

# default for most robots:
User-agent: *
Disallow: /cgi-bin/
Disallow: /volatile/
```

```
# special dispensation for MOMspider, our favorite
# link analyzer:
User-agent: MOMspider/1.00 libwww-perl/0.40
Disallow: /cgi-bin/
```

This, of course, assumes you are using MOMspider as your link analyzer. Table 6.11 gives some of the User-agent identifiers for existing robots (note: the User-agent identifier for a robot may change as the version number changes, but using a substring of the identifier—like "WebCrawler"—should work for any version).

Table 6.11

User-Agent Identifiers for Some Existing Robots

Robot's Name	User-agent identifier	For more information
JumpStation	JumpStation-Robot	http://js.stir.ac.uk/jsbin/jsii
RBSE Spider	RBSE Spider v 1.0	http://rbse.jsc.nasa.gov/eichmann/urlsearch.html
WebCrawler	WebCrawler/2.0 libwww/3.0	http://webcrawler.com/
The NorthStar Robot	NorthStar	http://comics.scs.unr.edu:7000/top.html
InfoSeek	InfoSeek Robot 1.11	http://www.infoseek.com
Lycos	Lycos/*version.number*	http://www.lycos.com/
Link Verifier	EIT-Link-Verifier-Robot/0.2	See Chapter 7
W3M2	W3M2/*version.number*	http://www-ihm.lri.fr/~tronche/W3M2/
MOMspider	MOMspider/1.00 libwww-perl/0.40	See Chapter 7

7

Maintenance and Reporting Tools

The major cost incurred in maintaining a Web server is not that of initial construction and content creation; it is in maintaining the infostructure once it has been created. This is especially true when multiple people are responsible for infostructure development, with varying degrees of time and skill to devote to the task. It is further complicated when the infostructure (invariably) has links woven to the outside world to documents that may or may not move due to circumstances outside of local control. Some of this maintenance can only be provided with proper application of care and diligence, but a great deal of it can be provided via automated tools that can analyze the state of your Web for you.

This chapter discusses tools that provide just this sort of functionality: tools that can check HTML, tools that can verify the integrity of hyperlinks, and tools that can analyze access and error logs. These tools are invaluable, especially as your infostructure grows—they can mean the difference between a promising start and a stagnant pond of stale information.

Unlike in other chapters, we have broken these tools down by purpose rather than by platform, primarily because many of these tools are available only for the Unix platform. Windows and Macintosh users are not out of luck, however; several of these tools are also available via form-based Web pages, or are written in portable Perl or C code. In addition, we have found and included both a Windows-based and a Macintosh-based log analysis tool. We have indicated for each tool on which platforms it can be used.

Checking HTML

An important part of maintaining your infostructure is ensuring that the HTML in your documents is correct. While Chapter 11 addresses some of the stylistic ways you can ensure this when composing your document, there are also tools available that will allow you to rigorously check your document once it is complete. These programs—much like "lint" programs that check source code for correctness—will examine your document and tell you if (and where) any HTML errors can be found.

One unofficial motto of the Internet is to be strict in what you produce, and lax in what you accept. You should strive to be careful in producing correct HTML, so that you will be in no danger of having documents that cannot be read and interpreted by any browser. By the same token, most browsers are very accepting of incorrect HTML, so even if you do not have strictly conforming documents, they will still be displayable (if not always as you expected).

Both of the HTML checkers we evaluate here are also available via a Web-based interface, which means that you can use them to check your HTML even if can't run them directly on your local machine. Please remember to be polite; remember, you are using someone else's resources that they are generously providing for free.

HTML Validation Service and Check Toolkit (Unix, or via the Web)

Features

The HTML Validation Service and Check Toolkit, made available by HalSoft, are front ends to an SGML parser (`sgmls`) that parses the HTML in your documents. They will tell you whether your use of HTML is technically correct (although they make no judgment about style). This includes checking whether you have used the correct syntax in tags (did you leave out a quote? did you forget an end tag?), and whether you have used elements in illegal ways (like putting an ADDRESS element inside of an A element, instead of the other way around).

Installation

Installation of the HTML Check Toolkit on your local machine is relatively straightforward, if you are using one of the supported platforms. HalSoft has provided a forms-driven interface for helping you through installation at

```
http://www.halsoft.com:80/html-tk/
```

If you point a forms-capable browser at this page, you'll find information about the HTML Check Toolkit and a section on *Downloading and Configuration.* Follow the instructions in that section. You will be asked for some information about yourself, and then you will be asked:

- Which flavor of Unix system are you using?

- Which directory should a symbolic link to the executable be made in? (`/usr/local/bin/` is a good choice.)

- Which directory should a symbolic link to the manual page be made in? (`/usr/local/man/man1` is a good choice.)

- What kind of compression would you like? (If you have the `gunzip` tool, select `gzip`; otherwise, select `compress`).

After this, you will be given the option to download the file. Further installation instructions are provided as part of the process— we won't waste space repeating them here. (One note: make sure you are using a forms-capable browser running on the Unix machine, so that the binary is downloaded to the correct machine.)

Use

Once you have installed it, you can test your HTML by typing

```
darwin% html-check somefile.html
```

However, before you can check *any* of your files, you will have to make sure that your files properly identify which level of HTML they conform to. You can do this with a public identifier as the first line in your document. The appropriate ways to declare the various versions of HTML are listed in Table 7.1.

In order to check a document for conformance to HTML 2.0, it must begin with the line ⟨!DOCTYPE HTML PUBLIC "-//IETF//DTD HTML 2.0//EN"⟩, as follows:

```
⟨!DOCTYPE HTML PUBLIC "-//IETF//DTD HTML 2.0//EN"⟩
⟨HTML⟩
⟨HEAD⟩
⟨TITLE⟩A Sample HTML 2.0 Document⟨/TITLE⟩
⟨/HEAD⟩
⟨BODY⟩

⟨H1⟩A Sample HTML 2.0 Document⟨/TITLE⟩

⟨P⟩This is a test. This is only a test. Had this
been real content, this paragraph would be
followed by something useful.

⟨/BODY⟩
⟨/HTML⟩
```

If this document is checked, you will see the following output:

```
html-check sample.html
sample.html ...
sgmls: SGML error at sample.html, line 8 at "⟩":
       TITLE end-tag ignored: doesn't end any open
       element (current is H1)
sgmls: SGML error at sample.html, line 10 at "⟩":
       H1 end-tag implied by P start-tag; not
       minimizable
```

Table 7.1		
Public Identifiers for HTML Documents	HTML 2.0	(!DOCTYPE HTML PUBLIC "-//IETF//DTD HTML 2.0//EN")
	HTML 3.0	(!DOCTYPE HTML PUBLIC "-//IETF//DTD HTML 3.0//EN")
	Netscape extensions	(!DOCTYPE HTML PUBLIC "-//Netscape Comm. Corp.//DTD HTML//EN")

Can you find the error? The output is cryptic, but it supplies one important piece of information: line numbers. In this case, the problem is on line number 8, and it's a `TITLE` end tag that doesn't end an open element . . . ah! That's because it should have been an `H1` end tag instead. This also explains the second error—the `H1` never ended (the ⟨/`TITLE`⟩ was simply ignored),—and having a paragraph in the middle of a heading is illegal.

Use (via the Web)

Instead of installing the HTML Check Toolkit locally, you can use the HTML Validation Service to check your documents (or to check portions of HTML). This can be beneficial if you are interested in only occasional use of the service, or if you do not have access to a Unix machine on which you can install it.

The URL of the service is

```
http://www.halsoft.com/html-val-svc/
```

You can use it either to check documents by URL or to check pieces of HTML (see Figure 7.1 (a) and (b)—both of these options are on the same document! Which you invoke depends on the submission button you select.). The first option is useful if you have a document (or set of documents) already available via a Web server: just enter the URL(s) in the text field, select the level of HTML you wish to check for, and select the Submit URLs for Validation button. (One nice feature of the Web version is that your documents do not have to have the `DOCTYPE` command to declare the level of HTML they conform to!)

For an added level of confidence, you can check the Strict check box, which will provide a much more rigorous parsing of your document. You can also have the report include the input, the parser output, or the formatted output, but none of these options is really necessary.

Once your document passes, you will see a check mark like that in Figure 7.2, along with the HTML code necessary for including the check mark in your document. You can (and should!) now insert the inlined image into your document, in order to show that your document is truly compliant.

(a)

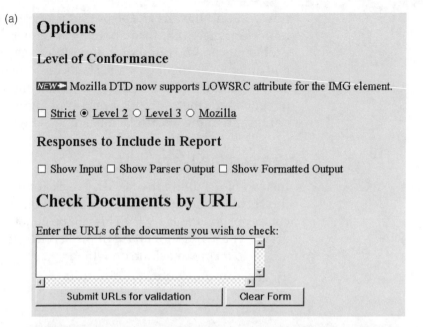

(b)

Figure 7.1

(a) Check Documents by
URL (b) Check Bits and
Pieces Interactively
(Netscape)

The second option is useful for checking small pieces of HTML, to quickly determine whether a given construction is valid. For example, which is correct:

```
⟨ADDRESS⟩⟨A HREF="/~tilt/"⟩Eric's Home
Page⟨/A⟩⟨/ADDRESS⟩
```

or

```
⟨A HREF="/~tilt/"⟩⟨ADDRESS⟩Eric's Home
Page⟨/ADDRESS⟩⟨/A⟩
```

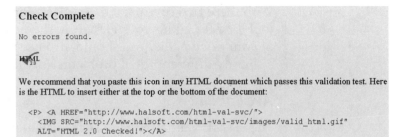

Figure 7.2
The Validated HTML
Check Mark (Netscape)

To find out, enter the first version into the "Check Bits and Pieces Interactively" section (Figure 7.1b) between the ⟨BODY⟩ and ⟨/BODY⟩ tags, and press the Submit HTML for Validation button. Then back up, clear the form, and do the same for the second version.

It turns out that the first version is correct, and the second is illegal! (Which is a little known fact to begin with—anchors can't contain every other kind of element; they can only contain character formatting elements or headers.)

Evaluation

The HTML Validation Service does what it sets out to do, which is to rigorously check your HTML against the HTML grammar. If your document passes, then it is legal. If it doesn't, browsers may still display it properly, but browsers that are less tolerant will have a harder time conveying your intentions (especially if the problem with the document is because of a typo or incorrectly placed tag).

The major difficulty with this service is that the output of the parsing can be cryptic. The best way to approach this is just to look at the first line number listed, find the error, and fix it. Then rerun the parse (sometimes errors can cascade, and fixing one will fix others). Repeat this process until your document passes.

The other difficulty is the need, when using the Check Toolkit locally, to use proper public identifiers for your documents. It's difficult to actually complain about this since, technically, HTML documents should contain this information anyway. But most don't, since browsers don't require it. At least it forces us to be honest about the underlying SGML base upon which HTML is built.

With these two caveats, the HTML Validation Service is a useful tool for debugging your HTML, and you should employ it on all of your documents. You should also use weblint, which checks for a slightly different set of problems, including stylistic ones (next).

Availability

The HTML Validation Service is available via the Web at

```
http://www.halsoft.com/html-val-svc/
```

The HTML Check Toolkit for Unix systems can be retrieved (also via the Web) from

```
http://www.halsoft.com/html-tk/
```

Both are freely available.

Weblint 1.007 (Perl, or via the Web)

Features

Weblint, written by Neil Bowers of Khoral Research, checks the syntax of your HTML documents, and also attempts to make stylistic suggestions, such as not using "here" as the text for an anchor, or recommending that you supply the ALT attribute for inlined images. (To understand why these things are important, see Chapter 11). It is a Perl program without any particular Unix dependencies, which means that—as long as you have a Perl interpreter—you can use it on any platform (see the Bibliography for locations of Perl interpreters). It's not a parser so much as it is a program that performs certain tests on your documents, a distinction no doubt of importance only to computer scientists. A list of the specific tests performed is included with the distribution.

Installation

To install weblint, first retrieve it via FTP from

```
ftp://ftp.khoral.com/pub/perl/www/weblint-1.007.tar.gz
```

You will need the "gunzip" tool to uncompress it.

Although a makefile has been included, it is useful primarily for installing the script (as in `make install`)—the script (a Perl program called `weblint`) can be used as is as soon as it has been untarred.

Use

Use is straightforward:

```
darwin% weblint some-html.html
```

If there are errors, weblint will tell you about them (in a somewhat friendlier fashion than the HTML Check Toolkit), including the line they are on. For example, if we run weblint on the following file:

```
⟨HEAD⟩
⟨TITLE⟩A Sample HTML 2.0 Document⟨/TITLE⟩
⟨/HEAD⟩
⟨BODY⟩

⟨H1⟩A Sample HTML 2.0 Document⟨/TITLE⟩

⟨P⟩This is a test. This is only a test. Had this
been real content, this paragraph would be
followed by something useful.

⟨/BODY⟩
```

You'll get the following response:

```
sample.html(1): outer tags should be ⟨HTML⟩ ..
⟨/HTML⟩.
sample.html(6): unmatched ⟨/TITLE⟩ (no matching
⟨TITLE⟩ seen).
sample.html(10): No closing ⟨/H1⟩ seen for ⟨H1⟩ on
line 6.
```

The first response should demonstrate that weblint, being from the same mold as the "lint" program for cleaning up C code, is picky. Even the HTML Check Toolkit, which performs a rigorous parsing, allows the omission of the HTML element (which is optional). Weblint does not just check for syntax, it also checks for stylistic considerations.

Use (via the Web)

It is also possible to use weblint via the Web:

```
http://www.unipress.com/weblint/
```

You can either enter the URL of a document you wish to check or some sample HTML code to be checked.

Evaluation

Weblint is a useful program to check for stylistic considerations and common errors. It is easy to use, and the output is straightforward. However, it is not perfect, and should not be used alone, since it does not actually parse the HTML for correct syntax. Instead, it runs a series of tests on the document being checked (a litany of bad practices, in a sense). For example, the

```
⟨ADDRESS⟩⟨A HREF="/~tilt/"⟩Eric's Home
Page⟨/A⟩⟨/ADDRESS⟩
```

or

```
⟨A HREF="/~tilt/"⟩⟨ADDRESS⟩Eric's Home
Page⟨/ADDRESS⟩⟨/A⟩
```

test (used previously with the HTML Validation Service) fails in weblint—proper context of elements is not one of the problems checked for. This isn't exactly a big deal, but you would be best served by employing both weblint and the HTML Check Toolkit since each checks for a slightly different set of errors. In a pinch, though, weblint is a good solution by itself, for if simplicity no other reason.

Availability

Weblint (and additional information) is available via the Web at:

```
http://www.khoros.unm.edu/staff/neilb/weblint.html
```

In addition, a Web-based interface is available from

```
http://www.unipress.com/weblint/
```

Weblint is freely available. A related program is webcheck, which uses weblint to check an entire site for good HTML (and mails the results of the check to the owners of the files checked). Webcheck is available at

```
http://coney.gsfc.nasa.gov/Mathews/misc/tools.html
```

Htmlchek 4.1 (Perl)

Availability

An additional HTML checking tool, which we will not evaluate here, is htmlchek. Htmlchek is similar to weblint, and is also Perl-based (so it can be used on a variety of platforms). More information about htmlchek is available via the Web at:

```
http://uts.cc.utexas.edu/~churchh/htmlchek.html
```

Verifying Links

Another topic of great importance is checking the internal consistency of your Web by ensuring that links between documents are still valid. As your document space grows, the number of links connecting documents will grow, and manual checking can be tedious and repetitive. Fortunately, programs are available that can explore your infostructure and follow each link to ensure that none is broken.

This is important for two reasons: first, it can be easy to create malformed links when authoring documents, and unless authors are diligent in checking, mistakes will slip by until some kind soul sends e-mail to the author of the page to let him or her know of the mistake. Second, even correct links to documents will break over time, as the remote documents move for various reasons. Setting up weekly automated checks of your infostructure can help prevent this from happening.

A note of caution: link verifiers work by searching your entire Web server. This means that they retrieve a document, find all anchors that it contains, and then retrieve all of the documents that are referenced. Then they repeat this process for each document just retrieved. This means that the verification program will be trying to retrieve large numbers of documents from your server in a short amount of time, which can place a large load on your server. For this reason, you should follow these guidelines with these programs:

- Use verification programs during off-hours, so that any strain you put on your server will be during times when no one else is trying to use it.

- Restrict access to verification tools to those who can use them responsibly—the last thing you need is for ten people to decide to simultaneously check the integrity of their home pages. Instead, if the program supports it, set up an automated site check that happens once a week and checks the entire site. If the program is form-based, use server security to password-protect use (see Chapter 9).

- Don't check other people's sites. This can use up a lot of network bandwidth.

- In general, employ common sense.

Link Verifier (Unix)

Features

Link Verifier, from EIT, is part of the Webmaster's Starter Kit (see Chapter 6). It is a maintenance tool designed to follow the links in an infostructure and to find, interactively, which ones are broken. Among other things, Link Verifier provides the ability to incrementally search your Web for broken links, and to verify links to documents on external Web servers. On top of this, it operates via a form-based interface, eliminating the need to set up configuration files and to work out command line interfaces.

Installation

Link Verifier is a precompiled CGI program made available by the folks at EIT (with no source available). As such, it is only available for Unix, and furthermore, it is only available for the flavors of Unix for which they have made it available. To install it, you must retrieve the files `webtestdoc.tar` and `verify_links.tar.Z` from the `ftp.eit.com` FTP site. The file `webtestdoc.tar` can be found in the directory `/pub/wsk/doc`. The file `verify_links.tar.Z` file can be found in the directory `/pub/wsk/`*system*`/webtest`, where *system* is the flavor of Unix you are using. (You can find out which systems are supported by looking at the contents of `/pub/wsk`).

NOTE: You must have permission to install CGI scripts to install Link Verifier.

After retrieving the proper files via FTP, move `webtestdoc.tar` to your server's root document directory, and move `verify_links.tar.Z` to the same directory your `cgi-bin` directory is in (probably your server's root directory). Uncompress and untar them. The documentation file will unpack into the directory `admin/webtest` (relative to your document root). The program itself will unpack into `cgi-bin/admin/webtest` (which is why it should be untarred from the same directory that your `cgi-bin` directory is in).

You will then be able to access the program via the URL

```
http://your.web.server/cgi-bin/admin/webtest/
verify_links
```

and the documentation via

```
http://your.web.server/admin/webtest/
verify_links.html
```

The documentation states that these URLs are placed deep in your server to minimize the chance that anyone but a Web administrator will employ Link Verifier, to prevent undue loads being placed on your (or other) servers. It might also be a good idea to password-protect the `/cgi-bin/admin/webtest/` directory (see Chapter 9, *Security*).

A word of warning: we had problems with the installation of Link Verifier. On some systems, it worked perfectly; on others, it would die inexplicably. Because it is precompiled (and documentation is sparse), we had no way of determining what was causing the problems. Our advice to you is to try it out on your system and see if it works. If it does, fabulous—as you'll see in the next section, it's a great way to interactively check documents. If it doesn't work, skip this section and take a look at one of the other link checkers—it's not worth the headache of trying to figure out what is breaking, especially when there are other tools available that can do the job just as well.

Use

To use Link Verifier, fire up a forms-capable Web browser and point it at

```
http://your.web.server/cgi-bin/admin/webtest/
verify_links
```

You will see something similar to Figure 7.3.

The following fields are available to you to fill in:

Starting Point: The document at which Link Verifier will start. It will test all links within *num* hops of this document (where *num* is the number in **Search Radius,** next). This should be a document on your local server.

Search Radius: The number of hops away from the specified **Starting Point** that Link Verifier will explore. If left blank, Link Verifier will assume 0 hops, and simply verify that the starting

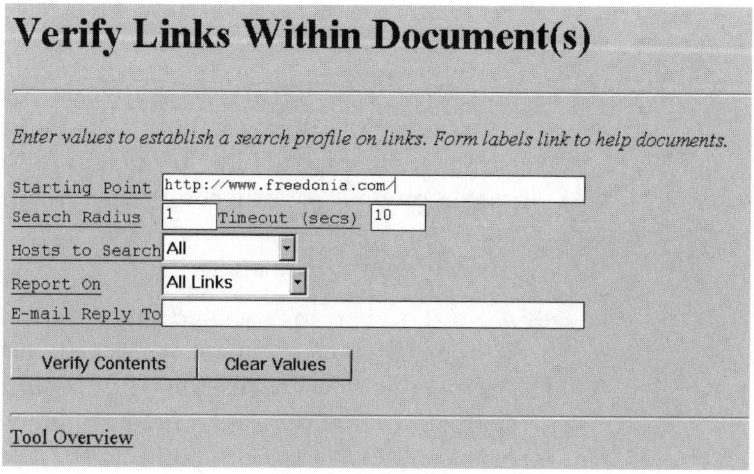

Figure 7.3
Link Verifier (Netscape)

point exists. You will have to experiment with this value, but you won't need to set it too high, as the number of links explored should grow exponentially with respect to this number. Try moderate values like 1 or 3 to begin with.

Timeout (secs):   Number of seconds Link Verifier will explore before interrupting the search and presenting the current results. You can use this to explore your Web incrementally. A button at the bottom of the returned results allows you to continue the exploration where you left off. Leaving this blank enables Link Verifier to explore until it has searched the entire search radius. 10 seconds is a good value for this.

Hosts to Search: Can either be set to **All** or **Local Server.** If set to **All,** Link Verifier will check links from local documents to remote documents to make sure they are correct, but it will *not* explore any of the links on the remote documents. This allows you to make sure your own documents are correct without accidentally unleashing Link Verifier on someone else's site. If set to **Local Server,** no links to remote hosts are checked. **All** is preferable, as links to remote sites are more likely to break than links to local sites.

Report On: Can either be set to **All Links** or **Problem Links.** If set to **All Links,** the resulting report will describe each link checked (which might be quite a few), whether they were broken or okay. If set to **Problem Links,** the resulting report will only list broken links. **Problem Links** is preferable, as you are probably only interested in what is broken.

E-mail Reply To: If this is set, the report will be e-mailed to the address given, instead of displayed in your browser. This allows Link Verifier to work in the background, and give you back control of your browser immediately. If not set, the results of Link Verifier will appear in your browser window after the search has been completed.

For example, if you were the Freedonia Web master, you might enter the values in Figure 7.4. You would set the starting point to `"http://www.freedonia.com/,"` the search radius to 3, the timeout to 10, the hosts to search to `"All"`, the type of links to report on to `"Problem Links,"` and no e-mail address to reply to. (However, since you are *not* the Freedonia Web master, you will set your starting point to your own Web site's address.) Then, you will press the `Verify Contents` button.

After 10 seconds or so, a result somewhat like Figure 7.5 will appear. The problem links are listed, along with the error that occurred when the link was tested, and the document the link is contained within. Some errors, like timeouts and "No Server," mean that no response occurred before Link Verifier gave up. You can test these manually by following the link given for the problem. For example, the URL `http://www.willamette.edu:80/htbin/finger?jtilton`, which had a "timeout error," can be tested by selecting the link and seeing whether the document does in fact exist. (It turns out that it does, and the Link Verifier just didn't wait long enough for it to show up.)

Other errors, such as `"404 Not Found"` indicate that the problem link points to a document that does not exist. In these cases, you would then bring up the document the link resides in, find the offending anchor, and fix it.

Since Link Verifier will usually "time out" before completing its exploration (based on the value you supply for the **Timeout** field),

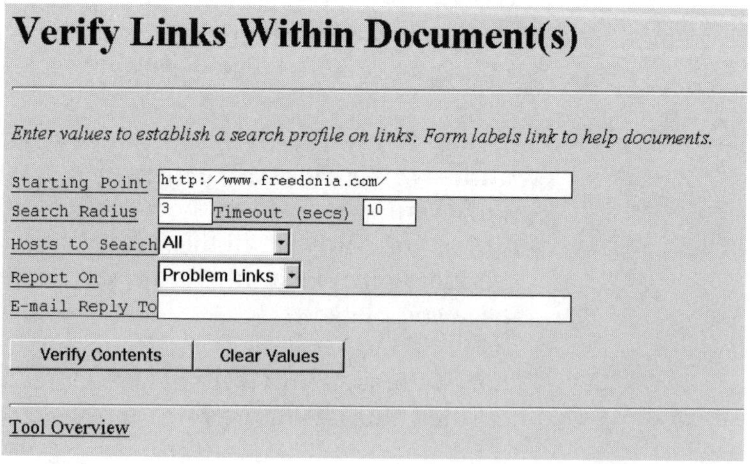

Figure 7.4

Sample Freedonia Web Search Setup (Netscape)

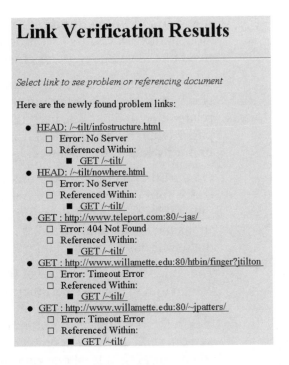

Figure 7.5
Broken Links in Freedonia
(Netscape)

you will be told something like, "You have the option to continue the suspended search. There are 69 unsearched links due to global timeout." Below this is will be a button labeled Continue Search. Selecting that button will cause Link Verifier to search for another 10 seconds (or however long you have set the timeout for).

NOTE: Link Verifier occasionally has problems, and "goes away" for a period of time longer than the specified timeout. If you abort the search (by pressing the Stop button on your browser), you may still need to kill the Link Verifier processes. Use the `ps` command to find processes named `verify_links`, and then use the `kill` command to abort them manually.

Evaluation

The two main points in Link Verifier's favor are that it is interactive, and that it can simply be dropped in to your server as a CGI script and run. The interactive nature of it makes link checking into a straightforward process: open up a browser and a telnet session, and work your way through a set of documents, fixing broken links as you come across them.

Since you can set the search radius, you can use Link Verifier to check limited sections of your infostructure, such as a collection of related documents (Eric used it to check the links in his personal pages when he moved them from Willamette to CMU, an application for which it worked wonderfully).

On the other hand, you will probably *not* want to use this tool to check your entire server. For one thing, it would take a very long time to do, and for another thing, one individual is seldom responsible for maintaining all documents on a server (especially if the server has user-supplied pages).

The "plug-and-play" nature of the package is also nice, if you want a tool that works and that works *now.* The fact that it is form-based means that there is no setup involved, outside of putting the files in the right place and pointing a browser at it. But if it doesn't work (a difficulty we experienced under the Linux platform, and when checking at least one experimental server), you have no way of finding out what is wrong. Again, in the majority of cases, it should work without a flaw, but if it doesn't, don't spend too much time trying to figure out why not; move on to another tool and be done with it.

All that being said, Link Verifier is a wonderful program, and you should give it a try. It does what it sets out to do—to provide an easy-to-use means of interactively checking links—and it does it well.

Availability

Link Verifier is available via FTP at

```
ftp://ftp.eit.com/pub/wsk/doc/webtestdoc.tar
```

and

```
ftp://ftp.eit.com/pub/wsk/system/webtest/
verify_links.tar.Z
```

where *system* is the flavor of Unix you are using. Look at the /pub/wsk directory to see which types are available. Source is not available, so you are limited to supported systems.)

Further information about Link Verifier is available on-line from

```
http://wsk.eit.com/wsk/dist/doc/admin/webtest/
verify_links.html
```

Link Verifier is freely available.

MOMspider (Unix)

Features

MOMspider (the Multi-Owner Maintenance Spider), written by Roy Fielding as part of the Arcadia project at the University of California, Irvine, is a tool for the automated checking of links in an infostructure. Unlike Link Verifier, MOMspider is not meant to be run interactively. Instead, it runs in the background, checking links throughout a set domain of documents. Instead of using a search radius, MOMspider's searches are limited by site or by document tree.

Installation

First, you will need to retrieve the MOMspider, via FTP. The FTP site is liege.ics.uci.edu, and MOMspider is in the directory /pub/websoft/MOMspider. You will want to get the file MOM-spider-1.00.tar.Z (the 1.00 reflects the version number, and may change). You will also want to get the file libwww-perl-0.40.tar.Z from the directory /pub/websoft/libwww-perl (on the same FTP site). Libwww-perl is a Perl programming interface for the Web that is used by MOMspider.

Installing MOMspider requires some mucking around with Perl—if you aren't familiar with Perl, the next two sections should help you get through it.

Installing libwww-perl

First, you will need to install libwww-perl. It can be placed anywhere, but a good spot to put it is in the standard include path for your Perl distribution. (You can find out the standard include path—the directories Perl automatically searches for libraries in—by typing

```
darwin% perl -e 'print "@INC\n"'
```

at a shell prompt.) A standard location is `/usr/local/lib/perl`.

If you do not wish to place libwww-perl in one of your include directories (in order to keep it in its own directory, for instance), you must set the environment variable `LIBWWW_PERL` to the name of the directory which libwww-perl is in before running MOMspider (or any other tool that requires libwww-perl).

For the moment, let us assume you will be placing libwww-perl in the directory `/usr/local/lib/perl/libwww-perl-0.40`. First, move the the distribution file to the directory `/usr/local/lib/perl`. Then uncompress and untar the file—the files will be unpacked into the directory `libwww-perl-0.40` by default.

Once you have unpacked the distribution, you will need to edit the `Makefile` in the newly created directory (and before you do this, you will need to make `Makefile` writeable with `chmod`). You will need to change the line

```
PERLBIN = /usr/bin/perl
```

to reflect the location of the Perl interpreter on your system. Some common values include

```
PERLBIN = /bin/perl
PERLBIN = /usr/local/bin/perl
```

(Of course, the default may be correct for your system.) Once you have set this value, type the following in the shell (while in the libwww-perl directory):

```
darwin% make
darwin% make config
```

Finally, be sure to set the environment variable `LIBWWW_PERL` to the directory that libwww-perl is in—in this case, you would use:

```
setenv LIBWWW_PERL /usr/local/lib/perl/libwww-perl -0.40   (in the C shell, or)
LIBWWW_PERL=/usr/local/lib/perl/libwww-perl-0.40; export LIBWWW_PERL
```
(in the Bourne Shell)

Remember, you will need to set this environment variable whenever you use MOMspider, which means you should either put it in your shell initialization file or create a script that runs MOMspider and set the environment variable from within it.

Installing MOMspider

MOMspider can be installed in any location. A good location is `/usr/local/etc/MOMspider-1.00` (where `1.00` reflects MOMspider's current version number). To install it there, move the distribution file to the directory `/usr/local/etc`, uncompress it, and untar it.

First, you will need to change the first line of the program `momspider` to reflect the location of the Perl interpreter on your system (see the preceding). For example, if the Perl interpreter is `/usr/local/bin/perl`, the first line of `momspider` should read:

```
#!/usr/local/bin/perl
```

(If it is not already, you should also make `momspider` executable.) Also, before running MOMspider, you will need to set the MOM-SPIDER_HOME environment variable equal to the directory that MOMspider is installed in (again, see the discussion of environment variables; in this example the value would be `/usr/local/etc/MOMspider-1.00`).

You will also need to change the global configuration file, `momconfig.pl`, to reflect your local site's configuration. The majority of sites will only require one change: the value of `LocalNetwork`. `LocalNetwork` defines the domain name of your local network, so that MOMspider knows what limits should be placed on itself. For example, if your Web server is `www.freedonia.com`, you will want to change the line

```
$LocalNetwork = '\.uci\.edu';
```

to

```
$LocalNetwork = '\.freedonia\.com';
```

Two things here are important: first, `momconfig.pl` is an actual Perl file. If you aren't familiar with Perl, the Bibliography has pointers to resources that can help you out (and Chapter 8 contains a brief overview). Second, any periods in the `LocalNetwork` value need to be preceded with a backslash (\) so that Perl will not interpret them as special characters.

Use

momconfig.pl sets MOMspider's defaults, but these defaults can be overridden through *instruction files.* An instruction file describes how MOMspider is to traverse an infostructure (or set of infostructures)—where the infostructure starts, what it is bounded by, the e-mail address of the infostructure's owner, and the sorts of actions that should be taken by MOMspider when encountering any number of interesting events.

For example, let's build a sample instruction file that will explore the Freedonia Web server. The organization of Freedonia's Web server is illustrated in Figure 7.6. As you can see, the Freedonia site contains several subsections, including the "Euphonium Player's Resources" (starting at the URL http://www.freedonia.com/euphonium/, and maintained by brianb@freedonia.com), and the "History of Freedonia" collection (starting at the URL http://www.freedonia.com/history/, and maintained by heathert@freedonia.com). In addition, there are several other documents that are not part of either of these subsections, but that still need to be checked.

What we would like MOMspider to do is to verify the links on this server, but—in the case of special collections—to send information about the integrity of the collection to the owner of the collection, *not* the Web administrator (who has enough to do already!).

The instruction file is composed of two parts: global directives and traversal tasks. Global directives are used to override the default configuration options in momconfig.pl. Available global directives are listed in Table 7.2. Most of the configuration options deal with MOMspider's behavior as a good Web traversal robot (see *Web Robots and robots.txt* in Chapter 6 for more information, and as Box 7.1, *The MOMspider Avoid Files*). We will not worry about modifying the global directives for this example. The supplied defaults should be fine.

What we *do* want to define in our instruction file are our traversal tasks, which are used to describe each collection of documents that we want. In this example, we will define a traversal task for both the "Euphonium Player's Resources" and the "History of Freedonia."

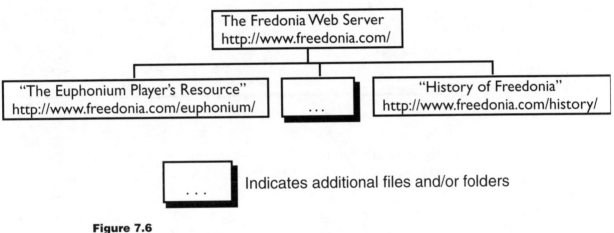

Figure 7.6

Infostructures in Freedonia's Web Server

Table 7.2

MOMspider Global
Configuration Directives

SystemAvoid *Pathname*	System-wide per-file avoid file. Default is `$MOMSPIDER_HOME/system-avoid`.
SystemSites *Pathname*	System-wide per-site avoid file. Default is `$MOMSPIDER_HOME/system-sites`.
AvoidFile *Pathname*	User per-file avoid file. Default is `$HOME/.momspider-avoid`.
SitesFile *Pathname*	User per-site avoid file. Default is `$HOME/.momspider-sites`.
SitesCheck *N*	Number of days to cache robot exclusion information (`/robots.txt`) for a site (see *Web Robots and robots.txt* in Chapter 6). Default is `15`.
ReplyTo *email-address*	E-mail address of the human being running MOMspider (so that webmasters can contact him or her if there are problems with MOMspider tromping on other sites). Default address is set by libwww-perl to *user@hostname*, and should only need to be set explicitly if the user MOMspider is run and cannot receive mail.
MaxDepth *N*	Maximum depth of any MOMspider search (in order to prevent runaway infinite loops). Default value is 20 (which should be more than sufficient).

The bare minimum traversal task for the "Euphonium Player's Resources" might look something like this:

```
⟨Tree
    Name        Euphonium-Resource
    TopURL      http://www.freedonia.com/euphonium/
    IndexURL    http://www.freedonia.com/euphonium/result.html
    IndexFile   /usr/local/etc/httpd/docs/euphonium/result.html
⟩
```

What does this mean? The angle brackets (⟨ and ⟩) delimit the task, so that multiple tasks can be defined in a single instruction set. The keyword `Tree` indicates the type of task this is; in this case, MOM-spider will only check the links of documents in the same directory (or in subdirectories) as the top document in this traversal.

The way that MOMspider works is to start at the `TopURL` for each task description, retrieve it, and find every anchor within that

Box 7.1 The MOMspider Avoid Files

The `SystemAvoid`, `SystemSites`, `AvoidFile`, and `SitesFile` are used by MOMspider to cache information between successive uses, in order to improve efficiency. `SystemAvoid` and `SystemSites` are both used to cache information each time MOMspider is run, while `AvoidFile` and `SitesFile` serve the identical purpose for individual users who run MOMspider.

What do these files do? The avoid files contain information about specific documents that should be avoided: for example, the URL of a CGI script that implements a chess game, which could potentially have a different virtual URL for each different move available (not to mention the extra stress on your server when MOMspider retrieves a large number of scripts that must be executed in a short time span). Similarly, the sites files contain information about specific sites that should *not* be indexed. All four of these files are built automatically by MOMspider when it finds a `robots.txt` file at the top level of the Web server it is searching (again, see *Web Robots and* `robots.txt` in Chapter 6 for an explanation of `robots.txt`).

Why are there system and user versions of these files? Again, MOMspider automatically generates these files, so the system and user versions should be identical. However, after MOMspider has generated a user's `AvoidFile` and `SitesFile`, he or she can then modify it by hand to add more documents or sites that should be avoided by MOMspider.

document. It then follows each of these anchors to make sure that it:

- Still exists.
- Has not been redirected to another location.
- Has not been changed recently.
- Has not expired (although expiration information is only supported by a few servers).

Then it checks each of these documents to see whether it is still within the valid search space. The top document is defined by `TopURL`, and here it is `http://www.freedonia.com/euphonium/` (it's worth noting that all URLs defined in traversal tasks must be *full* URLs). Since this is a `Tree` traversal, URLs such as

`http://www.freedonia.com/euphonium/opheicleide.html`

and

```
http://www.freedonia.com/euphonium/other-
gear/mouthpeices.html
```

are fair game for further exploration. But

```
http://www.freedonia.com/~brianb/
```

is not. Any documents that are still valid then have anchors extracted from them; these anchors are checked, and the process repeats.

`IndexURL` and `IndexFile` both describe the same document—the index document that MOMspider produces after traversing the collection of documents defined by this task. `IndexURL` gives the location of this document as a URL, and `IndexFile` gives the location of this document within the filesystem. *Both* forms are required. (Note that this must be a location to which MOMspider can write.)

Finally, the `Name` directive gives the name of the infostructure—in this case, `Euphonium-Resource`. This must be one word (that is, have no white space).

If we were to save this traversal task to the file `simple-instruct` (in the MOMspider directory), and then run MOMspider:

```
darwin% cd $MOMSPIDER HOME
darwin% ./momspider -i simple-instruct -e error-
log -o output-log
```

The command line option `-i` designates the instruction file to be used, `-o` designates the output log, and `-e` designates the error log. If you are running MOMspider interactively, you might omit `-e error-log -o output-log` so that you can watch what MOMspider is doing. However, if you are running MOMspider as a batch job (described in a moment), you'll want to use these options.

MOMspider would spend some time traversing the Web, and then produce a report on "Euphonium-Resource" at `http://www.freedonia.com/euphonium/result.html` which would look something like Figure 7.7.

MOMspider Index for Euphonium-Resource

Index started: Sun, 09 Jul 1995 17:53:53 (Mon, 10 Jul 1995 00:53:53 GMT)
by brianb@freedonia

- Summary of Results
- Broken Links
- Redirected Links
- Changed Link Destinations
- Old version of this index

Euphonia Rex

200 OK http://www.freedonia.com/euphonium/
Last-modified: Sat, 18 Jun 1994 07:03:30 GMT

- Image 200 OK euphonium.xbm
  Last-modified: Wed, 27 Oct 1993 01:03:57 GMT
- Link 200 OK bowman.html
  Last-modified: **Mon, 10 Jul 1995 00:53:36 GMT**
- Link 200 OK bowman.html#euph-p
  Last-modified: **Mon, 10 Jul 1995 00:53:36 GMT**
- Link **603 Timed Out** http://don.its.utas.edu.au/trom/
- Link **404 Not Found** /~jtilton/

Figure 7.7

Sample Report on
Euphonium-Resource
(Netscape)

Try this yourself, but do *not* use the traversal task as described here. Instead, pick a resource on your own server on your own site. Be sure to change all four entries to reflect the local resource.

Once you've generated a report, you'll notice that it is divided into four major sections: a summary of all links encountered (broken down by the page they were encountered on), a summary of broken links, a summary of redirected links, and a summary of recently modified links. Only the summary of all links is broken down by page. The other sections list the links in that category, with two anchors for each: the anchor around the word "Link" (or "Image," if it is a reference to an inlined image), which is an internal anchor to the point in the "summary of links" section where the link in question is listed; and the anchor around the URL, which points to the URL (so you can manually verify the document). The easiest way to use the report is probably to start in the "broken links" section, and check each broken link, using the "Link" anchor to find which document the broken reference is in.

Next, let's add the second Freedonian resource, the "History of Freedonia." This time, we're interested in using a few more of the features of MOMspider. For example, this resource contains links to several documents on other sites, and Heather T. wants to keep track of any changes in those documents. Furthermore, she'd like to be notified by e-mail of any changed or broken links, and not just check the result page MOMspider generates.

To accommodate this, we might use the following task:

```
⟨Tree
      Name              Freedonia-History
      TopURL            http://www.freedonia.com/history/
      IndexURL          http://www.freedonia.com/history/result.html
      IndexFile         /usr/local/etc/httpd/docs/history/result.html
      EmailAddress      heathert@freedonia.com
      EmailBroken
      EmailRedirected
      EmailChanged      7
      ChangeWindow      7
⟩
```

We have employed five new directives for this purpose (indicated in bold). Four of them deal with e-mail notification, and the fifth (ChangeWindow) deals with the result document that MOMspider will generate.

The EmailAddress directive specifies the e-mail address to which any notifications about links that have changed in some way should be sent. The next three (EmailBroken, EmailRedirected, and EmailChanged) specify the kinds of changes that should be considered interesting and worth mailing to the e-mail address that has been specified. EmailBroken notifies the owner of links that point to nonexistent documents. EmailRedirected notifies the owner of links that have been moved to new locations. EmailChanged specifies a window (in days)—if the document pointed to by a link has been modified within that time frame, the owner of the infostructure is notified. This window should be set to the number of days between running MOMspider. In this case, it will be run once a week, so the window is set to 7.

The `ChangeWindow` directive is similar to the `EmailChanged` directive, except that it is used for highlighting changed links in the result document (at `IndexURL`).

If we were to add this task to `simple-instruct` and run MOMspider again, MOMspider would generate two result files (one for `Euphonium-Resource` and one for `Freedonia-History`), and the owner of `Freedonia-History` would also receive e-mail notification of any interesting changes to her infostructure. In this example, there are two broken links, and one that has changed within the last week:

```
Date: Sun, 9 Jul 1995 17:55:54 -0700
From: Big Momma Webmaster ⟨web@www.freedonia.com⟩
Subject: MOMspider Index for Freedonia-History

This message was automatically generated by
MOMspider/1.00 after a web traversal on Sun, 09
Jul 1995 17:53:53

The following parts of the Freedonia-History
infostructure may need inspection:

Broken Links:
⟨http://www.black-hats.com/biscuits/⟩
⟨http://www.cs.cmu.edu/~jtilton/⟩

Changed Since Sun, 02 Jul 1995 17:53:53 :
⟨http://www.freedonia.com/~tilt/history/other.html⟩

For more information, see the index at
⟨http://www.freedonia.com/history/result.html⟩
```

Finally, since there are documents on the Freedonia Web server that are not part of either of these documents, but that we would like to verify nonetheless, we will add a final traversal task:

```
⟨Site
    Name            Freedonia
    TopURL          http://www.freedonia.com/
    IndexURL        http://www.freedonia.com/
    IndexFile       /usr/local/etc/httpd/docs/
    IndexTitle      MOMspider: The Freedonia Web Server
    EmailAddress    web@freedonia.com
    EmailBroken
```

```
    EmailRedirected
    EmailChanged        7
    ChangeWindow        7
    Exclude             http://www.freedonia.com/euphonium/
    Exclude             http://www.freedonia.com/history/
)
```

We have added only three new directives this time (again, highlighted in bold). First, this is a different type of traversal task: Site instead of Tree. This means that instead of being limited by being in the same directory as (or a subdirectory of) the TopURL, MOMspider will explore any document on the server www.freedonia.com.

In addition, we have specified a title for this traversal: "MOMspider: The Freedonia Web Server." This is the title that will be used for the result document (specified by IndexFile) and as the subject line for any e-mail messages generated. If IndexTitle is not supplied, this defaults to "MOMspider Index for *Name*" (with *Name* given by the Name directive). We've prefixed it with "MOMspider:" so that any e-mail messages generated will be easily identifiable.

The last, and most important, directive is Exclude. It prevents MOMspider from rechecking the two document trees we have already checked. The Exclude directive takes a URL prefix, and avoids rechecking any URL that begins with that prefix.

That's it. Table 7.3 lists the task directives. Our completed instruction file, after we take into account all that we've learned (with changes from the first tries highlighted in black), looks like this:

```
#
# Global configuration directives
#
MaxDepth 20

#
# The task descriptions:
#

# Euphonium-Resource collection
```

Table 7.3 MOMspider Task Directives	⟨Site	Start of task description of type *Site* (checks whole site).
	⟨Tree	Start of task description of type *Tree* (checks only documents subordinate to `TopURL`).
	⟨Owner	Start of task description of type *Owner* (checks only documents owned by `Name`. Only supported by WN server; see MOMspider documentation for more details).
	Name *name*	Name of the document collection. Required.
	TopURL *url*	Fully specified URL of entry point to the document collection. Required.
	IndexURL *url*	Fully-specified URL of the document where MOMspider will store results. Required.
	IndexFile *filename*	Filename of document where MOMspider will store results. Required.
	IndexTitle *string*	Name used as title for `IndexFile` and as subject for any e-mail generated.
	ChangeWindow *num*	Number of days within changed document is considered to be "recently changed." Default is 7.
	ExpireWindow *num*	Number of days within which expired document is considered to be "recently expired" (not supported by all servers).
	EmailAddress *address*	E-mail address to send e-mail notifications to. Required only if any of the next four directives are used.
	EmailBroken	Send e-mail notification for broken links.
	EmailRedirected	Send e-mail notification for redirected links.
	EmailChanged *num*	Send e-mail notification for documents that have been updated within the last *num* days.
	EmailExpired *num*	Send e-mail notification for documents that have expired within the last *num* days (not supported by all servers).
	Exclude *prefix*	Prefix of URLs that should not be checked.
	⟩	End of task description.

```
⟨Tree

    Name        Euphonium-Resource
    TopURL      http://www.freedonia.com/euphonium/
    IndexURL    http://www.freedonia.com/euphonium/result.html
    IndexFile   /usr/local/etc/httpd/docs/euphonium/result.html
    IndexTitle  MOMspider: The Euphonium Player's Resource
```

```
        EmailAddress        brianb@freedonia.com
        EmailBroken
        EmailRedirected
        EmailChanged        7
        ChangeWindow        7
)

# Freedonia-History collection
⟨Tree
        Name                Freedonia-History
        TopURL              http://www.freedonia.com/history/
        IndexURL            http://www.freedonia.com/history/result.html
        IndexFile           /usr/local/etc/httpd/docs/history/result.html
        IndexTitle          MOMspider: The History of Freedonia
        EmailAddress        heathert@freedonia.com
        EmailBroken
        EmailRedirected
        EmailChanged        7
        ChangeWindow        7
)

# The rest of the site, excluding Euphonium-Resource
# and Freedonia-History
⟨Site
        Name                Freedonia
        TopURL              http://www.freedonia.com/
        IndexURL            http://www.freedonia.com/
        IndexFile           /usr/local/etc/httpd/docs/
        IndexTitle          The Freedonia Web Server
        EmailAddress        web@freedonia.com
        EmailBroken
        EmailRedirected
        EmailChanged        7
        ChangeWindow        7
        Exclude             http://www.freedonia.com/euphonium/
        Exclude             http://www.freedonia.com/history/
)
```

For illustrative purposes, we've also added comments, and an example of how you would supply a global configuration directive. Comments are on lines by themselves that start with a "#" mark, and are ignored by MOMspider. Global configuration directives are on lines by themselves, and occur before the task descriptions.)

There are a few things to notice here: first in order to use MOM-spider effectively, your infostructure should be structured into independent directories. This is a good idea anyway (and it, along with some other ideas for structuring your server, are discussed in greater detail in Chapter 12). Second, you should create your instruction file in a bottom-up manner: start with the document collections in the deepest subdirectories and work your way up to the top level. In this way, MOMspider can better take advantage of information it has learned in earlier traversals as it gets closer to the end of the instruction file. Finally, be sure to Exclude any directories you have already searched from any traversals later in the file that might redo the work.

If you have several infostructure maintainers, and each one is only interested in checking subsections of the document tree, they can do this by creating an instruction file for just that subsection. A better idea, though, is to create a monolithic file (as in our example), and to MOMspider it once a week (say, Sunday morning at 1 A.M.).

To set up MOMspider to run automatically (once you have tested your instruction file and made sure it works), you will want to use the cron command. Create a shell script something like this:

```
#!/bin/sh
LIBWWW_PERL=/usr/local/lib/perl/libwww-perl-0.40
MOMSPIDER_HOME=/usr/local/bin/momspider-1.00
export LIBWWW_PERL; export MOMSPIDER_HOME
cd $MOMSPIDER_HOME
./momspider -i freedonia-instruct -e error-log -o output-log
```

Evaluation

MOMspider is near and dear to our hearts, because it was one of the first tools that specifically was for maintaining "infostructures" (and because it credits Eric for coining the term). In all seriousness, however, MOMspider is a powerful tool for checking the consistency of your Web. It goes beyond simply checking whether connections have been broken, and checks also for documents that have moved and for documents that have changed. Documents that have changed can be the most devious of infostructure errors—the link still works, but the content may no longer be what you expect it to be.

The fact that MOMspider can alert you to a document that has recently been modified means that you can stay on top of even this error. In addition, MOMspider is able to take advantage of information from prior invocations, including awareness of robot exclusion information provided by sites, making it more efficient and a good Net citizen.

MOMspider also has a few features that are not yet easily exploitable, but hopefully will be in the future. There is a third traversal type, Owner, that limits itself to documents that have an Owner: HTTP header supplied that matches the value of the Name directive (the Owner: header can be supplied by including the element ⟨META HTTP-EQUIV="Owner:" CONTENT="Your Name Here"; see Chapter 13 for more details). This allows you to define more arbitrary search spaces that aren't limited by directory structure. Unfortunately, the only server that can provide this information at present is WN. Similarly, MOMspider implements checking for documents that have expired, but the Expires: HTTP header is not in widespread use.

On the other hand, the feature-rich nature of MOMspider also makes it somewhat baroque to set up and use. Once you understand how the instruction file works, it becomes easy to create one that suits the needs of your site. However, the time invested in figuring out what is going on is an order of magnitude greater than the time invested in using Link Verifier. This is a relatively small consideration, however (and hopefully addressed somewhat by the tutorial given here!). If you want a truly powerful and automated link checker, you want MOMspider. It's worth the time and energy to set up, without question.

Availability

MOMspider (and more extensive documentation, fully explaining instruction files and command line options) is available via the Web at

```
http://www.ics.uci.edu/WebSoft/MOMspider/
```

MOMspider is freely available for use. Perl (4.036 or later) is required. The libwww-perl package is also required, and is available from

```
http://www.ics.uci.edu/WebSoft/libwww-perl/
```

WebView (Windows NT or 95, part of WebSite)

WebView, part of the O'Reilly WebSite package (see Chapter 6), is worth mentioning in this category, because it can serve as a link verification tool (among other things). The Find Node . . . item in the Search menu brings up the Find Node dialog box. Selecting Hyperlink and checking the Broken box (and leaving the String to Find: field blank) will find the next broken link in your server. You can find the next broken node with Find Next Node in the Search menu, and so forth. Unfortunately, WebView is only available as part of WebSite.

Analyzing Logs

A topic related to checking the contents of your web is keeping track of how your web is used. All servers keep logs of the accesses made, but as raw data these access logs are little better than vast tracts of wasted space on your hard disk. Fortunately, tools are available that can help to analyze these logs, allowing you to pinpoint which documents are the most heavily used, how much usage your server is experiencing during the course of the day, and what sites are most heavily using your server (among many other options). In addition, you can also track errors the server encountered, such as nonexistent documents, malformed URLs, or problems executing CGI scripts. (Other kinds of logs also exist; see Box 7.2.)

Box 7.2 Other Kinds of Log Files

Access and error logs are universally supported by servers; but they are not the only kinds of logs available. Some servers also support *agent* logs and *referer* logs. An agent log contains information about which agents have accessed your server. "Agent" here is roughly equivalent to either "client" or "browser"; Mosaic and Arena are examples of agents. Other programs that access servers, such as webspiders and link verifiers, also are agents; Lycos or MOMspider are good examples. The agent log gives you a good way to assess the kinds of browsers people are using to view your site, as well as a way to track whether your server is being hammered by somebody's poorly written Web spider software.

A referer log tracks how readers are getting to documents on your server. Each line in a referer log gives the location of a document on your server, along with the URL of the document that contained the link to the document. You can use this to determine who has created links to documents on your server (which is especially useful if you are moving a popular service or document, and you would like to notify people who have links to the service so they can update the links). And, yes, "reterrer" is mis-spelled intentionally. Software developers are not noted for their spelling ability.

Once you are armed with this information, you can then use it to decide where in your infostructure you should devote your attention. Are the documents and services you expected to be popular actually popular, and if not, what can you do about them? Are there large numbers of errors surrounding a particular document, set of documents, or script? Is some service *too* popular, and should you find a new home for it? (Of course, statistics are also useful for justifying the expense of maintaining a Web server, but you knew that already, didn't you?)

One problem with finding a log analysis program is that, at least at one point, each major server kept its logs in a different format from other servers. This meant that, if you were running NCSA httpd, you'd have to find an NCSA httpd log analysis program; and if you were running CERN httpd, you'd have to find a CERN httpd log analysis program. Fortunately, in early 1994 the various server authors got together and created the NCSA/CERN Common Logfile Format or, simply, the Common Logfile Format (CLF). Most servers now support this format, and the majority of log analysis programs expect it.

A related issue is cycling your logs as they get too large, so that they do not grow forever and clog up your hard disk. This was covered in Chapter 6.

Getstats (C)

Features

Getstats, from Kevin Hughes at EIT, can analyze logs in Common Logfile Format, as well as from GN, MacHTTP, or the Unix gopher. While intended for Unix platforms, it is written in non-Unix specific C code, so it should be usable on any platform as long as a C compiler is available (although specific Mac and Windows log analyzers are available, as detailed here). It can produce reports by month, week, day, hour; domains requesting files; and directory trees files are requested from; as well as a summary of errors within a given time frame.

Installation

Installation is relatively straightforward. Unlike most packages, getstats is composed of a single C source code file, on the FTP server `ftp.eit.com`, in the directory `/pub/web.software/getstats`; the file is named `getstats.NN.c` (where *NN* is the version number, as in `getstats.12.c`). Some other useful files are also in this directory; you'll probably at least want `domain.codes.txt` (for mapping top-level domain names onto the countries they represent).

Once you've retrieved these files and placed them in a directory by themselves (for example, a `getstats` subdirectory off your server's main directory), you will need to edit the `getstats.NN.c` file. It has several hard-coded configuration settings (eight pages worth!), some of which you'll need to change before you compile. While most of these options can be overridden with command-line options, you'll want to change:

```
#define SERVERSITE "http://www.eit.com/"
```

Notice that this is a C file, and that the options are preprocessor directives. Replace the text in the quotes with the URL for your server's main index document. Make sure to end the URL with a forward slash (/).

```
#define ROOTDIR "/usr/local/www"
```

Replace this with the directory where your server *data* begins (for example, `"/usr/local/etc/httpd/htdocs"`). This can be overridden with a command line option, but it is better to set a useful default now.

```
#define HOMEPAGE "/eit.home.html"
```

Replace this with the filename of your server's main homepage (for example, `/index.html`).

```
#define LOGFILE "/usr/local/etc/httpd/logs/access_log"
```

Replace this with the location of your server's log file. This can also be overridden with a command line option, but it is better to set a useful default now.

```
#define SERVERTYPE "NCSA"
#define COMMON 0
```

These two are related. If you are running Plexus, GN, or MacHTTP, you should set `SERVERTYPE` to `"PLEXUS"`, `"GN"`, or `"MAC"`, respectively. If you are running an NCSA server earlier than 1.2 or a CERN server earlier than 1.16b, you should set `SERVERTYPE` to either `"NCSA"` or `"CERN"`, respectively.

However, if you are running a server that supports the Common Logfile Format (including NCSA 1.2 or later, and CERN 1.16b or later), leave `SERVERTYPE` alone. Instead, set `COMMON` to 1.

```
#define DOMAINFILE NULL
```

If you retrieved `domain.codes.txt`, set this to the full pathname of the `domain.codes.txt` file. For example,

```
#define DOMAINFILE "/usr/local/etc/httpd/getstats/domain.codes.txt"
```

There are many other options too many to detail here. If you are curious, look through the first few pages of the getstats source code. Another option of interest is the number of accesses per hashmark in the hourly/daily/weekly/monthly reports; we had to set this number higher so that the bar graphs generated would scale well. Your mileage may vary.

Now that you have set the appropriate defaults, you are ready to compile it. The following should work:

```
darwin% cc getstats.12.c -o getstats
```

(assuming your C compiler is `"cc."`) This will leave you with the executable program `getstats`.

Use

After compilation (as described in *Installation*), you can get a concise listing of statistics simply by typing:

```
darwin% getstats
HTTP Server General Statistics
Server: http://www.freedonia.com/ (NCSA Common)
Local date: Sun Jul 02 14:23:21 PM PDT 1995
This report covers the day of 07/02/95.
All dates are in local time.
Requests last 7 days: 8577
New unique hosts last 7 days: 1222
Total unique hosts: 1222
Number of HTML requests: 1720
Number of script requests: 597
Number of non-HTML requests: 6260
Number of malformed requests (all dates): 801
Total number of all requests/errors: 9378
Average requests/hour: 651.8, requests/day: 9378.0
Running time: 1 minute, 9 seconds.
```

If this does not work (for example, if getstats cannot open the log file), go back over the options you have set, and recompile the source code.

Getstats offers a number of different report formats, and you can generate any or all of them by specifying them as comm and line options. A full list of command line options is available by typing

```
darwin% getstats -z | more
```

(The "| more" is included because the list of options is longer than 24 lines, and will doubtless not fit on most terminal windows.) A condensed list of command line options is in Table 7.4.

The first reports you will be interested in are the monthly, weekly, daily, and hourly reports. For these reports, a count of accesses is made for each unit (months, weeks, days, hours) since the log started. For example, the hourly report looks like:

```
darwin% getstats -h
[...concise report information...]
HTTP Server Hourly Statistics
Covers: 07/02/95 to 07/08/95 (7 days).
All dates are in local time.

Each mark (#) represents 20 requests.

07/02/95 (Sun)

   midnite:      191  :  ##########
   1:00 am:      147  :  #######
   2:00 am:      128  :  ######
   3:00 am:      386  :  ###################
   4:00 am:      177  :  #########
   [...]
```

As you can see, each hour from July 2 (to July 8th, although we won't show the entirety) is listed, along with the number of requests that occurred during that time.

Related to this are the daily summary and hourly summary reports:

```
darwin% getstats -hs
[...concise report information...]
HTTP Server Hourly Summary
Covers: 07/02/95 to 07/08/95 (7 days).
All dates are in local time.

Each mark (#) represents 200 requests.

   midnite:     1280  :  ######
   1:00 am:      985  :  #####
   2:00 am:      861  :  ####
   3:00 am:     2621  :  #############
   4:00 am:     1175  :  ######
   [...]
```

Table 7.4

Selected Command Line
Options for Getstats

Concise report	-c
Monthly	-m
Weekly	-w
Daily	-d
Hourly	-h
Daily Summary	-ds
Hourly Summary	-hs
Request report	
Sorted by request	-r
Sorted by accesses	-ra
Sorted by date	-rd
Sorted by bytes	-rb
Sorted by file size	-rf
Directory tree report	-dt
Error	-e
All Reports	-a
Logfile to use	-l
Take logfile from STDIN	-I
Generate HTML output	-ht

Note: case of command line option is important! -m is different from -M.

This is similar to the information in the hourly report, except that the entire week the server log spans has been broken down into 24 units. To wit, there have been 1,280 accesses between midnight and 1 A.M., when you add up the accesses in that hour from July 2, July 3, and so on. This report (along with the daily summary) is useful for analyzing patterns of usage on your server—when the heavy times are and when the light times are (good times to run automated link checkers and other automated programs that will use up processor time and server resources).

Another useful report that can be generated is the request report, which lists requests per-document accesses. This can be sorted in a number of ways; the most useful is by number of accesses:

```
[...concise report information...]
HTTP Server Request Statistics
Covers: 07/02/95 to 07/08/95 (7 days).
All dates are in local time.
Sorted by number of requests, 1443 unique
requests.
```

```
# of requests : Last Access (M/D/Y) : Request

  7564  :  07/02/95  :  /wdbin/play.pl
  3973  :  07/02/95  :  /cgi-bin/tic-tac-toe
  3125  :  07/02/95  :  /html-composition/strict-
                          html.html

  2100  :  07/02/95  :  /~tjones/Language-Page.html
  [...]
```

As you can see, on this server, the two most popular documents are CGI scripts, followed by *Composing Good HTML* and the *Human Languages Page* (we swear we didn't make these numbers up). If this server is running particularly slowly, it might because of those extremely popular (and pesky) CGI scripts. Related to this report is the directory tree report (-dt), which indicates accesses by directory.

Another useful option, if you are archiving log files, is to run several reports on an archived file:

```
darwin% getstats -ra -hs -l old-log.1294
```

or to do the same but generate HTML output for placing on your server:

```
darwin% getstats -ra -hs -l old-log.1294 -ht )
report-for-dec94.html
```

That should be enough to get you started using getstats. As you'll find, there are *plenty* of different options, including the ability to analyze within a certain date range or from a particular host.

Evaluation

Getstats can certainly fulfill your statistical analysis needs. It provides a huge number of features, and should with most server logs. The only drawback, if it can be called a drawback, is that it provides such a huge number of options that it can be somewhat daunting.

Availability

The source code for getstats is available via FTP at

```
ftp://ftp.eit.com/pub/web.software/getstats/
```

In addition, on-line reference documentation is available via the Web at

```
http://www.eit.com/software/getstats/getstats.html
```

As an added bonus, at least two packages are available that use the output of getstats to create graphs; see

```
http://www.tcp.chem.tue.nl/stats/script/
http://infopad.eecs.berkeley.edu/stats/
```

for more details.

Wusage 3.2 (C)

Features

Wusage, by Thomas Boutell, can analyze logs in Common Logfile Format, as well as from old-style NCSA, CERN, and Plexus servers. Like Getstats, wusage is intended for Unix platforms, but it is written in non-Unix specific C code and should be usable on any platform as long as a C compiler is available. It is meant to be run once a week on your log file, and will automatically maintain a statistics directory replete with graphs, charts, and previous statistics.

Installation

To install wusage, first download the package from the FTP site isis.cshl.org, in the directory /pub/wusage. The distribution file is wusage3.2.tar.Z (where 3.2 is replaced by the current version number). Uncompress and untar the distribution file (put it somewhere like /usr/local/etc/httpd/tools/ wusage3.2). The only thing you might have to change in the Makefile is the C compiler (for example, instead of CC=cc, use CC=gcc, depending on your site). Then go ahead and type

```
darwin% make all
```

This should leave you with the binary executable wusage.

Next, you will need to create the configuration file, `wusage.conf`. The distribution comes with a sample that you can modify. This configuration file has a definite order in which keywords must appear, but it is heavily commented (lines beginning with "#" are comments, and are ignored by wusage) to indicate where various configuration options should appear. In addition, each keyword should appear on a line by itself.

The entries you will want to change include:

```
#Type of server log: COMMON (all new servers),
#NCSA_HTTPD, CERN_HTTPD, or PLEXUS_HTTPD.
COMMON
```

If you have a server that supports the Common Logfile Format, which includes current versions of NCSA and CERN httpd, leave this as COMMON (the capitalization is required). If you have an old NCSA (before 1.2) or CERN (before 1.16b) server, use either NCSA or CERN.

```
#Name of your server as it should be presented
Quest
```

Change "Quest" to the name of your server (such as "Metanoia Bookworks").

```
#File to use as a prefix;
#MUST BE A COMPLETE FILE SYSTEM PATH.
/home/www/prefix
```

The prefix is inserted at the beginning of the usage statistics that wusage generates, and can be used for any sort of header information you would like to include. Since wusage generates HTML documents, this document can include HTML elements. If you've installed wusage in `/usr/local/etc/httpd/tools/wusage3.2`, a good value for this would be "`/usr/local/etc/httpd/tools/wusage3.2/prefix.`"

```
#File to use as a suffix;
#MUST BE A COMPLETE FILE SYSTEM PATH.
/home/www/suffix
```

This is the same as the prefix, but it is appended to the end. Sample `prefix` and `suffix` files are included in the distribution, and Boutell asks that you use the link to the wusage documentation that is included in the sample `suffix` file in your own `suffix` file. A good value for this would be `"/usr/local/etc/httpd/tools/wusage3.2/suffix."`

```
#Directory where html pages generated by usage program
#should be located
/home/www/web/usage
```

Wusage requires its own directory in your document space, where it will place statistics reports. If your document root directory is `/usr/local/etc/httpd/htdocs`, a good value for this would be `"/usr/local/etc/httpd/htdocs/usage."` Make sure that this directory is writeable by whichever user you will run wusage as, and that it is readable and searchable by the user that the Web server is run as (to wit, it should be world readable and searchable).

```
#URL to which locations of html pages should be appended
#for usage reports (the same as the first line, but in
#web space, not filesystem space)
/usage
```

This is a pointer to the same directory as described in the last paragraph. However, this pointer is relative to your Web—that is, if the directory you create would be accessed via the URL `http://www.freedonia.com/usage/` (replacing `www.freedonia.com` with your server name), you would set this to `"/usage"` (no trailing slash).

```
#Path of ncsa httpd log file
/home/www/ncsa/logs/access_log
```

This is the filename of your access log; if your server is in `/usr/local/etc/httpd`, then a good setting for this might be `"/usr/local/etc/httpd/logs/access_log."`

```
#Your top-level domain name (org, edu, com... just the topmost level)
org
```

Set this to your top-level domain name. www.freedonia.com would set this equal to "com."

Use

Once you have configured wusage, using it is easy. To invoke it, type

```
darwin% wusage -c wusage.conf
```

(Make sure that you have write access to wusage's usage directory, so that wusage will be able to create its reports and charts.)

After wusage finishes (which may take some time), you can view the results by checking the URL

```
http://www.freedonia.com/usage/
```

(Of course, you must change the server name to your own server, and if you are using a different directory, you must also change that. But you know what we mean.)

NOTE: If you don't have a week's worth of access information in your access log, you may not see a link to any reports on the index page. Try using the URL `http://www.freedonia.com/usage/week0.html` instead.

That's it. There are not a plethora of command line options (like in getstats). In fact, the best way to use wusage is to simply run it once a week, as a cron job.

Evaluation

Where getstats is feature-full, wusage is relatively straightforward. It can be run once a week as a cron job, and forgotten about. It will maintain the statistics directory and do all other associated work (with the exception of cycling your log files) for you. On the other hand, if you need specific statistical information, wusage is not the package for you.

A good strategy, especially if wusage generates usable weekly statistics for your site, is to use wusage for weekly statistic generation. Then, use getstats for specific analysis and extraction.

Availability

The source code for Wusage is available via FTP at

```
ftp://isis.cshl.org/pub/wusage/wusage3.2.tar.Z
```

In addition, on-line reference documentation is available via the Web at

```
http://siva.cshl.org/wusage.html
```

VBStats 3.1 (Windows)

Features

VBStats, by Robert Denny, is an HTTP log file analyzer and reporter for Windows HTTP servers. VBStats takes normal Common Logfile Format access logs (such as those created by WinHTTPD), imports them into a Microsoft Access database, then builds HTML pages with graphs of access per week/day and top 10 lists for various statistics (most requested page, most frequent server, and so on) which you can link to your server's homepage.

VBStats provides automatic graphing of server accesses, automatic indexing by week, ability to restrict reports from including pages/directories, and includes the WinCron program that allows scheduling of other programs.

Use

VBStats is particularly easy to use, thanks to a usually intuitive GUI. The VBStats package comes in PKZIP format—unzip it into a temporary directory and run SETUP.EXE from Windows. This sets up the VBStats group in Windows, copies the necessary files from the temporary directory, and optionally runs the Setup Wizard for VBStats (discussed next).

VBStats comes with five programs. The Setup Wizard configures VBStats for use with your server, letting you specify the server name, location of the log file, and style of graph (among other things). LogToDB takes the log file specified by the Setup Wizard and imports it into the database that VBStats uses to keep track of access logs. The Restricter allows you to specify files or directories that should not show up in the report (HTML) pages. The Reporter parses through the database and builds a report page for each completed week for which statistics exist, as well as an index page that graphs server usage from the beginning to the end (dates) of the database, and points to all the weekly pages. The Maintenance Utility allows you to purge old data from the database (statistics occurring before a particular date), compress the database (after a purge, so that the database starts at record 1), and remove placeholder information from the database (which is added after each completed week, so that the reporter doesn't need to recalculate weeks for which report pages already exist).

To use VBStats, first run the Setup Wizard and fill in all the information it asks for. You should only need to run it once unless you need to change the information. In the future, you merely need to run LogToDB to import the latest HTTP log data, then Reporter to generate report pages for the new dates. Reporter will not generate a page for a week that has not yet come to an end (based on your system's time), so doing this more than once a week is unnecessary (unless you change the restrictions via the Restricter). The index page and weekly report pages are put into the directory specified in the Setup Wizard, which you can link to from your server's homepage to give visitors access to your server's statistics.

It is recommended that you not use the current, live access log (typically "access.log") to update the database, because the HTTP server is constantly updating the file. In the Setup Wizard, you have the option of having the Reporter signal the HTTP server to cycle out its current log file (which the HTTP server does by changing its name and starting a new log file). The log-cycling tool with Windows httpd (see Chapter 6) will rename the log file to "access.001"; by checking the "Cycle Logs" option in the Setup Wizard and giving the correct log file name, Windows httpd and the Reporter should have no trouble operating together.

WinCron, a shareware program, is provided with the VBStats package (this WinCron has not been registered—if you use it and like it, please support the author, Mark Woodward, according to the information listed in the About... option in the Help menu). WinCron allows you to schedule programs to run at particular times, provided your system is running at the time. For HTTP servers, this is not a problem as the computer is running almost constantly. As an example of its use, you could set up WinCron to automatically run LogToDB and Reporter every Monday morning at 2 a.m. to set up the report pages for the previous week. To set up this operation, run WinCron and select "Weekly Event..." from the Selection menu. Change the "Startup Directory" to the location of the VBStats package (that is, "C:\VBSTATS"), and enter the path to LogToDB in the "Command Line." Finally, set the day and time you want the operation to run, and select the OK button. Next, schedule a similar event that just runs the Reporter (with a Startup Directory equal to the location of the VBStats package) and occurs approximately 15 minutes later (to give LogToDB enough time to complete the database update). Leave WinCron running constantly, and these two operations will occur automatically on the day and time you specified every week.

Evaluation

VBStats is very clean and easy to use. It has a simple, easy-to-understand interface, and it does what it does very well. If you want or need stats pages for your Web server, then this package will work well for you. It gets the job done without a lot of additional features that you may not ever use. If you need a package that does more than graph day-to-day server usage and build a few selected top 10 lists, you'll have to look elsewhere because that's the extent of VBStats' functionality. However, for most users, this is more than enough from a statistics package.

Availability

VBStats 3.1 is free, and is available via the Web from

```
http://www.city.net/win-httpd/lib/util-support/
vbstat31.zip
```

WebStat
(Macintosh)

Features

WebStat is a standalone HTTP log file analysis tool for MacHTTP/WebSTAR, written by Phil Harvey. It provides formatted server statistics for usage times, client domains, and file accesses.

It provides some customization of report formatting, the ability to exclude specified client domains for reports, and can be used in conjunction with Cron (described in a moment) to schedule automatic generation of log reports.

Use

WebStat comes as a package of files, including WebStat, WebStat.config, and WebStat.format. Configuration of WebStat is not done through the standard Macintosh interface, but through editing of the WebStat.config text file. Everything, however, should work properly using the defaults, except, perhaps, the path for your log file; this is specified with the LOG directive in the WebStat.config file.

To run WebStat, simply double-click on the program's icon; it will read in its configuration file, and generate a log report with the filename specified in WebStat.config (the default file is WebStat.html), in the format given in WebStat.format. The report file can then be viewed with your preferred Web browser.

A supplementary program, Cron, allows you to schedule programs to run at particular times, provided your system is running at the time. For HTTP servers, this is not a problem as the computer is running almost constantly. Cron uses the same format as the Unix cron utility.

You can create crontab entries to run regular reporting or maintenance utilities, such as WebStat, or a small MacPerl script, such as the following one to rotate WebSTAR logs:

```
# rotatelog.pl
# rotates WebSTAR logs
#
```

```perl
# $logdirpath should point to the directory of your logs
# $logname should be the name of your server log
# $serverpath should be the full path pointing to WebSTAR
#

$logdirpath = "Macintosh HD:www:";
$logname = "WebSTAR.log";
$serverpath = "Macintosh HD:www:WebSTAR□";


#
# get the current date to include it in the old log's name
#

($sec, $min, $hour, $day, $month, $year, $wday,
$yday, $isdst) = localtime(time);

$month++;

if ($month < 10) {$month = "0$month"; }
if ($day < 10) { $day = "0$day"; }

$rotlogname = "WebSTAR_" . $year . $month . $day
. ".log";

#
# if the rotated log file already exists, don't
write over it
#

if (-e "$logdirpath$rotlogname") { die
"$logdirpath$rotlogname already
exists\n"; }

#
# turn WebSTAR logging off, rotate the log, then
turn logging back on
#

&MacPerl'DoAppleScript("tell application
\"$serverpath\"\n Suspend Logging
true\n end tell");

rename("$logdirpath$logname","$logdirpath$rotlogname");

&MacPerl'DoAppleScript("tell application
\"$serverpath\"\n Suspend Logging
false\n end tell");
```

```
#
# quit MacPerl
#

&MacPerl'Quit(2);
```

We can then run the preceding script at a regular interval to rotate logs. For example, to rotate logs every Sunday at 2 A.M., we can put the following entry in our crontab file:

```
0 2 * * 0 nobody open rotatelog.pl
```

where, in order, 0 is the minute, 2 is the hour, * is the day of the month (any day), * is the month of the year, and 0 is the day of the week (0-6, with 0 being Sunday), "nobody" is a meaningless placeholder for compatibility with the Unix crontab format, "open" is the command to execute, and "rotatelog.pl" is the name of the file. This assumes that "rotatelog.pl" lives in the same folder as cron; if it doesn't, you'll need to supply a full path. This also assumes you've checked the box in the Scripts section of MacPerl's Preferences to Run scripts opened from the Finder, and that AppleScript is installed.

Evaluation

WebStat is fairly straightforward, and does its job well. The lack of a GUI front end for configuration is un-Maclike, but probably very reasonable given the task being performed. Source code is provided for those who might wish to tailor the program to their specific needs.

ServerStat, by J. Eric Bush, is based on the WebStat source. It parses GopherSurfer logs as well as MacHTTP/WebSTAR logs, and provides a graphical front end to WebStat. It is also recompiled to be PowerPC-native. It was still in beta at the time of this writing.

Availability

WebStat 2.3.4 is freeware, and available at

```
http://www.freedonia.com/utilities/
```

Table 7.5 Other Log Analysis Packages			
	wwwstats	http://www.ics.uci.edu/ pub/websoft/wwwstat	A Perl-based package for analyzing Common Logfile Format (CLF) files.
	gwstats	http://dis.cs.umass.edu/stats /gwstat.html	Generates charts and graphs from wwwstats output.
	analog	http://www.statslab.cam.ac. uk/~sret1/analog/	A self-described "fast" C-based log analyzer for CLF files.
	WebStat	http://www.pegasus.esprit. ec.org/people/sijben/statistics/ advertisment.html	Python-based CLF analyzer.
	Yahoo's list	http://www.yahoo.com/ Computers/World_Wide_Web/ HTTP/Servers/Log_Analysis_ Tools/	Up-to-date on-line list of log analysis tools.

More information on ServerStat can be found at

```
http://www.ericse.ohio-state.edu/ss.html
```

cron 1.0d16 is freeware, and available at

```
http://gargravarr.cc.utexas.edu/cron/cron.html
```

Other Log Analysis Packages

Some other log analysis packages are available, and are detailed in Table 7.5.

Other Tools for Your Server

There are many other sorts of tools that can enhance the functionality of your server; many more than we can mention here. However, we can provide some pointers so that you can explore these areas on your own.

Table 7.6		
Resources for Adding Searching to Your Server	Harvest	http://rd.cs.colorado.edu/harvest/
	Using WAIS with HTML	http://www.eit.com/software/wwwwais/wwwwais.html
	"How to do a searchable database"	http://www2.ncsu.edu/bae/people/faculty/walker/hotlist/isindex.html
	On-line list of search resources	http://www-rlg.stanford.edu/home/jpl/websearch.html

Searching Tools

Although they do not fall under the rubric of maintenance or reporting tools, searching tools can greatly enhance the functionality of your server. Table 7.6 lists some resources for search tools (also see the review of WN in Chapter 6).

General Resources for Server Tools

Finally, a good general resource for server tools is Yahoo, especially

```
http://www.yahoo.com/Computers/World_Wide_Web/
Programming/
```

8

CGI: Extending Your Web with Dynamic Documents

What Is a CGI Script?

Until now, we have talked extensively about creating and maintaining what is essentially a static body of information, with an emphasis on the creation and maintenance of documents over the (relatively) long term. This is fine for information that is essentially static (such as as a research papers, documentation, or background information about a company or university), but makes impossible certain other kinds of information, such as a search index or a constantly updated stock quote site.

Fortunately for people who have the desire to build these more complex kinds of pages, most, if not all, HTTP servers now include support for CGI. CGI stands for Common Gateway Interface. It provides, as the name implies, a "gateway" between the World Wide Web and any other type of service. These gateways are in the form of programs that take information from a non-Web source and turn into a Web document in a dynamic, "on-the-fly" manner.

While this is intended to provide a way to make interfaces to non-Web information services available on the Web, it has much deeper ramifications. An HTTP server that supports CGI has the ability to dynamically create Web documents of any kind. Instead of a URL pointing to a static document, it can point to an executable program that returns an HTML (or any format) document. These executable programs, called *CGI scripts,* can do anything your programming abilities will allow: create a searchable index to your server, generate customized views of documents at the request of users, and even dynamically balance the load of supplying information onto two or more Web servers.

243

NOTE: CGI scripts are not the only way to create dynamic documents, although they are the most common. An alternate method, server-side include (SSI), allows you to embed commands to the server in your HTML; the server will execute these commands when the document is retrieved. This can be used to include other files (such as a standard document footer) or other dynamic information (such as when the document was last modified). The exact mechanism by which SSI works varies from server to server—see your server document for details. Another option is Java, a language developed by Sun Microsystems for creating downloadable applications which are embedded in HTML documents. See Appendix D for more information.

The rest of this chapter will require that you have a basic working knowledge of the C or Perl programming languages. While there is great deal of flexibility in which programming languages you can use in creating scripts, these are the two most popular choices. Perl, in particular, is an excellent choice for creating powerful programs quickly and easily; it is available for nearly every platform, and has a syntax recognizable to anyone familiar with C. If you are unfamiliar with Perl or C, the references in the Bibliography can help you get started.

Anatomy of a CGI Script

CGI scripts are invoked whenever they are requested from the server, that is, whenever a URL is selected that points to the script. Unlike other kinds of documents, which are simply returned to the client, a CGI script is first run, and then the output of the script is returned to the client. The notion here is that the document is created *dynamically*—the output of the script, whether it be an HTML document, a GIF or JPEG image, or some other type of document, is what is displayed by the browser. To the browser—and to the reader—the fact that the document was created by a program instead of a human is largely immaterial.

What sort of document is returned is, of course, dependent on what information is fed to the CGI script before it is run. There are many means of providing the information (and some of them are described in detail in this chapter), but there are two basic mechanisms: standard input and environment variables. Standard input is a familiar concept to C (and Perl) programmers; it is the input stream from which C programs expect input to come, whether that stream is fed by a file, another program, or by a human. Environment variables should also be familiar, especially to Unix programmers; these are variables passed to programs that describe the environment in which they are running. The CGI standard defines a set of environment variables that are passed to CGI scripts, giving the script information about how it was invoked and what is expected of it.

The idea is the same for all three major HTTP server platforms—Unix, Macintosh, DOS/Windows—but the implementation is different because of differences in interprocess communication and operating systems. We will first discuss CGI programming under the Unix operating system, to give a general explanation, then extrapolate to Macintosh and DOS/Windows servers. Don't worry, it turns out that CGI remains pretty much the same no matter what platform you are programming on.

Unix

For security reasons, CGI scripts are usually contained within a central directory, to which only limited access is available. This is intentionally different from the standard document-type identification (by file extension) where any kind of document can be in any directory. This is so that you can provide the ability for users to provide their own Web documents, without having to provide the ability for users to provide scripts. This is important because scripts, especially on any multiuser machine, can have glaring security holes if written improperly. Because they will be run with the same user permissions as the Web server, they will have access to everything that the server does, which may include quite a few things. (For this reason, it's always a good idea to make sure anything run by the HTTP server runs as a user such as "Web" with very limited access; this way, if a script does break and give the

Box 8.1 Running CGI More Securely

CGI scripts can provide incredibly useful functionality, but they can also present a danger to your system security. Because CGI scripts can be invoked by users outside of your system, it is possible for an insecurely written script to have security holes which could allow others to cause damage to your web, or to give outsiders access to your machine.

CGI-wrap is a tool which will run a user's CGI scripts with the user ID and permissions of that user. This doesn't prevent them from writing insecure scripts, but it does limit any resulting damage. Any runaway CGI script can only do as much damage as that user can do. It should be noted that just because scripts are run with the user ID of your users, they are still not safe. If such a script is compromised, an attacker might still conceivably be able to gain access to such vital system files at the password file. CGI-wrap is available at:

    http://www.umr.edu/~cgiwrap/

taintperl is an alternate Perl compiler which comes with the Perl distribution. It is based on the notion that any command line variable, environment variable, or user input is "tainted", and cannot be used in any command which invokes a subshell, or modifies processes, files, or directories. Furthermore, any variable which is set using any of these tainted variables also becomes tainted. You can explicitly untaint variables after you have checked them to verify that they are, in fact, safe. (see the Bibliography for information about how to get the Perl distribution for the platform.)

We recommend that you at least use taintperl for CGI scripts, in order to better ensure their security. To use it under Unix, replace the line

    #!/bin/perl

at the start of your Perl-based CGI scripts with

    #!/bin/taintperl

(Note that these lines may differ based on where Perl is on your system). In addition, if you are intending to allow your users to write scripts, use CGI-wrap as well as require that they use taintperl.

---

client access to the Web account, an invader won't be able to do much more than change your Web documents).

Scripts can be written in any programming language that result in a Unix executable, including C, Perl, and shell scripts. C programs will have to be compiled into an executable before they can be used. Perl and shell scripts are usually self-executable, so they're always ready to go. Perl is one of the most popular languages for writing CGI scripts in both the Macintosh and Unix environments for a variety of reasons:

- It's free.

- It's easy to learn and use (especially if you know C—Perl is like C, only without C's problems).

- It has powerful text manipulation, database, and indexing routines built in.

- Perl scripts can usually be run on all three major platforms (Macintosh, DOS/Windows, Unix) with little or no additional programming.

- It's still free.

We have chosen to use Perl for presenting most examples in this chapter, but the programming principles will hold for whatever is your language of choice. Several good books are available on the subject of Perl. Also, free Perl interpreters are available for Unix, Macintosh, and DOS. See the Bibliography for information about Perl books, as well as for common Perl FTP sites on the Internet.

A Minimal CGI Script (the Content-Type: Header)

Here is a minimal CGI script, written in Perl, which simply returns an HTML document:

```
#!/bin/perl
#The above line attempts to execute the Perl interpreter located in
#the /bin directory. You may need to change the path name if your
#Perl executable is not kept in /bin.
#
#HELLO_WORLD.pl - sample CGI script

print "Content-type: text/html\n\n";
print "<h1>Hello World</h1>\n";
print "and good morning to you.\n";
```

If this program were put in a cgi-bin directory, then linked to the client (user) on the other side of the Web, you would see something akin to Figure 8.1. As you can see, the HTML embedded in the print statements in HELLO_WORLD.pl was sent to the Web browser exactly as a normal HTML document would have been, which is what the Web client on the other end thinks it is. The most important line of HELLO_WORLD.pl is this one:

```
print "Content-type: text/html\n\n";
```

All documents published on the Web have a *MIME type* associated with them. MIME stands for Multipart Internet Mail Extension, and provides a means for representing document formats so that Internet clients (including mail readers and Web browsers) can handle documents. Under normal circumstances, the MIME type is determined by the extension of the document's filename (for example, ".html," " ".txt," or ".gif").

This automatic typing doesn't happen with scripts, because they can potentially return any file format as their output. Because of this, the script has to tell the client what kind of information it is sending back. The most common types you'll probably use are text/html, for producing HTML markup; and text/plain, for producing "plain" (without HTML) text, although a CGI script that produced images might use image/gif or image/jpegif. (Actually, technically, they aren't MIME types, but *Internet Media Types*, a MIME-like system. Since this is splitting hairs, however, you'll have to check out the explanation of MIME, MIME types, and Internet Media Types in Appendix B).

HELLO_WORLD.pl produces HTML, so it begins by outputting a Content-type of text/html followed by *two newline characters* ("\n\n"). The two newlines are necessary to create a blank line between the Content-type and the actual document. The blank line is needed because the first line is actually part of the HTTP header, not the document itself. By providing a blank line, clients can then distinguish the end of the HTTP header, and the beginning of the document. The rest of HELLO_WORLD.pl simply prints HTML, which the server sends back to the client. This is what a Web client would actually receive from HELLO_WORLD.pl:

Figure 8.1

Hello World!
(Netscape)

Hello World

and good morning to you.

```
[other http headers supplied by server]
Content-type: text/html

⟨h1⟩Hello World⟨/h1⟩

and good morning to you.
```

Redirection (the Location: Header)

The previous example is fine for producing static documents, but it fails to take advantage of the power of scripting. So now, let's add some of the functionality of Perl to a script:

```
#!/bin/perl
#RANDOM_URL.pl - sample CGI script

$r=int(random(5));
$host_address=,"www.somewhere.com";
$html_pages[0]=,"~tjones/";
$html_pages[1]=,"~jtilton/";
$html_pages[2]=,"~csteadman/";
$html_pages[3]=,"~bfrench/";
$html_pages[4]=,"~bob/info.html";

print "Location: http://$host_address/$html_pages[$r]\n\n";
```

RANDOM_URL.pl, when invoked, will randomly choose a URL based on the information in $host_address and the @html_pages array, and cause that page to be displayed. Instead of having this script print out an HTML page, it replaces Content-type: with Location:, the HTTP redirection header. Location: URL causes the client to go to URL and display that page, instead of waiting around for the script to return additional HTML. The client then gets the Content-type from the new document, and everything is happy. Since the script is telling the client to load some other document, there is no need to print out any HTML from the script itself. However, we could have easily used Content-type instead of Location in RANDOM_URL.pl, and replaced the print line in with:

```
print "Content-type: text/html\n\n";
print "⟨h1⟩Random URL⟨/h1⟩";
print "This script has generated a ⟨a
href=\"http://$host_address/$html_pages[$r]\"⟩ran-dom URL⟨/a⟩. Don't
you wonder where it goes?\n";
```

This would give the client an opportunity to select a link to go to the random URL. To make this a more useful script, you could have it read a list of URLs from a file and randomly pick one—that way you wouldn't have to rewrite the program every time you added a new URL to the random list.

This example demonstrates that CGI scripts are useful for even more than simply returning documents, due to the fact that they can also generate HTTP headers.

NOTE: While the CGI script can generate HTTP headers, it does not generate *all* of the HTTP headers that are seen by a client. Some headers are prepended by the server before the output of the client is returned. However, some servers, such as NCSA httpd, can run special "nph" scripts, which are responsible for printing *all* HTTP headers, giving the script author a very fine level of control over what is returned to the client. See your server documentation for more details.

Sending Information to a Script

Many scripts allow you to interact with them—you can search through some data, fill in a form, or play a game. Obviously, there's something more going on with these scripts than the sample scripts in the last section. What you select on the screen or type into a box is sent to the script, which is doing something with that information. There are three different ways to send information to a script: through additional path information, through a query string (most often produced by a document containing the ISIN-DEX element), or through a form. The differences between the three methods are described in the next few sections.

Extra Path Information (the `PATH_INFO` Environment Variable)

A URL to a script looks like this:

```
http://some.address.com/some/path/some-script
```

If we're sneaky and add extra path information after the script name, like this:

```
http://some.address.com/some/path/some-
script/more/path/info
```

then the server is smart enough to realize that extra information has been sent in the URL, so it pulls the extra data (in this case, **/more/path/info**) off the URL and puts it in an environment variable string called PATH_INFO.

Both DOS and Unix use environment variables as a means of passing information to programs about the environment that they are in. In Unix, some common environment variables are user name, home directory, and terminal settings. In DOS, they more usually contain directories where a particular program can be found. Unix generally uses many more environment variables than DOS. The CGI interface defines several environment variables that are used to pass information to CGI scripts, such as the extra path information just described. (A complete list of environment variables used by the CGI interface is given in Table 8.1.)

In order to use the path information, you need to extract it from the environment. In C, the procedure call to do this is getenv:

```
char pathstr[100];
strcpy (pathstr, getenv("PATH_INFO"));
```

In Perl, environment variables are stored in an associative array called %ENV, so to pull the data out of the PATH_INFO environment variable:

```
$pathstr=$ENV{'PATH_INFO'};
```

If we used our previous sample URL, the variable pathstr (or $pathstr) would now contain the string /more/path/info, which you can break apart and do with whatever you want.

What *can* you do with it? Path information can't be entered by users (unless they like typing in their own URLs all the time), so you don't generally use it for getting info from someone. Figure 8.2 shows an example where this could be useful. If the client selects English, we want to display the date in English; if the client selects Spanish, we want to display the date in Spanish. (Times will be the same, because they're just numbers.) Instead of writing

Table 8.1

CGI Environment
Variables

SERVER_SOFTWARE	Name and version of the server invoking the CGI script (format is `name/version`; for example, `NCSA/1.4.1`).
SERVER_NAME	Hostname, DNS alias, or IP address of the server.
GATEWAY_INTERFACE	Version of the CGI specification supported by the server (format is `CGI/revision`; for example `CGI/1.1`).
SERVER_PROTOCOL	Name and version of protocol used to submit the CGI request (format is `protocol/revision`; for example, `HTTP/1.0`).
SERVER_PORT	The port number to which the request was sent.
REQUEST_METHOD	The method with which the request was made. HTTP methods include `"GET,"` `"POST,"` `"HEAD,"` etc.
PATH_INFO	The extra path information, as given by the client. See *Extra path information,* earlier.
PATH_TRANSLATED	A server-translated version of `PATH_INFO`, after virtual-to-physical mapping has been done.
SCRIPT_NAME	A virtual path to the script being executed, used for self-referencing URLs.
QUERY_STRING	The query information. See *Input from the user,* earlier.
REMOTE_HOST	The hostname of the machine making the request. If the server does not have this information, it should set REMOTE_ADDR and leave this unset. (Often REMOTE_HOST is set to the value of REMOTE_ADDR in this case).
REMOTE_ADDR	The IP address of the remote host making the request.
AUTH_TYPE	The type of protocol-specific authentication method used to validate the user (used if the server supports user authentication and the script is protected).
REMOTE_USER	The username the user has been authenticated as, if authentication has been performed by the server.
REMOTE_IDENT	The remote username retrieved from the server (if the HTTP server supports RFC 931 identification).
CONTENT_TYPE	The content type of the data supplied to the script (for queries that have attached information, such as via `POST`).
CONTENT_LENGTH	The length of the supplied content in bytes.
HTTP_*headername*	Any HTTP headers supplied by the client are also supplied, with the `"HTTP_"` prefix prepended. For example, the `USER_AGENT` and `ACCEPT` headers are supplied as `HTTP_USER_AGENT` and `HTTP_ACCEPT`.

Select one of the following links to get the current date and time displayed in that language:

Figure 8.2

The Current Date/Time
Server, in English or
Spanish (Netscape)

Date/time in English

La fecha y tiempo en español

two separate scripts, one that prints in English and one in Spanish, we can write one script and send it extra path information. Here is the HTML code behind the preceding:

```
〈html〉〈head〉〈title〉The Current Date/Time Server〈/title〉〈/head〉
〈body〉
〈h2〉Select one of the following links to get the current date and
time displayed in that language:〈/h2〉
〈a href="http://www.somewhere.com/cgi-
bin/CURRENT_TIME.pl/english"〉Date/time in English〈/a〉〈p〉
〈a href="http://www.somewhere.com/cgibin/CURRENT_TIME.pl/spanish"〉La
fecha y tiempo en español〈/a〉
〈/body〉〈/html〉
```

The name of the script is CURRENT_TIME.pl and in the links, we send either "/english" or "/spanish" to it in PATH_INFO. So here is a Perl program to handle this:

```
#!/bin/perl
#CURRENT TIME.pl - displays the current time in either Spanish
# or English, depending on what is in the environment string
# PATH INFO.

#We do this to avoid trying to copy an empty string
if ($ENV{"PATH INFO"})
{
    $pathstr5$ENV{"PATH INFO"};
}
else
{
    #If PATH INFO is empty, don't put anything in $pathstr
```

```
      $pathstr5"";
}

($seconds,$minutes,$hours,$monthday,$month,$year,$weekday,$yearday,
$isdst)=localtime(time);

@English_days=("Sunday", "Monday", "Tuesday", "Wednesday",
"Thursday", "Friday", "Saturday");

@Spanish_days=("domingo", "lunes", "martes", "miércoles", "jueves",
"viernes", "sábado");

@English_months=("January", "February", "March", "April", "May",
"June", "July", "August", "September", "October", "November",
"December");

@Spanish_months=("enero", "febrero", "marzo", "abril", "mayo",
"junio", "julio", "agosto", "septiembre", "octubre", "noviembre",
"diciembre");

print("Content-type: text/html\n\n");

if ($pathstr, eq "/english") || $pathstr, eq "")
#If English was specified, or if there was no path
# information, print it in English
{
   print "⟨h2⟩Today is $English_days[$weekday],
$English_months[$month] $monthday. The time is
$hours:$minutes:$seconds⟨/h2⟩\n";
}
else #Otherwise print it in Spanish
{
   print "⟨h2⟩Hoy es el $Spanish_days[$weekday], el $monthday de
$Spanish_months[$month].";
   if ($hour==1)
   {
     print "Es $hours:$minutes:$seconds⟨/h2⟩\n";
   }
   else
   {
     print "Son $hours:$minutes:$seconds⟨/h2⟩\n;
   }
}
```

Path information is also used frequently for on-line games on the Web, such as tic-tac-toe. The tic-tac-toe board could be an array of inlined images, each with a link around it. In the URL of the link, you could include some information about which image is being selected (maybe by numbering them) in the path information. The script can then know which image was selected, and act accordingly.

Input From the User (the `QUERY_STRING` environment variable)

A query string is the simplest way to get a short piece of information from the user. It is accessed the same way as the path information, except that the name of the environment variable is QUERY_STRING instead of PATH_INFO. The query information is also passed as part of the URL, except, instead of being passed off as additional path information, it is separated by a question mark:

```
http://some.address.com/some/path/some-
    script?query-string-info
```

For an HTML document to ask the user to enter information, it must include the ⟨ISINDEX⟩ tag. This either gives users a small box in which they can type information (in a graphical browser like Netscape), or otherwise informs them that they are viewing a searchable document (in Lynx, for example, you can search a document containing ⟨ISINDEX⟩ by pressing the "s" key). You can't just put an ⟨ISINDEX⟩ tag in just any document, though; it must be in a script, because when the user types something into the text box and sends it to your server, the *same* URL is called again, only with query string information this time. Here is a sample Perl program that uses the query string and the ⟨ISINDEX⟩ tag:

```perl
#!/bin/perl
#QUERY_STRING_EXAMPLE.pl - a short and sweet
example of how
# to use ⟨ISINDEX⟩ and QUERY_STRING.


#We do this to avoid trying to copy an empty
string
if ($ENV{"QUERY_STRING"})
{
```

```
    $query-string=$ENV{"QUERY_STRING"});
}
else
{
    #If QUERY_STRING is empty, don't put anything in
    # $query-string
    $query-string="";
}

print "Content-type: text/html\n\n";

if (!$query-string)
{
    #If $query-string is empty, give the client a chance to
    # type something in by printing a document with an
    # <ISINDEX> tag in it.
    print <<end_of_page
<html>
<head>
    <title>ISINDEX</title>
    <isindex>
</head>
<body>
    <h1>This is a searchable index. Please enter some text.</h1>
</body>
</html>
end_of_page
;
}
else
{
    #Else $query-string isn't empty, so print out whatever
    # is in it.
    print <<end_of_page
<html>
<head>
    <title>ISINDEX Results</title>
</head>
```

```
⟨body⟩
    ⟨h1⟩You typed $query_string. How very clever of you.⟨/h1⟩
⟨/body⟩
⟨/html⟩
end_of_page
;
    #NOTE: Your script doesn't have to be quite this snooty.
}
```

When the script first gets loaded by the user, he or she has not had a chance to enter anything into the query string, so the environment variable QUERY_STRING is empty. The script then prints out "This is a searchable index. Please enter some text," and the user is given a text box to type into and a button marked Submit, as seen in Figure 8.3.

After the user has entered something into the text box and pressed the Submit button, the script gets called again. The browser appends the information that was entered by the reader to the URL of the document; if the reader entered "Kansas," the script would be referenced with the URL

```
http://www.freedonia.confcgi-bin/isindex-sample?KANSAS
```

The server takes the query string information and places it in the QUERY_STRING environment variable. The script recognizes that QUERY_STRING contains information, and executes the code that prints out the contents of QUERY_STRING to show how smart it is. In a real world situation, you could link this to some a text file or database, and instead of just printing the query string you would use it to search the text file or database and return (to the client) whatever it found.

This is a searchable index. Enter search keywords: ▏

Figure 8.3
An ISINDEX Query Page
(Netscape)

This is a searchable index. Please enter some text.

One important thing about the query string is that it gets *URL encoded* before it gets put into the QUERY_STRING environment variable. This means that certain characters (such as the ampersand and equal sign) in the string will have been translated into hexadecimal numbers, and spaces will (usually) be translated into the plus sign (other times they may be translated into their hexadecimal value of "%20"). For more on URL encoding and how to take care of it, read the next section.

PATH_INFO and QUERY_STRING are only two of the environment variables used by CGI to pass information to scripts. Table 8.1 describes the other environment variables available.

The Mother Lode of Information—Handling Forms Via GET, and POST

The query string is nice, but it is still rather limited. The user can only enter a word or a sentence, a number, or a combination of the two, and the data supplied can be no longer than 255 characters in length. For simple searches that's okay, but you've probably seen elaborate e-mail forms where you can type in an entire letter, *and* your name *and* your e-mail address, *and* vote for your favorite Smurf. Or maybe you've run across cute little check boxes or radio buttons or lists you can select from, and you send all that information to the server and it does something with all of it.

Welcome to the world of forms. A form is a subsection of an HTML document that lets you specify text boxes, text fields, lists, and buttons to display on the page, lets the user type something or press buttons, then sends the whole mess to a script, which then takes all that information and does something with it. A common use of forms is for e-mail comments—users get to enter their e-mail address, name, and a message that gets e-mailed to whomever the script says (usually the person who wrote the script, but not always). Forms came with HTML 2.0, and were a particularly powerful addition to the original HTML set. The rest of this section deals with how to get the information out of these forms and use it constructively (for information on building the forms themselves see *Designing Forms,* later in the chapter).

Each element in a form has its own name, given as an attribute of the element, like this: ⟨INPUT NAME= "age"⟩. When the data from a form gets sent to its script (which is specified in the ACTION attribute of the FORM element, as explained in *Designing Forms)*, it looks like this: name1=value1&name2=value2... where *name1* is one of the names of the form elements, and *value1* is what the user typed in or selected (in a list or set of buttons) for that element (and so on). Simple? Here's an example form:

```
⟨form method=POST action="http://www.somewhere.
com/cgi-bin/cgi-mail.pl"⟩

Please select who you want to send mail to:
⟨select name="towhom"⟩
⟨option⟩Eric Tilton
⟨option⟩Carl Steadman
⟨option⟩Tyler Jones
⟨/select⟩
⟨p⟩

Type in your message here:⟨P⟩
⟨textarea name="message" rows=10 cols=60⟩
⟨/textarea⟩⟨P⟩

Please enter your e-mail address: ⟨input
name="username"⟩⟨P⟩
Please enter your name: ⟨input name="realname"⟩⟨P⟩

⟨Input TYPE="submit" VALUE="Send this message"⟩⟨br⟩
⟨Input TYPE="reset" VALUE="Erase this form"⟩
⟨/form⟩
```

which would look something like Figure 8.4 when viewed with a Web browser.

Fictional user Mr. X now comes to this page, and does the following: selects to mail to Carl Steadman, enters the message "Hello Carl," enters his e-mail name as "X@X.com" and his real name as "X." Finally, he selects the Send this message button at the bottom of the form, which calls up the script "cgi-mail.pl" on the server at "www.somewhere.com" in the directory "cgi-bin." Got all that? Here is the data that the script gets:

```
towhom=Carl+Steadman&message=Hello+Carl&username
=X@X.com&realname=X
```

It's your job as the CGI programmer to do something with that. But first, some explanations are in order. Notice that the words on

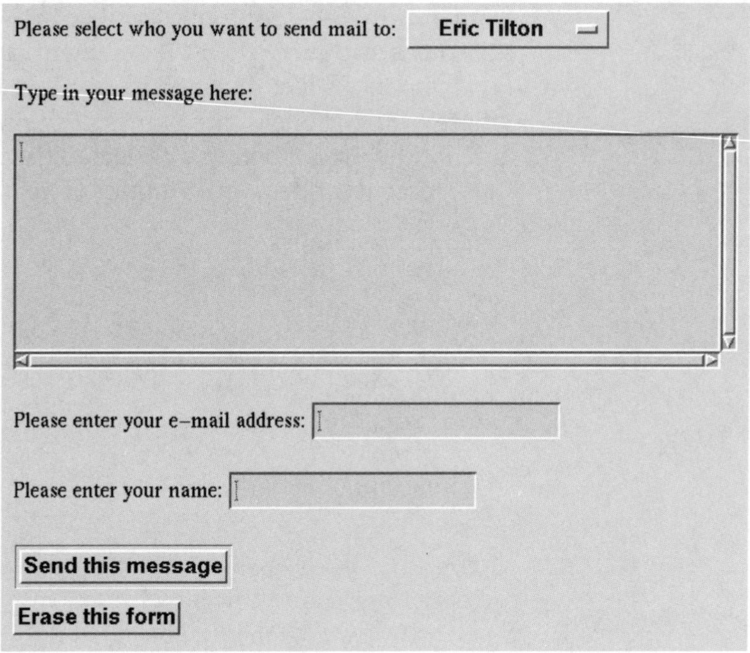

Figure 8.4

A Simple HTML Form
(Netscape)

the left-hand side of each equals sign (`towhom`, `message`, `user-name`, and `realname`) match the NAME attributes from the elements in the form. These are referred to as the names of the various fields and buttons of the form. On the right-hand of each equals sign is what the user typed in or selected from a menu (`"Carl Steadman,"` `"Hello Carl,"` `"X@X.com,"` and `"X"`). These are called the *values* from the form, and there's one value for each name (each `"name=value"` part in the preceding string is called a name/value pair; each name/value pair is separated by an ampersand (&) for easy separation).

Notice how the values entered for each element are encoded here; the element with the NAME of `towhom` had the value of `"Carl Steadman,"` the element with the NAME of `message` had the value `"Hello Carl,"` the element with the NAME of `username` had the value `"XX.com,"` and the element with the NAME of `realname` had the value `"X."` Go back and look at the form again, and notice how the NAME attributes correspond to the encoded data.

Well, the values are *almost* what the user typed on the form. Take a look at the value for `"towhom"` at the beginning of the data string. It reads: `towhom=Carl+Steadman`, when user X actually typed in `Carl Steadman`. There is a "+" in the message value. Part of the form processing procedure, which occurs before the data is sent to the script, is URL encoding of the data, which is what you see in this example. In URL encoding, spaces are translated into plus signs (+), and certain other characters (such as ampersands and equal signs) that occur in the form data are translated into their hexadecimal ASCII values, with a "%" before the number to signify that a hexadecimal-encoded character follows (the general form of hexadecimal encoding is `%xx`, where xx is replaced by a two-digit hexadecimal number). Spaces can also be translated into hexadecimal instead of plus signs, in which case they become `%20`, as in `Carl%20Steadman`. It is the duty of your script to decode any plus signs and hex-coded values in your data before it gets used for anything important (see Appendix A for more information on URL encoding and hexadecimal values for characters).

This may sound like a lot of unnecessary programming, but there is a reason for doing this encoding. What if the data that some user typed in contained an ampersand? Your script would happily assume that a new name/value pair was going to appear, and act accordingly, effectively splitting a single value into two or more pieces that will never get associated with each other again. You could run into the same problems if there were an equal sign in the string, or various other characters that might wreak havoc with the data you expected to get. So the URL encoding is supposed to help you down the road, but it does mean you'll have to add an extra step to your CGI programs that deal with forms.

To decode the data, split the name/value pairs at each ampersand, and split each pair into a name and a value (by splitting at the equal sign), you can write all the code by hand and reinvent the wheel. But that's not something I suggest. You'd be better off downloading one of the CGI libraries available for C or Perl. These are publicly usable source code listings that you can add to any C or Perl program to quickly and painlessly take your form data string and parse it into a nice clean data structure for you. (See the Bibliography for the locations of some CGI libraries, and the Examples section to see a CGI library in action.) In Perl, one typically uses associative arrays to store the name/value pairs (the keys of the array are the names), while in C a common data structure is an array of records with name and value fields (that is, `array[0].name` and `array[0].value`). You of course are welcome to do it any way you want. The C code is too long to include here, but the Perl routine to take care of splitting form data is relatively short:

```
#Read form data into $form_data.
read(STDIN, $form_data, $ENV{'CONTENT_LENGTH'});

#Split the string at each "&", put all name/value pairs into
# the array @name-value-pairs.
@name-value-pairs=split(/&/,$form_data);

#Loop through each pair (which right now looks like
# "name=value"), split into name and value, and decode them.
foreach $pair (@name-value-pairs)
{
   #Split the string at the "=", copy what's to the left into
   # $name, what's to the right into $value.
   ($name, $value) = split(/=/, $pair);

   #Translate all "+" into spaces in the name field.
   $name=~ tr/+/ /;
   #Translate all "%##"s into the corresponding characters
   $name=~ s/%([a-fA-F0-9][a-fA-F0-9])/pack("C",
    hex($1))/eg;

   #Do the same for the value field.
   $value=~ tr/+/ /;
   $value=~ s/%([a-fA-F0-9][a-fA-F0-9])/pack("C",
   hex($1))/eg;

   #Finally, put the name and value into an associative array
   # indexed by the names of the form.
   $form{$name} = $value;
}
```

By the end of either the C or Perl routines, you will have a set of data from the form, which you can manipulate in any way you see fit. So, working with our current example, the parsed information from Mr. X would now be represented like this (in Perl):

```
$form{'towhom'}="Carl Steadman"
$form{'message'}="Hello Carl"
$form{'username'}="X@X.com"
$form{'realname'}="X"
```

This all assumes that you know how to get the form data *into* your script in the first place. There are two ways for your script to retrieve the data, and they depend on which method, GET or POST, was specified in the FORM element. Recall that the form start tag looks like this: ⟨FORM METHOD=[GET|POST] action="URL"⟩, where you can use *either* GET or POST (but not both).

NOTE: GET and POST are shown in all capital letters for a reason: they are *required* to be in all capital letters. Remember this, because it will cause problems later if you forget.

If the method of a form is GET, then the data from the form will be put into the environment variable QUERY_STRING, just like the data from an ⟨ISINDEX⟩ page. Be sure to review the QUERY_STRING section of this chapter for copying data out of the QUERY_STRING environment variable.

If the form's method is POST, then the data is sent to the script via standard input, also known as STDIN (a built-in file handle in C and Perl); and another environment variable, CONTENT_LENGTH, is set to the length of the data in bytes. The data coming from STDIN may or may not be terminated with a newline (return, '\n') or end-of-file marker, so it is important to use the CONTENT_LENGTH to figure out how many bytes to read from STDIN. Here is C code to retrieve form data sent via POST:

```
int content-length;
char *form_data=(char *)malloc(sizeof(char)*100);

content-length=atoi(getenv("CONTENT_LENGTH"));
fgets(form_data, content-length+1, stdin);
```

And to do the same in Perl:

```
read(STDIN, $form_data, $ENV{'CONTENT_LENGTH'});
```

The main difference between GET and POST is that GET information is encoded in the URL, while POST information is sent as an additional part of the HTTP request. Because URLs are limited in length (because of practical requirements on the size of URLs that servers expect, URLs cannot support information that might be encoded by a highly complex form), there are limits to how much information can be sent via GET. On the other hand, POST information can be of arbitrary length. For this reason, POST is usually the method of choice for submitting information from forms.

From here, the data in form_data needs to be split up into the name and value pairs as described earlier, and then used to do something productive. Perhaps you use what the user entered to update (or search) a database. Maybe you use it to send mail to someone (as in an on-line comment form). The possibilities are limited only by your skill as a C or Perl (or other language) programmer from this point.

(At this point, you should either read the upcoming *Macintosh* or *DOS/Windows* sections, if you are interested in CGI programming on either of these platforms, in order to learn how they differ from the information already presented. Otherwise, you can proceed to *Designing Forms,* to learn how to create forms, now that you know how to receive and interpret the information from them.)

Macintosh

CGI programming on the Macintosh is very similar to CGI programming under Unix. C, Perl, AppleScript, or other executable programs go in a folder under the Mac HTTP server folder (see Chapter 6 for information on setting up MacHTTP servers), and when a client requests a URL that names a CGI script, the script is run and its output is sent back to the client. As with Unix, CGI scripts may be written in any Macintosh programming language that can produce a Macintosh executable.

Writing Perl scripts on the Macintosh is almost identical to writing Perl scripts under Unix. First, you must find a copy of MacPerl and the MacPerl CGI extension (see the Bibliography for FTP locations). Install MacPerl as per the instructions that come with it (it should be a self-extracting archive, making installation simple). Next, extract the Perl CGI extension, which should give you a folder with four or five files, including one named "MacHTTP CGI Script." Copy that file into the "MacPerl Extensions" folder in the

MacPerl folder or in the Preferences folder. Now, when you run MacPerl, you should be able to choose "File," "Save As...," and select to save as a "MacHTTP CGI Script." Any MacPerl script you write with the intent of being a CGI script will have to be saved as a "MacHTTP CGI Script" for MacHTTP to use it.

To write a CGI script using MacPerl, pay close attention to the examples and instructions given in the Unix section of this chapter. Environment strings/variables are handled in the same manner by the Mac version of Perl; file operations are the same between Mac and Unix Perl; and most other nonplatform-specific operations (for example, executing another program from within Perl) are the same on both Mac and Unix. There are two important, but simple, differences, involving the path_info variable and reading form data.

Under Unix, additional information can be placed after the script name in a URL, such as:

```
http://www.somewhere.com/some/path/some-
script/more/path/info
```

Unix HTTP servers realize that some-script is the name of a CGI script, and put the rest of the information in the URL (namely /more/path/info) into the environment variable path_info. MacHTTP doesn't do this—it interprets the /more/path/info to be part of the pathname of the script, so it ends up looking for a CGI script called info that's contained in a directory that (probably) doesn't exist, namely /some/path/somescript/more/path. Instead, MacHTTP looks for a dollar sign ($) after the script name. Data coming after the dollar sign (but before a question mark; data after a question mark is the query_string) is put into the path_info environment variable. So for this URL example to work properly on a MacHTTP server, the URL would have to be changed to:

```
http://some.address.com/some/path/some-
script$/more/path/info
```

Then, when some-script is executed, it can pull /more/path/info out of the path_info environment variable. This does not represent a CGI programming change—all the correct data is in the same environment variable as under Unix—but it does require a change in any HTML pages that will be calling on a MacHTTP server.

Additionally, MacPerl and Perl under Unix differ in their handling of form data. When a script is receiving data from a form using the POST method (which means the script needs to read the form data from standard input), Perl under Unix uses this routine to read the data:

```
read(STDIN, $form_data, $ENV{'CONTENT_LENGTH'});
```

Mac Perl uses this routine instead:

```
sysread(STDIN, $form_data, $ENV{"CONTENT_LENGTH"});
```

With that change (where necessary), the example scripts given in the Unix section and at the end of this chapter will run on a Macintosh Web server with MacPerl installed.

DOS/Windows

At the programming level of CGI, there is little difference between DOS and Unix. The difficulty lies in setting up *wrapper scripts,* which allow DOS CGI applications to access environment variables—standard in (STDIN) and standard out (STDOUT) like a "normal" CGI script. (And even that isn't too difficult, once you've got the hang of it.) Because Windows isn't itself an operating system, CGI applications under Windows HTTP must be run by DOS (specifically, by COMMAND.COM in a DOS virtual machine), which means you can't access Windows applications from these kinds of CGI scripts.

Windows HTTP comes with its own built-in method for executing CGI scripts, the CGI-DOS interface. Under Windows HTTP's CGI-DOS, when a request is made for a CGI script, the .PIF file HSCRIPT.PIF is run from Windows (creating a DOS virtual machine; that is, a DOS shell in Windows). This .PIF file runs a DOS .BAT file, which sets up the necessary environment strings, and text redirection then executes the requested CGI script. Or rather, it executes the wrapper script requested by the client. A wrapper script is a DOS .BAT file that executes the actual script, and redirects output from that script into the file given by the environment variable OUTPUT_FILE. The server then returns whatever data is in the OUTPUT_FILE to the client when the script exits.

Here is a sample wrapper script for the CGI script called CGI1.pl (the wrapper script is named CGI1.BAT):

```
C:\PERL\PERL.EXE C:\PERL\CGI1.pl > %OUTPUT_FILE%
```

CGI1.BAT would live in the HTTP root for the Windows server (typically \httpd). When executed, it runs the Perl program CGI1.pl (note that in DOS Perl, the Perl program is executed directly, and the name of the script is sent as a parameter) and redirects anything returned by the script into the file specified by the %OUTPUT_FILE% (this means "the environment variable OUTPUT_FILE" in DOS). When the script exits, the contents of OUTPUT_FILE are sent back to the client as expected. The CGI script itself should operate exactly as it would on a Macintosh or Unix server, namely by sending its data directly to standard out (STDOUT), which is typically done just by printing the data (as in print "<h1>Header</h1>").

The reason for OUTPUT_FILE and the redirection of the data from the script is because Windows can't directly access standard in or standard out from a DOS virtual machine. By the CGI 1.0 definition, a script's output should go to standard out to be picked up by the HTTP server (and sent to the client). Since Windows can't grab standard out, the only way Windows can get the data is if it is put into a file that Windows can then read (and send to the client). The same is true for data going *to* a script, namely form data being sent using the POST method. Again, by the CGI definition, form data being sent via POST should be sent on standard in to the script. (Data being sent via the GET method is contained in the environment variable QUERY_STRING, so it isn't a problem.) Since Windows can't give the script data via standard in, Windows HTTP creates a form-content file (which contains all the data from the form) and puts the name of the file into the environment variable CONTENT_FILE.

For a script to receive form information (from a form using the POST method) in this manner, the wrapper script needs to look like this:

```
C:\PERL\PERL.EXE C:\PERL\CGI1.pl < %CONTENT_FILE% > %OUTPUT_FILE%
```

The Perl script is run, but receives the contents of the CONTENT _FILE through standard in, and all output from the script goes out through standard out and into OUTPUT_FILE. Through these two environment variables (which your CGI scripts should not need to reference) and the text redirection, the CGI scripts themselves can operate exactly the same as on the other platforms.

To use the wrapper scripts, they need to go into the CGI-DOS directory on the Windows HTTP server. URLs should access the wrapper scripts directly, as in:

```
<a href="http://www.somewhere.com/cgidos/cgi1.bat">Try me</a>
```

> **NOTE:** When using DOS Perl to write CGI scripts, you should always use forward slashes when referencing filenames. For example, to open the file C:\PEOPLE\TEXT\DATA.TXT in DOS Perl, the command would look like: open(FILE, "C:/PEOPLE/TEXT/DATA.TXT");.

There are alternate CGI methods available for Windows HTTP, including a Perl shell called CGI-DOS, which works much like the preceding, and WIN-CGI, which uses Visual Basic under Windows (instead of a DOS virtual machine) for CGI scripts, which has the benefit of allowing your CGI scripts to access Windows programs (such as a database) but is much more difficult to program. References to CGI-DOS and WIN-CGI are given in the Bibliography.

Designing Forms

HTML forms allow you to get specific information from a user and send it to a script for processing. Using form elements, you can design a page with a series of text boxes, menus, and buttons, for users to fill in and submit. Once submitted, a CGI script takes the data and does something with it. It could mail the information to you (or someone else), it could update a database (or return the results of a database search), or it could return a file (image,

HTML, text) based on what was chosen in the form. Forms have many uses in the HTML world, from e-mail forms to order forms to on-line voting—whenever you need information from the user.

An HTML form is actually a subsection of a regular HTML document. You can have any number of forms in a single document, but the forms cannot overlap. A form is surrounded by the FORM element (see Chapter 13 for the descriptions of all HTML form elements), like this:

```
⟨FORM METHOD=POST ACTION="http://www.somewhere.com/cgi-bin/cgi1.pl"⟩
[Form elements, additional text and HTML]
⟨/FORM⟩
```

Between the start and end FORM tags, any additional body HTML elements are allowed, except another FORM tag. The FORM start tag contains two pieces of information: METHOD=POST or METHOD=GET specify how the server should send the form data to the CGI script. If the method is POST, the form data will be sent to the script via standard in (STDIN), and the length (in characters) of the form data will be given by the environment variable CONTENT_LENGTH. If the GET method is specified, the form data will instead be contained in the environment variable QUERY_STRING. The only difference between these two methods is how the CGI script accesses the form data. The URL in ACTION="*URL*" points to the CGI script to which the form data should be sent (when the form is submitted).

The CGI script needs to be able to handle the form data by the proper method—either GET or POST. If the FORM element uses a method of GET, but the CGI script was written expecting the data to come from a POST, the script will not find the form data. While it is possible to write CGI scripts so that they accept via either GET or POST, it shouldn't be necessary if you're sure to use the same method in the FORM element as you do in the CGI script (although many CGI libraries exist that can handle both GET and POST transparently). Also, notice that GET and POST are used in all capital letters.

NOTE: Many (if not all) servers expect GET and POST, not get or Get or any other combination of upper- and lower-case letters. If you use anything other than all-uppercase GET and POST, your form (or rather, the CGI script which handles the form) may not function.

Your form must contain a Submit button, which is created using an INPUT form element of type submit (⟨INPUT TYPE=submit⟩). When the Submit button is pressed by the user, the form data is gathered, the CGI script is invoked, and the data is sent to the script. Without a Submit button, the CGI script will never be invoked, so you might have a nice-looking form but it won't actually do anything. In addition, you may have a Reset button, also formed with the INPUT form element (⟨INPUT TYPE=reset⟩). The Reset button, when selected by the user, erases all data that the user has entered, and resets all fields and buttons to their default text or state. The locations of the Submit and Reset buttons are not important, but conventionally are placed near each other at the bottom of the form.

HTML Form Elements

The main HTML form elements are INPUT, SELECT, and TEXTAREA. The INPUT element can be a small (one-line) text-entry box, a password entry box (where typed characters are not echoed to the screen), or check boxes or radio buttons. Figure 8.5 shows the different types of INPUT element styles displayed on a graphical Web browser. The SELECT element is a menu of options, from which one or more items can be selected. The TEXTAREA element is a larger (multiline) text-entry box. Figure 8.6 shows the

- Text input field: |Text
- Password input field: |*****
- Radio buttons: ◆Red ◇White
- Checkboxes: ▪Purple ⬜Pink
- Submit form button: **Submit Query**
- Reset form button: **Reset**|

Figure 8.5
INPUT Fields (Netscape)

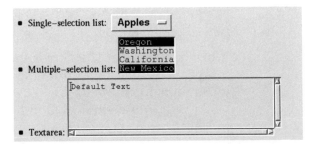

Figure 8.6
SELECT Lists and
TEXTAREA Field
(Netscape)

two types of SELECT menus (in the first, only one item from the menu can be selected; in the second, any number of menu items may be selected) and a TEXTAREA. HTML 3.0 adds a variety of new form elements, including new types for the INPUT element and a drawable figure input element. Because these new form elements are not currently implemented, they will not be discussed here, but their eventual use is likely to be similar to the current form elements.

The INPUT *Form Element*

The INPUT element is used like this:

⟨INPUT NAME="*name*" TYPE=*type other-ATTRIBUTES*⟩

name is the name of the form element, and must be unique within the form (other forms in the same document may share names), except with radio buttons. *type* is the type of INPUT element that this form element will be—text, password, radio, check box, and so on. *other-parameters* may include MAXLENGTH, SIZE, VALUE, and CHECKED, among others (see *Form Elements* in Chapter 13), which specify default sizes or attributes for the form element. The VALUE parameter is especially important. In text-type input fields (TYPE=text or TYPE=password), the VALUE parameter specifies the default text to be displayed in the input field (if there is no VALUE parameter, there is no default text). For check box and radio button types (TYPE=checkbox or TYPE=radio), the VALUE parameter contains the value for the button when selected (unselected buttons are not sent as part of the form data). For form Submit and form Reset buttons (TYPE=submit or

TYPE=reset), the VALUE parameter specifies the name to be displayed on the button.

When data from an INPUT element is sent to a CGI script, the form data uses the NAME from the INPUT element and the value of the input field. The value can either be the data that was entered by the user into a text field, or the value of the VALUE parameter for check box or radio buttons. Text entry fields with no text in them are sent as is; check box or radio buttons that are not selected are not sent. Here is a sample of form data from an INPUT element:

```
username=Tyler+Jones
```

Examples of the INPUT Form Element

To make an input field suitable for having users enter their names:

```
Please enter your name: 〈INPUT NAME="user-name"
TYPE=text SIZE=30〉
```

To make a set of radio buttons, of which only one can be selected at a time, with the first button selected by default:

```
My favorite color is:
〈INPUT NAME="color" TYPE=radio VALUE="red" CHECKED〉Red
〈INPUT NAME="color" TYPE=radio VALUE="purple"〉Purple
〈INPUT NAME="color" TYPE=radio VALUE="brown"〉Brown
```

Because the name of each field is the same ("color"), only one button will be selected at a time, and only the selected button will be sent with the form data to the script (if a second button is pressed by the user, the first button becomes unselected and the second button becomes the new selected button). The values of each button will tell the script which button was selected when the form was submitted. Without the values, the script would not be able to discern which of the three buttons was selected. The button with the value of "red" includes the CHECKED attribute in the INPUT element. This causes that button to be selected by default (when the page is first displayed, and when the form is reset).

To make a form submission button:

```
⟨input type=submit value="Press here to submit
this form"⟩
```

When the form is displayed, the submission button will have "Press here to submit this form" written on it.

The SELECT *Form Element*

The SELECT form element is used like this:

```
⟨select name="name"⟩
⟨option⟩Option 1
⟨option⟩Option 2
⟨option⟩Option 3
⟨/select⟩
```

There can be any number of ⟨option⟩ tags in the list. This example list allows one and only one of the list items to be selected, and is typically displayed as a drop-down menu on graphical Web browsers. By including the MULTIPLE attribute in the SELECT tag (as in ⟨SELECT NAME="name" MULTIPLE⟩), any number of list items may be selected. As with the INPUT element, *name* must be unique within the form—no form elements should have the same name (excepting, as mentioned before, certain cases involving radio buttons).

When data from a SELECT element is sent to a CGI script, the form data uses the NAME from the SELECT element and the value of whichever list item was selected. The value is either the value of the VALUE attribute for that list item, or the text of the list item if the VALUE attribute is not defined (see example below). In the case of a multiple-selection list (such as the SELECT tag with the MULTIPLE attribute), each list item that was selected is sent individually, each using the NAME of the SELECT element. This can confuse some form-data extraction routines in CGI scripts, because multiple entries in the form data have the same NAME value (this is the only case where you would expect this to happen; any other time the form data has multiple entries with the same NAME value, someone didn't design the form correctly), so each new piece of data overwrites the previous data. The Perl code given in the Unix section for parsing form data has this problem. If you will be using multiple-selection lists in a form and subsequent CGI script, be sure to modify the data parsing code to handle this situation. To modify the Perl parsing code, you could change the line that reads:

```
$form{$name} = $value;
```

to something like this:

```
if ($form{$name}) #If this form element name already exists
{
    #Append the data in this form element to whatever data already exists.
    $form{$name} .= "\t$value";
}
```

This modification will create a tab-separated list of data with the same NAME values (that is, a multiple-selection list), which will have to be split apart later (in order to use the individual list items). Data from a regular (single-selection) SELECT element might look like this:

```
Favorite+colors=Red
```

Data from a multiple-selection SELECT element might look like this:

```
Favorite+colors=Red&Favorite+colors=Blue&
Favorite+colors=Purple
```

Examples of the SELECT Form Element

A single-selection list without VALUE attributes for list items:

```
⟨SELECT NAME="Favorite color"⟩
⟨OPTION⟩Red
⟨OPTION⟩Blue
⟨OPTION⟩Green
⟨OPTION⟩Purple
⟨/SELECT⟩
```

To make the preceding a multiple-selection list, change the first line to:

```
⟨SELECT NAME="Favorite color" MULTIPLE⟩
```

The same single-selection list with VALUE parameters for list items:

```
⟨SELECT NAME="Favorite color"⟩
⟨OPTION VALUE="1"⟩Red
⟨OPTION VALUE="2"⟩Blue
⟨OPTION VALUE="3"⟩Green
⟨OPTION VALUE="4"⟩Purple
⟨/SELECT⟩
```

When the data from this form element is sent to a CGI script, instead of being Red, Blue, Green, or Purple, the data will be 1, 2, 3, or 4. This can be used to abbreviate the data.

The TEXTAREA Form Element

The TEXTAREA element is used like this:

```
⟨TEXTAREA NAME="name" ROWS=5 COLS=50⟩Default text
⟨/textarea⟩
```

The ROWS parameter specifies how many rows tall the text input box should be (when displayed). Similarly, COLS specifies how many columns wide the text box should be. As with the other form elements, *name* should be unique within the form. TEXTAREAs have no limit on how much text may be entered into them—browsers typically render them as scrollable to allow users to edit text that has scrolled outside the box. Any text between the start and end tags is considered default text and will be initially placed inside the text box when the form is displayed (default text is editable). If you don't require any default text, place the start and end TEXTAREA tags right next to each other.

Data from a TEXTAREA, when sent to a CGI script, is similar to data sent from an INPUT element. The NAME of the element is followed by whatever text was entered to the input box, as in:

```
textfield=Dear+Mom,+Today+I+went+to+the+zoo+
with+my+roommate...
```

Example Form

The following form contains examples of the different types of form elements just described. Figure 8.7 shows a screen shot of the form as it would be displayed using a graphical Web browser.

```
⟨HTML⟩
⟨HEAD⟩
⟨TITLE⟩Example HTML Form⟨/TITLE⟩
⟨/HEAD⟩
⟨BODY⟩
⟨p⟩This is an example HTML form. Please fill in the information below
and press the SUBMIT THIS FORM button at the bottom of the form. Or,
you may use the RESET THIS FORM button to erase what you have
entered.

⟨HR⟩
```

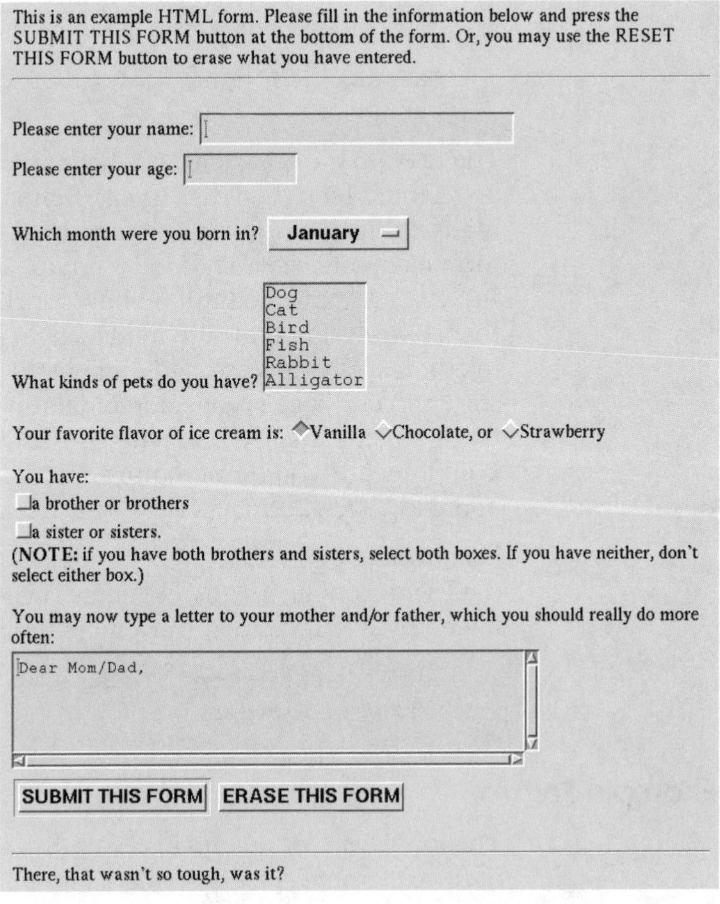

Figure 8.7

Example HTML Form
(Netscape)

```
⟨FORM METHOD=POST
ACTION="http://www.somewhere.
com/cgi-bin/example-form.pl"⟩
Please enter your name: ⟨INPUT NAME="name"
SIZE=30⟩⟨BR⟩
Please enter your age: ⟨INPUT NAME="age" SIZE=10⟩

⟨p⟩Which month were you born in? ⟨SELECT NAME="birthmonth"⟩
⟨OPTION⟩January   ⟨OPTION⟩February   ⟨OPTION⟩March
⟨OPTION⟩April     ⟨OPTION⟩May        ⟨OPTION⟩June
⟨OPTION⟩July      ⟨OPTION⟩August     ⟨OPTIOn⟩September
⟨OPTION⟩October   ⟨OPTION⟩November   ⟨OPTION⟩December
⟨/SELECT⟩

⟨p⟩What kinds of pets do you have? ⟨SELECT NAME="pets" MULTIPLE⟩
⟨OPTION VALUE="d"⟩Dog        ⟨OPTION VALUE="c"⟩Cat
⟨OPTION VALUE="b"⟩Bird       ⟨OPTION VALUE="f"⟩Fish
⟨OPTION VALUE="r"⟩Rabbit     ⟨OPTION VALUE="a"⟩Alligator

⟨/SELECT⟩

⟨p⟩Your favorite flavor of ice cream is:
⟨INPUT NAME="icecream" TYPE=radio VALUE="vanilla" CHECKED⟩Vanilla
⟨INPUT NAME="icecream" TYPE=radio VALUE="chocolate"⟩Chocolate, or
⟨INPUT NAME="icecream" TYPE=radio VALUE="strawberry"⟩Strawberry

⟨p⟩You have:⟨BR⟩
⟨INPUT NAME="brother" TYPE=checkbox⟩a brother or brothers⟨BR⟩
⟨INPUT NAME="sister" TYPE=checkbox⟩a sister or sisters.⟨BR⟩
(⟨STRONG⟩NOTE:⟨/STRONG⟩ if you have both brothers and sisters, select
both boxes. If you have neither, don't select either box.)

⟨p⟩You may now type a letter to your mother and/or father, which you
should really do more often:⟨BR⟩
⟨TEXTAREA NAME="letter" ROWS=10 COLS=50⟩Dear Mom/Dad,
```

```
〈/TEXTAREA〉
〈INPUT TYPE=submit VALUE="SUBMIT THIS FORM"〉 〈INPUT TYPE=reset
VALUE="ERASE THIS FORM"〉
〈/FORM〉
〈HR〉
p〉There, that wasn't so tough, was it?
〈/BODY〉
〈/HTML〉
```

CGI Script Examples

This section gives CGI script examples for common uses of CGI scripts, including 〈ISINDEX〉, forms, and dynamic documents. These are written in Perl under the Unix operating system, but will run under DOS/Windows with no changes and under Macintosh with the change mentioned in the Macintosh section of this chapter (except as noted).

Example with 〈ISINDEX〉—States and Capitols

```
#!/bin/perl

#Print the MIME header print "Content-type: text/html\n\n";

#If there is nothing in the QUERY_STRING environment variable,
# print a page with ISINDEX in the head of the document and tell
# the user what to do.
if (!$ENV{'QUERY_STRING'})
{
    #The next line says "print until you see the word 'end_of_page'"
    print 〈〈end_of_page
〈html〉
```

```
〈HEAD〉
   〈TITLE〉ISINDEX Sample CGI Script〈/TITLE〉
   〈ISINDEX〉
〈/HEAD〉
〈BODY〉
〈H2〉States and Capitols〈/h2〉
This is a searchable index of state capitols. Type in the name of a
state, and I'll tell you the name
of the capitol city.
〈/BODY〉
〈/HTML〉
end_of_page
;
}
else
#Else there was data in QUERY_STRING, so search the database (text file)
# for the state and print it's capitol city.
{
   $state_name=$ENV{'QUERY_STRING'};
   #Translate any plus signs in the query_string into spaces. Remember
   # that the query_string gets URL encoded just like form data.
   $state_name=~ tr/+/ /;
   if (!open(FILE, "capitols.txt"))
   {
      print "ERROR: Couldn't open capitols.txt data file. Aborting.");
      exit(0);
   }
   while (〈FILE〉)
   {
      chop;
      ($state, $capitol) = split(/=/,$_);
      $states{$state}=$capitol;
   }
   close(FILE);
   print 〈〈end_of_page
〈HTML〉
〈HEAD〉
   〈TITLE〉ISINDEX Sample CGI Script Results〈/TITLE〉
```

```
</HEAD>
<BODY>
end_of_page
;

    #If the state the user entered is in the database,
    # print the capitol city.
    if ($states{$state_name})
    {
        print <<end_of_page
<H2>The state of $state_name was in my database.</H2>
The capitol of $state_name is $states{$state_name}.
end_of_page
;

    }
    else
    #Else the state wasn't in the database, so let the user
    # know they probably made a typo.
    {
        print <<end_of_page
<H2>I've never heard of $state_name.</H2>
Are you sure that $state_name really exists?
end_of_page
;

    }
    print <<end_of_page
</BODY>
</HTML>
end_of_page
;
}
```

The `capitols.txt` *File*

```
Alabama=Montgomery
Alaska=Juneau
Arizona=Phoenix
Arkansas=Little Rock
California=Sacramento
```

```
[...]
Oregon=Salem
Pennsylvania=Harrisburg
[...]
Wyoming=Cheyenne
```

Changes for Macintosh

None required. The data file `capitols.txt` must be located in the same folder as the CGI script. To turn this into a CGI script, run MacPerl, enter the text of the script, then do a Save As to a MacHTTP CGI Script.

Changes for DOS/Windows

Create a wrapper script that looks like this:

```
c:\perl\perl c:\httpd\cgi-dos\isindex.pl ) %output_file%
```

where `isindex.pl` is the name of the CGI script, and the paths to both the Perl interpreter and the CGI script are correct for your system. Place the wrapper and CGI scripts in the `\httpd\cgi-dos` directory. Change the line of the Perl script that reads:

```
open(FILE, "capitols.txt")...
```

to:

```
open(FILE, "c:/httpd/cgi-dos/capitols.txt")...
```

or change the path to wherever the data file is located on your system. Remember to use forward slashes!

Example Handling Forms

This script will print out all data coming from a form. It won't actually *do* anything with the data—that is left for you to decide and fill in where necessary.

```
#!/bin/perl

#Print out a MIME content-type
print "Content-type: text/html\n\n";
```

```
#Get the form data from either standard in or the QUERY_STRING
# environment variable
    #If the environment variable CONTENT_LENGTH is defined, take the form
    # data from standard in
if ($ENV{'CONTENT_LENGTH'})
{
    read(STDIN, $buffer, $ENV{'CONTENT_LENGTH'});
}
else
    #Else take the form data from the QUERY_STRING environment variable
{
    $buffer=$ENV{'QUERY_STRING'};
}

#Split the name-value pairs from the form data at each ampersand ('&')
@pairs = split(/&/, $buffer);

#Now, for each name=value pair, split at the equal sign ('='). The name
# will become an associative array key, the value will become the data
for
# that key. Then, decode the URL-encoded names and values.
foreach $pair (@pairs)
{
    ($name, $value) = split(/=/, $pair);

    #Un-URL-encode plus signs and %-encoding
    $value =~ tr/+/ /;
    $value =~ s/%([a-fA-F0-9][a-fA-F0-9])/pack("C", hex($1))/eg;

    #If this name already has an entry in the associative array, then
    # append the new data onto the old, separated by a comma. This should
    # only happen with multiple-selection lists.
    if ($form_data{$name})
    {
        $form_data{$name} .= ",$value";
    }
    else
```

```perl
    #Else create an entry in the associative array.
    {
        $form_data{$name} = $value;
    }
}

#Print out a title and other introductory information
print <<end_of_page
<HTML>
<HEAD>
    <TITLE>Form Data Results</TITLE>
</HEAD>
<BODY>
<H2>Form data results</H2>
Following is a list of all the data that was
entered in the form.
<HR>
end_of_page
;

#Now print out the form data, sorted alphabetically by name

foreach $key (sort (keys (%form_data)))
{
    print "$key = $form_data{$key}\n";
}

#Lastly, print out the tail information for the HTML page
print "</body></HTML>\n";
```

Changes for Macintosh

Change the line of the script that reads:

```perl
        read(STDIN, $buffer, $ENV{'CONTENT_LENGTH'});
```

with:

```perl
        sysread(STDIN, $buffer, $ENV{"CONTENT_LENGTH"});
```

Changes for DOS/Windows

Create a wrapper script that looks like this:

```
c:\perl\perl c:\httpd\cgi-dos\form-data.pl < %content_file% > %output_file%
```

where `form-data.pl` is the name of the CGI script, and the paths to both the Perl interpreter and the CGI script are correct for your system. Place the wrapper and CGI scripts in the `\httpd\cgi-dos` directory.

Example of Distributing Load

A Web service may be too popular for the server it's being run on. When the server gets overloaded, everything runs slower, causing even more overload. To alleviate this problem, the service needs to run on more than one machine, so that the machines can each handle a smaller percentage of the total use of the service. One common method of distributing load is to put a note on the main server that mentions the availability of *mirrors*, additional sites hosting the same data or service, for the user to connect to (instead of using the main server). But this still requires the user to connect to the main site (at least the first time), then choose a mirror. (In the future, users may use the mirror for all of their work, thereby alleviating the main site even more.) However, through CGI and the `Location:` HTTP directive, a script can be used instead to automatically route accesses through a set of mirrors, in round-robin format, to distribute the total work load approximately evenly over all available mirrors. A mirror may be an additional computer located at your site set up with the same information, or it may be a site located somewhere else entirely, also set up with the same information. The sites used in this example are fictitious, but the implementation is still valid.

```perl
#!/bin/perl

#Initialize variables containing the paths and names of files which this
# script uses.

#The tracking file keeps track of which entry in the list of servers was
# last used.
$tracking_file="tracking/tracking.txt";
#The server file contains a list of servers (URLs) to cycle through.
$server_file="distribute-servers.txt";
```

```perl
#$servernum counts how many servers are in the list.
$servernum=0;

#Try to open the server file; if it can't be opened, print an error page
# and exit.
if (!open(SERVERS, $server_file))
{
   print "Content-type: text/html\n\n";
   print <<end_of_page
<HTML>
<HEAD>
   <TITLE>Load Distribution Error</TITLE>
</HEAD>
<BODY>
   <H2>Load Distribution Error</H2>
   There has been an error in the load distribution script. The
server file
   "distribute-servers.txt" could not be opened.
   Please contact the owner of this page.
</BODY>
</HTML>
end_of_page
;
   exit(0);
}
#The server file was opened okay, so read the list of URLs contained
# therein.
while (<SERVERS>)
{
   chop;
   if ($_ ne "")
   {
      $servers[$servernum++]=$_;
   }
}
close(SERVERS);

#If there were no URLs in the server file, print an error page and
# exit.
if ($servernum<=0)
```

```
{
    print "Content-type: text/html\n\n";
    print <<end_of_page
<HTML>
<HEAD>
    <TITLE>Load Distribution Error</TITLE>
</HEAD>
<BODY>
    <H2>Load Distribution Error</H2>
    There has been an error in the load distribution script. There
are no
    sites in the file "distribute-servers.txt" in the current
directory.
    Please contact the owner of this page, bob\@freedonia.com.
</BODY>
</HTML>
end_of_page
;
    exit(0);
}

#Open the tracking file and read out the number of the last URL we
# re-directed to.
open(TRACKING, $tracking_file);
read (TRACKING, $last_server, 10);
close(TRACKING);

#Add one to the tracking number, so that this time we'll re-direct
# the client to the next URL in the list. If we go past the
# end of the list, start back over at the first URL.
$this_server=$last_server+1;
if ($this_server )= $servernum)
{
    $this_server=0;
}

#Write the tracking number back to the tracking file. If we
# can't open the tracking file, print an error page and exit.
```

```
if (!open (TRACKING, ")$tracking_file"))
{
    print "Content-type: text/html\n\n";
    print <<end_of_page
<HTML>
<HEAD>
    <TITLE>Load Distribution Error</TITLE>
</HEAD>
<BODY>
    <H2>Load Distribution Error</H2>
    There has been an error in the load distribution script. The
tracking file
    "tracking.txt" could not be opened for output. Please contact the
owner
    of this page, bob\@freedonia.com.
</BODY>
</HTML>
end_of_page
;
    exit(0);
}
#Else
print TRACKING "$this_server";
close(TRACKING);

#Finally, if everything else has worked correctly,
print out a re-direction
# HTTP header so that the client will
automatically go to a new URL.
print "Location: $servers[$this_server]\n\n";
```

Notes for Unix

The `tracking/tracking.txt` file must be readable and writable by the script.

Changes for Macintosh

Change the line that reads:

```
$tracking_file="tracking/tracking.txt";
```

to:

```
$tracking_file="tracking.txt";
```

The files `tracking.txt` and `distribute-servers.txt` must be located in the same folder as the CGI script. To turn this into a CGI script, run MacPerl, enter the text of the script, then do a Save As to a MacHTTP CGI Script.

Changes for DOS/Windows

Create a wrapper script that looks like this:

```
c:\perl\perl c:\httpd\cgi-dos\distribute.pl ) %output_file%
```

where `distribute.pl` is the name of the CGI script, and the paths to both the Perl interpreter and the CGI script are correct for your system. Place the wrapper and CGI scripts in the `\httpd\cgi-dos` directory. Change the line that reads:

```
$tracking_file="tracking/tracking.txt";
```

to:

```
$tracking_file="c:/httpd/cgi-dos/tracking.txt";
```

and the line that reads:

```
$server_file="distribute-servers.txt";
```

to:

```
$server_file="c:/httpd/cgi-dos/distribute-servers.txt";
```

Or, for both these lines, change the pathnames to wherever you place these data files on your system. Remember to use forward slashes!

9

Security

Security is a slippery issue, especially on the Internet. As an infostructure maintainer you are faced with a few conflicting goals: making some information freely available, keeping other information available only to authorized users, and keeping some information hidden away from everybody. The first and last goals are easy; making information available is what this book is about, and keeping information from everyone is easily accomplished by not putting it on an Internet-connected computer in the first place. It's the middle task that is complicated.

There are two points at which you need to be concerned about your data falling "into the wrong hands" (as it were). The first is by your system's security being compromised, allowing an external intruder access to some or all of your filesystem. This can happen any number of ways, and most of those ways do not fall under the provenance of this book. However, the issues in this area that are directly related to running a Web server are covered in the next section *System Security* (and we have listed some books that address the subject of general system security in more depth in the Bibliography). Related to this is the ability to restrict access to data served by your server, limiting access to specific authorized users, or to certain authorized hosts or domains. This is covered in *Access Control and Basic Authentication* a little later.

The second point is when your data is being transmitted over the network, where it is possible for unintended recipients to intercept the data being sent from your Web server to readers. Unless you are using TCP/IP tools that support encryption, all data you send across the Internet (whether it be via HTTP or through a telnet session) is sent in the clear. *Clear data* is data that can be read or interpreted by anyone who sees it; for example, the clear text sent in a telnet session includes the keystrokes you type and the responses you receive from the remote system. *Encrypted data* is data that is encoded with some sort of shared secret between the sender and the recipient, and that is gibberish to anyone who does not know the secret. An encrypted telnet session transmits the same data that a clear one does, but an idle passerby who happens to read the packets being exchanged between you and the remote system would not be able to decode them into a recognizable form (unless he or she knew the secret!).

This includes things like login names, passwords, and any potentially sensitive data you care to transmit. This means that even if you utilize basic name/password authentication schemes to restrict access to data, that data is still effectively made public when it is transmitted across the network. (This isn't quite as bad as it sounds—for one thing, the data is not actually transmitted to every host on the Internet, just to those routers and LANs used to relay it from you to your readers. But it's still dangerous.) The solution to this is to encrypt the data before it is sent, which is covered in *Encryption and Authentication*.

So do you need security? That depends on how important it is to you that your data remain private. If your infostructure is serving information with no restrictions, then you only need to worry about system security. If you are planning on accepting or transmitting sensitive information (including credit card numbers), you'll want a server that can support encryption. If you are planning on maintaining a user database, and do simple tracking of who is using your site for demographic purposes, encryption is probably a bit overpowering (and you'll want to think seriously about the wisdom of using a medium like the Web—which is essentially stateless—to maintain any sort of stateful connection which implied by someone "logging in" to a service).

Of course, the best way to achieve security is not to put your machine on the network in the first place, but that's not a viable option if you want to place your infostructure on the Internet.

System Security

Unix

Most system security problems revolve around Unix systems, simply by virtue of the sheer number of daemons and servers and users and groups and passwords and . . . well, you get the picture. The problem is not that Unix lacks security facilities, but that managing the security facilities can be a complex and daunting task. While we can't help you with all of these problems (since most of them are out of the scope of this book), we can help you with the ones that relate to running an httpd.

Make sure to use Unix to your advantage, not to your detriment. With NCSA httpd, it is possible to start the server as root, and to have it change the user it is running as (see Chapter 6 for more details). The best approach to running your httpd is to create a new user called `"web,"` and to put it in the group `"nogroup"` (or the equivalent), giving it virtually no permissions.

Next, create a group, `"webfolks,"` and add any users who will be doing development work on your main infostructure to this group. Make sure the document tree is owned by the "webfolks" group, so that any subdirectories and documents created will also be owned by "webfolks." Then make sure that these documents have the group read and write permissions turned on, and that they are globally readable (so that the Web server can read them).

What's the advantage to this? Well, first, it means that you can have a team of maintainers, rather than a single one. Second, if your Web server is compromised, it will only be able to read or write to those things that are globally readable or writable. Consider what might happen if the server were run as root, and it turned out there was a security flaw in the server that allowed outsiders to cause httpd to arbitrarily execute programs and write to files.

In addition, you want to think twice before enabling things like server-side includes and CGI scripts for the general user populace (see *Access Control* and *Basic Authentication*). Any script that gets run gets run with the same permissions as the user web, which can lead to nastiness like launching remote xterms to give someone else shell access to your site. If your UserDir directive is set to `public_html`, you can add the following entry in your `access.conf` to sanely identify what your users can do from their directories (notice the use of the "*" wildcard):

```
⟨Directory /*/public_html*⟩
AllowOverride None
Options Indexes
⟨/Directory⟩
```

Also, make sure that you aren't running a server with known security holes (NCSA httpd 1.3 and earlier fits this definition).

Windows and Macintosh

Macintosh and Windows systems are not immune to security problems—in fact, because of the complete lack of any security functionality in the operating system, you are much more reliant on the server you are running to be secure. Under Unix, if someone can fool the server, they are still limited by the access permissions of the server itself. In Windows or MacOS, there are no such guarantees.

Access Control and Basic Authentication

Most servers provide site-based access control and "basic"-level authentication (see Box 9.1), allowing you to restrict accesses to pages, based on two criteria:

• Host and domain names.

• Users (who are verified by means of passwords) or groups of users.

You can use this information to allow or deny access to documents on your server, based on who is trying to access it, and from where they are trying to access it. This can be useful if you have internal information that should not be accessed from out-of-site, if you want to make information available to a small group of people, or if you want to restrict access for other sites that have been abusing the services you have been making available.

This access control means simply that if you restrict access to information based on domain or user, any client attempting to access the information that does not meet the criteria you have specified will *not* be served the information. Any client that does meet the criteria will be served, at which point the document will still be transmitted in clear text across the Internet. Still, this level of access control can be very useful, especially if your main intent is to dissuade idle browsers from poking into information they should not be poking into. Simply preventing information that should remain local from being accessed from off-site will effectively prevent anyone from outside your local network to read the data—they'll never have the chance to intercept and read it!

NCSA & Windows httpd

NCSA and Windows httpd share an almost identical scheme for implementing access control (although Windows httpd provides a slightly more limited set of features). Both have an `access.conf` file that describes the global access configuration (although Windows httpd calls it `access.cnf`), and both have local per-directory access configuration files. The local configuration files are placed in the directory that they affect, and can override the global configuration file (although you can globally prevent any overriding you wish to). The NCSA local access configuration files are named `.htaccess`; the Windows httpd files are named `#htaccess.ctl` (note that any of these filenames can be changed via your server's configuration files—we prefer to assume, of course, that you've used the default values).

These access control files (ACFs) define an access policy on a per-directory basis. This means you cannot allow clients on the machine `good-ship.lollipop.com` to retrieve the document "`stuff.html`" but not to retrieve the document "`secret-stuff.html`" if these documents are both in the directory "`mixed-bag.`" The security directives you provide for a given directory apply toward all documents in that directory.

Building the global `access.conf` file

The global `access.conf` file is much like the other configuration files (`httpd.conf` and `srm.conf`, described in Chapter 6); it contains a list of directives (listed in Table 9.1), one on a line. Blanks lines and comments (lines beginning with "#") are ignored (see Figure 9.1).

The major difference is that `access.conf` also supports what are known as *sectioning directives.* A sectioning directive contains other directives, providing information that applies to all other directives in the section. `Directory`, the first sectioning directive, defines a directory to which all of the other directives within the section refer. Like an HTML element, the `Directory` sectioning directive has a start and end tag, and looks something like this:

```
⟨Directory some-directory⟩
[...any directives which apply to some-
directory...]
⟨/Directory⟩
```

(You cannot nest `Directory` directives.)

some-directory refers to the absolute filename of the directory within your filesystem, not to its URL. Any directives contained within `Directory` apply to *some-directory* and any of its subdirectories. This means you can create a default access configuration for your DocumentRoot directory and have it apply to the

```
# access.conf: Global access configuration
# Online docs at http://hoohoo.ncsa.uiuc.edu/
# I suggest you consult them; this is important and confusing stuff.

# /usr/local/etc/httpd/ should be changed to whatever you set ServerRoot to.
<Directory /usr/local/etc/httpd/cgi-bin>
Options Indexes FollowSymLinks
</Directory>

# This should be changed to whatever you set DocumentRoot to.

<Directory /usr/local/etc/httpd/htdocs>

# This may also be "None", "All", or any combination of "Indexes",
# "Includes", or "FollowSymLinks"

Options Indexes FollowSymLinks

# This controls which options the .htaccess files in directories can
# override. Can also be "None", or any combination of "Options", "FileInfo",
# "AuthConfig", and "Limit"

AllowOverride All
--More--(77%)
```

Figure 9.1

Example `access.conf`

Table 9.1

ACF Configuration
Directives
(NCSA/Windows httpd)

[N=NCSA httpd, W=Windows httpd, G=Global ACF, L=Local ACFs] Directive Name	N	W	G	L	
⟨Directory *directory-name*⟩...⟨/Directory⟩	X	X	X		Sectioning directive that contains other global ACF directives. All global ACF directives contained by the `Directory` directive apply only to that directory (and its sub-directories). Required.
Options *option1 option2 ...*	X	X	X	X	Takes any of the options `None`, `All`, `Indexes`, `FollowSymLinks`, `SymLinksIfOwner-Match`, `ExecCGI`, `Includes`, and `IncludesNoExec`.
None	X	X	X	X	Enables no options.
All	X	X	X	X	Enables all options.
Indexes	X	X	X	X	Allows automatic indexing of directories for which no `index.html` file exists.
FollowSymLinks	X		X	X	Allows httpd to resolve symbolic links (which may potentially lead outside of virtual document tree).
SymLinksIf-OwnerMatch	X		X	X	Allows the server to only follow symbolic links for which the target file/directory is owned by the same user ID as the link.
ExecCGI	X		X	X	Allows CGI scripts (files ending with `.cgi`) to be executed in this directory, even though it is not a CGI directory.
Includes	X		X	X	Allows server-side includes to be performed.
IncludesNoExec	X		X	X	Allows server-side includes, but disables the `exec` include (which runs a specified program and includes the output).
AllowOverride *option1 option2...*	X	X	X		Takes any of the options `None`, `All`, `Options`, `FileInfo`, `AuthConfig`, and `Limit`.
None	X	X	X		Allows no overrides or local ACFs.
All	X	X	X		Allows local ACFs to override all globally set options.
Options	X	X	X		Allows local ACFs to use the `Options` directive to override the global `Options` directive.
FileInfo	X	X	X		Allows local ACFs to use the `AddType` directive.
AuthConfig	X	X	X		Allows local ACFs to use `AuthName`, `AuthType`, `AuthUserFile`, and `AuthGroupFile` directives (see Table 9.2).

Continued.

Table 9.1
continued

[N=NCSA httpd, W=Windows httpd, G=Global ACF, L=Local ACFs] Directive Name	N	W	G	L	
Limit	X	X	X		Allows local ACFs to use the AddType directive.
AddType	X	X	X	X	This directive works exactly as it does in the resource configuration file (see Table 6.5).
DefaultType	X			X	This directive works exactly as it does in the resource configuration file (see Table 6.5).
AddEncoding	X		X	X	This directive works exactly as it does in the resource configuration file (see Table 6.5).
AddDescription	X	X		X	This directive works exactly as it does in the resource configuration file (see Table 6.5).
AddIcon	X	X	X	X	This directive works exactly as it does in the resource configuration file (see Table 6.5).
IndexIgnore	X	X	X	X	This directive works exactly as it does in the resource configuration file (see Table 6.5).
DefaultIcon	X	X	X	X	This directive works exactly as it does in the resource configuration file (see Table 6.5).
ReadmeName	X	X	X	X	This directive works exactly as it does in the resource configuration file (see Table 6.5).

bulk of your infostructure. So, if your DocumentRoot is `/usr/local/etc/httpd/htdocs`, you would start with

```
<Directory /usr/local/etc/httpd/htdocs>
</Directory>
```

Next, you will want to set some defaults. This is done with the `Options` and `AllowOverride` directives. The `Options` directive is a catchall, allowing you to turn on and off specific features of httpd on a per-directory basis. Some of these features must be explicitly enabled, such as allowing the server to generate an index of a directory if no `index.html` file exists, or allowing CGI scripts to be executed from within directories (Table 9.1 lists possible values for the `Options` directory). So, if you wanted to allow automatic indexes to be generated (so that you can provide a directory full of documents without creating a preprepared index file), and to use server-side includes (disallowing, of course, the ability to execute programs and including the output), but you do *not* want to allow CGI scripts to be in directories with documents, you might use:

```
⟨Directory /usr/local/etc/httpd/htdocs⟩
Options Indexes IncludesNoExec
⟨/Directory⟩
```

Since `Indexes` and `IncludesNoExec` are included, these options are activated. Since the others are not, they are not activated.

NOTE: Why would we want to turn on server-side includes, but without allowing the ability to run programs and include the output? For that matter, why disallow CGI scripts in document directories? Because, especially if you have a large user base contributing to your infostructure, it is better to disallow the opportunity for anyone to write a program that will be executed by your Web server. This is not because your users will be intentionally malicious (although they might be); it is more because they might inadvertently create CGI or other scripts that can inadvertently provide a security hole.

The `Options` values that you set will apply to the directory you specify, as well as to all subdirectories. It is possible to override these options using the local ACFs, but you can control the extent to which overriding can occur via the `AllowOverride` directive. Unlike `Options`, `AllowOverride` can only be used within the global ACF, providing the Web administrator with final control over what is and isn't allowed.

For example, to allow local ACFs to override the global `Options` directive, and to provide their own `Limit` information (see *Allowing and Denying Access to Information by Site*, next), you would use:

```
⟨Directory /usr/local/etc/httpd/htdocs⟩
Options Indexes IncludesNoExec
AllowOverride Options Limit
⟨/Directory⟩
```

To allow local ACFs to override any global defaults, use:

```
⟨Directory /usr/local/etc/httpd/htdocs⟩
Options Indexes IncludesNoExec
AllowOverride All
⟨/Directory⟩
```

To disallow local ACFs altogether, use:

```
⟨Directory /usr/local/etc/httpd/htdocs⟩
Options Indexes IncludesNoExec
AllowOverride None
⟨/Directory⟩
```

A list of all `AllowOverride` values is provided in Table 9.1. Be careful in how you allow overrides; for example, permitting `Options` to be overridden means that a local ACF can let CGI scripts be allowed from within that directory.

How do you deal with this confusing mess, then? A good way is to recognize that you (probably) have three distinct domains in your infostructure. The first is your main document tree, which you probably have set up to be modifiable only by you and, possibly, by a small group of trusted Web maintainers. If your DocumentRoot is `/usr/local/etc/httpd/htdocs`, you would set up a fairly liberal global access control policy:

```
⟨Directory /usr/local/etc/httpd/htdocs⟩
Options All
AllowOverride All
⟨/Directory⟩
```

The second segment is your CGI scripting area. If you have made a separate area for this, again restricted to a small group of people, you might set an access policy like this:

```
⟨Directory /usr/local/etc/httpd/cgi-bin⟩
Options Indexes FollowSymLinks
⟨/Directory⟩
```

This allows you to make symbolic links in the CGI directory to other programs elsewhere on your fileserver. (There is no need to set `ExecCGI` since this is already a CGI directory.)

Finally, your third segment consists of the mini-infostructures produced by your user base (if you have a user base, and if you allow them to maintain their own Web spaces). If you have set UserDir to `public_html`, you might use something fairly restrictive like:

```
〈Directory /*/public_html*〉
  AllowOverride None
  Options Indexes
〈/Directory〉
```

Notice the use of the "*" wildcard character to match any directory that contains the string `"/public_html."`

Then, if you have specific users whom you trust to create CGI scripts, you can enable them to do so on a user-by-user basis:

```
〈Directory /home/billg/public_html/cgi-bin〉
AllowOverride None
Options Indexes ExecCGI
〈/Directory〉
```

This allows `billg` (whose home directory is `/home/billg`) to create a `cgi-bin` subdirectory in his `public_html` directory, where he can put CGI scripts.

NOTE: When using `ExecCGI` to enable CGI scripts in what are otherwise document directories, be sure to end the CGI scripts with the extension `.cgi`, which distinguishes them from other (static) documents.

There are a few other directives listed in Table 9.1, the remainder deal with overriding defaults set in the resource configuration file, which are described in the table. They can be used in local as well as global configuration files (as indicated in the table), and work exactly the same way as they do in the resource configuration file.

Allowing and Denying Access to Information by Site

Table 9.2 lists the other directives which can be used in ACFs. Unlike those listed in Table 9.1, these can all be used in both the global and local ACFs, and are all available in both NCSA and Windows httpd. Also, unlike those in Table 9.1 (which deal primarily with overriding default configuration options for specific directories), these directives relate specifically to allowing and denying access to information on your site.

Table 9.2

ACF Access Control
Directives

General Access Control directives	
⟨Limit *method1 method2* ...⟩...⟨/Limit⟩	Sectioning directive that contains the Order, Deny, Allow, and Require directives. method1, et al., are a list of HTTP methods (including GET, POST, and PUT) which this directive affects. See *Allowing and Denying Access to Information by Site* for more details.
Order *first,second*	Describes order in which access policies by site will be described. *first* and *second* can be either Allow or Deny.
Deny *site*	Denies access to this directory to a site.
Allow *site*	Allows access to this directory to a site.
Require *type entity1 entity2* ...	Requires that the client accessing the site be authenticated as being the *entity* of type *type*. See *Allowing and Denying Access to Information by User* for more details.

User and Group directives (See *Allowing and Denying Acess to Information by User* for more details.)	
AuthName *name*	Name of the authentication realm.
AuthType *type*	Type of authentication used (must be Basic).
AuthUserFile *filename*	Full pathname of password file used for authentication.
AuthGroupFile *filename*	Full pathname of group file used for authentication.

The most important directive in this set is Limit, which is a sectioning directive (like the Directory directive, just described). It describes which clients can access a particular directory, in conjuction with the Order, Deny, Allow, and Require directives.

The syntax of the Limit directive is somewhat rigorous. First, the opening element of the directive must contain information about which retrieval methods this applies to:

```
⟨Limit GET⟩

⟨/Limit⟩
```

In this case, the directive will affect any accesses made with the HTTP GET protocol (used for retrieving any documents from your server). Note that the capitalization of GET is important. The other options are POST (currently used for submitting form-based information—see Chapter 8) and PUT (currently not implemented, but which will eventually be used for putting information onto servers).

Second, the opening ⟨Limit⟩ directive must be followed by the Order directive. The Order directive specifies the order in which the following Deny and Allow directives will appear. It can be used in two ways (note that there is no space after the comma):

- Order deny,allow: In this form, the Deny directives will first describe which domains will *not* be allowed access to this information. Next, the Allow directives are used to describe the exceptions to these rules. This ordering is useful for describing a very restrictive access policy—first, you deny everyone access, then you make exceptions for those who are allowed to access the directory.

- Order allow,deny: In this form, the Allow directives will first describe which domains are allowed to access the directory, and then the Deny directives will list exceptions. This is useful if you are planning on excluding a relatively small number of sites from accessing a directory—for example, if the yahoos at Miskatonic University are abusing your on-line archive of movies and tying up your connection to the outside world with frivolous downloads. You could deal with them by allowing everyone access, and then denying it to any machine in the .miskatonic.edu domain.

The Order directive is followed by the Deny and Allow directives (in the order you have specified in the Order directive!). The Deny and Allow directives can contain a full host name, a domain name, and IP address (full or partial), or the keyword all.

To put this all together, here are some examples. First, to only allow access to the directory /usr/local/etc/httpd/htdocs/ local for local machines, you might use (assuming, of course, that your local domain name is freedonia.com):

```
⟨Directory /usr/local/etc/httpd/htdocs/local⟩
[...any configuration directives...]
⟨Limit GET⟩
Order deny,allow
Deny all
```

```
Allow .freedonia.com
</Limit>
</Directory>
```

Notice the "." in ".freedonia.com"—this indicates that this is a domain name, and not the full name of a machine. Also notice the enclosing `Directory` directive. The `Limit` directive does not exist in a vacuum; in the global ACF, it must be used in a `Directory` directive, just like any other directive.

For another example, if we wanted to deny access to those yahoos at Miskatonic, we might use something like:

```
<Directory /usr/local/etc/httpd/htdocs/noyahoos>
[...any configuration directives...]
<Limit GET,POST>
Order allow,deny
Allow all
Deny .miskatonic.edu
</Limit>
</Directory>
```

Notice here that we included two methods in the `Limit` directive: GET *and* POST. This means that these limits apply both for retrieving documents and for submitting form information (as opposed to the last example, where it only applied to retrieving documents).

Allowing and Denying Access to Information by User

The `Allow` and `Deny` directives are fine for broad, site-level access control, but they don't provide the ability to fine-tune that control to a person-by-person level. To that end, both NCSA and Windows httpd provide the ability to do user authentication. The four User and Group directives in Table 9.2—`AuthName`, `AuthType`, `AuthUserFile`, and `AuthGroupFile`—enable this level of authentication, in conjunction with the `Require` directive.

`AuthName`, `AuthType`, `AuthUserFile`, and `AuthGroup-File` allow you to describe a set of users and groups of users (sometimes referred to as an *authentication realm*), out of which specific users and groups are allowed to access the directory in question.

For example, your authentication realm might include the users `sara`, `george`, `allison`, `bill`, `hrothgar`, and `pat`. It might also define two groups of users: the `techheads` (which include `sara`, `allison`, and `bill`), and the `coffeejockeys` (which include `george`, `allison`, and `pat`). (Notice that at least one user, `allison`, is in both groups, while another, `hrothgar`, is not in a group at all!)

To define such an authentication realm, we would need to set up a password and a group file for the realm. The password file is of a similar format to the Unix password file, including the name of the user and the encrypted password:

```
sara:AsZcoikRa9YKE
george:Japl8mqI9WiTY
allison:nP0MhVKsbmlnQ
bill:YLOPC6AZU7cFM
hrothgar:vTPkzibTiSIBs
pat:qn6cfbzTFlA5A
```

To manage this file, you use the `"htpasswd"` program (included in the `support` directory of both the NCSA and Windows httpd distributions). `htpasswd` takes two arguments, the name of the password file and the name of the user being added (or edited into) the password file. So, to create a new password file, you might use:

```
darwin% htpasswd -c /usr/local/etc/httpd/conf/ourusers sara
Adding password for sara.
New password: (type the new password here - it will not be echoed)
Re-type new password: (re-type the new password - it will not be echoed)
```

The `-c` flag means that `htpasswd` will create a new password file. Note that we recommend you use the `conf` subdirectory to store your password and group files, making it easier to keep track of them.

To add another user to your (now created) password file, you would omit the `-c` flag:

```
darwin% htpasswd /usr/local/etc/httpd/conf/ourusers hrothgar
```

```
Adding user hrothgar
New password: (type the new password here - it will not be echoed)
Re-type new password: (re-type the new password - it will not be echoed)
```

> You can edit a user's password with the same command; to edit hrothgar's password, you would use:

```
darwin% htpasswd /usr/local/etc/httpd/conf/ourusers hrothgar
Changing password for user hrothgar
New password: (type the new password here - it will not be echoed)
Re-type new password: (re-type the new password - it will not be echoed)
```

> Once you have created your users, you can also place them into groups. Groups are useful if you have a set of people who will be accessing some shared sets of documents; if you create a group including all of them, you won't have to explicitly list each of them in the ACFs every time you want to give them all access to a directory. The group files are even simpler than the password files. For example, to create our `techheads` and `coffeejock-eys` groups, we would create a file called `ourgroups` in the `/usr/local/etc/httpd/conf` directory that looked something like this:

```
techheads: sara allison bill
coffeejockeys: george allison pat
```

> As you can see, the format is groupname: *user1 user2 ... userN,* with usernames separated by spaces.
>
> Finally (for NCSA httpd), make sure that your Web server can read these files by making them globally readable.
>
> **NOTE:**   There is no requirement for user and password files to be in a special directory. We have chosen to do so in these examples because separating them makes them easier to maintain; and by placing them in a directory that is not served by httpd decreases the chance that your users' passwords will be compromised.
>
> Once you have set up your authentication realm, you can use it to restrict access to directories on a per-user level. For example, to

use the password and groups files we have set up, we will use the four user and group authentication directives like so:

```
⟨Directory /usr/local/etc/httpd/htdocs/coffeestuff⟩
AuthUserFile /usr/local/etc/httpd/conf/ourusers
AuthGroupFile /usr/local/etc/httpd/conf/ourgroups
AuthName OurFolks
AuthType Basic

⟨Limit GET,POST⟩

⟨/Limit⟩
⟨/Directory⟩
```

(We will fill in the `Limit` directive in a moment.) Let's take a look at what the four directives do. The first two, `AuthUser-File` and `AuthUserGroup` should be straightforward—each gives the full pathname of the user or group file that we wish to use for authenticating people who will be accessing the directory.

The third is very simple. `AuthName` gives the name of the authorization realm itself. This is actually completely at your whim; the name you give here does not match up to anything, and is used only by the client. The client, at its option, will display the value of `AuthName` to the user when the user is prompted for a name and password.

Why bother, then? Well, if you are maintaining separate authentication realms, the visual cue offered by `AuthName` will allow users to know which name and password pair they should use to access this particular document. You should pick an authorization realm name for each pair of password and group files, and use it consistently in your ACFs. In this case, we chose OurFolks as the name of the realm.

Our final directive, `AuthType`, is simpler yet, because there is only one type: `Basic`. At some later point, NCSA httpd may support encrypted authentication, and at that point you could use the name of that type of authentication there. But for now, you must supply the "`AuthType Basic`" line, because there is no default value for `AuthType`.

After using these four directives to define your authorization realm, you can then choose users from within that realm who are allowed to access this document. Continuing with our example, it seems only fair that the `coffeejockeys` group should be allowed to access the `coffeestuff` directory. As you may recall, our `coffeejockeys` are `george`, `allison`, and `pat`:

```
⟨Directory /usr/local/etc/httpd/htdocs/coffeestuff⟩
AuthUserFile /usr/local/etc/httpd/conf/ourusers
AuthGroupFile /usr/local/etc/httpd/conf/ourgroups
AuthName OurFolks
AuthType Basic

⟨Limit GET,POST⟩
require user george
require user allison
require user pat
⟨/Limit⟩
⟨/Directory⟩
```

This is the final directive: `require`, which can be used to specify a `group` or a `user` that is authorized to access documents in this directory. The syntax of `require` is:

```
require type entity1 entity2 ... entityN
```

type can be either `"user,"` `"group,"` or `"valid-user."` Any number of entities of that type (that is, any number of users or groups) can be specified, each separated by a space, after the `type` keyword. Thus, instead of listing the three users on separate lines (as we did previously), we can list them with one `require` directive:

```
require user george allison pat
```

Of course, we can do this a different way, because the `coffeejockeys` are already defined as a group:

```
⟨Directory usr/local/etc/httpd/htdocs/coffeestuff⟩
AuthUserFile /usr/local/etc/httpd/conf/ourusers
AuthGroupFile /usr/local/etc/httpd/conf/ourgroups
AuthName OurFolks
AuthType Basic

⟨Limit GET,POST⟩
require group coffeejockeys
```

```
require user hrothgar
⟨/Limit⟩
⟨/Directory⟩
```

What's this? How did `hrothgar` end up in there? Well, `hroth-gar` is a big guy, and he didn't want to be left out, and as it turns out we can mix and match `require` directives to our hearts' content. In fact, it turns out that there's been a little in-office revolution, and all the users in our authentication realm want to be able to look at this nifty `coffeestuff`. Fortunately, that's what the third type of `require` directive is for:

```
⟨Directory usr/local/etc/httpd/htdocs/coffeestuff⟩
AuthUserFile /usr/local/etc/httpd/conf/ourusers
AuthGroupFile /usr/local/etc/httpd/conf/ourgroups
AuthName OurFolks
AuthType Basic

⟨Limit GET,POST⟩
require valid-user
⟨/Limit⟩
⟨/Directory⟩
```

The `valid-user` format implies that any user who appears in the password file is allowed to access these pages.

So what happens when `hrothgar` decides he wants to look at `http://www.freedonia.com/coffeestuff/`? If he has a browser that supports user authentication (and most do), he'll be prompted for his "OurFolks" realm name and password. After entering it (correctly), the httpd daemon will serve him the pages.

Of course, if he enters it incorrectly, he won't be served the pages. NCSA and Windows httpd aren't scared of `hrothgar`.

Building a Local `.htaccess` File

While the global ACF can be used to control access policies for any directory, a global ACF used for such fine control would quickly become very large. Also, since it is a global configuration file, the server would need to be restarted each time the global ACF was modified.

An alternate solution is to use local ACFs. These files reside in the directory that they control, and are equivalent to a global ⟨Directory⟩...⟨/Directory⟩ directive for that directory. Thus, the following entry in the global ACF:

```
⟨Directory /usr/local/etc/httpd/htdocs/coffeestuff⟩
AuthUserFile /usr/local/etc/httpd/conf/ourusers
AuthGroupFile /usr/local/etc/httpd/conf/ourgroups
AuthName OurFolks
AuthType Basic

⟨Limit GET,POST⟩
require group coffeejockeys
require user hrothgar
⟨/Limit⟩
⟨/Directory⟩
```

would be equivalent to the following local ACF file (in its entirety!) in the directory /usr/local/etc/httpd/htdocs/coffeestuff:

```
AuthUserFile /usr/local/etc/httpd/conf/ourusers
AuthGroupFile /usr/local/etc/httpd/conf/ourgroups
AuthName OurFolks
AuthType Basic

⟨Limit GET,POST⟩
require group coffeejockeys
require user hrothgar
⟨/Limit⟩
```

Notice that the only difference is that there is no containing ⟨Directory /usr/local/etc/httpd/htdocs/coffeestuff⟩...⟨/Directory⟩ directive.

To create a local ACF, you create a file called .htaccess (for NCSA httpd) or #haccess.ctl (for Windows httpd) in the directory that will be affected. There are a few limitations; the most important of these is that the only options allowed in a local ACF are those options that are explicitly allowed in the global ACF (via the AllowOverride directive). Thus, in order to include local ACFs in your main document tree that allow access control, you would need to include

```
⟨Directory /usr/local/etc/httpd/htdocs⟩
AllowOverride Limit AuthConfig
```

```
[...remainder of /usr/local/etc/httpd/htdocs
configuration directives...]
</Directory>
```

By explicitly allowing `Limit` and `AuthConfig`, the local ACFs in the main document tree can then do site-by-site and user-by-user access control. Other options that can be allowed in local ACFs (via the `AllowOverride` directive) are `Options` (allowing the `Options` directive to appear in local ACFs), `FileInfo` (allowing the use of the type mapping directives in local ACFs), `None` and `All` (both of which should be self-explanatory).

Note that the preceding `AllowOverride` command does *not* allow users to override the global ACF in their local directories. In that case, you would need to provide an `AllowOverride` in the `<Directory /*/public_html*>` directive.

MacHTTP/WebSTAR

Compared to NCSA and Windows httpd, the MacHTTP (and WebSTAR) access control configuration is a piece of cake. Instead of having a separate global access control file, the MacHTTP access control directives are contained in the `MacHTTP.config` configuration file (see Table 9.3; see Tables 6.9 and 6.10 for other `MacHTTP.config` directives).

The following sections describe how to use the access control directives. The discussions also apply to WebSTAR, although in WebSTAR the directives are modified via the WebSTAR Admin program, rather than by directly editing the `MacHTTP.config` file.

Table 9.3
MacHTTP.config Access Control Directives

Directive	Description
ALLOW *address*	Allows host with names or IP addresses that match *address* (or partially match *address*) to connect to the server.
DENY *address*	Disallows host with names or IP addresses that match *address* (or partially match *address*) to connect to the server.
REALM *substring realm-name*	Provides basic authentication for any URL matching *substring* for users in the authentication realm *realm-name.*

Allowing and Denying Access to Information by Site

Unlike NCSA or Windows httpd, MacHTTP is restricted to allowing or denying access based on machine address to the entire server, not just to documents or directories. This means that if you include any `ALLOW` or `DENY` directives in `MacHTTP.config`, they'll apply to *everything* on the server. In order to provide a finer grain of control (for example, to have some documents globally accessible and other documents only locally accessible), you'll need to run more than one server, each configured differently.

The usage of the `ALLOW` and `DENY` directives is very straightforward. If you use them, then they are evaluated in the order in which they appear. Before any `ALLOW` or `DENY` directive is evaluated, it is assumed that all hosts are first denied. Thus, the series

```
ALLOW .freedonia.com
DENY coffeejockeys.freedonia.com
```

would imply that the only people who can access documents on your server are those accessing it from within the domain ".freedonia.com" (unless they're from that pesky rogue machine, `coffeejockeys.freedonia.com`).

With this scheme, it is easy to restrict access to a small number of hosts, but it is harder to allow access to all but certain specific machines. The technique recommended by the Security Tutorial that comes with MacHTTP is to use:

ALLOW 1
ALLOW 2
ALLOW 3
ALLOW 4
ALLOW 5
ALLOW 6
ALLOW 7
ALLOW 8
ALLOW 9
DENY yahoos.miskatonic.edu

How does this work? Well, the first nine `ALLOW` directives effectively amount to allowing everyone (the more clean `"ALLOW *"` is not valid syntax, for some strange reason), since at least one of the nine digits will match the (numeric) IP address of the client accessing your server. The DENY directive then winnows out specific hosts that are not allowed access. This is a hack, but you take what you can get.

Allowing and Denying Access to Information by User

MacHTTP does provide more sophisticated access control via user- and group-based authentication. This is accomplished through the third access control directive, REALM. REALM that defines an authentication realm—a set of users that are allowed to access documents in that particular authentication realm. The actual users' names and passwords are defined via Passwords... in the Edit menu. To add a new user, you enter the user's name and password, and use the Realms pop-up menu to select a realm in which the user will exist. You can also edit a user's name and password by selecting it from the scrolling list of users presented.

The syntax of the REALM directive itself is

```
REALM substring realm-name
```

If the substring matches the URL being retrieved from the server, that URL is assumed to be in the realm realm-name. The server will require that the user retrieving the document authenticate him- or herself as being one of the users in realm-name.

For example, if you define the realm coffeejockeys, which includes the users george, allison, and pat, you might use the following REALM directive:

```
REALM coffee coffeejockeys
```

Since the substring is "coffee," the following URLs would require authentication for the realm coffeejockeys:

```
http://www.freedonia.com/coffee/index.html
http://www.freedonia.com/coffee/related/java.html
http://www.freedonia.com/history/coffee-and-
freedonia.html
```

as each contains the substring coffee. Thus, if a reader attempted to retrieve the URL http://www.freedonia.com/coffee/related/java.html, he or she would have to authenticate him- or herself as being george, allison, or pat.

As you may notice from the three example URLs given, this is also not quite as sophisticated an authentication scheme as offered by NCSA and Windows httpd. Any URL anywhere on the server may match the substring, and thus require authentication, which means that you need to exercise control over which strings you pick and which filenames you use. On the other hand, compared to the NCSA/Windows httpd authentication mechanism, this is very easy to use.

Encryption and Authentication

Basic authentication and access control are useful mechanisms; but because basic authentication relies on clear text transmission by both client and server, the username, the password, and the document being retrieved are all sent in readable form across the network. Obviously, if you have data that requires serious protection, basic authentication is not a powerful enough solution.

To that end, two major standards for providing encryption for HTTP requests have been proposed: Secure Sockets Layer (SSL), and Secure Hypertext Transport Protocol (S-HTTP). Neither is a standard (yet—see Box 9.1), but most servers are moving toward implementing *both* protocols in order to hedge their bets. Which one "wins" will depend on which one is most widely supported by client software, because your readers, not just your server, must be able to use the encryption method for it to do any good at all.

Secure Sockets Layer

Secure Sockets Layer (SSL) is a protocol developed by Netscape Communications Corporation as a means of ensuring secure application-layer transport of information over TCP/IP. This means that SSL is not tied directly to HTTP; instead, it works at a layer below. This means that SSL can be used underneath other Internet protocols, such as gopher, telnet, or NNTP (the network news transport protocol).

Most encryption mechanisms rely on there being some "secret" that is shared by both the sender and the recipient. In traditional

Box 9.1 So What's the Standard, Anyway?

If you slip on to any of the `comp.infosys-tems.www.*` newsgroups, you'll probably still find heated discussion about how "Netscape is at it again," using the popularity of its browser to subvert the standards-making process, and to make SSL the de facto security standard before it even makes it through the W3C. And depending on how you look at it, this assessment is right—or dead wrong.

The misconception at work here is that the major competitor to SSL, S-HTTP, is an openly developed standard endorsed by the W3C (the World Wide Web Consortium, the standards-making body for the Web), while SSL is a fresh young upstart of the same level of vileness as Netscape-enhanced HTML. It turns out, though, that S-HTTP is nothing of the kind; it is, in fact, just another proposed standard, this time from Enterprise Integration Technologies and Terisa.

In fact, a strong claim could be made that the only "standard" is Basic authentication, the unencrypted authentication scheme already implemented by most servers and clients. In the world of the Web, it's currently hard to find any standards at all—even the HTML 2.0 specification (as we write this) is still just a draft, if a very stable one.

Don't despair, however. Whichever standard the W3C comes out in favor of, most commercial servers seem to be moving toward supporting *both* SSL and S-HTTP, including Netscape's Commerce Server, O'Reilly's WebSite, and Open Market's Secure Web Server. And most browsers will probably move toward this as well. Anyone providing encryption is (most likely) a commercial venture that wants to retain your business, so no matter what happens, your vendor will (probably) take care of you.

encryption, the information is encrypted by some secret key, and can later be decrypted by the same secret key. Thus, for individuals to share information, they must also know the same secret key. The problem with this is in sharing the secret key—how can you safely transmit the key to the other individual?

Public-key encryption technology addresses this problem. It relies on a two-key system: a public key and a private key. These keys are generated in such a way that a message encrypted with the public key can *only* be decrypted by the matching private key; and, vice versa, a message encrypted with the private key can *only* be decrypted by the matching public key. The trick is that the keys are generated such that knowing one key does not enable you to learn what the other key is. In this way, you can safely transmit your public key to anyone, over an insecure network, and then use your private key to securely encrypt transmissions to them.

SSL is based on public-key encryption technology. It is responsible for negotiating the level of security between the two communicators, and for using public and private key information to set up and maintain a secure data stream. Once SSL has been invoked, any further information sent on that stream is encrypted from prying eyes. To the two individuals communicating, however, it appears to be a simple TCP/IP data stream. Thus, it can then be used for any protocol—such as HTTP. User authentication information (such as names and passwords), documents retrieved, and any other information passed along (such as credit card numbers) are encrypted as they pass over the network.

Your readers do not have to do anything special in order to employ SSL—they must simply use a client that supports it (such as Netscape or Emacs-w3, at this writing). On the other hand, as a server maintainer, you must not only obtain a server that supports SSL (currently Netscape's Commerce Server), but you must also generate a public/private key pair. The catch is that the public-key technology involved is licensed by Netscape from RSA (`http://www.rsa.com/`), and you will have to pay a fee for the certificate which validates your key (preventing other servers from impersonating you).

Further information about the Netscape Commerce Server is available at:

    http://www.netscape.com/

(Also see the review in Chapter 6.)

More information about the SSL protocol is available at

    http://home.netscape.com/newsref/std/

S-HTTP

Secure Hypertext Transfer Protocol (S-HTTP) is a protocol developed by Enterprise Integration Technologies (EIT) and Terisa Systems for transmitting information securely via the HTTP protocol. The main difference between S-HTTP and SSL is one of philosophy—while SSL secures the entire transmission channel, S-HTTP encrypts the document itself being transmitted. Like SSL, S-HTTP relies on public-key technologies. Unlike SSL, S-HTTP sends key information as part of HTTP itself, rather than negotiating encryption before the HTTP connection is even made.

Your readers do not have to do anything special to employ S-HTTP, other than using a client that supports it (currently this includes Spry's AIR Mosaic). You will need to use a server that supports S-HTTP (currently this includes Spry's Internet Office Server and Open Market's Secure Web Server).

More information about Spry's Internet Office Server is available at:

```
http://www.spry.com/sp_prod/officeserver/svrsheet.
html
```

More information about Open Market's Secure Web Server is available at:

```
http://www.openmarket.com/omi/products/secureweb.
html
```

More information about the S-HTTP protocol is available at:

```
http://www.terisa.com/
```

10

Publicizing Your Infostructure

You've spent almost a month perfecting your Web site. Everything has been spellchecked; you've triple-checked your CGI scripts and imagemaps; the 3-D rendered buttons have that "just-waxed" shine to them; and your site is filled to the brim with content. Finally, you sit back and watch the access log, ready for the world to come beating a path to your virtual doorstep. You wait. And wait. And wait. After a week without so much as a digital nibble, you start wondering what's wrong. Is your Internet connection down? Did you forget to change the file permissions on your HTML documents? Did everyone on the Internet suddenly go to bed?

Not even close. What you forgot to do was *advertise* your new infostructure space. Even a Web site that held the cure for cancer, 10 guaranteed get-rich-quick schemes, *and* undeniable proof that UFOs exist isn't going to get many visitors, and certainly not droves and droves of them, if it isn't advertised.

Advertising your Web on the Internet and Elsewhere

Advertising on the Internet isn't as simple as sending e-mail to everyone announcing the availability of your new site. If it were, everyone would get hundreds of e-mail messages a day just regarding new Web pages. This and other "brute force" methods of Web announcing (including sending a message to all known newsgroups) are neither efficient nor accepted—the Internet community hates this kind of broadband junk mail. Despite what some claim, junk mail (and Usenet articles) will more likely

317

provoke complaints and avoidance of your site, rather than increasing your readership and popularity.

Fortunately, precedent and planning have created a number of acceptable, high-visibility methods for advertising new Web sites and services on the Internet, ranging from mailing lists to newsgroups to Web pages devoted to nothing but announcing new and improved places on the World Wide Web and Internet. Through these, it is easy to get out there and get noticed by a large number of people. After all, what use is a Web site if nobody ever sees it?

What Do You Have to Offer?

Before you even begin to think about advertising your infostructure, you need to determine what it is that your site has that other people are going to be interested in. If your site consists solely of pictures of your pet turtle because you couldn't think of anything more useful to publish on the Web, perhaps it isn't the right time to promote it everywhere. If, on the other hand, your site contains information about your company or institution, a product or products, a service, idea, or other kinds of promotional materials, then advertising your site is probably the right thing to do.

As more and more information gets published on the World Wide Web and the Internet in general, what a site has to offer (its "content") is going to determine its success (if it doesn't already). A list of your favorite links on the Web might be interesting once, but when the novelty wears off, who is going to want to come back to it? The World Wide Web is well past the stage when anyone can put anything on a Web page and people will visit it, just because it is new. The Web is now used for research, business, advertising, education, politics, communication, and entertainment by millions of people around the world, and they are constantly hungry for information that they can use.

Thus the importance of content, of having something that people will be interested in and want to come back to. However, don't let this scare you off. Just because your Web site doesn't offer foreign language training or marriage counseling on-line doesn't mean people won't find it interesting. But it does mean you have to discriminate between information and hype. Do you genuinely offer something to people who are visiting your site, or is it just eye candy? There's no governing body of "content police" on the Internet who are going to tell you that your site isn't interesting and doesn't have anything to offer, then take away your access—you have to be your own judge of what you publish.

Once you've thought about what your site has to offer, or perhaps gone back and added some content so that people will now find your site interesting and useful, it's time to take the plunge and put your name out there on the digital newswire.

Starting Points: Announcing Your Web

As with any new product, business, or service, your first action should be to announce the availability of your Web. This is the fastest way to reach the most people, and for some things this may be all that you need. Once word of your Web is out there, many things start to happen on their own, including word of mouth and eventual inclusion in various Web indices. How far the news of your Web goes on its own, once it's announced, is largely dependent on how many people think what it has is interesting or useful enough to remember and, therefore, tell others about. But no matter how far news of your site might spread, an announcement is the best, and simplest, form of advertising your Web.

NCSA's What's New with the World Wide Web

The NCSA *What's New* site accepts submissions of new, moved, or updated Web sites, and routinely releases these submissions via the *What's New* Web page. This site was one of the first, and remains one of the foremost, Web announcement methods on the Internet. Submissions can be made by e-mail or through a form at the site. At this writing, NCSA generates a new list of announcements every Monday, Wednesday, and Friday. Lag time for submissions is approximately two weeks from when you submit your announcement until when it appears. Announcements made to the NCSA *What's New* page automatically get indexed into the W3 Catalog, a Web-searchable archive of Web sites, so that your site is available to searchers almost immediately after your announcement comes out.

What's New is available via the URL

```
http://www.ncsa.uiuc.edu/SDG/Software/Mosaic/Docs/
whats-new.html
```

and the W3 Catalog is at

```
http://cuiwww.unige.ch/w3catalog
```

Usenet Newsgroups: comp.infosystems. www.announce

The comp.infosystems.www hierarchy of newsgroups has grown substantially in the last year, and is up to 15 newsgroups at this writing. Announcements of various servers and sites can still be found in the other comp.infosystems.www newsgroups, but the preferred location is through comp.infosystems.www.announce, a moderated newsgroup specifically for announcing new, moved, or updated Web sites. Lag time is shorter here than at NCSA, but it still may take a week or more for your submission to be posted to the newsgroup (as is the way with moderated newsgroups).

The moderator must okay all submissions, so if your notice is not formatted according to the guidelines for submission, it will be returned to you without being posted. It is a good idea to follow the newsgroup for a few weeks, and to read the FAQ, before posting your announcment. The audience of this newsgroup is approximately as large as that of the NCSA *What's New* page, though its throughput is slightly less—typically between 200 and 400 announcements are posted weekly.

The comp.infosystems.www.announce charter (and further information about the group) is available via the Web at

```
http://www.halcyon.com/grant/charter.html
```

Net-Happenings

Net-Happenings is a Usenet newsgroup (`comp.internet.net-happenings`), a Web site, and a mailing list; in addition, various archives containing Net-Happenings announcements are available. Net-Happenings is a service of InterNIC Directory and Database Services, moderated by Gleason Sackman, whose purpose is to announce new, updated, and interesting Internet services, servers, and sites along with a variety of Internet media. Its function is similar to the previous two resources, except that it covers a wider variety of Internet resources, not just new or updated Web sites.

The Net-Happenings Web site includes a searchable index of previous announcements and an on-line submission form with which you can make your own announcement. All submissions are checked by Gleason Sackman before they are posted to the Web site, newsgroup, and mailing list. The format for submission is similar to the previous resources, which includes a URL, brief description, and a subject heading. Announcements are posted to the Web site twice daily during the week, and generally range from 10 to 50 announcements per day.

The Net-Happenings Web site is at

```
http://www.mind.net/NET/
```

Announcements by Subject: Newsgroups and Mailing Lists

If your Web site (or some subset of it) has a particular audience in mind, there are further announcement possibilities for contacting just those individuals who are most likely to be interested in what your site has to offer. For example, a Web site covering the chemistry department of a university may want to announce its existence to other chemists on the Internet. Or, a site that offers an on-line chess game would want to let other chess players know that the site existed. This kind of specificity can only be achieved through newsgroups and mailing lists, because these are the only forms of mass media on the Internet. Only those people who are genuinely interested in the subject matter read newsgroups such as `sci.chemistry` (a chemistry-related newsgroup) or are subscribers to mailing lists such as `Chess-L` (a chess-related mailing list). So if your site fits in with a particular subject area, this is a good way to reach additional folks who might actually be interested in what your site has to offer.

Finding the Right Newsgroup

Your Internet provider will carry some subset of all the existing newsgroups in the world (or may possibly carry every single newsgroup available everywhere), if you have access to newsgroups at all (and not everyone does). If you can obtain a list of newsgroups your service provider carries, you may have to go through it by hand, looking for newsgroups that fit a particular subject. If you can get an electronic list, do a keyword search for something dealing with your subject. To announce a Web site devoted to dogs, for instance, you might do a newsgroup search for "dog," "canine," and "pets." If you can't find a way to look through your local newsgroups, here are two Web sites that list newsgroups and descriptions for newsgroups that those sites provide (and to which you might also have access):

- Oxford University Library's Automation Service, Newsgroups Available at Oxford

  `http://www.lib.ox.ac.uk/internet/news/`

- University of Illinois Find-News Script

  `http://www.cen.uiuc.edu/cgi-bin/find-news`

It is acceptable to find a few newsgroups to which you wish to post your announcement. It is not acceptable to send your announcement to *every* newsgroup. This is akin to sending an unwanted e-mail message to everyone on the Internet. Only a small percentage of the newsgroup population may want to read your announcement, and everyone else will become irate. But a properly placed announcement to a few newsgroups whose readers may be interested in your site will not cause anyone hard feelings or be seen as a waste of bandwidth.

Once you think you have found newsgroups with appropriate titles or descriptions, it is a good idea to read the newsgroup for a few weeks, and to read the FAQ (Frequently Asked Questions list; many are available from the Oxford site just given) for the newsgroup (which is usually posted monthly, or more frequently, to the newsgroup). These will give you an idea of what people are talking about over the newsgroup, so you can ensure that your post will be appropriate. It is very important to do this, otherwise you will end up alienating more potential readers than you attract. Being a good Net citizen is important.

Once you are sure that you have a list of appropriate newsgroups to which you want to send your announcement, use your favorite Usenet news program to send out your announcement. Be concise and factual—don't spend 50 lines describing your site and all it has to offer in big, flowery language if you can do it in 20 lines. Focus on why people reading the newsgroup should be interested in your site and what it has for them. Posting to appropriate newsgroups can significantly increase your audience if done correctly.

Finding the Right Mailing List

Mailing lists, or listservs, are similar to newsgroups except that all communication is by e-mail. One person will send a message to the listserv address, and everyone else who subscribes to the mailing list will receive a copy of the message. Replies get sent back to the listserv address and are again distributed to everyone. The audiences for mailing lists generally aren't as large as for newsgroups, but mailing list subscribers tend to be more devotional about a subject, with fewer "lurkers" (individuals who read messages but never actually post to a mailing list or newsgroup).

As with finding the right newsgroup, you'll need to do some searching by keywords relating to your subject or subjects to find the appropriate mailing list. Mailing lists are a bit harder to find than newsgroups, so you'll want to find several of the (semi)inclusive lists available. One of the best sites to search for appropriate mailing lists is Nova Southwestern University's searchable index of Dartmouth College's mailing list database, at:

```
http://alpha.acast.nova.edu/listserv.html
```

The index will search mailing list titles and descriptions for a keyword or phrase, and return address and description information for matching mailing lists. Another good on-line resource is PAML, the list of Publicly Available Mailing Lists. A Web version of PAML is located at

```
http://www.neosoft.com/internet/paml/index-
index.html
```

Finally, there are mailing lists that announce new mailing lists, such as NEW-LIST. You can subscribe to NEW-LIST by sending a message with the body "SUBSCRIBE NEW-LIST Jane Patterson" (replacing "Jane Patterson" with your own name) to "LISTSERV@vm1.nodak.edu." NEW-LIST also supplies two excellent articles providing further information on finding mailing lists, which you can retrieve by sending either of the following two commands in the body of a message to LISTSERV@vm1.nodak.edu:

```
GET NEW-LIST SEARCHES
GET NEW-LIST WOUTERS
```

Once you have found mailing lists that look appropriate for your subject matter, subscribe to them and read the list for a few weeks. As with newsgroups, this gives you a better idea of what people on the list are actually discussing. Once you're sure the mailing lists are appropriate, send a well-thought-out announcement to each mailing list, following the rules for announcing to newsgroups—namely, to be short and to-the-point. You don't need to overwhelm anyone with your verbosity—give an overview of your site and why people might find it interesting, and let the readers of the newsgroup or mailing list decide for themselves.

It is even more important to be careful with mailing lists than with newsgroups, as your messages go directly to people's e-mail boxes. Don't abuse the services of e-mail list providers.

Where Are You? Or, Making Yourself Easy to Find

Announcements hit one breed of Internet surfer—those who keep an eye on the "what's new" resources, looking for new information and sites as soon as they come out. Another breed, the researchers, use the various Web indices to search for information and sites when they need them, so they're not likely to pay much attention to the constant announcements of things they don't need right now. There's a little bit of both breeds in all of us, which is why, after announcing your Web, you should consider submitting it to some (or all) of the more popular Web indices on the Internet.

Web indices generally fall into two categories. The first type of index is the kind the WWW Virtual Library and Yahoo are most famous for—an organized, subject-oriented list of links to sites and servers. These are similar to the yellow pages of the phone book, where each subject heading contains links to sites also dealing with that subject. The second type, the crawlers, worms, and URL archives, function in a much different way. Their content is usually not categorized into subjects; instead, you use keywords to search through titles of Web documents, URLs, or even the text of entire HTML pages, to find locations that might have what you need. These kinds of indices are less user-friendly than subject-oriented indices, but their scope can expand much further than human-assisted subject indexing lists can, because no judgment has to be made about where a new site belongs in relation to other sites, or even if the new site contains useful information or not. Both kinds of indices are useful for different reasons, so it is doubtful that one will ever take over the other.

Subject-Oriented Indices

Subject-oriented indices organize Web pages and sites according to what is the main focus of their content. This makes for more organized browsing, because users can stroll from subject to subject and find a list of related items, or even find new subjects that sound interesting. Before submitting to a subject-oriented index, you'll need to determine the subject area or areas for the page or pages you plan on submitting. If your site is the homepage for a university or business, then try a subject like "education" or "commercial." By "try," we mean that you should browse through the index you plan on submitting to before you actually go through with it. Look for the subject that fits your page or pages, or use the index to narrow down your subject. "Education" may be further subdivided into "K-12," "Secondary School," and "Universities." If you have already made an announcement about your site or page, you may also find that it's already listed in the index you're planning to submit to. If this is the case, and you want to replace the listing with your own, be sure and mention that you want to *update* an entry in the index, not just add a new one.

The World Wide Web Virtual Library

The WWW Virtual Library is a subject-oriented index maintained by volunteers and sponsored by the World Wide Web (W3) Consortium. Individuals volunteer to maintain a particular subject index by collecting links for the index, updating its pages, and generally being referred to as the list's "owner." Because it takes a volunteer to maintain a particular subject, not every conceivable subject may yet have its own index. If this is the case, you may opt to become the owner of a new list covering your subject. You can check the on-line documentation at the WWW Virtual Library, or send e-mail to `www-request@mail.w3.org` for information about starting a new subject index at the Virtual Library.

If your subject is indexed at the WWW Virtual Library, contact the owner of the index to get your site added to that list. All WWW Virtual Library pages should include an e-mail address to contact the owner, and the WWW Virtual Library site includes a list of owners' addresses, along with the page(s) they maintain, for easy reference. The information an owner may want will vary from owner to owner, so it is best to include, in your e-mail, the URL of the site you wish to add and a brief description of the site (what it has that relates to the subject whose owner you are e-mailing. Be sure to include your proper e-mail address, so the owner can contact you for more information regarding your site. Once you have contacted the owner of a subject, it is usually just a matter of time before your site appears on the subject index.

The Virtual Library is available at

```
http://www.w3.org/hypertext/DataSources/bySubject/
Overview.html
```

Yahoo

The largest and best organized subject index on the World Wide Web, Yahoo has made a business of indexing the Web. Additions to Yahoo come from submissions and various other sources, such as Web announcements. Yahoo has an extensive hierarchy of subjects, where you're bound to find almost anything you might possibly build a Web page around. If you don't find a fitting subject, Yahoo will add a subject heading to its index for you.

Submitting to the Yahoo index involves finding the correct subject heading in its hierarchy, and following the "Add" link at the top of the Web page. By filling out the on-line form, you submit your site to the Yahoo index, where it will be reviewed and added under the proper subject. If your subject doesn't exist, Yahoo suggests you submit your site from a nearby subject, and mention in the submission that you would like to create a new subject. In addition, you can modify an existing link via the "Suggest" link at the top of any Yahoo page.

Yahoo is available via the Web from

```
http://www.yahoo.com/
```

New Riders Official World Wide Web Yellow Pages

The New Riders Yellow Pages is just that—a printed index, organized by subject, of resources and services available via the World Wide Web, published by the Macmillan Publishing Company, USA, and authored by Andrew Busey, Larry Colker, and Hank Weghorst. The 1995 edition contains four million resources in 500 pages, and is available in most chain bookstores for easy access. While print media may not seem the best method by which to search for something on the Internet, a well-organized resource in a familiar format will appeal to users. These are the assets of the New Riders Yellow Pages: most children and adults are familiar with yellow pages directories in general, and the New Riders Yellow Pages are clearly laid out and organized for even novice users of the Internet. The New Riders Yellow Pages are currently in their third edition.

Submission to the New Riders Yellow Pages is through the on-line Web form listed here. Submission requirements include title, URL, contact address (owner), subject, and a brief description. Submissions are reviewed before being included in the Yellow Pages, and the owner will be contacted when the entry is approved. Because index is in the print medium, you may have to wait for six months to a year for your entry to appear in the next edition of the New Riders Yellow Pages. You should submit to this resource in conjunction with the previous, Web-based indices, because the previous indices are more quickly updated, faster to search, and used by more people on the Internet.

```
http://www.mcp.com/nrp/wwwyp.submit.html
```

Document-Oriented Indices

Document-oriented indices organize Web pages and sites by the words in their titles, URLs, or entire documents, and allow keyword searching on the resulting database. For example, a search for "flugbog" would return a list of links to pages (or titles, or URLs, depending on the search index) that contained the word "flugbog." This kind of index is less hospitable to the casual browser, but is very useful when trying to find pages that may mention a particular subject. (Try doing a search for your name and see what happens.)

When submitting to a document-oriented index, you typically just give the URL of the document(s) you want to index. There is no subject evaluation involved, so descriptions or other information about the site is unnecessary. Oftentimes, the software that performs the indexing on your page will also follow any links in the page, indexing them as well (and subsequently indexing any links found on these pages, and so on). These are *recursive* indexers. The Web *spiders* and *worms* are examples of such, which index documents by following all possible links in documents they find. Obviously, indexing entire documents is much more space-consuming than just indexing document titles or URLs, so the former is much less common on the Web than the latter, but is, usually, much more informative.

Lycos

Lycos is one of the largest Web document indexes available. It indexes the entire text of documents, and makes that index searchable by keywords. As of this writing, the Lycos server claims to have indexed 4.24 million Web documents. Lycos is a recursive indexer, and will use submitted URLs as starting points for a recursive index search (indexing all pages reachable from that URL, plus pages reachable from those pages, and so forth).

While Lycos finds most pages serendipitously (by exploring the Web), you can "suggest" starting points for Lycos to index, so that your pages can be added to Lycos even more rapidly. Lycos also allows URLs to be removed from its index by specifying a partial URL to match to pages in the database. This can be useful if you no longer wish to have your pages indexed by Lycos (for legal or policy reasons, or because the document is no longer available at that location).

Lycos is available via

```
http://www.lycos.com
```

The WWW Worm (Oliver McBryan)

The WWW Worm is another recursive indexer that indexes URLs, document titles, document citations (documents in which a particular URL is mentioned), and citation hypertext (the actual text of the citation link). These items are keyword searchable, such as searching by the key "or.us" in URLs to find Web servers in Oregon. As of this writing, the WWW Worm claims to have indexed three million documents. Submission to the WWW Worm includes a starting URL and a one-line description of the URL (the "citation hypertext" for the starting URL). The WWW Worm will recurse through all locatable pages (that aren't already in the database) and index them as well.

The WWW Worm is available via

```
http://www.cs.colorado.edu/home/mcbryan/WWWW.html
```

Submit It! (Scott Bannister)

Submit It! isn't an index in itself, but it will help you get in touch with more indices than can be mentioned here. Submit It! is a service that takes data about your site and submits it to various Web indices and announcers by building submit requests to each index/announcer you choose. At this writing, Submit It! includes these indices:

- Yahoo
- Starting Point
- EINet Galaxy
- WebCrawler
- Lycos
- Harvest

and these announcement services:

- NCSA *What's New* with the World Wide Web
- What's New Too!

Submit It! is a faster way to submit your site to these locations than by submitting to each site manually. Be sure to deselect any locations to which you have already submitted your site, such as NCSA *What's New* if you have already announced there.

Submit It! is available via the Web at

```
http://www.cen.uiuc.edu/~banister/submit-it/
```

Staying Around: Advertising Over Time, On and Off the Internet

Once the initial announcement of your site has worn off, newcomers will be guided primarily by your inclusion in various indices, either those mentioned previously or smaller, personal indices (such as hotlists and bookmarks) which are very popular on the Web. For some, if not most, sites (services or businesses, for example), continuing to advertise over time is both useful and important. New Internet users surface every day, and they may be too late to see your announcement or may not know how to use the Web indices to find you. A different kind of advertising is going to keep people noticing your site for the first time.

This other kind of advertising involves using routine tools and services to subtly plug your Web site. By adding your URL to your `.signature` file (a short file that typically gets appended to e-mail messages and Usenet postings), everyone with whom you communicate via e-mail has a chance of visiting your site, provided they know what to do with a URL. If you have a Unix account on the Internet, you can add your URL and a brief description of your site to your `.plan` file (typically a file that is displayed when another Internet user uses the "finger" command to get information about you at your Internet site). Business cards and official letterhead are also becoming common locations for URLs among the technoluminati in the business world. Basically, any method by which you routinely transfer information to other people can be used to include your URL for others to see, but the sources just noted are by far the most common. For businesses that use traditional media for advertising, URLs are popping up in more and more newspaper, magazine, mail, and TV advertisements, which is yet another avenue to pursue (if you have an advertising budget).

The goal when using these secondary advertising methods is to be subtle yet noticeable—don't make your URL the sole point of the communication; let it ride along to be picked up if someone is interested, and to keep your site in circulation after the initial announcement. These secondary methods are by no means necessary to the successful advertising of a Web site, but they will certainly spread word of your site to audiences that the primary advertising methods (announcements, indices) may not reach.

Because of the transient nature of the Internet—the fact that next month several hundred or several thousand people who have never been on the Internet will join the millions already there—it may also be useful to follow up the announcement of your site made to newsgroups and mailing lists. A good rule of thumb is to resend a notice of your site to the appropriate newsgroups or mailing lists approximately every 12 months to reach the new users who have joined the Internet. Follow-up notices occurring too close together (less than six months apart) will not reach as many new users, and will annoy the regulars on those services.

As a last note on following-up, many universities provide accounts for their students who may not have Internet access during the summer months (approximately May through August or September). A follow-up notice made during that time will have disappeared from Usenet or the mailing list long before students have a chance to read it, so timing notices during the fall, winter, or spring months gives you the best chance of reaching the greatest possible audience. Of course, timing your initial announcement accordingly is also a valuable idea, but in practice it is difficult to schedule when a Web service will become operational, and waiting several months before announcing may not be worth the extra audience (a follow-up notice in six months would be appropriate in this case).

On the Move: When Documents Change Location

While it would be nice that if after something was put on the Web it always stayed at the same place, this isn't always possible. If for some reason you must leave your current Internet service provider, you'll probably want to take all your Web documents with you. Or if your site gets a new server to handle the WWW, the URLs to all your documents will change. There are various other reasons why documents or services you provide will have to change their URLs. During the moving phase, all links that reference your old site will be pointing to documents that no longer exist. If your old URL was "www.somewhere.com" and now all your documents are at "www.anywhere.com," anyone trying to access the documents at the first address will be met with a "can't find file" error from the server at that site. This can be very frustrating for clients who have no idea where to find you anymore.

The first thing you will want to do is to set up redirection information so that readers attempting to access the original location will be pointed to the new location. There are two approaches to this. The first is to replace the original page with a document like this:

```
⟨HTML⟩
⟨HEAD⟩
```

```
⟨TITLE⟩The Flugblogs Page has moved!⟨/TITLE⟩
⟨/HEAD⟩
⟨BODY⟩
⟨H1⟩The Flugblogs Page has moved!⟨/H1⟩
⟨P⟩ "This document is no longer here. It can now
be found at
⟨A HREF="http://www.flugblogs.com/"⟩http://www.
flugblogs.com/⟨/A⟩ --
please update your references!

⟨P⟩ (⟨EM⟩Flugblogs⟨/EM⟩, the computer programmer's
favorite breakfast cereal!)

⟨HR⟩

⟨P⟩ This page moved July 27, 1995
⟨ADDRESS⟩⟨A HREF="http://www.flugblogs.com/~bob/"⟩
Bob Crusade,Flugblogs Information Maintainer,
bob@flugblogs.com⟨/A⟩⟨/ADDRESS⟩
```

This approach has the advantage of being obvious—it will be clear to readers and to link maintainers that this document has been moved. Some of this information will trickle back to the maintainers of links, and solve some of your moving problem.

Another approach is more subtle and transparent—using redirection. This uses the HTTP Location: header to inform browsers that the document has been moved. Browsers that support this header (which by now includes most browsers) then retrieve the new document, without the reader ever being aware that the document has been moved. This is useful for moving documents from one part of your server to another, or in any situation where you can guarantee that the original server will continue to provide redirection pointing to the new locations of your documents. Using redirection is discussed in Chapter 6, in the *Virtual document tree* sections for the respective servers.

Once the move is complete, you should use the methods mentioned in this chapter, especially the announcing and indexing sections, to announce that your site, services, or pages have moved to a new URL, and to change the links in any major indices (WWW Virtual Library, Yahoo, and so on) to your new URL. This way you reach the most users, notifying them that your pages have moved before they even know it themselves, thus saving a lot of time later because people or indices don't have to try and figure out where you've moved to.

Reannounce your new URL to the announcement services as a *moved* URL, so people realize they'll need to change their links to your site. Resubmit your site to any indices you originally submitted to, being sure to mention it's a *changed*, not a new, URL. It may seem like a lot of extra work, but remember that by moving your pages or sites, you're essentially creating brand new pages or sites to which nobody knows the address. To make sure that people continue to have access to your services, you should run through these steps again, lest your new site continue on unnoticed and unvisited.

Part III

Style Guide

No matter how well armed you are with technical knowledge, there are still traps and pitfalls you can fall into while creating your infostructures. Most of these revolve around style issues. How should a certain element be used? How can multimedia be employed tastefully? How should I organize my infostructure so that it makes sense to my readers? What you need is a style guide to the vagaries of information publishing.

This section is that style guide. It discusses what you should and shouldn't do, and why. We start in Chapter 11 by discussing the elements of style for the document and move on to stylistic considerations for your web as a whole in Chapter 12. In some cases, our recommendations are motivated by technical considerations; in others they are motivated by personal preference. We think that all of these are useful guidelines and we hope you will give them due consideration before setting off to build your web.

11

Document Style Considerations

The World Wide Web has been a wildly successful experiment. It has filled a need for both information users and for information providers; it is a tool that allows information to be deployed to a wide variety of people over wide geographic distances, regardless of what kind of computer they may be running. All that is required to publish information is any one of a number of Web servers, and all that is required to view that information is any one of a number of Web clients.

This is both an opportunity and a challenge. So far in this book we have discussed ways in which you should construct your infostructure so that it is easily usable by your audience and easily maintainable by you. Now we must discuss the ways in which you construct your markup so that it is readable and usable to a wide range of browsers.

It is important to note again at this point that HTML provides a device-independent way of describing information. The elements of HTML describe *what* your information is, not *how* it should be displayed. This is a subtle point, and perhaps the most important one of this entire book. HTML will let you describe some information as a header, or some other information as an address. It will not let you describe text as 24-point Helvetica, right-justified. Your challenge is to provide professional page layout and design *without* using the traditional tools of professional page layout and design. Sound like a paradox? Not really. All it involves is a bit of trust.

The trust you must have can be summarized by the following rule:

- *If* you mark up a document so that your information is labeled as what it is instead of as how it should be displayed,

- *Then* browsers will render it in a way that is appropriate and professional-looking.

With the current diversity of clients for the Web (and we can only expect to see more), it has become important to write HTML that will look good on any client, and not just on the specific client to which the author may have access. You must trust your markup. There is no way to anticipate how every browser will (differently) render your HTML. If you follow this rule you will get the best possible rendering with all browsers, instead of for just one.

To this end, there are a few solutions. One approach is software based—a "lint"-like program for catching semantic and syntactic errors in HTML, and perhaps even correcting them. In Chapter 7, we reviewed several HTML checking programs available that do exactly this. Another approach is the one taken by this chapter—a style guide that points out common errors you might make in the composition of HTML, and that recommends good practices to follow.

This chapter is divided into three main sections. The first section discusses good practices to follow in creating your documents. The second discusses common errors and things to avoid when composing HTML. The final section discusses style sheets, which provide a mechanism for greater control over how a document is rendered.

Bear in mind when following these guidelines that your document may not end up looking the best it possibly can on a particular browser. However, it also will not look ugly on any browser, which is the risk you take if you disregard these recommendations and tweak your markup code for, say, Netscape. Unfortunately, Netscape may render things differently from Lynx, which may render things differently from Mosaic, and so on and so forth. Even within a particular browser, a user may chose font or style preferences different from the ones that you might assume. What these guidelines should do, if followed, is make a better presentation for the most browsers (instead of the best presentation for only one), and ensure that your documents reach the widest audience possible.

Good Practices

This section presents good practices for the generation of any HTML document. Specifically, this includes anything that should routinely be done in the creation of documents for the benefit of both reader and author.

How to Use Non-standard HTML

There are at least three major flavors of HTML currently in practice as this is being written: HTML 2.0, HTML 3.0, and the Netscape extensions to HTML 2.0. HTML 2.0 is the closest thing to current practice that is available, and can be assumed to be "safe" for all browsers.

On the other hand, the HTML 3.0 and the Netscape extensions are not widely implemented, let alone standardized. Under most circumstances, this would be a good reason not to use them until they are more widely available, but there is the mitigating circumstance that all of the Netscape extensions (and some of HTML 3.0, most notably tables) are supported by one of the most popular Web browsers . . . Netscape!

What should be done about this? Many Web authors take the approach that, since most people use Netscape, it's acceptable to use the Netscape elements, even if it is to the detriment of people using other browsers. Others take the approach that nothing more than HTML 2.0 should ever be used, which means that any benefit that might be derived from these enhancements is lost.

The best road is the middle. Two good rules of thumb are:

- If two or more popular browsers support the extension, it's probably fine to use. For instance, both Netscape and Mosaic (and Arena) now support tables, so any tables you use will be available to most of your audience.

- If the extension is not widely supported, and it will not adversely affect your document if missing, it's probably fine to use. For instance, the FONT element changes the font size of text in the Netscape Navigator, but not in any other client. However, other clients will simply *ignore* tags they do not understand, so the text in the FONT element will still be readable. On the other hand, if the MATH element is ignored by a browser, the browser will display gibberish.

In general, try to think about the effect that the nonstandard elements will have if they are not recognized. These elements can be used intelligently, and on browsers that recognize them, can dramatically enhance the presentation of your page. If it is not possible to use the elements in such a way that rendering is still good on all clients, think about providing multiple copies of the document (for instance, providing a version of the table using the PRE element), and possibly using content-negotiation on the server to provide the reader with the correct version of the document (see Chapter 6).

Also, think about whether there is more than one way to accomplish what you are trying to do, and whether a way exists that will accommodate more of your readers. For example, the Netscape method for centering text is to use the CENTER element, while the HTML 3.0 method is to use the ALIGN attribute. Netscape supports limited use of the ALIGN attribute, which means that

```
<P ALIGN="center">This is my centered text.</P>
```

will work in any browser which supports centering. In fact, Netscape is beginning to support more and more of HTML 3.0; a good strategy is to attempt the HTML 3.0 elements first, and to only resort to Netscape-specific elements if absolutely necessary.

A final thought on the subject: try to avoid banners in your document that claim that your document is "Enhanced for Netscape" or "Enhanced for HTML 3.0." Rather, try to build your document so that if a reader reads it in (for example) Netscape, it will be obvious that it uses the new elements to good effect, and if readers read it in another browser, they can remain blissfully unaware of what they cannot see, and still be impressed by what they do see.

Signing and Time-stamping Documents

One problem that faces anyone trying to find information using the Internet is the question of "authoritativeness." The relative ease with which WWW servers can be set up and populated with information means that the traditional checks of the publishing process cannot act to filter out information that is inaccurate or misleading. In addition, it can often be hard to tell how current information found on-line is, or how actively it is maintained and updated.

One thing that you can do to assist Web users is to sign and date all documents in your infostructure, so that people viewing the documents can form some impression of the authority of the document (that is, how recent it is, and how reliable the information provider is). This is not a complete solution, but it is a large step forward. Some editors, such as HTML-helper-mode (see Chapter 4) will do this automatically.

For example:

```
⟨HR⟩
Last modified: March 6, 1995
⟨ADDRESS⟩
⟨A HREF="http://www.willamette.edu/~jtilton/"⟩
James Eric Tilton⟨/A⟩⟨BR⟩
⟨A HREF="mailto:jtilton@willamette.edu"⟩jtilton@
willamette.edu⟨/A⟩
⟨/ADDRESS⟩
```

Some notes about this example:

- The date is given in an unambiguous format: "March 6, 1995." Why is this better than the more economical "3/6/95?" One reason is that for some of your audience, especially those from Europe, this means "June 3, 1995."

- A link to a home page is provided. If a reader is interested, he or she can follow it to find more information by this author. This provides a consistent centering function that helps keep a reader from becoming disoriented (See *Main Roads and Scenic Paths* in Chapter 12).

- A `mailto:` link anchors the document to the mail address of its creator. The `mailto:` URL specifies an e-mail address. Most browsers support this, allowing the reader to send e-mail to the address specified. This can be a useful way to get feedback. In addition, the `mailto:` link is separated from the link to the homepage by a ⟨BR⟩, so that the two links can be easily distinguished.

Another option for signing a document is to encode information about the author in the document's header information. You can do this by including a LINK element of type `made` in your HEAD element. For example:

```
⟨HEAD⟩
⟨TITLE⟩This is my Title⟨/TITLE⟩
⟨LINK REV="made"
HREF="mailto:author@some.site.org"⟩
⟨/HEAD⟩
```

This example uses the LINK element, which may be unfamiliar to you. It is equivalent to the A element; that is, it provides a link to some other object. However, since it is part of the HEAD information (which is information *about* the document, rather than part of the document itself), this is a link from the *entire* document to another object. (Anchors, on the other hand, are links from some small subset of the document, like a word or a phrase, to another document). This link, like most other HEAD information, is typically not displayed by a browser or followable by a reader.

The fact that it is not displayed does not make it useless, however. Many browsers, such as Lynx, supply a "reply to author" function. The information about who the author is comes from using the LINK as shown in this example. Other applications that can make use of the information include Web spiders and other maintenance tools, which can benefit from having authority information in machine-readable format.

The format of the LINK element is the same as that of the A element. Notice the use of the REV attribute, which describes this relationship as a REVerse relationship of the type `made`. This means that this document was made by the object at the other end of the anchor.

Device Independence Through Better Printing

One promise of the widespread availability of personal computers has been the reduction of our reliance on paper. In some ways, this promise has been realized; many trees (and municipal landfills) are no doubt grateful that many of us are now committing our words to e-mail instead of to a handwritten or typewritten letter or memo. On the other hand, until video display technology produces results indistinguishable from paper, we will no doubt continue to print out hard copy. It's hard to curl up with a notebook at night, especially if it has a coaxial cable jutting out the back. Because of this, many people will want to print out the documents that you have provided electronically. In effect, they will want to take the document you have woven into a part of a web, and make it into a standalone document.

Fortunately, HTML is well-suited for this. A document in HTML can theoretically be rendered in many more formats besides on a screen. Print is one obvious alternative, although speech and braille are also possible and desirable. We bring this up because it is important to consider ways other than on-screen that a reader may encounter your documents. Given that, thinking about your document as something that might be printed can be a very useful tool for creating documents that aren't tied to the specific requirements of a browser or display hardware.

Taking Advantage of Prose

One of the advantages of the World Wide Web over similar infosystems, like Gopher, is that the Web makes no distinction between what a menu is and what a document is. For instance, in Gopher, a document is "dead"—it can't lead anywhere—and, in order to continue exploration, a reader must return one step back to a menu. In the same vein, a Gopher menu provides only limited information about where links lead: often a menu item must be retrieved and explored before any sense can be made of whether it is appropriate to what a reader seeks.

On the other hand, a Web document is "live"—there's no clear dividing line between a menu container and its contents. This is a liberating distinction, as a document can now be as verbose as necessary in providing context for links. Consider the difference between the two documents in Figures 11.1 and 11.2.

Figure 11.1

A Menu List without Context (Lynx)

```
Here is a list of my favorite links:
    * What's New at NCSA
    * Yahoo
    * What's Cool/What's Not
    * The Fine Art Forum Online Art Resources Directory
```

Figure 11.2

A Prose Description of Resources (Lynx)

```
There are several online resources for finding new and exciting Web
sites. They include What's New at NCSA, a collection of pointers to
new sites which have become available in the past month; Yahoo, a
subject-oriented catalog of Web pointers; What's Cool/What's Not, an
entirely subjective but entirely amusing daily update on the state of
the 'net; and the Fine Art Forum Online Art Resources Directory, the
definitive list of art online.
```

The second example is much more satisfying, because it is more than simply a list of pointers. Instead, an effort has been made to integrate the list into prose that is (presumably) better tied into the subject of the document as a whole.

This is not to say that it is always preferable to force what is more naturally a menu into prose for the sake of prose. If you are creating a document that serves as a jumping-off point for other resources, your readers might not want to get into the thick of text to find the resource they're searching for. In this case, a definition list may be more appropriate, as shown in Figure 11.3. This is a nice compromise, giving context without becoming buried in a forest of words.

```
There are several online resources for finding new and exciting Web
sites. They include:

What's New at NCSA,
        a collection of pointers to new sites which have become
        available in the past month,

Yahoo,
        a subject-oriented catalog of Web pointers,

What's Cool/What's Not,
        an entirely subjective but entirely amusing daily update on the
        state of the 'net, and,

the Fine Art Forum Online Art Resources Directory,
        the definitive list of art online.
```

Figure 11.3

A Menu Using a Definition List (Lynx)

Meaningless Link Text

When creating documents, make sure that your links are meaning-ful—that is, that they avoid on-line-specific references, and that they don't detract from readability. The text of your links should flow well in the context of the rest of your text, and your text should also be able to stand alone as a printable document. You should at all costs avoid the "Click Here" syndrome, as shown in Figure 11.4.

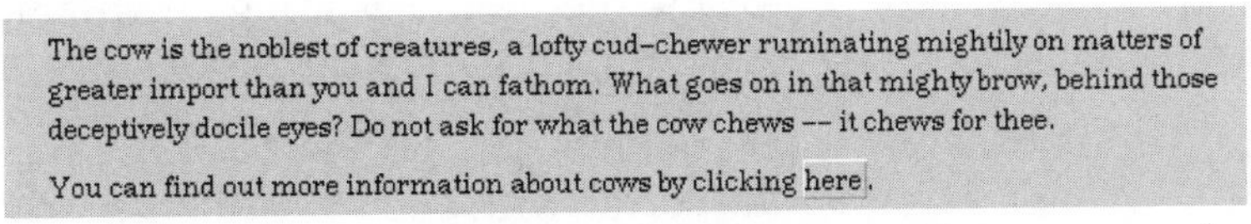

Figure 11.4

The "Click Here" Syndrome (Arena)

The cow is the noblest of creatures, a lofty cud-chewer ruminating mightily on matters of greater import than you and I can fathom. What goes on in that mighty brow, behind those deceptively docile eyes? Do not ask for what the cow chews — it chews for thee.

You can find out more information about cows by clicking here.

Figure 11.4 is also bad because it refers to "clicking," which as-sumes that everyone is using a mouse with their browser, which is not always the case. A much better alternative is demonstrated in Figure 11.5.

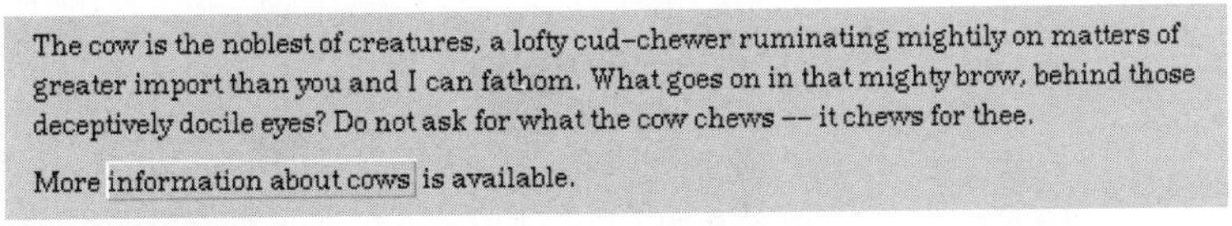

Figure 11.5

Meaningful Link Text (Arena)

The cow is the noblest of creatures, a lofty cud-chewer ruminating mightily on matters of greater import than you and I can fathom. What goes on in that mighty brow, behind those deceptively docile eyes? Do not ask for what the cow chews — it chews for thee.

More information about cows is available.

Another point to consider about the choice of words selected for link text ("information about cows," in Figure 11.5), is that often this link text may be what is used as information for a reader's bookmark or hotlist entry. When the word "here" is used as link text, the hotlist may become cluttered with entries that read only "here," instead of with information about what the link is actually about.

Organization through Outlining

Headers provide a useful way to provide an outline for your doc-ument. Headers of level 1 (H1) indicate major points, while head-ers of level 2 (H2) provide subtopics to those points, and so on. It is important to remember that the purpose of these headers is not to provide specific kinds of fonts or layout, but rather to organize a document into sections. To that end, here are some recommendations about heading usage:

- A heading should not be more than one level below the heading that precedes it. That is, an H3 element should not follow an H1 element directly.

- Also, one version of the HTML specification declares that "a heading element implies all the font changes, paragraph breaks before and after, and white space (for example) necessary to render the heading." Extra highlighting elements are discouraged within the header, like EM or B.

- Do not mark up text as H2 or H3, simply because it provides the correct size and style of fonts on the browsers used by local readers. On another browser, that same text may be incredibly grotesque and large, not providing the desired effect at all. Figures 11.6 and 11.7 demonstrate this effect.

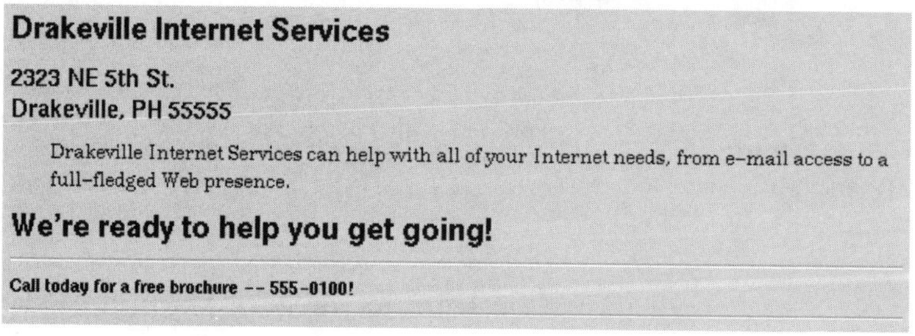

Drakeville Internet Services

2323 NE 5th St.
Drakeville, PH 55555

Drakeville Internet Services can help with all of your Internet needs, from e-mail access to a full-fledged Web presence.

We're ready to help you get going!

Call today for a free brochure -- 555-0100!

Figure 11.6
Expected Headline
Rendering (Arena)

Physical versus Logical Character Emphasis

Since HTML is designed to be a device-independent language for describing the content of documents, most of the elements within it aren't intended to give direct control to the author over how the final page layout will look. The major exceptions to this are in the character highlighting elements.

There are two types of character highlighting elements, physical and logical. The physical styles involve things like "italic font" and "boldface"; while the logical styles are things like "emphasis,"

Drakeville Internet Services

**2323 NE 5th St.
Drakeville, PH 55555**

Drakeville Internet Services can help with all of your Internet needs, from e-mail access to a full-fledged Web presence.

We're ready to help you get going!

Call today for a free brochure -- 555-0100!

Figure 11.7
Unexpected Headline Rendering (Netscape)

"citation," and "strong." It is strongly recommended that you employ the logical styles rather than the physical styles in your documents. Using the I element to render text in italics will only be effective on those browsers that are capable of displaying italics—which all browsers are not guaranteed to be able to do. It is far better to encode semantic content—to describe things in terms of logical styles—and then allow the browser to display that semantic structure as best it can, given its display capabilities.

So, instead of

    ⟨I⟩italics⟨/I⟩

you might use

    ⟨EM⟩emphasized⟨/EM⟩

or a

    ⟨CITE⟩citation⟨/CITE⟩

And instead of

    ⟨B⟩bold⟨/B⟩

you might use

```
⟨STRONG⟩strong⟨/STRONG⟩
```

This also leaves the possibility open in the future for more sophisticated uses of semantic encoding, which has much more inherent meaning than font styles like bold or italic. For example, the Lycos indexing system can take advantage of semantic encoding to create abstracts of documents.

NOTE: Before you stop using B and I altogether, however, here's another viewpoint to consider. One argument against logical character styles is that it turns out to be a bottomless pit, a fruitless attempt to define logical styles for every possibility. Physical styles, combined with their context, seem to provide a much richer set without a huge number of tags. Consider the large space of context that can be implied with only the typographical conventions of **bold** or *italic*. The only problem is that contextual space needs to have a human being to interpret it, which would make some kinds of computer-based rendering difficult, if not impossible (such as speech synthesis).

A Picture is Worth a Thousand Words (Which is Why It Takes a Thousand Times Longer to Load . . .)

The title of this section is somewhat facetious, but only somewhat. It's becoming more obvious from current Web development efforts that the main attraction of the Web is not hypertext, and that it's not an easy interface; the main attractions are the flashy graphics and the alluring promise of multimedia. We shall heroically refrain from commenting on whether this is a good or a bad thing, for the fact remains that on-line multimedia is here to stay. What we *will* comment on is the issues that must be considered to use multimedia for best effect.

The first set of issues revolves about the faux sense of page design you can get by using inline images. An early example of this was one of the early commercial forays into the Web by a graphic design house that advertised professional layout services for on-line brochures. Staff members spent quite a bit of time designing graphics images of the proper width so that they could achieve page-layout effects like right justification and centering, and created pages that were fairly well-designed. However, they got bitten because this design relied on a browser's window being the default width of X Mosaic. With a wider window, the carefully aligned logo in the upper right corner was immediately followed by the image that should have been left-justified on the following line.

Current browsers implement some better forms of layout control for images. For example, an author can specify the way that text will flow around an image with an ALIGN element. Figures 11.8 and 11.9 exemplify this; the former has no text-flow information, and the latter does. This is not perfect, as using the ALIGN tag can cause strange stair-stepping effects if there is not enough text separating two images, as Figure 11.10 illustrates. Fortunately, stair-stepping can be avoided through the use of the CLEAR attribute. The CLEAR attribute specifies that an element should not be displayed until it has a clear margin to one side or the other—that is, that if there is an image that text is flowing around, this element should be displayed below this image. For example:

```
⟨IMG SCR="biscuit.gif" ALIGN="left"⟩ This is a
biscuit.
⟨BR CLEAR="left"⟩ ⟨IMG SCR="basket.gif" ALIGN=
"left"⟩ This is a basket.
```

In this example, the BR element is displayed when the left margin is again clear, and there is no stair-stepping effect. While this is a contrived example, it should demonstrate how you can use CLEAR to provide the correct layout cues to browsers. While HTML 3.0 supports CLEAR in several elements, the Netscape Navigator currently only supports clear on the BR element. See Chapter 13 for more information on the CLEAR attribute.

If the desired effect is of images with captions, a table is probably the best approach for layout purposes (Figure 11.11). See the IMG, FIG, and TABLE elements in Chapter 13 for more information.

A cat for all seasons...

Your author has always appreciated animals of the feline persuasion: lions, tigers, and the powerful and respected tabby. From an early age, he knew that the dog need not apply to be *his* best friend, and that in the end he must find himself a cat woman.

This picture was taken one moonlit night. Perhaps your author should get out more often.

Figure 11.8

IMG without the ALIGN Element (Netscape)

A cat for all seasons...

Your author has always appreciated animals of the feline persuasion: lions, tigers, and the powerful and respected tabby. From an early age, he knew that the dog need not apply to be *his* best friend, and that in the end he must find himself a cat woman.

This picture was taken one moonlit night. Perhaps your author should get out more often.

Figure 11.9

IMG with the ALIGN Element (Netscape)

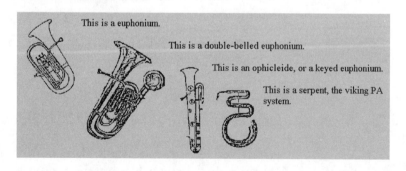

This is a euphonium.

This is a double-belled euphonium.

This is an ophicleide, or a keyed euphonium.

This is a serpent, the viking PA system.

Figure 11.10

Stair-Stepping Due to ALIGN (Netscape)

Another consideration is the duplication of effort. Many authors swear by colored bullets and colorful horizontal rules, implementing both effects by using inlined images rather than the structural markup. Doing this can leave the portion of your audience that is unable (or unwilling) to view inlined images out of the loop, and can also negate some of the benefits provided by structural

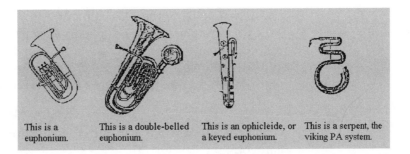

This is a
euphonium.

This is a double-belled
euphonium.

This is an ophicleide, or
a keyed euphonium.

This is a serpent, the
viking PA system.

markup. There is also an unexpected side effect to using many small images: the current way that Web clients retrieve documents requires that a separate connection to a Web server be initiated for each image. The time involved in negotiating this connection may actually be longer than the time involved in retrieving the image itself. Consider whether the effect achieved by the "enhanced" layout justifies the cost.

Another concern is the size of images. With the increasing home popularity of the Internet, more and more users are purchasing dial-up connections of one sort or another. This may be of the strict "shell-account" variety, which means that your readers will not see images at all; or they may be of the SLIP/PPP variety, which means that your readers will have an average of only 14,400 bits of information per second sent to them. This is not a large number, and huge images can take minutes to load. Bear this in mind when selecting images; will the image take so long to load that your reader will go somewhere else rather than wait?

The image size issue can be alleviated in several ways. First, the increasing popularity of the JPEG format (see the discussion of image formats in Chapter 2) means that images can be compressed to much smaller sizes, which provides dramatic speed-up in image load time. Even better results can be achieved by using fewer colors (grey scale, rather than full 24-bit color, for example). Another approach is to use a small set of navigational icons that appear on every page in your Web. Most browsers now cache documents and images; using the same icons (and using the *same* URL to refer to them, perhaps by maintaining an /icons directory on your Web server) means that the reader will only incur the cost of downloading once.

Also, when using the `IMG` element, use the `ALT` attribute, which allows alternate text to be specified for an inlined image. This is especially useful for images that have specific meaning (and provide a link to other documents), as that meaning can be lost on those who do not have images loaded. For example:

```
⟨IMG SRC="http://www.miskatonic.edu/icons/next.gif"⟩
```

can be better represented with the addition of the following `ALT` attribute:

```
⟨IMGSRC="http://www.miskatonic.edu/icons/next. gif"ALT=" [Next Page]"⟩
```

as shown in Figures 11.12 through 11.16.

Hypertext Bound

On the other extreme, you can flow all the text to a book-length work into a single file, creating a content listing at the beginning of the document which links to sections within the document, delineated by the appropriate headings and divider bars. From the user's perspective, however, it's just as easy to get lost within the text as the prior example: instead of a maze of text, as before, we now have a crush of text, without the benefit of pagination to form physical, if not logical, breaks in the text, as we would if it were a printed work. However, if you see the document as primarily being printed and used as a paper resource -- perish the thought -- this way of organizing the text might be most appropriate.

Obviously, you need to find functional units that make sense within the logical structure of your document in order to decide how to divide it across a file system or database that stores your hypertext. Your goal should always be to allow the reader to find the information she is seeking easily and quickly, while maintaining the context of that information within the larger whole of your hypertext.

Back Up! **Next Page!**

Last modified: May 25, 1995
tilt+@cs.cmu.edu

Figure 11.12

The Document as
Expected (Netscape)

Finally, don't rely entirely on imagemaps and graphic logos to build your site. There are a few sites that have almost no textual content whatsoever; when visited by readers who do not (or cannot) load images, there is no information available. This is not to say that imagemaps must be avoided altogether. Instead, provide alternate means of navigation that supplement the imagemap, such as explanatory text that follows your map.

Hypertext Bound

On the other extreme, you can flow all the text to a book-length work into a single file, creating a content listing at the beginning of the document which links to sections within the document, delineated by the appropriate headings and divider bars. From the user's perspective, however, it's just as easy to get lost within the text as the prior example: instead of a maze of text, as before, we now have a crush of text, without the benefit of pagination to form physical, if not logical, breaks in the text, as we would if it were a printed work. However, if you see the document as primarily being printed and used as a paper resource -- perish the thought -- this way of organizing the text might be most appropriate.

Obviously, you need to find functional units that make sense within the logical structure of your document in order to decide how to divide it across a file system or database that stores your hypertext. Your goal should always be to allow the reader to find the information she is seeking easily and quickly, while maintaining the context of that information within the larger whole of your hypertext.

Last modified: May 25, 1995
tilt+@cs.cmu.edu

Figure 11.13

Inlined Images Off/No ALT Tag (Netscape)

```
the appropriate headings and divider bars. From the user's
perspective, however, it's just as easy to get lost within the text as
the prior example: instead of a maze of text, as before, we now have a
crush of text, without the benefit of pagination to form physical, if
not logical, breaks in the text, as we would if it were a printed
work. However, if you see the document as primarily being printed and
used as a paper resource -- perish the thought -- this way of
organizing the text might be most appropriate.

Obviously, you need to find functional units that make sense within
the logical structure of your document in order to decide how to
divide it across a file system or database that stores your hypertext.
Your goal should always be to allow the reader to find the information
she is seeking easily and quickly, while maintaining the context of
that information within the larger whole of your hypertext.

[IMAGE] [IMAGE]

Last modified: May 25, 1995
    tilt+@cs.cmu.edu
```

Figure 11.14

Text Browser/No ALT Tag (Lynx)

Obviously, you need to find functional units that make sense within the logical structure of your document in order to decide how to divide it across a file system or database that stores your hypertext. Your goal should always be to allow the reader to find the information she is seeking easily and quickly, while maintaining the context of that information within the larger whole of your hypertext.

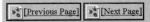 [Previous Page] [Next Page]

Figure 11.15

Inlined Images Off/ALT Tag Supplied (Netscape)

```
Obviously, you need to find functional units that make sense within
the logical structure of your document in order to decide how to
divide it across a file system or database that stores your hypertext.
Your goal should always be to allow the reader to find the information
she is seeking easily and quickly, while maintaining the context of
that information within the larger whole of your hypertext.

[Previous Page] [Next Page]
```

Figure 11.16

Text Browser/ALT Tag Supplied (Lynx)

Common Errors

This section details common errors in HTML composition that may lead to documents that are not fully device-independent. The behaviors of these errors are undefined, so certain browsers may render them as intended but not all browsers are guaranteed of doing so. Therefore, these mistakes should be avoided, even if your browser of choice renders your documents correctly.

These errors are, for the most part, artifacts of "raw" HTML authoring. Web development has suffered from a lack of good authoring tools, a situation that only now is beginning to be rectified. Many of these errors involve typos or simple mistakes, although others deal with more fundamental conceptual problems.

Paragraph Break Errors

The P element, the paragraph break, may be the most misused element of all (although the BLINK element vies closely for this honor). Errors involving the P element are the most common culprits in cases of ugly HTML rendering. If you fix nothing else, fix these.

Perhaps the biggest misconception about the P element is that it signals an end of paragraph, rather than a paragraph break. According to the specification, "⟨P⟩ is used between two pieces of text that otherwise would be flowed together." In most cases this is not important—functionally, a ⟨P⟩ serves as an end-of-paragraph marker. However, in certain contexts, use of ⟨P⟩ should be avoided, such as directly before or after any other element that already implies a paragraph break. To wit, the P element should not be placed either before or after the headings HR, ADDRESS, BLOCKQUOTE, or PRE. It should also not be placed immediately before or after a list element of any stripe. That is, a ⟨P⟩ should not be used to mark the end of text for LI, DT or DD. All of these elements already imply paragraph breaks.

Some clarifications on the preceding might be in order. One is the difficulty of rendering appropriate white space by a browser. While it is true that all of the entities mentioned imply a paragraph break, this only occasionally means that they also imply white space between sections; actually, this depends on the browser. So, while you might feel inclined to add a ⟨P⟩ in order to fix white space problems, please think twice and avoid it if you can. In another browser, you may create several lines of unsightly white space.

There is a distinct difference between how the original HTML specification and how HTML 2.0 and HTML 3.0 handle the P element. In the original, the P is empty. It does not contain the paragraph, as one might logically expect; instead, it signals a break between paragraphs. In 2.0 and 3.0, this is rectified, and the P element contains the entire paragraph. This means that instead of being placed between paragraphs, it should be inserted before the paragraph it contains. This also means that there is now an end tag for the P element, ⟨P⟩ which goes at the end of your paragraph. However, most current browsers, despite being largely HTML 2.0 compliant, still treat the P element as if it were a paragraph break (as described earlier in this section). Why? Because although HTML 2.0 was designed to reflect the current state of HTML, the designers of the specification took the opportunity to change the usage of the P element. The upshot of this is that even though this idiom is first introduced in HTML 2.0, it should more properly be considered an idiom of the 3.0 specification.

The authors of the HTML 2.0 and HTML 3.0 specifications claim that this change will not affect the bulk of existing HTML, and, for the most part, this is accurate. For example, you do not need to worry about inserting ⟨/P⟩ tags at the end of each paragraph, because the next ⟨P⟩ tag implies the end of the previous P element. However, an issue that still remains open is what to do with the start of a series of paragraphs. Should you put a ⟨P⟩ tag at the front, in conformance with the coming 3.0 specification, or leave it out, to conform with the current standards?

It is becoming clearer that this treatment of P will become de facto in the next year or so, which makes it probably best to conform with the 3.0 specification and place a ⟨P⟩ in front of each paragraph. Most browsers do collapse extra white space, and when HTML 3.0 becomes widespread you won't be left with a large number of legacy documents.

Character and Entity Reference Errors

Simply put, a character reference and an entity reference are ways to represent information that might otherwise be interpreted as a markup tag. For example, consider the rendered HTML document in Figure 11.17.

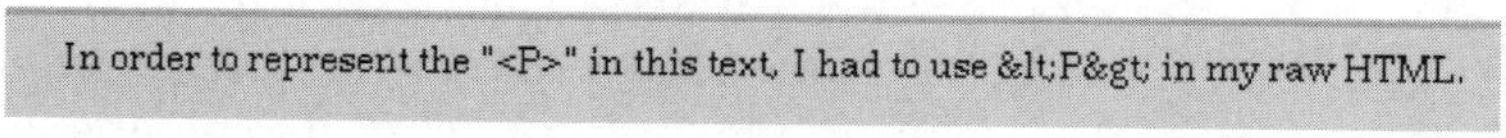

Figure 11.17

Properly Escaping Character Entities (Arena)

In order to represent the "<P>" in this text, I had to use <P> in my raw HTML.

The source that produces this document, which uses entities, looks like:

```
In order to represent the &quot;&lt;P&gt;&quot; in
this text, I had to use &amp;lt;P&amp;gt; in my
raw HTML.
```

In this example, the < becomes "⟨", the > becomes "⟩", the " becomes a quotation mark, and the & becomes "&" (which is needed in order to represent the text < in the document without the text being turned into "⟨"). There are currently five entities for this purpose in HTML, as well as several entities that allow encoding of the ISO Latin-1 Character Set. See Appendix C for more details.

The most common error in the use of entities is to leave off the trailing semicolon. Also, no additional spaces are needed before or after the entity/character reference. Here are some examples of incorrect usage:

```
Doug &amp Chris went out for a walk.
A paragraph break can be represented with
&quote; &gt; P &lt; &quote;
```

Can you spot the errors in these examples? They are:

- In the first line, "`&amp`" needs to have a semicolon after it.

- In the third line, "`&quote;`" should be `&quot;` (this is subtle and annoying, much like the UNIX system call, `creat()`).

- There should be no spaces in the third line, which should read: `&quot;&gt;P&lt;&quot;`.

URL Errors

Another misunderstood aspect of Web document composition is in the creation of URLs.

Directory Reference Errors

One gray area involves references to directories. It is possible to request an index of a directory from an HTTP server. The typical response from the server is to either return a pregenerated index document (which is often the document "index.html" in the referenced directory), or to construct an HTML document on the fly, which contains a listing of all files in the directory. However, when making such a directory reference, it is important to make sure to have a trailing slash on the URL. That is, if you were to request the index of Willamette University's directory of HTML documentation, you would want to refer to it as `http://www.willamette.edu/html-composition/`, not as `http://www.willamette.edu/html-composition`.

Many servers are able to catch these errors and provide redirection to the proper URL, but it's best to get the URL right in the first place, notably because not all browsers support transparent redirection.

Not Using Fully Qualified Domain Names

Problems can arise when the hostnames in URLs aren't fully qualified. Within a local network, a machine can often be simply referred to by its hostname. For example, the domain `miskatonic.edu` might have in it a WWW server with the hostname `www`. Readers within that domain can refer to the machine by this name. However, the server's fully qualified domain name is www.miskatonic.edu. This fully qualified domain name provides enough information so that any host, anywhere on the Internet, can find this particular machine.

What happens is that an HTML author might construct a link that looks like this:

```
⟨A HREF="http://www/~jtilton/metanoia/"⟩Metanoia-A Change In
Spirit⟨/A⟩
```

which produces a link to "Metanoia—A Change In Spirit" that will only work for people in the local network that that machine is on. A correct link would look like this, instead:

```
⟨A HREF="http://www.miskatonic.edu/~jtilton/metanoia/"⟩Metanoia-A
Change In Spirit⟨/A⟩
```

which would allow all of the readers who are interested in Metanoia—even those living in Freedonia—to actually follow the link.

Along those same lines, be careful in using URLs of the scheme "file:." It's possible to have a reference to file://localhost/some/file/pathname. What this does is reference the file described on the local host of whoever is browsing the document. Which is why a reference to ⟨A HREF="file://localhost/etc/motd"⟩the message of the day⟨/A⟩ will display the message of the day on your machine, not the message of the day on my machine. However, this makes several assumptions about your reader's local machine and network that you probably shouldn't be making. Unless you know what you are doing (and probably even then), references of this type will really mess up your Web.

Missing Quotes in Start Tags

One common error, especially with the current lack of widely available and useful authoring tools, is to leave off a quote in the attributes of tags. For example, this reference to the euphonium, king of instruments, should look like:

```
⟨A HREF="http://www.cs.cmu.edu/~tilton/euphonium/"⟩
```

but people composing "raw" HTML from a text editor will often instead type

⟨A HREF="http://www.cs.cmu.edu/~tilton/euphonium/⟩

It's likely that by the end of that huge URL, the author had forgotten that it was quoted. The behavior of browsers upon encountering this varies; some display a proper link, but you can't follow it, while others actually eat up huge portions of the following text, thinking that everything up to the next quotation mark is part of the URL.

Missed End Tags

Many of the HTML elements contain information within them. For example, ⟨EM⟩emphasized text⟨/EM⟩ would be rendered as emphasized text. There is a start tag (⟨EM⟩), some content (which may include text, and in some cases, other nested elements), and an end tag (⟨/EM⟩, indicated by the ⟨/). A common mistake is to miss the / in the end tag. All elements (except empty elements, discussed next) must be terminated by an end tag, otherwise, undefined behavior may occur.

Some HTML elements may be empty, such as ⟨P⟩ and ⟨HR⟩ (see Chapter 13 for an extended discussion on element content). If this is the case, there is no need for an end tag.

Using White Space Around Element Tags

In general, the use of white space around element tags should be avoided. For example, if white space immediately follows a start tag, the style changes implied by that element may be applied to the initial space as well. For instance,

```
You really should
⟨A HREF="http://www.willamette.edu/~jtilton/"⟩
CZeCh THIZ OuT ⟨/A⟩ !
```

would be rendered in Netscape as shown in Figure 11.18, and in Lynx as shown in Figure 11.19.

On some browsers, there may be white space around the anchor, which adds unwanted unsightliness to the rendering, and may

Figure 11.18

Improper Use of White
Space (and Spelling and
Punctuation, too)
(Netscape)

You really should <u>CZeCh THIZ 0uT</u> !

Figure 11.18

Improper Use of White
Space (and Spelling and
Punctuation, too)
(Netscape)

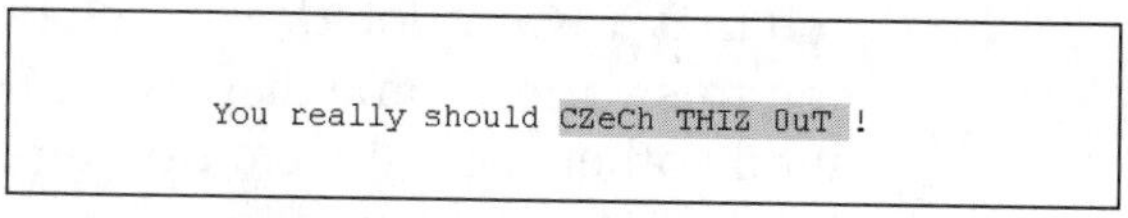

Figure 11.19

Improper Use of White
Space (Lynx)

```
You really should CZeCh THIZ 0uT !
```

lessen the impact of the document. (This comment really applies to white space immediately following start tags, and immediately preceding end tags).

Stylesheets

The point has probably been well made by now that HTML is not a very good vehicle for providing specific information about layout and presentation. There are no mechanisms for authors to specify how they want specific elements rendered, or to control aspects of page layout. While one of the strengths of HTML is this very independence from presentation details, it has become clear that some form of presentation control is needed.

Stylesheets are the answer to this problem. They provide the other half of the equation, the half that is currently not provided by HTML. While HTML provides information about content, stylesheets provide information about how to render specific elements.

Unfortunately, while several mechanisms for providing stylesheets are under development, there is no clear standard at the time of this writing. We cannot tell you which stylesheet mechanism(s) will become standard, but we can tell you about the current contenders. Keep your hopes up, though, because of the importance of stylesheets, it is highly likely that a usable standard will emerge within the next year.

Some Stylesheet Proposals

In these proposals, the stylesheets contain information about how elements should be rendered, whether this is font information, justification information, and so on. At the time of this writing, the syntax for these stylesheets has not yet been fully designed.

Arena/Cascading Stylesheets

The Arena browser is currently the only browser that supports a stylesheet mechanism, and that mechanism is currently only very limited and very experimental. The mechanism involves "cascading stylesheets," which means that the several different stylesheets, each with a different order of importance, are combined in order of importance to create a presentation style. Readers can specify their preferences for rendering, as can document authors, and these preferences are merged to produce the final document.

DSSSL/DSSSL Lite

DSSSL is the Document Style Semantics and Specification Language, which has emerged from the SGML community as a potential stylesheet mechanism. Because it is complex, work is being done to create DSSSL Lite, a modified subset of DSSSL which can be easily implemented by client programmers and easily used by HTML authors.

Alternatives to Stylesheets

While stylesheets are not currently usable, there are alternatives in existing specifications, which can be used with existing browsers. While the HTML 3.0 enhancements described next are not yet widely propogated, it is likely that they will be soon; and the Netscape enhancements are already available (and some are likely to be integrated into the evolving HTML 3.0 specification).

HTML 3.0

While HTML 3.0 does include the STYLE element for supporting whatever mechanism is eventually deployed for stylesheets, HTML 3.0 also provides some new elements for greater control over presentation. These elements include BANNER, BIG, SMALL, TABLE, MATH, and TAB.

- The BANNER element provides a means for a banner of HTML that will always remain on the screen. This might be a copyright notice, a toolbar, or any other content that should always be available.

- The BIG and SMALL elements allow for rendering text as bigger or smaller, as compared to the default text size.

- The TABLE and MATH elements provide for a more sophisticated means of layout. The TABLE element allows the author to specify a spreadsheet-style arrangment, with cells that can contain text, images, and even input elements for FORMs. The MATH element allows for the description and rendering of complex mathematical formulae.

- The TAB element allows the author to specify tab stops within the document.

In addition, some entities have been added, such " ace;" to provide finer control over spacing. For more information about these additional elements and entities, see Chapter 13 and Appendix C.

Netscape

The Netscape approach cannot be called a stylesheet, per se. Rather, as of the 1.1 release of Netscape Navigator, Netscape has provided several "enhanced" elements to help control presentation. These elements include FONT, BASEFONT, IMG, and BODY.

Chapter 13 describes the FONT and BASEFONT elements, which allow changing the size of font within a document; it also describes the additions to the IMG element, which has been enhanced to provide text flow around images in documents.

Chapter 13 also describes the enhancements to the BODY element, which allows control over the background. Authors are allowed to provide a background color or image for their documents. In addition, authors can specify different colors for hypertext links, in case the default colors do not have sufficient contrast to the new background color.

NOTE: Be careful when changing colors for hypertext links. Most browsers take the approach of using a bright color (such as bright blue), which has high contrast to the default page background, for links that have not yet been followed; and of using a dull color (such as dark blue), which has less contrast to the default page background, for links that have already been followed. Readers have become used to this high-contrast/low-contrast visual cue, and changing the link colors can confuse readers. The best approach is not to change the link colors unless you have to. With most background colors, the defaults should still be fine. If you do need to change the link colors, use a color that is bright and in high contrast to the background color, for links to pages that have not yet been visited. Use a duller version of that same color for links that have already been followed.

12

Web Style Considerations

In Chapter 5 we discussed some of the issues you should take into account in planning your web. Now, we will return to that subject, this time with an eye toward the architecture, rather than the administration, of your infostructure.

Organization

When organizing your infostructure, there are several important issues. They include:

Present a clear ordering—by subject (table of contents), or
of information   some other form of reasonable entry
                     into the infostructure. Some useful
                     forms are:

- Table of Contents

- Searchable Index

- What's New (with the organic nature of on-line documents, a time-oriented ordering will help infonauts quickly orient themselves with what is new and/or changed in otherwise familiar territory)

Readers need to be able to find what they are looking for, and a good overview that allows them to quickly find a particular topic or document is invaluable.

Only make a document as long as it needs to be. If a document can be logically decomposed into more than one file, do so, but only decompose a document if the narrative branches from the linear structure of the current document. An example of this is breaking up a book-length work into chapters, and further breaking up these chapters into sections. Because of the length of time involved in retrieving documents, making the document available in readable chunks means that the reader can use the information without becoming overwhelmed by loading times and correspondingly large amounts of information presented in a single, huge, scrolling document.

Correspondingly, make sure a document is richly cross-referenced, so that if readers want to ask, "Why?" they can. If you can split up supplementary information into separate documents, do so. This allows the reader to follow a main flow of narrative, but still be able to look up evidence and additional related stories and information as necessary. But don't put in so many links that the reader gets lost trying to follow them all.

Provide a clear, consistent navigation structure. Readers should always be able to easily navigate to all documents that immediately relate, but they should also always be able to get any other document in the infostructure with a minimum of fuss. Always provide access to the original table of contents, or its equivalent. This is especially important when others create links to documents in your Web, but do not necessarily create links to your main entry points; readers can find themselves in the middle of what is obviously a larger document, but without any means of finding additional information. See *Main Roads and Scenic paths*, next.

Design Goals

Importance of Content

Anyone working with HTML for any length of time will soon realize that the markup language is composed of containers, which label content. It should be obvious, then, that your Web should be primarily about this content, whatever it may be.

That's not to say that content only lies between HTML tags; content is also found within other media types, of course, and, depending upon the type of information you provide, sounds or images may be more important to both you and your readers than other types of media.

Web sites, however, should be driven by content, not by vanity or the need or desire to make a buck. Whatever your background, you have real "content"—information, discussion, narrative, ideas—to publish on the Web. People *will* visit your site to find this content. Provide it. Focus your site around it.

The largest threat to the Web is that as it becomes insanely popular, instead of becoming a worldwide information repos-itory, as its founders and proponents have hoped, it is becoming a large intertwined mass of self-referential sites unwittingly involved in meta-discussions on the nature of the Web: homepages that say little more than "This is my homepage" (or "our homepage," in the case of the corporate or organizational "presence"), with a collection of links that (virtually) point to the same collections of sites as the last page you visited.

Main Roads and Scenic Paths: Issues of Navigability

As readers attempt to sail the seas of your infostructure, it is important that you provide useful ways for them to move around in your infostructure. Many readers complain about the proliferation of links in documents, providing so many choices that it becomes impossible to decide where to go next. The blessings of hypertext—leaving control in the hands of the reader—can also be a curse, as the original thrust of the narrative becomes awash in sidetracks and dead ends.

A means of approaching this problem is to use the metaphor of "main roads" and "scenic paths." This means categorizing the kinds of links that you can include into two major groups: those that are recommended next destinations, and those that lead into explanatory sidetrails and divergences. As an example, a main path through a hypertext version of this book would be the linear progression from Chapter 1 to Chapter 13. A scenic path, on the other hand, would be a reference from Chapter 6's description of CGI functionality in various HTTP servers to Chapter 8's extended discussion of CGI scripting.

This is not to say that there is a single main path through a document—there can be several (just as there are several ways to read this book, including reading the first three parts in any order, and referring to Part IV (the HTML reference) as needed via sidetrails). And sidetrails include references outside of the immediate document, such as bibliographic references. In addition, sidetrails can become main paths if the trail leads to another document instead of to self-contained explanation.

The point, however, is that a document (in the extended sense of several HTML pages collected and interlinked) should contain at least one or more author-defined main paths through the text, in order to provide a guidepost for those exploring the information. These main paths should take the form of "next" and "previous" anchors, links back to the table of contents and index from any point within the document, and pointers to alternate main paths that are available (where appropriate).

Although hypertext is based on notions of nonlinear text, readers *do* make it linear as they read through it. And it doesn't hurt to provide at least one sensible linear pathway through the document for readers who aren't interested in wandering around in hyperspace.

Consistency

Consistency is what brings your site together so that it becomes a cohesive whole—it can unite otherwise disparate topics or content areas, and give your site a distinctive feel in comparison to other sites, a sense of personality. Consistency also lends to the maintainance of a site. If you have a certain way of doing things site-wide, it becomes much easier to make significant changes without putting a great deal of time into it. You can achieve site-wide consistency a number of ways, described in the following sections.

Headers and Footers

A standard site-wide graphical banner or text-based header can be used to easily identify the site or sponsoring organization. Your header doesn't necessarily need to be static across the site; you can easily share dimensions and a primary graphic element across banners while making each one relate specifically to the content at hand.

Footers can be used in the same way. A standard method to sign documents and/or a standard text-based or graphical menu bar can easily pull a site together, not only as a design element, but also as an easy way to always navigate to the table of contents or index of a site.

Server-side includes, supported by most HTTP servers, can simplify some of this work, allowing you to create generic headers and footers, which can be modified once and thereafter included in all of your documents.

Graphic Elements

A unifying theme for graphic elements throughout the site easily pulls it together into a whole. A shared motif, such as bubbles, signposts, or a corporate logo, works, as does a site-wide color scheme or page backgrounds. You can rely on sizing and positioning of graphic elements or textual elements, as well, to achieve a unified feel.

Personality and Style

Beyond images and design elements, sites come together because of personality and style. A consistent feel or attitude of a site, conveyed across textual and graphic elements, can not only make each piece seem as if it's part of a larger unit, it can also attract readers who share the same attitude or outlook (or are fascinated by yours). The best sites on the Web aren't necessarily the most polished, but those that pull readers back again and again not only because of informational content but also because of the voice with which that content is presented.

In documents in which each should have its own personality, such as user home pages, you can still pull all these different personalities and outlooks together by presenting a com-mon theme or launching point. All the users of a particular Internet service provider, for example, have something in common by the sheer fact of their being there. And by providing a top page view to user-maintained areas, the service provider has begun to form a community around which a commonality can develop.

Persistent URLs

Although Universal Resource Names, or URNs, are being developed in order to provide a naming system for documents that is independent of the actual server being used, at this point it remains desirable to use URLs as if they refer to the same resource persistently through time.

As a content provider, you can help provide those who make links that point to your site by developing a file structure that will allow you to manage content as it grows and develops. If your Web space is based on a hierarchical filing system, you can avoid major reorganization of that file system by:

- Thinking not only about organizing your current content, but how you should plan to develop and expand that content in the future.

- Creating a filespace that is neither too shallow nor too deep for your content.

An example might be an organization that has just created a new division, Foobar. Currently, there's little information to publish about Foobar on the Web; Foobar has a mission statement and little else. Though it might seem logical to create a file, "foobar.html," to hold the mission statement, and to store it in the same directory as your main organization's Web, it might be wiser to create a subdirectory named foobar that could then contain foobar.html and other files, as Foobar expands. This way, links don't have to be changed or redirected down the road when Foobar adds additional files and perhaps chooses to design and administer its own Web space. If part of Foobar's mission statement is to spin off into its own organization, you might even create a directory on the same level as the parent organization's, to signify within the URL path the relative autonomy of the division and its future direction.

Another way to manage URLs is to publicize only a few well-known entry points to your Web; for example, the top view, or table of contents page, and perhaps an index page, or a FAQ page.

When URLs do change, it's important that you not only provide links from the old URLs to the new ones (or redirect the URLs to the new ones), but that you also make an attempt to notify those that have links into your Web space through general announcements (see Chapter 10) or contact directly those who have well-known links to your documents (such as Yahoo or Lycos).

Seamlessness

Your Webspace should not only be consistent with itself internally, it should make references between the site and the outside world appear seamless. A good case in point is the corporate site that has made its product information available via the Web, but, under the link for Ordering Information, only provides an 800 number in order to purchase the advertised commodity (and remember, this is a *World Wide* Web: 800 numbers aren't very useful for those outside the United States). Or consider the homepage for a band that doesn't provide any audio clips of the band's songs, but just a thumbnail image of the cover art from its most recent album, available through some obscure indie label. Or how about the online newspaper that provides news coverage, but doesn't push the envelope and provide a real way to participate in the political process.

Seamlessness is about bridging the gap between the world you create within your Web and the world outside it. Often, this means not carrying over from traditional broadcast media restrictions or limitations that fail to make sense in interactive media.

Macrocosms and Microcosms

The Big Picture: Entire Server Structure

A site-wide strategy to organize information is never easy to invent, but vitally important to your site's success as a place where information is retrieved and used, versus simply being an area in which content is stored.

Finding a Metaphor

Of course, there's no single recipe or structuring mechanism that you can apply to all types of content to give you a well-designed Web site. That comes from thinking about the nature of your site and your content, and the logical divisions around which your content can be organized. However, finding an existing metaphor that you can work within while also pushing its boundaries can be an effective way to plan for the organization of a site. There are many obvious metaphors upon which to base a Web site: think of your content as organized like a book, building, or branching tree.

The Book Metaphor: Pages of Content

Books lend themselves easily to the Web and, in fact, many books have been "ported" to the Web, for better and for worse. Books have tables of contents and indices, for quickly locating information; parts, chapters, sections, and subsections, for organizing content; and footnotes, endnotes, and bibliographies, for displaying links to other content. Collections of books become "libraries," complete with card catalogs and help desks.

However, books also have pages that display content statically, while computer displays have a single, dynamic screen. A book metaphor quickly falls apart when applied to the Web on a page level: you could choose to consider a single HTML document a "page," causing you to break up content into arbitrarily small and hard-to-manage, difficult-to-navigate pieces; or you could think of text and graphics currently displayed on a screen as a "page," which could easily drown the user in a sea of text without the benefit of traditional navigational tools such as page breaks and page numbering. The screen is not a page.

The Building Metaphor: Content as Artifice

Sites can also be thought of as being housed in a building, a collection of buildings, or along some other spacial metaphor. The information you hope to store and manage is divided for the user along content areas, which is housed in different "buildings," which can then be further subdivided into "rooms." Obviously, this can be effective for some types of content, such as for a large corporate site with many divisions, or a museum or gallery. Basically, any information that can be mapped onto a spatial plane consistently lends itself to this sort of view.

At the same time, a spacial metaphor in a largely text-driven medium, as the Web is today, is often hard to pull off convincingly. VRML (Virtual Reality Markup Language) and other such developments will allow for the creation of virtual spaces; even then, the connecting points between rooms or buildings—hallways and walkways—need to be considered thoughtfully. It's also the case that, at many sites, the metaphor is dropped too quickly; you're asked to select a content area built upon a clickable map-based view, but then you're dropped into pages of descriptive text. Not only can this be disconcerting for a user, it points out the fact that oftentimes resources aren't allocated wisely across a Web site, with too much attention and time spent on the top page of a site in comparison to the remainder of the site.

The Branching Metaphor: Regimented Growth

A third way of thinking about a site to use a branching metaphor, where all content springs from a common root and then branches out into many divisions and content areas. This is an obvious metaphor to use for Web sites built atop filesystems, since most filesystems share this organization of directories (or folders) branching into subdirectories (or subfolders), and so on.

A branching metaphor shouldn't be pursued over the linear flow of information, however; too many branches can be confusing or frustrating for a user, especially if navigating those branches requires repeated jumps to a monolithic top structure. In general, there some key issues you should keep in mind when organizing a site on a macro level, including:

Provide a main entry point, or top view, that makes it easy for users to find the content they're most interested in. At times, you'll know exactly what a user is looking for: if you run a site that provides audio clips of theme songs from popular cartoon series of the '70s, users probably expect to find a listing of available audio samples or a link to such a listing from your site's top page. Other times, you can't be expected to know: for a site covering a wide diversity of subjects, it may be necessary to provide a search mechanism or usercustomizable top view in order for users to navigate your site comfortably.

Offer multiple paths to the same content. Not all readers seek the same information in the same way. A good glossary or index will cross-reference information: for example, you may be told to look under "automobiles" if you seek information under "cars." That same information could probably be found by looking through a table of contents. With hypertext links, you can refer to the same information in many ways. Do so, where it facilitates users without overwhelming them.

Keep in mind, too, that a site, whether it be a filesystem or a database, need not be organized as the user sees it; the underlying structure doesn't have to be identical to the structure that the user navigates. However, a close relationship between the two can make it easier to maintain a site, as content is revised and expanded. A change in one part of your Web space can have an impact on other parts of your site that share links or other references. The easier it is for you to see these relationships while maintaining these underlying documents, the more likely it becomes that your site as a whole is kept up to date and cohesive.

The Little Picture: A Document Corpus

Many of the decisions you make on a site-wide level to organize content carry over to the management of documents, whether they are single pages of HTML or a collection of such pages that cover a single topic. These things include such obvious carryovers as having an overview of the information presented within the document available to the reader at the top page, or expected entry point; making links available at appropriate points (usually, at the tops or the bottoms of pages) to bring the reader back to the overview of the document; and keeping your collection of documents uniform in terms of both content and form.

Much of the management of documents, though, is the management of links. Hypertext is all about links—this should be patently obvious to most. But *producing* hypertext is all about managing links from the perspective of your potential reader. Too often, Web documents fail by not managing links effectively—either by delivering screensful of ever-scrolling text, or providing index-card-sized groupings of hypertext that link in a myriad of directions to other index-card-sized groupings of hypertext. Neither end of the spectrum allows the user to easily navigate the content presented; in one case, the user becomes disoriented in a sea of text; in the other, in an ocean of links. Worse yet, documents can become so overseasoned with random and senseless connections to every possible place that the reader becomes lost in a sea of text *and* links!

The key to managing links in your documents (besides simply verifying that they are correct, which is covered in Chapter 7) is to organize them into classifications, and to employ links of various classifications in a reasonable and intelligent way. The next few sections describe some of the various classifications of links.

Footnotes

There are two traditional purposes for footnotes: for bibliographic references and for further commentary and/or elaboration of points within the main text. Links to short explanatory text within a hypertext document can be useful to readers, if it's clear from context that the link is a digression.

Within your documents, the footnote style of link should be regarded as an explanatory link that elaborates on the current discussion without drawing the reader away from the main text. A footnote will draw the reader away temporarily, explain something, and then allow the reader to return to the main flow of text. While a footnote might offer further links to further explanations of greater depth, the footnote itself is usually nothing more than a brief explanation or glossary-style definition.

You can achieve this effect in context by linking from a phrase (as in the lemming example, next) to a short explanation or parenthetical remark that explains the text in question. If you are to trying to acheive a more traditional effect, you can also use numbered note references, either by using a number surrounded by brackets ([1]), or by using the SUP element in HTML 3.0.

HTML 3.0 also defines the FN element for use in footnotes, which, "when practical, [should be] rendered as pop-up notes":

```
⟨P⟩Nothing is certain about the ⟨A HREF="#FN1"⟩
lemmings⟨/A⟩, other than that they left as they
came, with nothing but a silly grin and some lemon
pies.

⟨FN ID="fn1"⟩Lemmings: Small rodents that like to
leap off cliffs if necessary for retrieving a
really nice lemon pie.⟨/FN⟩
```

Whole Documents

Where the footnote provides brief elaboration, the link to a whole document (whether it be to a single document, or to the entry point for a collection of documents) provides new potential for exploration. This is the most common sort of link, that which provides a connection between your document and the outside world.

This sort of link should be used with care. It has the potential to draw your reader completely away from your document, by providing supplementary information that takes longer to read than the original document. It is better to use footnote-style links for explanation and elaboration, and from there to use links to outside documents to provide further reference information for the curious (and insatiable) reader. Another danger is that of peppering your document with random hypertext links that readers feel they must follow, without actually providing further explanations or further reading that's germane to the context or the point of your own document.

On the other hand, if you are referring directly to another on-line document, this is the kind of link to use. By providing direct access to supplementary material for your readers, you can give them as much or as little detail as they are willing to plow through.

Indices

Another form of link is the index. Unlike the previous two classifications, which provide further information for readers as they advance through the text, the index allows readers to enter the text from whatever point they desire, so that they can get right to the meat of what they are interested in. An index allows the reader to cut through the author's predesigned tour of the information, and get right to that vital information on the wildebeest's dietary habits.

There are several variations on this. The most popular is the full-text searchable index, allowing readers to query a database of keywords and retrieve those portions of your text that contain those keywords. Several software packages provide this kind of functionality; several are listed at the end of Chapter 7 (in addition to the built-in searching facilities of WN, described in Chapter 6).

Another variation is often found in books (such as this one) that contain an enumerated list of keywords. This differs from an index where the *reader* supplies the keywords so that the author can provide a selection of keywords that are particularly useful for finding information. This is important—picking proper keywords can be an arcane art, sometimes requiring intimate knowledge of the contents of the collection being searched. Especially if the collection is a large one, most keywords will return a large number of documents that may be only partially related to what the reader had in mind.

Yet another variation provides even more refinement and selection: the table of contents. A table of contents is a form of index, organized by broad topic. Consider providing not just one, but multiple tables of contents for your documents, especially if there is more than one reasonable way in which to read the information.

Portability between Server Platforms

One of the advantages of HTML, which most Web documents consist of, is that it is based upon a number of other clearly defined, widely supported, nonproprietary formats, such as ISO Latin-1 and Internet Media Types (itself based on MIME). This approach makes it much more likely that, a decade from now, your documents will not be part of some legacy system that is, at best, difficult to maintain and expand.

If your documents do have that kind of life span, however, it's probable that they will reside on multiple hosts in that time frame, perhaps concurrently, in the case of popular sites that are mirrored. A little attention to the requirements of different filesystems during the initial planning of your site could save a lot of time spent renaming files and links in the future.

About filesystems: some make the argument that Web servers should sit atop *databases*, instead of filesystems; databases certainly allow nonhierarchical relationships between pieces of content and make it easier to provide *dynamic* documents (documents that alter their appearance or content based upon the user accessing the data or other conditions) than traditional filesystem-based approaches. By the time this book sees print, there will certainly be several HTTP-serving database systems that address "automatically" many of the issues raised in this chapter.

There are some very compelling reasons for using a database over a filesystem. A database-oriented system might be utilized to maintain linkages as documents move and change; to track documents as they grow old, alerting maintainers to update the documents periodically so that they do not suffer "bit-rot"; and to generate multiple representations of a collection of information dynamically (allowing your readers to order your document collections in ways that make sense to them). However, a database approach is not required to get some of this functionality; Chapter 7 discusses tools that also do these sorts of things.

But this automation may not come cheap; there will always be a learning curve to mastering any system, proprietary or nonproprietary, and the skills learned from managing a proprietary system are not easily transferred to other systems. You, as an information provider, must rely on your database solutions vendor to understand your needs and continue to build the feature-set of the system to satisfy them as you develop and grow. You may be risking the future of your documents by marrying your content to a single-vendor methodology for some short-term gains in manageability and ease of publishing content.

Do keep these considerations in mind. One fear we have is that the Web, as it moves forward almost exponentially, may lose any sense of history as links fail and documents drop out of view, because the cost of maintenance and "keeping up" has grown too great. Pick simple solutions over complex ones.

Naming Space

So far, most Web servers have been Unix-based, and have used the naming space associated with that operation system. Many servers have since been developed for other platforms, however, and it's no doubt prudent that, as you create documents, you do not adhere to a naming space for a particular platform such that you make it difficult to move your documents to another platform.

- Some filesystems have naming spaces that are case-sensitive. Unix is a good example of an OS that would consider "document.html" a different file from "Document.html," while other filesystems, such as MacOS, make no such distinction—both names would refer to the same file. For the sake of portability, it's probably best to keep all the file and directory names within your Web structure lowercase. An added benefit is that this makes your URLs much more human-communicable: when case is significant, it's much easier to read an all-lowercase URL over the phone than one that contains both uppercase and lowercase characters.

- Some filesystems require file extensions to properly type files. Servers running under MacOS could serve up files with proper Content-type headers based upon the file's creator and file type stored in the file's resource fork; other filesystems use extensions to do this typing. It's always wise to use the appropriate file extension for the content type—such as .gif for GIF files—whenever possible.

- Some filesystems are restricted to a limited number of significant characters. DOS and Windows, of course, allow only eight characters, plus three characters for the file extension. Generally, filenames less than 32 characters should be fairly cross-platform, except for DOS/Windows (although Windows 95 and NT eliminate this restriction). If you think your files may ever need to live on a DOS or Windows server, you may need to restrict yourself to 8 + 3 character filenames.

- Almost all filesystems define special characters. Almost all OSs allow certain special characters in filenames, while disallowing others; MacOS, for example, allows spaces in filenames, while Unix doesn't. It's best to avoid all characters except for the letters a through z, the numbers 0 through 9, and the underscore, hyphen, and period.

Developing Content

Uniqueness

Uniqueness may not be seen as an important design goal at first glance; after all, uniqueness—not duplicating efforts by creating or compiling same or similar content—may appear to be more of a community issue than an organizational one.

Providing a unique resource, however, increases traffic to your site, and adds to the authoritativeness of your content (see the next section). It will also require support, and a popular, unique resource can have a spillover effect on the other content you provide on your site, especially if your site has a consistent feel and character.

In addition, redoing what has already been done elsewhere can add to frustration on the part of readers. Providing yet another list of exciting on-line resources means that there is simply more of the same sort of content available, which readers must then evaluate and compare to other such resources. Providing a unique resource (or a resource in short supply) means that you are adding to the content of the network, instead of duplicating it.

How do you check for uniqueness of content? There are many search mechanisms on the Web, some of them mentioned in Chapter 10, *Publicizing Your Web*. You can also check in relevant newsgroups and mailing lists.

You can also produce your content so that it leans toward providing unique, value-added content. Instead of simply providing a list of poetry sites, say, you could provide a list of poetry resources that you find particularly compelling, with descriptions of why you think they are compelling. Adding value and content means that you are being a good network citizen, leaving the community with more than you found it.

Authoritativeness

Authoritativeness has always been a fallacy, except when read as author-itativeness; whatever claims to authority you or your organization have ultimately boil down to status and reputation within the community. You become a reputable source not by being nonrefutable, but by putting a stamp on what you write, by claiming authorship and, thereby, author-ity.

This means that readers must take greater responsibility for critically analyzing what documents they come across. But it also means that you must be responsible in establishing credentials for what you claim, providing source material and raw data to justify your conclusions.

In some sense, this is the result of all of the things we discuss in this book. In building and maintaining your infostructure, you are aiming for authoritativeness; for documents that are well thought out and well designed, that do not become stale or inaccurate, and that remain both internally and externally consistent. Your mission now is to use the tools we have provided to place the stamp of authority and relevance on your own works, and to create infostructures on the Web that are compelling and creative. Good luck!

Part IV

HTML Reference

HTML Reference Guide

Introduction to the Hypertext Markup Language (HTML)

HTML is the fundamental language that Web documents are written in. HTML uses *tags* interspersed among the text of a document to provide information about the content of the document. Tags are used to encode information about the type of content represented by each section of the document; this may be formatting information (such as bold or italic), structural information (such as headings and titles), or linking information (such as anchors between documents).

A tag is a set of words or characters enclosed between the less than (⟨) and greater than (⟩) symbols. This separates the tag from the actual text of a document, and allows browsers to recognize where a tag starts and stops. Nothing that is enclosed between angle brackets will be displayed—if the browser doesn't recognize a tag, it ignores it.

Each tag corresponds to an *element* of HTML. An element is the basic building block of HTML. For example:

```
The ⟨A HREF= "http://www.freedonia.org/")Freedonia
Web Server⟨/A⟩ is filled with 27 essential vitamins
and minerals, including Vitamin X!
```

Here, the tags are ⟨A HREF5"http://www.freedonia.org/⟩ and ⟨/A⟩, and the element as a whole is

```
⟨A HREF="http://www.freedonia.org/"⟩Freedonia Web
Server⟨/A⟩
```

385

The difference between a tag and an element is subtle, but important: an element is the container for text, and a tag is what delimits the start and end of an element.

Most elements use a *start tag* and an *end tag* to specify range of text included in the element. A start tag has the form ⟨element-name [attributes]⟩, and the end tag has the form ⟨/element-name⟩. The EM element, which specifies emphasized text, is used like this:

```
⟨EM⟩Emphasize this text⟨/EM⟩, but not this text.
```

The start tag is ·EMÒ, and the end tag is almost the same, ·/EMÒ. When a browser finds a start tag, it knows that everything following the tag is part of the element described by that tag, and it will render that text appropriately.

Elements can take *attributes*, which are name/value pairs included in the start tag for the element. The A element, for example, takes the HREF attribute (among others). Attributes can take certain well-defined values, each of which affects how the element is interpreted. The HREF attribute modifies the A element by providing a destination for the anchor that the A element defines. The attribute is included in the start tag like this:

```
⟨A HREF5"http://www.freedonia.org/"Ò
```

Each attribute is listed after the element's name in the tag, separated by white space. The attribute's name is listed, followed by an equal sign (5), followed by the value of the attribute. For example, the option REV attribute in the A element is inserted as:

```
⟨A HREF5"mailto:tilt@cs.cmu.edu" REV5"made"Ò
```

Note that quotes surrounding the attribute value are not required, but they are recommended.

Some elements are empty, which means that they have a start tag, but no end tag, and no content. An example of this is the HR element, which is rendered as a horizontal rule. There is no content contained by this horizontal rule, so there is no need for an end tag. The HR element can be inserted in your document with one tag: ⟨HR⟩. In contrast, other elements, such as the list elements, have a start tag, an end tag, and one or more subordinate elements within them that specify where a new line in the list should go. These subordinate elements are usually indicated only by a start tag, because the end of the element is clearly indicated by context. For example, the OL element (which represents an *ordered list*) contains multiple empty LI elements, each of which represents a new item in the list:

```
⟨OL⟩
⟨LI⟩This is list item 1
⟨LI⟩This is list item 2
⟨LI⟩Even though this line is longer than one page
line, it will still all be displayed as list item
3.
⟨/OL⟩
```

Elements can be inserted most places within the HTML document, including within other elements, but there are certain restrictions. The HTML document itself is composed of two main sections, the HEAD, and the BODY. The head section of an HTML document contains the document's title, a base URL, revision notes, and anything else that gives information about the document itself. The body section contains the actual content of the document; this is what will actually be displayed by the browser. All of the HTML tags (except for the comment tag) have a particular section of the document to which they belong. For example, the TITLE element should only be used in the head, and the IMG element should only be used in the body. In the reference section, next, any element that should be placed in the HEAD of an HTML document will be noted.

The remainder of this chapter is a reference to the elements that are available in HTML, a concise list of tags (including HTML 1.0, HTML 2.0, HTML 3.0, and the Netscape-specific tags), their syntax, and how they are commonly used and rendered (for an introduction to using HTML to build documents, see Chapter 3). For ease of reference, the elements have been listed in alphabetical order. The elements that relate to forms, tables, and mathematical equations have been placed in separate sections following the main reference section.

Key

Each entry in the HTML Reference follows the format shown in Figure 13.1. The name of the element is given and, if needed, a more descriptive name is provided in parentheses. The common syntax follows. Next is a short description of the element's purpose and usage. Finally, if necessary, a list of additional attributes that the element takes is given, with a description of each attribute's use.

To the left of each entry, icons (as shown in Table 13.1) indicate special conditions under which that element or attribute may be used. Specifically, any elements that are HTML 3.0 or Netscape-

---

A. [ICONS] ELEMENT (Full Name of Element)

```
Syntax
Description of the element's syntax
Common uses:
If appropriate, common idioms of this element's use
```

A description of the element's purpose and usage.

I. Additional Attributes:

If appropriate, a description of attributes taken by the element.

Figure 13.1
Sample Entry

Table 13.1
Icons for HTML 3.0, Netscape, and HEAD Elements

 This element or attribute is part of HTML 3.0, and will be available to HTML 3.0 conformant clients. At the time of this writing, HTML 3.0 is still very much in development and may change drastically in the final version, although some features (such as tables) are in widespread use.

 This element or attribute is part of the Netscape-specific extensions to HTML, and at the time of this writing is only recognized by the Netscape Navigator Web client.

 This element belongs in the HEAD element of an HTML document.

Table 13.2 Additional Typographic Conventions		
	content	any text and/or additional HTML tags
	text	any text (but not HTML tags)
	url	any URL
	name	a string consisting of a sequence of letters, digits, periods, or hyphens (but no white space)
	char	any single character
	num	any number
	attributes	a list of attributes, as described in the *Attributes* section for this element.
	[ ]	text within brackets is optional
	[ ]*	text within brackets can be repeated 0 or more times
	*[text1	text2]*	Either *text1* or *text2* must appear, but not both.

specific have been marked as such, as well as any elements that should only be used in the HEAD of a document. Table 13.2 is a key to additional typographic conventions used in this chapter to describe the syntax of HTML elements.

HTML Reference

The ID, LANG, CLASS, CLEAR, NOWRAP, and MD Attributes

HTML 3.0 adds the following attributes to almost all elements. For brevity, their descriptions are given here instead of with each HTML 3.0 element. Each element that accepts one of these attributes will list the attribute name under the *Additional Attributes* of the element.

```
ID="name"
```

ID allows this element to become the destination of a link by letting an A element point to it (as in ⟨A HREF="#name"⟩). This is similar to the ⟨A NAME="name"⟩ tag functionality in previous editions of HTML.

```
LANG="text"
```

text specifies that the language and country indicated by the element should be considered, for purposes of hyphenation, quotation marks, and so on, if the browser supports this. An example of LANG value is "en.uk," which stands for English, specifically the style of English spoken in the United Kingdom. Optionally, just the language code may be given, as in "en." Language codes are governed by ISO 639, country codes by ISO 3166.

```
CLASS=text
```

text is a space-separated list of SGML *name* items, which subclasses the element within the scope of the document. This can be used to apply a style to an element, or to restict searches or other operations to relevant areas of the document. For example, a search engine for biology journal articles may only want to search divisions (see DIV) or paragraphs (see P) that are in the ABSTRACT class.

```
CLEAR=text
```

This does one of two things, depending on the value of *text*. If *text* is one of LEFT, RIGHT, or ALL, the text associated with the element is displayed below any floating images (or tables or input boxes) aligned with the left, right, or both margins, respectively. Normally, text is displayed alongside a floating image; if the text continues beyond the bottom of the image, the text is displayed in the (now free) left- or right-hand margin.

If the CLEAR attribute is used by an element, the text associated with that element will *not* be displayed alongside a floating image currently occupying the left- or right-hand margins. Instead, the text will be displayed below the image(s), in the now free left- and/or right-hand margin. If *text* is a value surrounded by quotation marks (such as "100 pixels"), the text associated with the image will be displayed alongside a floating image as long as that much space exists before the bottom of the image. For example,

```
CLEAR="25 pixels"
```

indicates that the content of the element should be displayed alongside a floating image as long as the current position for displaying text is more than (or exactly equal to) 25 pixels from the bottom of the floating image. If there is not enough room, no part of the text is displayed alongside the floating image; it is all displayed below the image.

    NOWRAP

If present, this indicates that the text associated with the element should not be automatically wrapped to fit within the current display window. The ⟨BR⟩ tag may be used to specify where line breaks occur; otherwise, no line breaks will be added by the browser.

    MD="*text*"

text is a message digest or checksum associated with a file pointed to by any attribute that uses a URL (including the A element, IMG element, and any element that uses the SRC attribute). The message digest or checksum is created for the file pointed to, and is checked against a recalculated checksum each time the URL is retrieved. This way, an author can be sure that what is being pointed to by a URL is always the same—if the target file is changed, the checksum will be different and the browser should notify the user viewing the page.

The Comment Tag

    Syntax:
    ⟨!-- content --⟩

Any characters contained within the *comment tag* will not be displayed. This tag can be used to store revision information in a document:

    ⟨!-- This document last updated on 1-25-95 by
    Tyler Jones --⟩

or to stop sections of an HTML document (including other HTML tags) from being displayed:

    ⟨!--
    This part of the document used to get displayed,
    but ⟨EM⟩not anymore!⟨/EM⟩
    --⟩

NOTE: Comment tags *cannot* be nested. The first $--\rangle$ in the document will end the comment, so this:

```
⟨!-- This comment surrounds another comment ⟨!--
but the comment will end here --⟩ instead of here
--⟩
```

will not work; "`instead of here --⟩`" will be outside of the comment. Unlike most HTML elements, the comment element does not actually have a start and end tag; any commented text must be contained within the tag itself.

A

A (anchor)

```
Syntax:
⟨A [HREF|NAME]="text ")text⟨/a⟩
```

```
Common uses:
⟨A HREF="url ")text⟨/a⟩
⟨A HREF="url#name")text⟨/a⟩
⟨A HREF="#name")text⟨/a⟩
⟨A NAME="name")text⟨/a⟩
```

The anchor element represents one end of a connection between two documents. This is the mechanism by which HTML provides hypertext functionality. The text between the start and end tags is displayed as a link on the page. When the text is selected by the user, the document referenced by *url* is retrieved.

The first three forms, containing the HREF attribute, provide an anchor *to* another document. The first form references the object specified by the URL given. The second and third forms reference a specific fragment within the document named by the URL. In the second form, the URL is given; in the third, it is not, and the fragment is assumed to be in the current document. By referencing a fragment, a specific portion of a document may be linked to, rather than the entire document. In practice, this means that the referenced portion will be displayed when the page is brought up, rather than the beginning of the document being displayed.

In order to provide fragment names, the final form defines an anchor destination inside a document. By providing a NAME attribute, an anchor can be what is pointed to, rather than being what is doing the pointing. The value of the NAME attribute matches the fragment description given in the second and third forms.

It is possible for an anchor to have both an HREF attribute (that is, be the start of a link) and a NAME attribute (be the destination of a link) at the same time.

```
Example:
Lizards, especially ⟨A HREF="http://www.freedonia.org/fun/salamander.
html"
NAME="lizard"⟩the mighty salamander⟨/A⟩, can be fun as well.
```

> **NOTE:**　The text within an anchor cannot include HTML. This means that if you would like, for example, a header to also be an anchor, the A element must be within the H2 element.

Additional Attributes

METHODS="*text*"

text is a white space-separated list of HTTP methods supported by the object pointed to by this link.

REL="*text*"

text is a comma-separated list of relationship values between the current document and the document that is pointed to by this link.

REV="*text*"

text is a comma-separated list of relationship values between the current document and the document that is pointed to by this link. Semantically, REV is the opposite of the REL attribute, and describes the relationship values that the other document would put in a REL link to this document.

SHAPE="*text*"

When an anchor element is used within a ⟨FIG⟩, the SHAPE attribute is used to specify an area within the image that, if clicked on, links to the URL speficied by the A element (a *"hotzone"*). *text* may be one of:

- `default`—the default menu item to select if the user clicks on an area outside of any hotzones.

- `circle x, y, radius`—defines a circle-shaped hotzone in the image, with the center at *x, y,* and with a radius of *radius.*

- `rect x, y, width, height`—defines a rectangle-shaped hotzone in the image, with the upper left corner at *x, y,* and of size *width, height.*

- `polygon: x1, y1, x2, y2,..., xn, yn`—defines an n-sided polygon-shaped hotzone in the image. Each *x, y* pair represents a point connected by a line to the previous and the following pairs. The *n*th point is considered to connect back to the first point, automatically closing the polygon.

In all cases, *x* and *y* may be specified in pixels as integers, or on a scale from 0.0 to 1.0 across and down the image, where 0.0 indicates the left or top edge of the image, and 1.0 indicates the right or bottom edge of the image. (For example, the point (0.5, 0.5) would be the exact center of any image.) If a user clicks in an area that is part of two or more hotzones, the distance from the mouse click to the centers of all applicable hotzones is calculated, and the nearest hotzone is considered selected. In this way, hotzones may overlap without the figure failing.

> `TITLE="text"`

text is the title of the document pointed to by this link. In the event that that document doesn't have a TITLE element, the value of this attribute may be displayed as the title of the document.

> `ID, LANG, CLASS, MD`

ABBREV (abbreviation)

> *Syntax:*
> `⟨ABBREV⟩content⟨/ABBREV⟩`

The content of the `ABBREV` element is an abbreviation.

Additional Attributes

```
ID, LANG, CLASS.
```

ABOVE

See the section *Math Elements*.

ACRONYM

Syntax:
⟨ACRONYM⟩*content*⟨/ACRONYM⟩0

The content of the ACRONYM element is an acronym.

Additional Attributes

```
ID, LANG, CLASS.
```

ADDRESS

Syntax:
⟨ADDRESS⟩*content*⟨/ADDRESS⟩

The ADDRESS element indicates authorship information relating to the current document; specifically, it is intended to indicate an address at which the author may be reached.

Additional Attributes

```
ID, LANG, CLASS, CLEAR, NOWRAP
```

ARRAY

See the section *Math Elements*.

ATOP

See the section *Math Elements*.

AU (author)

Syntax:
⟨AU⟩*content*⟨/AU⟩

The content of the AU element is the name of an author.

Additional Attributes

```
ID, LANG, CLASS
```

B

B (bold)

```
Syntax:
⟨B⟩content⟨/B⟩
```

The B element indicates text that is to be displayed bold.

Additional Attributes

```
ID, LANG, CLASS
```

BAR

See the section *Math Elements*.

BASE

```
Syntax:
⟨BASE HREF="url"⟩
```

The BASE element defines the URL of the document itself, for use in situations where the document may be out of context and the URL may not be obvious. This can happen when the document has been retrieved with a different URL than expected (which can be a side effect of CGI scripts and imagemaps), or if the document is a mirror of a master document that exists elsewhere. This can be useful for correctly resolving relative URL references in such a document; if there is a BASE element supplied, the URL provided is used to dereference relative URLs.

BASEFONT

```
Syntax:
⟨BASEFONT SIZE=num⟩
```

The BASEFONT element changes the default font size for all subsequent text and for all relative font size changes to the text (see the

FONT element) to *num*. Valid values are from 1 to 7, inclusive (1 being smallest, 7 being largest). Default size is 3.

BANNER

> *Syntax:*
> ⟨BANNER⟩*content*⟨/BANNER⟩

The BANNER element allows you to specify text or images that stay in the display window when the page is scrolled through. For example, the content of the BANNER element might be a copyright notice or a navigation toolbar. The BANNER element may only occur directly after the BODY element.

Additional Attributes

> ID, LANG, CLASS.

BELOW

See the section *Math Elements.*

BIG

> *Syntax:*
> ⟨BIG⟩*content*⟨/BIG⟩

The content of the BIG element is displayed in a larger font than normal text.

Additional Attributes

> ID, LANG, CLASS

BLOCKQUOTE

> *Syntax:*
> ⟨BLOCKQUOTE⟩*content*⟨/BLOCKQUOTE⟩

The BLOCKQUOTE element indicates text and/or HTML between the tags that is a single, continuous block (one or more sentences or paragraphs) quoted from another source. In the HTML 3.0 specification, the BLOCKQUOTE element is being deprecated in favor of the BQ element, which has the same semantics (but a shorter name).

BODY

> *Syntax:*
> ⟨BODY⟩*content*⟨/BODY⟩

Surrounds the body section of an HTML document. Only elements that can be used in the body section should be used between the start and end body tags. The meat of your document goes between the body start and end tags—the text and HTML that will be displayed by a browser as your "page." (See the note under HTML). Only one BODY element can be used per document.

Additional Attributes

    BACKGROUND=" *url* "

url points to an image file to display (tiled) in the normal background of the browser's display window.

    BGCOLOR=" *#rrggbb* "

rrggbb is a hexadecimal triple that specifies a background color in terms of red intensity (*rr*), green intensity (*gg*), and blue intensity (*bb*). For example,

    ⟨BODY BGCOLOR="#A000A0"⟩

produces a nice purple color (with red and blue values of A0, and no green value).

    ALINK="#rrggbb"

rrggbb is a hexadecimal triple that specifies the active link color (see the BODY attribute for an example). It should be used to ensure that active links have sufficient contrast to the background color.

    LINK="#rrggbb"

rrggbb is a hexadecimal triple that specifies the default link color (see the BODY attribute for an example). It should be used to ensure that links have sufficient contrast to the background color.

```
VLINK="#rrggbb"
```

rrggbb is a hexadecimal triple that specifies the color for visited links (see the BODY attribute for an example). It should be used to ensure that visited links have sufficient contrast to the background color.

```
TEXT="#rrggbb"
```

rrggbb is a hexadecimal triple that specifies the color for text (see the BODY attribute for an example). It should be used to ensure that the body text has sufficient contrast to the background color.

```
ID, LANG, CLASS.
```

BOX

See the section *Math Elements*.

BQ (blockquote)

```
Syntax:
⟨BQ⟩content[⟨CREDIT⟩content⟨/CREDIT]⟨/BQ⟩
```

See BLOCKQUOTE. The optional CREDIT element (new in HTML 3.0) defines the source of the quote, so that it may be displayed differently from the rest of the quote.

Additional Attributes

ID, LANG, CLASS, CLEAR, NOWRAP

BR (line break)

```
Syntax:
⟨BR⟩
```

The BR element ends the current line, and begins the next text line. This element is different from the P element in that the P element implies a line of white space before the next line begins.

Additional Attributes

```
CLEAR=[LEFT|RIGHT|ALL]
```

Used in conjunction with floating images (see the IMG element). Breaks the line at the tag and begins displaying text again once the left (CLEAR=LEFT), right (CLEAR=RIGHT), or both (CLEAR=ALL) margins are clear of floating images.

ID, LANG, CLASS, CLEAR

BT (bold, upright font)

See the section *Math Elements.*

C

CENTER

Syntax:
⟨CENTER⟩*content*⟨/CENTER⟩

The content of the CENTER element is centered (horizontally) in the display window.

CAPTION

Syntax:
⟨CAPTION⟩*content*⟨/CAPTION⟩

Used by the FIG and TABLE elements to define caption text for a figure or table. See the section *Table Elements.*

Additional Attributes

ALIGN=[TOP|BOTTOM|LEFT|RIGHT]

Specifies where to display the caption—above, below, left, or right of the figure or table.

ID, LANG, CLASS

CITE

Syntax:
⟨CITE⟩*content*⟨/CITE⟩

The CITE element describes a citation of another source, such as a book title or author name.

Additional Attributes

ID, LANG, CLASS

CHOOSE

See the section *Math Elements*.

CODE

> *Syntax:*
> ⟨CODE⟩*content*⟨/CODE⟩

The CODE element describes a sample of source code. Unlike the PRE element, this is an example of code within a paragraph or other block of text.

Additional Attributes

ID, LANG, CLASS

CREDIT

> *Syntax:*
> ⟨CREDIT⟩*content*⟨/CREDIT⟩

The CREDIT element is used within the BQ and FIG elements to specify the source (author or copyright holder) of the quotation or image.

Additional Attributes

ID, LANG, CLASS

D

DD (definition for definition list)

See *DL*.

Additional Attributes

ID, LANG, CLASS, CLEAR

DDOT (double dots)

See the section *Math Elements*.

DEL (deleted text)

Syntax:
⟨DEL⟩*content*⟨/DEL⟩

The DEL element represents deleted text, as might be used in a legal document to show revisions.

Additional Attributes

ID, LANG, CLASS.

DFN (defining instance)

Syntax:
⟨DFN⟩*content*⟨/DFN⟩

The DFN element represents the defining instance of a term. This is similar to usage in textbooks, where the introduction of key terms is often reflected with bold or italic text.

Additional Attributes

ID, LANG, CLASS

DIR (directory list)

Syntax:
⟨DIR⟩
[⟨LI⟩*content*]*
⟨/DIR⟩

The DIR element describes a list of items containing up to 20 characters each. Since each item is relatively short, a directory list may be arranged in columns. The use of DIR is discouraged; you should use UL or OL instead. See UL for a *longer* discussion of the use of list elements.

Example:
⟨DIR⟩
⟨LI⟩Item 1
⟨LI⟩Item 2
⟨LI⟩Item 3
⟨/DIR⟩

DIV (document division)

Syntax:
⟨DIV⟩*content*⟨/DIV⟩

The DIV element is used in conjunction with the CLASS attribute to define a "container" for a section of text, such as a paragraph, chapter, appendix, forward, or sentence. Through this mechanism, HTML can be extended by the author to support arbitrary structures without having to explicitly add them to the specification.

Additional Attributes

ALIGN=[LEFT|RIGHT|CENTER|JUSTIFY]

Specifies the alignment for paragraphs within the division to be against the left margin, right margin, centered within the display window, or justified when lines must wrap around the right margin.

ID, LANG, CLASS, CLEAR, NOWRAP.

DL (definition list)

Syntax:
⟨DL⟩
[⟨LH⟩*content*⟨/LH⟩]
[⟨DT⟩*content*
⟨DD⟩*content*]*
⟨/DL⟩

The definition list has two subordinate elements to indicate lines, DT (Term) and DD (Definition). The DL element is meant to function like a glossary list, where you first list a term; then its definition is displayed on the next lines, indented by a half-inch. Each term is preceded by a ⟨DT⟩ tag. Each definition is preceded by a ⟨DD⟩ tag. End tags for the subordinate elements are not necessary—the end of a subordinate element is implied by the beginning of the next subordinate element.

HTML 3.0 adds the optional *line header* (⟨LH⟩) element to ⟨DL⟩ which defines a title for the list, to be displayed at the top of the list in an appropriate font. The ⟨LH⟩ tag must occur immediately after the ⟨DL⟩ tag.

```
Example:
⟨DL⟩
⟨LH⟩A WWW Glossary⟨/LH⟩
⟨DT⟩HTML
⟨DD⟩HTML, the Hypertext Markup Language, is a way
to provide platform-independent markup for
documents, and to link those documents together.
⟨DT⟩HTTP
⟨DD⟩HTTP, the Hypertext Transport Protocol, is a
protocol for serving HTML and other documents to
Web browsers.
⟨/DL⟩
```

Additional Attributes

```
COMPACT
```

When present in the ⟨DL⟩ tag, forces less white space to be displayed between list items.

```
Example:
⟨DL COMPACT⟩
⟨DT⟩Apple
⟨DD⟩An apple is a fruit.
⟨DT⟩Orange
⟨DD⟩An orange is another fruit.
⟨/DL⟩
```

```
ID, LANG, CLASS, CLEAR
```

DOT (single dots)

See the section *Math Elements*.

DT (term for definition list)

See *DL*.

Additional Attributes

```
ID, LANG, CLASS, CLEAR
```

E

EM (emphasis)

> *Syntax:*
> ⟨EM⟩*content*⟨/EM⟩

The content of the EM element is considered to be emphasized. This is generally rendered as underlined or italic text.

Additional Attributes

ID, LANG, CLASS

F

FIG (figure)

> *Syntax:*
> ⟨FIG SRC="*url*"⟩
> [⟨CAPTION⟩*content*⟨/CAPTION⟩]
> [⟨CREDIT⟩*content*⟨/CREDIT⟩]
> [⟨OVERLAY SRC="*url*"⟩]
> content
> ⟨/FIG⟩

Displays the image file pointed to by *url* at the current point in the document, allowing text to be displayed alongside the image ("flowing" text). The text and/or HTML between the tags will only be displayed on nongraphical browsers, but may specify clickable areas (hotzones) within the image itself. The optional CAPTION element surrounds text and/or HTML to be displayed as a caption for the image. The optional CREDIT element surrounds text and/or HTML that defines the owner, author, or copyright holder of the image. The contents of both CAPTION and CREDIT will be displayed on either graphical or nongraphical browsers. The optional OVERLAY element specifies an additional image file to display on top of the first image.

To turn the figure into an imagemap (an image that can be clicked on when viewed through a browser, such that different URLs are loaded depending on where on the image the mouse click occurred), the HTML within the FIG element must contain one or more A elements with HREF and SHAPE attributes. The SHAPE attribute defines an area within the image that can be clicked on (a hotzone), and the HREF attribute defines a URL to load when that hotzone is selected (when a mouse click occurs within the area defined by the SHAPE parameter).

Additional Attributes

ALIGN=[BLEEDLEFT|BLEEDRIGHT|CENTER|JUSTIFY|LEFT|RIGHT]

Defines how to display the image specified by the SRC attribute. BLEEDLEFT and BLEEDRIGHT display the image flush with the left or right window border, respectively. LEFT and RIGHT display the image flush with the left or right text margin, respectively. CENTER displays the image centered between the left and right text margins. JUSTIFY scales the image to occupy all the space between the left and right text margins, increasing or decreasing the image's size as necessary. The default is center alignment.

HEIGHT=*num*

Specifies the display height of the image, which may be scaled up or down (increased or decreased in size) to fit. *num* may be in pixels or en units, as defined by the UNITS attribute.

IMAGEMAP="*url*"

url specifies a CGI script to send mouse click and drag information to.

NOFLOW

When present, specifies that text should not flow around the image. Text that follows the FIG element will be displayed below the image, instead of alongside it. This is the default if the ALIGN attribute is set to center or justify.

UNITS=[PIXELS|EN]

Specifies the type of units the WIDTH and HEIGHT attributes will be specified in. One en is equal to half the point size of the current font.

WIDTH=*num*

Specifies the display width of the image, which may be scaled up or down (increased or decreased in size) to fit. *num* may be in pixels or en units, as defined by the UNITS attribute.

ID, LANG, CLASS, CLEAR, MD

FN (footnote)

Syntax:
⟨FN⟩*content*⟨/FN⟩

Generally used with the ID attribute as a destination for an anchor surrounding a word or phrase and offering additional information about that word or phrase. Where possible, footnote text may be displayed as a pop-up note in the window.

Additional Attributes

ID, LANG, CLASS.

FORM

See the section *Form Elements.*

FONT

Syntax:
⟨FONT SIZE=*num*⟩*content*⟨/FONT⟩

The content of the FONT element is displayed using a font of size *num* or, if *num* begins with a "+" or "−," that many sizes larger (+) or smaller (−) than the default font size. Valid size values are from 1 to 7, inclusive (1 is smallest, 7 is largest). The default font size is 3, which can be changed using the BASEFONT element. See also *BASEFONT.*

Example:
⟨P⟩This uses absolute font sizes: "The ⟨FONT
SIZE=6⟩rain⟨/FONT⟩ in ⟨FONT SIZE=5⟩Spain⟨/FONT⟩
falls mainly on the ⟨FONT SIZE=2⟩plain⟨/FONT⟩."

⟨P⟩This uses relative font sizes: "The ⟨FONT
SIZE=+3⟩rain⟨/FONT⟩ in ⟨FONT SIZE=+2⟩Spain⟨/FONT⟩
fall mainly on the ⟨FONT SIZE=-1⟩plain⟨/FONT⟩."

H

H1, H2, H3, H4, H5, H6 (headers, level 1-6)

Syntax:
⟨H1⟩*content*⟨/H1⟩ (also ⟨H2⟩, ⟨H3⟩, ⟨H4⟩, ⟨H5⟩, ⟨H6⟩)

The header elements display the text between tags as a "header," generally rendered as a bold font larger than normal text (how much larger depends on the level), with a blank line before the start tag and after the end tag (separating it from any other text nearby). Level 1 (H1) is the largest (much larger than regular text), and ranking decreases to level 6.

Headers provide a means for structuring your document into logical sections. They are not intended for providing font size control within your document, and this sort of usage can often backfire. See Chapter 11 for a discussion on how to handle headers properly.

Additional Attributes

```
ALIGN=[LEFT|RIGHT|CENTER|JUSTIFY]
```

Specifies how to align the text of the heading. Left and right align the heading text with the left and right margins, respectively. Center centers the heading text between the left and right margins, and justify adds spacing between letters and words such that the heading text stretches from the left text margin to the right text margin.

```
DINGBAT="text"
```

text specifies an HTML 3.0 icon entity to display as a bullet at the head of the heading text.

```
SEQNUM=num
```

num specifies the heading counter for this heading. By default, heading counters for each style of heading (H1 through H6) start at 1 at the beginning of the document, and increase each time a heading of that type is encountered. The heading counter for a heading style is reset to 1 when a heading of a higher level is encountered; that is, when an H3 is encountered, the heading counters for H4, H5, and H6 are reset to 1. If SEQNUM=num is present, the current heading is reset to *num,* and counting continues from *num* until a heading of a higher level is encountered.

```
SKIP=num
```

Causes the current heading counter (for this heading style) to be increased by *num.*

```
SRC="URL"
```

url points to an image file to display as a bullet at the head of the heading text.

```
ID, LANG, CLASS, CLEAR, MD, NOWRAP.
```

HAT (circumflex)

See the section *Math Elements*.

HEAD

> *Syntax:*
> ⟨HEAD⟩*content*⟨/HEAD⟩

Surrounds the header information for an HTML document. Only elements that can be used in the head section (such as those that specify information about the document as a whole) should be used between the ⟨HEAD⟩ and ⟨HEAD⟩ tags. The TITLE element is required to appear here. (See the note under HTML).

HR (horizontal rule)

> *Syntax:*
> ⟨HR⟩

The HR element results in a solid line across the width of the page, resizing itself automatically to the width of the display window.

Additional Attributes

```
SIZE=num
```

num indicates the thickness of the solid line—the larger the number, the thicker the line will be.

```
WIDTH=num
```

num indicates the width of the solid line. *num* may be either an exact measurement in pixels, or a percent (0-100) relative to the width of the display window (so, WIDTH=50% would indicate that the line should always be half the width of the display window). The default width is the width of the display window.

```
ALIGN=[left|right|center]
```

Align the solid line with either the left-hand side of the display window, the right-hand side of the window, or the center of the window. Defaults to center. Only applicable when the WIDTH of the line has been changed.

> NOSHADE

In most graphical browsers, the solid line has shadows along all four edges to give it the appearance of being three-dimensional. The NOSHADE attribute stops this fancy shading from being displayed, resulting in a flat solid line.

> SRC="*url*"

url points to an image file to use as the horizontal rule (instead of the default shaded line).

> ID, CLASS, CLEAR, MD

HTML

> *Syntax:*
> ⟨HTML⟩*content*⟨/HTML⟩

Surrounds an entire HTML document to specify that the content of the document is HTML-encoded text. The ⟨HTML⟩ tag should be the first thing in your document, and the ⟨/HTML⟩ tag should be the last. There should not be any text nor tags ouside of these tags.

NOTE: The HTML start and end tags, like the HEAD and BODY tags, can be omitted. This practice is not recommended, however. For example, if information about the document itself is properly contained in the HEAD element, agents that are only interested in that information (for caching purposes, for example) will be able to extract that information without having to process the the BODY information.

I

I (italic)

> *Syntax:*
> ⟨I⟩*content*⟨/I⟩

The I element indicates text that is to be displayed in italics.

Additional Attributes

ID, LANG, CLASS

IMG (image)

Syntax:
⟨IMG SRC="*url*" [ALT="*text*"]
[ALIGN=[TOP|MIDDLE|BOTTOM]]⟩

The IMG element displays the image pointed to by *url* as part of the current document at this point in the document, aligning it with the top, middle, or bottom of the current line of text, or displaying *text* from the ALT attribute if the document is being viewed through a nongraphical browser (such as Lynx). The ALT and ALIGN attributes are optional, but use of the ALT attribute, at least, is highly recommended.

Example:
⟨IMG SRC="http://www.freedonia.org/images/wonder-squirrel.jpg" ALT="[A Well-Composed Shot of Skippy, the Wonder Squirrel]"⟩ Skippy, the Wonder Squirrel, often is seen relaxing by the pool after a long day of hunting Internets with Team Twinkie.

Additional Attributes

ISMAP

If the ISMAP attribute is supplied, the image is treated as an imagemap. See Chapter 8 *(CGI)* for examples of use.

ALIGN=[LEFT|RIGHT|TOP|MIDDLE|BOTTOM]

Specifies how to align the image on the page. LEFT and RIGHT align the image against the left or right text margin, respectively, and allow subsequent text to flow alongside the image. TOP, MIDDLE, and BOTTOM align the top, middle, or bottom of the image with the current text baseline.

ALIGN=[LEFTvBRIGHT|TEXTTOP|ABSMIDDLE|ABSBOTTOM|BASELINE]

These additional ALIGN values are used by Netscape. LEFT and RIGHT produce floating images, aligned with the left- or right-hand margin, allowing text to wrap around the right- or left-hand side of the image. TEXTTOP, ABSMIDDLE, and ABSBOTTOM align the image with the absolute top, middle, or bottom of the current line of text (based on any font size changes in the line). BASELINE is identical to bottom alignment.

NOTE: It is worth noting that the ALIGN attributes, for both HTML 3.0 and Netscape, will cause a "stair-stepping" effect, as further images will also be affected by the flowing text implied by ALIGN (see Chapter 11 for more details). This can be prevented by using the CLEAR attribute in the first element which you wish to not be flowed around any other images or figures (described earlier in this chapter). Netscape supports only the CLEAR attribute for the BR element.

BORDER=*num*

num is the thickness of the border around an anchored image. A thickness of 0 indicates no border.

SRC="*url*"

url points to the image file to be displayed.

UNITS=[pixels|en]

Specifies which units the WIDTH and HEIGHT attributes will be specified in. Default is pixels.

VSPACE=*num* or HSPACE=*num*

Used only by floating images (see ALIGN) to control how much blank space should be retained above and below (VSPACE) or to the left and right (HSPACE) of a floating image when wrapping text around the image.

WIDTH=*num* or HEIGHT=*num*

num specifies the suggested display width or height of the image, in the units specified by the UNITS attribute.

WIDTH=*num* or HEIGHT=*num*

num indicates the width or height of the image (in pixels). These can be used by Netscape to speed up page display, because the size of the image can be calculated, and enough space reserved in the page, before the image has been loaded from the server.

NOTE: The difference between the WIDTH and HEIGHT attributes under HTML 3.0 and under Netscape is that HTML 3.0 uses the UNITS attribute to determine what the value of WIDTH and HEIGHT attributes refer to, whereas in Netscape the values refer either to pixels or to a percentage.

ID, LANG, CLASS, MD

INPUT

See the section *Form Elements.*

INS (inserted text)

> *Syntax:*
> ⟨INS⟩*content*⟨/INS⟩

Text in between the tags is considered "inserted" text, as might be used by a legal document to show revisions.

Additional Attributes

ID, LANG, CLASS

ISINDEX

> *Syntax:*
> ⟨ISINDEX⟩

The ISINDEX element indicates that the document is a searchable index of some kind. The client may request a search performed on the document, usually by allowing the user to enter one or more keywords. The document must be able to accept keywords, usually by means of a CGI script. For more information on the ISINDEX element, see Chapter 8, *CGI.*

In many browsers, the user will be able to enter keywords directly into the document itself, by means of a text entry box. Some browsers will place this box whereever the ⟨ISINDEX⟩ tag appears in your document, so—while it is technically a HEAD element—you can place it either in the HEAD or BODY portion of your document.

Additional Attributes

```
PROMPT="content"
```

In many browsers, users are given a prompt where they can enter text. In Netscape Navigator, the PROMPT attribute lets you specify what the prompt says. The prompt defaults to "This is a searchable index. Enter search keywords:"

ITEM (array item)

See the section *Math Elements*.

K

KBD (keyboard)

```
Sample:
⟨KBD⟩content⟨/KBD⟩
```

The KBD element indicates text that should be typed in by a user, as in instruction manuals.

Additional Attributes

```
ID, LANG, CLASS
```

L

LANG (language context)

```
Syntax:
⟨LANG LANG="name"⟩content⟨/LANG⟩
```

The content of the LANG element is considered to be in the language *name*. See the LANG attribute in the section *The ID, LANG, CLASS, CLEAR, NOWRAP, and MD attributes*.

Additional Attributes

```
ID, CLASS
```

LEFT

See the section *Math Elements*.

LI

Syntax:
⟨LI⟩*content*

Used only in UL or OL context. Specifies a new list item (which may have a bullet or number placed before it, depending on the list type and attributes). As a subordinate element, there is no need for a ⟨/LI⟩ end tag; instead, the end of the element is implied by the next ⟨LI⟩ start tag. See UL and OL.

Additional Attributes

SRC=*url*

url points to an image file to use as the bullet for this list item (only in UL context). Overrides the SRC or DINGBAT attribute in UL.

DINGBAT="text"

text specifies an HTML 3.0 icon entity to display as the bullet for this list item (only in UL context). Overrides the SRC or DINGBAT attribute in UL.

SKIP=*num*

Causes the current list counter to be increased by *num* (only in OL context). num is added to the counter from the last list item (or from 1 if this is the first list item, as subject to the SEQNUM and CONTINUE attributes of the OL element), and the new number is used as the list counter for the current list item and the remainder of the list as normal.

ID, LANG, CLASS, CLEAR, MD

LINK

Syntax:
⟨LINK HREF="*url*"⟩

The LINK element is used to indicate a relationship between this document and another, such as a "next" or a "parent" document. It is equivalent to the A element, except that it indicates a relationship between the whole document and the object specified by the URL, rather than just the text contained by the A element.

Unlike the A element, the LINK element usually does not provide a clickable region that can take you to another document. Rather, LINK is useful for describing semantic relationships between documents, such as authorship and prior revisions.

```
Example:
⟨HEAD⟩
⟨TITLE⟩Yet Another Fine Mess⟨/TITLE⟩

⟨LINK REV="made" HREF="mailto:jtilton@willamette
.edu"⟩
⟨!--
This LINK is a "REV"erse relationship between this
document and the object specified in the HREF
attribute. Since this is of type "made", it means
that this document was made by the object specified
by the URL, one "jtilton@willamette.edu". If it
had been a REL relationship, then this document
would have made jtilton@willamette.edu, instead.
And then where would we be?
--⟩

⟨/HEAD⟩
```

LH (list header)

```
Syntax:
⟨LH⟩text⟨/LH⟩
```

The LH element describes a caption for the list elements UL, OL, or DL.

M

MATH

See the section *Math Elements*.

MENU (level 0)

```
Syntax:
⟨MENU⟩
[⟨LI⟩content]
⟨/MENU⟩
```

The MENU element is similar to the DIR and UL elements, except that lines are expected to be less than the width of the page. The use of the MENU element is discouraged; UL or OL should be used in its place. See UL for a longer discussion on the use of list elements.

```
Example:
⟨MENU⟩
⟨LI⟩Lions
⟨LI⟩Tigers
⟨LI⟩Bears
⟨/MENU⟩
```

META

```
Syntax:
⟨META [HTTP-EQUIV="text"] [NAME="text"]
[CONTENT="text"]⟩
```

The META element provides a means for providing meta-information that cannot be provided with existing HEAD elements. This meta-information is either provided as an HTTP header (if the HTTP-EQUIV attribute is present), or else is extracted by the client. In order to be provided as an HTTP header, the server must be aware of the META element.

Additional Attributes

```
HTTP-EQUIV="text"
```

The HTTP-EQUIV attribute specifies the HTTP header that the CONTENT information should be provided in.

```
NAME="text"
```

The NAME attribute gives a name to the meta-information. If no name is specified, the HTTP-EQUIV value is assumed to be the name.

```
CONTENT="text"
```

The CONTENT attribute describes the value of the meta-information.

N

NOBR (no break)

> *Syntax:*
> ⟨NOBR⟩*content*⟨/NOBR⟩

The content of the NOBR element will always be displayed on a single line (with no line breaks anywhere in the text), even if it will not fit within the width of the display window. Use this element judiciously, as not all readers will want to resize their client window just to be able to view your page layout. See WBR.

NOTE

> *Syntax:*
> ⟨NOTE⟩*content*⟨/NOTE⟩

The NOTE element indicates an admonishment, note, or caution.

Additional Attributes

> CLASS=*name*

name specifies the type of the note (warning, caution, or note). Some browsers, such as Arena, associate an image with these note types.

> SRC="*url*"

url points to an image file to display at the head of the note text (as a bullet) or alongside the note text (as a floating image).

> ID, LANG, MD

O

OL (ordered list)

> ⟨OL⟩
> [⟨LH⟩*content*⟨/LH⟩]
> [⟨LI⟩*content*] *
> ⟨/OL⟩

The OL element is similar to the UL element except that the items in the list are considered to be in an important order (such as sequential steps or in order of priority). List items are typically rendered with a number preceding the item, rather than a bullet. See UL for a longer discussion of the use of list elements.

HTML 3.0 adds the LH element that defines a list header to be displayed above the first item of the list (see LH). In addition, in HTML 3.0, the stylesheet is responsible for the numbering style for each item of the list—the default is the Arabic numeral set (1, 2, 3 . . .).

```
Example:
⟨OL⟩
⟨LI⟩Item 1
⟨LI⟩Item 2
⟨LI⟩Item 3
⟨/OL⟩
```

Additional Attributes

COMPACT

If present, specifies that the list should be displayed "compactly." This can include reducing white space between list items and reducing the font size of the list.

CONTINUE

If present, causes the list to continue numbering where the last OL element left off. By default, each OL element is numbered from 1.

SEQNUM=*num*

num specifies the number from which the list should start counting. By default, each new OL list starts numbering at 1. If a SEQNUM is given, the list will start counting from *num*.

START=*num*

num is the number the list should start counting at. OL elements default to begin at 1. By specifying a START of some other number, the list will begin counting at that number. The symbols used will depend on the TYPE set (defined next).

TYPE=[A|a|I|i|1]

In most browsers, each OL element (including lists embedded in other lists) numbers its list using regular numerals (1, 2, 3 . . .). By specifying a TYPE for an OL element, you can choose what style of counter to use. Type A marks each list item with an uppercase letter (A, B, C . . .). Type a uses lowercase letters (a, b, c . . .). Type I uses uppercase Roman numerals (I, II, III, IV . . .). Type i uses lowercase Roman numerals (i, ii, iii, iv . . .).

The TYPE can also be changed in each individual LI element, to change the numbering style for that list item and all subsequent items (until another TYPE is given).

```
Example:
⟨OL TYPE=A⟩
⟨LI⟩ Pick up laundry
⟨LI⟩ Buy comic books
⟨LI TYPE=1⟩ Get Confused
⟨/OL⟩
```

VALUE=*num*

num is the number that the list item should be given. This is only valid in the LI element. It changes the value of that list item to *num*, and continues to count from *num* for subsequent list items (unless they're renumbered again using the VALUE attribute). Thus, you could number your list items "1, 3, 5, 7, 9" by giving each LI element a different VALUE.

```
Example:
⟨OL⟩
⟨LI VALUE=4⟩Check auxiliary fuel systems
⟨LI VALUE=3⟩Check food supplies
⟨LI VALUE=2⟩Check oxygen supplies
⟨LI VALUE=1⟩BLAST OFF!
⟨/OL⟩
```

OPTION

See the section *Form Elements*.

OVER

See the section *Math Elements*.

OVERLAY (figure overlay image)

```
Syntax:
⟨OVERLAY⟩
```

The OVERLAY element is used within a FIG element to specify an additional image file to display overlaid on top of the FIG's image file.

Additional Attributes

HEIGHT=*num*

Specifies the display height of the image, which may be scaled up or down (increased or decreased in size) to fit. *num* may be in pixels or en units, as defined by the UNITS attribute.

IMAGEMAP="*url*"

url specifies a program to send mouse click and drag information to.

SRC="*url*"

url points to an image file to display as the overlaid image.

UNITS=[pixels|en]

Specifies which type of units the WIDTH and HEIGHT attribute will be specified in. One en is equal to half the point size of the current font.

WIDTH=*num*

Specifies the display width of the image, which may be scaled up or down (increased or decreased in size) to fit. *num* may be in pixels or en units, as defined by the UNITS attribute.

X=*num*

num specifies the number of horizontal units (as given by the UNITS attribute) to offset the overlaid image from the left-hand edge of the FIG's image.

Y=*num*

num specifies the number of vertical units (as given by the UNITS attribute) to offset the overlaid image from the top edge of the FIG's image.

P

P (paragraph)

⟨P⟩*content*[⟨/P⟩]

The P element indicates a paragraph. There are two interpretations of this element: in one, it is an empty element, and only indicates a paragraph break; in the second, it is a container for the paragraph as a whole. See Chapter 11 for a discussion of how to deal with the P element.

Additional Attributes

ALIGN=[LEFT|RIGHT|CENTER|JUSTIFY]

Specifies how to align the text of the paragraph. LEFT and RIGHT align the lines within the paragraph with the left or right text margins, respectively. CENTER aligns the lines within the paragraph centered between the left and right text margins. JUSTIFY adds spacing between letters and words such that each line within the paragraph stretches from the left text margin to the right text margin.

ID, LANG, CLASS, CLEAR, NOWRAP

PERSON

Syntax:
⟨PERSON⟩*content*⟨/PERSON⟩

Text in between the tags is considered to be a person's name (and possibly includes additional information about the person).

Additional Attributes

ID, LANG, CLASS.

PRE (preformatted)

Syntax:
⟨PRE⟩*content*⟨/pre⟩

The content of the PRE element will be displayed as it appears, including white space, tabs, and carriage returns. It is rendered in a monospace font, in order to preserve text columns. The only HTML elements that can be used within the PRE element are the A element and the character formatting elements. Paragraph formatting elements (such as P, H1, and ADDRESS) may not be used.

```
Usage:
⟨PRE⟩
This text will
  be displayed exactly
    like this.
⟨/PRE⟩
```

Additional Attributes

```
WIDTH=num
```

num is the maximum length (in characters) of any line of text within the PRE element. This may be used by browsers to optimize font size and other display characteristics of the preformatted text, so that it will fit in the width of the displayed page.

```
ID, LANG, CLASS, CLEAR
```

Q

Q (quote)

```
Syntax:
⟨Q⟩content⟨/Q⟩
```

The content of the Q element is a short quote (longer quotes should use the CITE element), and should be displayed appropriately with respect to the LANG attribute.

Additional Attributes

```
ID, LANG, CLASS
```

R

RANGE

```
Syntax:
⟨RANGE⟩
```

```
Common uses:
⟨RANGE FROM=name1 UNTIL=name2⟩
```

The RANGE element marks an area of the document, for example highlighting areas that match a search criterion. *name1* corresponds to some element in the document that occurs at the beginning of the area to be marked, which has a matching ID=*name1* attribute. Similarly, *name2* corresponds to some element (with an ID=*name2* attribute) in the document that occurs at the end of the area to be marked. All displayable text between these two elements is considered marked.

Additional Attributes

```
FROM=name
```

name corresponds to some other element in the document with a matching ID=*name* attribute. The point at which the element occurs is considered to be the beginning of the marked area.

```
UNTIL=name
```

name corresponds to some other element in the document with a matching ID=*name* attribute. The point at which the element occurs is considered to be the end of the marked area.

```
ID, CLASS
```

RIGHT

See the section *Math Elements*.

ROOT

See the section *Math Elements*.

ROW (array row)

See the section *Math Elements*.

S

S (strikethrough)

```
Syntax:
⟨S⟩content⟨/S⟩
```

The content of the S element will be rendered using the "strike-through" attribute of the font, that is, with a horizontal line through the center of each character.

SAMP (sample)

Syntax:
⟨SAMP⟩*content*⟨/SAMP⟩

The SAMP element indicates a sequence of literal characters.

Additional Attributes

ID, LANG, CLASS

SELECT

See the section *Form Elements.*

SMALL

Syntax:
⟨SMALL⟩*content*⟨/SMALL⟩

The content of the SMALL element is displayed in a smaller font than normal text.

SPOT

Syntax:
⟨SPOT ID=*name*⟩

The SPOT element is used to insert an ID somewhere in the document where it is needed (such as for the A or RANGE elements) but where it is not practical to use another element's ID attribute (or when there are no nearby elements).

SQRT

See the section *Math Elements.*

STRONG

Syntax:
⟨STRONG⟩*content*⟨/STRONG⟩

The STRONG element indicates that text should be considered "strongly emphasized." This is most commonly rendered in bold type.

Additional Attributes

ID, LANG, CLASS

STYLE

Syntax:
⟨STYLE NOTATION="*text*"⟩
text
⟨/STYLE⟩

The STYLE element allows stylesheet information to be included in an HTML document. The NOTATION attribute specifies a stylesheet notation. At the time of this writing, no standard had yet been reached on stylesheet notation (see Chapter 11 for more information on stylesheets).

SUB (subscript)

Syntax:
⟨SUB⟩*content*⟨/SUB⟩

The content of the SUB element is displayed as subscripted text, that is, below the normal baseline and possibly in a smaller font. See the section *Math Elements* for information on how SUB is used in the context of the MATH element.

NOTE: The SUB element can be used outside the context of the MATH element.

Additional Attributes

ID, LANG, CLASS

SUP (superscript)

Syntax:
⟨SUP⟩*content*⟨/SUP⟩

The content of the SUP element is displayed as superscripted text, that is, above the normal baseline and possibly in a smaller font. See the section *Math Elements* for information on how SUP is used in the context of the MATH element.

NOTE: The SUP element can be used outside the context of the MATH element.

Additional Attributes

ID, LANG, CLASS

T

TAB

Syntax:
⟨TAB⟩

If used with the ID attribute, this element specifies a tab stop that subsequent TAB elements can use. If used with the TO attribute, the element causes subsequent text to begin at the tab stop position given in the TO attribute.

Additional Attributes

ALIGN=[LEFT|RIGHT|CENTER|DECIMAL]

Specifies the alignment style of the text associated with the TAB element. LEFT and RIGHT align the text following the TAB element (up until the next TAB element or line break) flush left or flush right, respectively, against the tab stop specified by the TO attribute. (If the TO attribute is missing, text is aligned flush left or right with the text margin of the display window.)

CENTER aligns the text following the TAB element at the tab stop specified by the TO attribute (or centered between the left and right text margins if the TO attribute is missing). DECIMAL searches the text following the TAB element for the first occurrence of the decimal point character (as specified by the DP attribute), and aligns that character with the tab stop specified by the TO attribute. Text before the decimal point character is displayed to the left of the tab stop, and text after the decimal point character is displayed after the tab stop. If an alignment is not possible (no occurrence of the decimal point character in text following an alignment of decimal, or proper alignment would cause the current text to overlap existing text), the TAB element is rendered as a single space and no tab or alignment is performed.

```
DP="char"
```

char specifies the decimal point character that an ALIGN=DECIMAL should look for. The default is the period (.). The default decimal point character may be changed by the language context of the text (as specified by the LANG attribute of a surrounding element).

```
ID=name
```

name is a unique identifier (for the entire document) that the TO attribute can later use. TAB elements using an ID attribute set tab stops—no actual tab movement takes place.

```
INDENT=num
```

num specifies how far in en units to indent the current line before the tab stop. Has no effect if used with the TO attribute.

```
TO=name
```

Causes the text following the TAB element to be aligned (as per the ALIGN attribute) with the tab stop previously defined with ID=*name*.

T (upright font)

See the section *Math Elements*.

TABLE

See the section *Table Elements*.

TD

See the section *Table Elements*.

TEXT

See the section *Math Elements*.

TEXTAREA

See the section *Form Elements*.

TH

See the section *Table Elements*.

TILDE

See the section *Math Elements*.

TITLE

> Syntax:
> ⟨TITLE⟩*text*⟨/TITLE⟩

The TITLE element describes the title of the document, which is generally displayed as the name of the browser's window or somewhere near the top of the window (although it is not guaranteed that it will be displayed at all). More important, the title is used for bookmark lists, and for many automated applications where the document is referred to by a name. The title should be short, descriptive, and to the point.

TR

See the section *Table Elements*.

TT (teletype)

> Syntax:
> ⟨TT⟩*content*⟨/TT⟩

The contents of the TT element should be displayed using a monospaced (fixed-width) font. (Normal text displayed by a graphical browser uses a proportionally spaced font.)

Additional Attributes

ID, LANG, CLASS

U

U (underline)

> *Syntax:*
> ⟨U⟩*content*⟨/U⟩

The content of the U element should be displayed as underlined or in italic if underlining is not available.

NOTE: Many browsers render links with underlines, which can make underlined text that is not a link confusing to the reader. Use the U element judiciously.

Additional Attributes

ID, LANG, CLASS

UL (unordered list)

> *Syntax:*
> ⟨UL⟩
> [⟨LH⟩*content*]
> [⟨LI⟩*content*]*
> ⟨/UL⟩

The UL element, like all list elements, describes a sequence of items. In each of these elements, there is a containing element (UL, OL, DIR, DL, and so on) that describes the scope of the list, and then a sequence of subordinate elements (LI, for most list elements, or DT and DD, for the definition list) that describes individual elements. The subordinate elements do not require an end tag, although they are not empty; rather, the end of on subordinate element is clearly defined by the start of the next subordinate element.

HTML 3.0 adds the optional *line header* (⟨LH⟩) tag that defines a title for the list, to be displayed at the top of the list, without a bullet, in an appropriate font. See LH.

List elements, in general, can be nested within each other. This means that a UL element can contain a sublist, which may be an embedded UL, OL, or any other type of list element.

> *Example:*
> ⟨UL⟩

```
⟨LI⟩Dogs
⟨LI⟩Cats
⟨LI⟩Other beasties:
⟨UL⟩ ⟨!— this is a sub-list: —⟩
⟨LI⟩Politicians
⟨LI⟩Administrators
⟨/UL⟩
⟨/UL⟩
```

Additional Attributes

COMPACT

If present, this specifies that the list should be displayed "compactly." This can include reducing white space between list items and reducing the font size of the list.

DINGBAT=" *text* "

text specifies an HTML 3.0 icon entity to use as the bullets for this list.

PLAIN

If present (⟨UL PLAIN⟩), no bullets will be displayed. The list items will be displayed as expected.

SRC=" *url* "

url points to an alternate image to use for the bullets in this list. Embedded UL elements may use different images by specifying different SRC files.

WRAP=[VERT|HORIZ]

WRAP specifies that the list should be displayed in multiple columns. WRAP=VERT specifies that list items should displayed down the page, then across to a new column and down again, repeating until all list items are displayed. WRAP=HORIZ specifies that list items should be displayed across the page, then down one line and across the page again, until all list items are displayed. The browser determines how many columns to use.

```
Example of WRAP=HORIZ:
   1   2   3   4   5
   6   7   8   9   10
```

Example of WRAP=VERT:
```
1  3  5  7  9
2  4  6  8  10
```

TYPE=[DISC|CIRCLE|SQUARE]

In most graphical browsers, when you indent unordered lists, the topmost (outermost) level uses filled-in circles (discs) as its bullets, the next level uses open circles, and the third level uses filled-in squares. By specifying a TYPE in the UL element, you can choose which type of bullets the list should use.

The TYPE can also be changed in each LI element to change the bullet type for that list item and all subsequent items, until another TYPE is given. Thus, a single UL element could use any combination of the previous three bullet types.

```
Example:
⟨UL TYPE="square"⟩
⟨LI⟩Flatland
⟨LI⟩Squareland
⟨LI TYPE="circle"⟩Circleland
⟨/UL⟩
```

ID, LANG, CLASS, CLEAR, MD

V

VAR (variable)

```
Syntax:
⟨VAR⟩content⟨/VAR⟩
```

The VAR element indicates the name of a variable. See CODE.

Additional Attributes

ID, LANG, CLASS

VEC

See the section *Math Elements*.

W

WBR (word break)

Syntax:
⟨WBR⟩

The WBR element is used inside of the NOBR element. It defines a place in the text where the browser may, if it needs to, break the line of text (in the event that the line is too long to fit within the width of the display window). See NOBR.

Form Elements

The FORM element provides a useful tool for describing user-interface elements in the context of an HTML document, including text input fields and pull-down menus. When coupled with a CGI script, forms allow your readers to interact with documents in your Web. See Chapter 8, *CGI*, for more information about using FORMs with CGI scripts.

The elements described in this section only have meaning within the FORM element. That is, they must be used within the ⟨FORM⟩ and ⟨/FORM⟩ tags, like this:

```
⟨FORM ACTION="http://www.freedonia.org/cgi-
bin/take-input.cgi"⟩
Name: ⟨INPUT NAME="name"⟩
⟨/FORM⟩
```

FORM

Syntax:
⟨FORM ACTION="*url*"⟩*content*⟨/FORM⟩

The FORM element contains a single form. Forms may not be embedded—you cannot have a form within a form—although several forms may be present inside a single document. *url* (the value of the ACTION attribute) is the URL of a CGI script to call when the form is submitted. When a form is submitted, only the form fields that lie between the start and end tags for that form are sent to the CGI script—fields outside of the tags are ignored.

Additional Attributes

METHOD=[GET|POST]

Indicates which method the server should use to send the form information to the CGI script specified in the ACTION attribute of the form. GET (in all capital letters) sends the form information as the query string (the QUERY_STRING environment variable). POST sends the form information via standard input, and sets the environment variable CONTENT_LENGTH to the exact number of bytes being sent.

POST is preferable to GET, as the amount of information that can be submitted by GET is limited to the size of URL that the server can support.

ENCTYPE=*text*

text is a MIME-type describing the type of encoding to be done to the form data. This only applies to forms that use the POST method. The default is application/x-www-form-urlencoded, and is the only supported encoding type at this time.

INPUT

Syntax:
⟨INPUT *attributes*⟩

The INPUT element is used only inside of a FORM element. It allows a user to enter or select information (to be sent to a CGI script as part of the form data).

Additional Attributes

ALIGN=[LEFT|RIGHT|TOP|MIDDLE|BOTTOM]

For input fields that use images (of the types SCRIBBLE, IMAGE, RESET, and SUBMIT), specifies the alignment style of the image. LEFT and RIGHT align the image against the left or right text margin, respectively, and allow subsequent text to be displayed to the side of the image (a "floating" image). TOP, MIDDLE, and BOTTOM specify whether the top, middle, or bottom of the image should be aligned with the current text baseline.

ACCEPT="*text*"

text is a comma-separated list of MIME types that the FILE input field type will allow to be sent. Used to restrict the kinds of files that may be attached via the FILE input field.

CHECKED

If a RADIO button or CHECKBOX INPUT type includes the CHECKED attribute, the button or box defaults to being selected when first displayed or when the form is reset.

DISABLED

If present, indicates that the input field is not modifiable by the user. The field's text may appear greyed out, or the field may just not be selectable.

ERROR="*text*"

text is an error message explaining why the input field's data is incorrect to the user. If this attribute is not present, the field's data is assumed to be correct. This can be set by a CGI script that analyzes the data after a submission, and redisplays the form if incorrect data is present.

MAX=*num*

num specifies the maximum allowable value in a RANGE type input field.

MAXLENGTH=*num*

num is the maximum number of characters to accept in this text entry field. This attribute is only valid for single-line text or password INPUT types.

MIN=*num*

num specifies the minimum allowable value in a RANGE type input field.

NAME=*name*

name is the name for this INPUT element. Names should be unique inside each form (that is, all fields should have different names), with the exception of radio buttons. Different radio buttons with the same NAME are considered to be grouped, such that only one button of the group can be selected. The NAME value is used when sending form data to a CGI script, such that the script can tell which data came from which field.

SIZE=[*num*|*num*,*num*]

Only used for text, password, and range INPUT types. *num* specifies the length of the text entry box (in characters) or, if two values are specified, the width and height of the multiple-line input box (this is only valid for text INPUT types).

 In HTML 3.0, if the input box is displayed in a fixed-width font, *num* is the width in characters. If the input box is displayed in a variable-width font, *num* is the width in en units.

 SRC="*url*"

url points to an image file to be used by this input field. For IMAGE or SCRIBBLE types, the image is displayed as the input field. For submit or reset INPUT types, the image is used as the Submit or Reset button, with the button label as specified by the VALUE attribute.

TYPE=[CHECKBOX|FILE|HIDDEN|IMAGE|PASSWORD|RADIO|
RANGE|RESET|SCRIBBLE|SUBMIT|TEXT]

- CHECKBOX type produces a single-toggle type (on or off) check box.

- FILE type allows a user to attach one or more files to the form, which will be submitted along with the form. The ACCEPT attribute may be used to limit the types of files that may be attached.

- HIDDEN input types do not display their data (which is specified by the VALUE attribute) nor allow the data to be modified by the user; it remains part of the form and is submitted with all other form data. This field can be used to save state information from one HTTP request to another.

- IMAGE type displays an image (as specified by the SRC attribute) that functions as the Submit button—when the user clicks on the image, the form data is submitted as with the submit input type—except that the coordinates where the user clicked are also sent (similar to an imagemap or figure).

- PASSWORD type is similar to the TEXT type, except that text entered is not displayed (so that passwords are not displayed in the clear).

- RADIO type produces a single-toggle type (on or off) radio button. Other RADIO input elements with the same NAME are considered grouped such that only one button in the group can be on at a time (selecting another radio button in the same group turns off any other button currently turned on, and changes the current radio button to the on position).

- RESET produces a similar button to the SUBMIT type that resets all fields in the form, and sets all radio buttons or check boxes to their default selection.

- RANGE type allows the user to enter a numeric value between the upper and lower limits set by the MAX and MIN attributes.

- SCRIBBLE type displays an image (specified by the SRC attribute) and the user is able to use the mouse or other pointing device to draw on the image (by clicking and dragging). For nongraphical browsers, this is rendered as a text type input field.

- SUBMIT type results in a button that, when selected, causes the form data to be sent to the CGI script specified by the FORM element. Multiple SUBMIT type inputs are allowed in forms in HTML 3.0, but the NAME attribute needs to be specified, otherwise the submit name (which Submit button was selected) will not be sent as part of the form data. Normally, the submit type does not use the NAME attribute.

- TEXT type produces a text entry field (length determined by the SIZE attribute).

VALUE="*text*"

The *text* in a text or password INPUT type indicates the default text to be displayed in the text entry field. For submit or reset INPUT types, *text* specifies the name to display on the Submit or Reset button (defaults are Submit and Reset, respectively). For radio buttons and check boxes, *text* specifies the value of the button or check box if it is selected. Radio buttons and check boxes that are not selected when the form is submitted are not sent to the CGI script, so the VALUE is the only way for the CGI script to know which buttons or boxes were selected.

```
ID, LANG, CLASS, MD
```

OPTION (selection list option)

> *Syntax:*
> ⟨OPTION⟩text

Only occurs within the SELECT element. Specifies the start of a new menu item in a selection list—*text* becomes an item on the list.

Additional Attributes

DISABLED

If present, the menu option should not be selectable.

ERROR="*text*"

text is an error message explaining why the menu's selections are incorrect to the user. If this attribute is not present, the menu's selections are assumed to be acceptable. This can be set by a CGI script that analyzes the menu after a submission, and redisplays the form if incorrect data is present.

SELECTED

If present, indicates that this menu option should be initially selected (when the form is displayed or reset). By default, none of the menu items is initially selected.

SHAPE="*text*"

When the SELECT element uses the SRC attribute to specify an image to display as the menu, the SHAPE attribute is used to specify an area within the image (a hotzone) that, if clicked on, causes one of the menu items to be selected. *text* may be one of:

- `default`—the default menu item to select if the user clicks on an area outside of any hotzones.

- `circle x, y, radius`—defines a circle-shaped hotzone in the image, with the center at *x, y*, and with a radius of *radius*.

- `rect x, y, width, height`—defines a rectangle-shaped hotzone in the image, with the upper left corner at *x, y*, and of size *width, height*.

- `polygon: x1, y1, x2, y2, . . ., xn, yn`—defines an n-sided polygon-shaped hotzone in the image. Each *x, y* pair represents a point connected by a line to the previous and the following pairs. The *n*th point is considered to connect back to the first point, automatically closing the polygon. In all cases, *x* and *y* may be specified in pixels as integers, or on a scale from 0.0 to 1.0 across and down the image, where 0.0 indicates the left or top edge of the image, and 1.0 indicates the right or bottom edge of the image. (For example, the point (0.5, 0.5) would be the exact center of any image.) If a user clicks in an area that is part of two or more hotzones, the distance from the mouse click to the centers of all applicable hotzones is calculated, and the nearest hotzone is considered selected. In this way, hotzones may overlap without the figure failing.

`VALUE="text"`

text specifies the value of the option, to be sent to the form, if it is selected. By default, the text following the OPTION element is sent to the form. The VALUE attribute can be used to give each OPTION a numerical value or abbreviation, to simplify the CGI script's job.

`ID, LANG, CLASS`

Select

```
Syntax:
⟨SELECT NAME="name"⟩
[⟨OPTION⟩content]
⟨/SELECT⟩
```

The SELECT element is used within a FORM element to produce a selection list (a list of items that the user can select from, similiar in style to a pull-down menu). Each line of text after an ⟨OPTION⟩

tag will become one item in the list, and the user can select one (or more) of the items in the list to be sent to the CGI script specified by the action of the form (preceded by the name of the selection list). See Chapter 8, *CGI*, for more information on using the SELECT element.

Additional Attributes

ALIGN=[LEFT|RIGHT|TOP|MIDDLE|BOTTOM]

Specifies the alignment style of the image (as given by the SRC attribute). LEFT and RIGHT align the image against the left or right text margin, respectively, and allow subsequent text to be displayed to the side of the image (a "floating" image). TOP, MIDDLE, and BOTTOM specify whether the top, middle, or bottom of the image should be aligned with the current text baseline.

DISABLED

If present, specifies that the menu should not be selectable or modifiable by the user.

ERROR="*text*"

text is an error message explaining why the menu's selections are incorrect to the user. If this attribute is not present, the menu's selections are assumed to be acceptable. This can be set by a CGI script that analyzes the menu after a submission, and redisplays the form if incorrect data is present.

MULTIPLE

Specifies that multiple list items may be selected. By default, only one list item can be selected. If MULTIPLE is present, any number of list items may be selected, and all selected list items will be sent to the CGI script (as separate NAME=VALUE instances).

SIZE=*num*

num is the numer of lines of the list to display at a time. If SIZE is 1 or not specified, most browsers display the list as a drop-down menu. If SIZE is greater than 1, most browsers will display the list as a scrollable list, such that only SIZE options are visible at any time.

SRC="*url*"

url points to an image to be displayed instead of the menu in graphical browsers. Users can then click on areas of the image (hotzones) to select menu items. Hotzones are then defined by the SHAPE attribute of the OPTION element. This exactly parallels the FIG element.

UNITS=[PIXELS|EN]

Specifies the units that the HEIGHT and WIDTH attributes are given in. Default is pixels.

WIDTH=*num*

num specifies the desired display width (in units specified by the UNITS attribute) of the image (given by the SRC attribute).

ID, LANG, CLASS, MD

TEXTAREA

⟨TEXTAREA NAME="*word*" ROWS=*rowsnum* COLS=*colsnum*⟩*text*⟨/TEXTAREA⟩

The TEXTAREA element is used only within a FORM element. Displays a text entry box *rowsnum* rows high and *colsnum* columns wide, with *text* as the default text within the text entry box. Allows the user to enter text to be relayed to a CGI script via the action of the form.

NOTE: This element is similar in functionality to the INPUT element with the "text" type. However, if you wish to have multiple input lines, this element is preferable to use, because INPUT does not handle fields with long text values very well.

Additional Attributes

ALIGN=[LEFT|RIGHT|TOP|MIDDLE|BOTTOM]

Specifies the alignment style of the text box. LEFT and RIGHT align the text box against the left or right text margin, respectively, and allow subsequent text to be displayed to the side of the image (a "floating" text box). TOP, MIDDLE, and BOTTOM specify whether the top, middle, or bottom of the text box should be aligned with the current text baseline.

DISABLED

If present, specifies that the text box should not be selectable or modifiable by the user.

ERROR="*text*"

text is an error message explaining why the text box's data is incorrect to the user. If this attribute is not present, the data is assumed to be acceptable. This can be set by a CGI script that analyzes the data after a submission, and redisplays the form if incorrect data is present.

ID, LANG, CLASS

Table Elements

HTML 3.0 provides a means for presenting tabular data, and for some control over presentation—the TABLE element. It is used in conjuction with the other table-specific elements introduced in HTML 3.0, allowing for sophisticated arrangement of rows and columns of data in cells that can include text, images, and even form input elements.

The elements described in this section can only be used in the context of the TABLE element. In order to use these elements, you must surround them with the 〈TABLE〉 and 〈/TABLE〉 tags. For example:

```
〈TABLE〉
〈TR〉 〈TH〉 Bats as big as houses 〈TH〉 Houses as big
                                          as bats
〈TR〉 〈TD〉 42                        〈TD〉 19
〈/TABLE〉
```

CAPTION

Syntax:
〈CAPTION〉*content*〈/CAPTION〉

Used by the FIG and TABLE elements to define caption text for a figure or table.

TABLE

Syntax:
⟨TABLE⟩
[⟨TR⟩*content*]
⟨/TABLE⟩

A table is an array (or matrix) of cells (or boxes), where each cell either contains data or is empty. The TABLE element surrounds a single table. Each ⟨TR⟩ tag signals the start of a new row of cells. Cells are defined by the ⟨TH⟩ and ⟨TD⟩ tags, and the text associated with them. Cells may contain images, text, additional HTML, forms, and even embedded tables.

Additional Attributes

ALIGN=[BLEEDLEFT|BLEEDRIGHT|LEFT|RIGHT|CENTER| JUSTIFY]

Defines how to display the table. BLEEDLEFT and BLEEDRIGHT display the table (starting with the first column for BLEEDLEFT, or last column for BLEEDRIGHT) flush with the left or right window border, respectively. LEFT and RIGHT display the table flush with the left or right text margin, respectively. CENTER displays the table centered between the left and right text margins. JUSTIFY scales the table to occupy all the space between the left and right text margins, increasing or decreasing the table's size as necessary. With BLEEDLEFT, BLEEDRIGHT, LEFT, or RIGHT alignment, subsequent text and HTML (that which occurs after the ⟨/TABLE⟩ tag) will be displayed alongside the table (if room exists), creating a "floating" table. With CENTER and JUSTIFY alignment, subsequent text is displayed below the table. The default is CENTER alignment.

BORDER

If present, specifies that table and cell borders should be displayed.

COLSPEC="*text*"

text specifies the alignment pattern for the columns of the table. *text* is given as a space-separated list of alignment-type followed by the width of the column (in units specified by the UNITS attribute). Alignment type can be one of L (left alignment—aligns the contents of the column with the left column border), R (right alignment—aligns the contents of the column with the right column border), C (center alignment—aligns the contents of the column centered between the left and right column borders), J (justify alignment—formats the data in the column to take up the space from the left column border to the right column border), or D (decimal alignment—aligns all data in the column such that the decimal character, as specified by the DP attribute, is in the same horizontal position). For example:

```
COLSPEC="L10 L15 R10"
```

specifies that the table has three columns; the first column should be 10 units wide, and data in that column should be aligned against the left border; the second column is also aligned against the left border, but it is 15 units wide; and the third column is 10 units wide, and data is aligned against the right border.

```
DP="char"
```

char specifies the decimal point character for decimal alignment (specified in the COLSPEC attribute). The default is the period (.). The default decimal point character may be changed by the language context of the text (as specified by the LANG attribute of a surrounding element).

```
NOFLOW
```

If present, specifies that subsequent text and/or HTML should not be displayed to the left or right of the table, even if the table has an ALIGN of left, right, bleedleft, or bleedright. Subsequent text will be displayed below the table.

```
UNITS=[EN|RELATIVE|PIXELS]
```

Specifies the type of units that the WIDTH and COLSPEC attributes will be given in. En units are one-half the current point size (of the current font). Relative units specifies that the values given by the WIDTH and COLSPEC attributes will be fractions, and should be considered fractions of the display window and the table width, respectively. For example, if a table had a width of 0.5 in relative units, the table's width would always be half the display window's width.

```
WIDTH=num
```

num specifies the width of the entire table in units defined by the UNITS attribute.

```
ID, LANG, CLASS, CLEAR, NOWRAP
```

TD (table data)

```
Syntax:
⟨TD⟩content
```

The TD element is only used within the TABLE element. Text and/or additional HTML following the tag (up to the next ⟨TD⟩, ⟨TH⟩, or ⟨TR⟩ tag, or the ⟨/TABLE⟩ tag) should be displayed within a cell of the current table.

Additional Attributes

```
ALIGN=[LEFT|RIGHT|CENTER|JUSTIFY|DECIMAL]
```

Specifies the horizontal alignment of the data in the cell. LEFT and RIGHT align the data against the left or right cell border, respectively. CENTER alignment centers the data between the left and right cell borders. JUSTIFY alignment spreads the data between the left and right cell borders such that it takes up all horizontal space in the cell. DECIMAL alignment aligns data such that the decimal character, as specified by the DP attribute, is in the same horizontal position in all cells in the column. By default, table data cells are center aligned.

```
AXES="text"
```

text is a comma-separated list of axis names (see the AXIS attribute under TH) specifying the row and/or column headers to which the current cell belongs. This can be used when rendering the document to speech to identify the position of the cell in the table.

```
COLSPAN=num
```

num specifies how many columns (below and including the current cell) this cell spans. Default is 1 (current cell).

```
DP="char"
```

char specifies the decimal point character for decimal alignment (specified in the ALIGN attribute). The default is the period (.). The default decimal point character may be changed by the language context of the text (as specified by the LANG attribute of a surrounding element).

```
ROWSPAN=num
```

num specifies how many rows (to the right of and including the current cell) this cell spans. Default is 1 (current cell).

```
VALIGN=[TOP|MIDDLE|BOTTOM|BASELINE]
```

Specifies the vertical alignment of the data in all cells in the row. (This can be overridden for individual cells by the VALIGN attribute in the ⟨TD⟩ or ⟨TH⟩ tags.) Top and bottom align the data in the cell against the top or bottom cell border, respectively. Middle alignment centers the data in each cell vertically between the top and bottom cell borders. Baseline specifies that the first line of text in each cell should use the same baseline. By default, table data cells are top aligned.

```
ID, LANG, CLASS, NOWRAP
```

TH (table header)

Syntax:
⟨TH⟩*content*

Only used within the TABLE element. Text and/or additional HTML following the tag (up to the next ⟨TD⟩, ⟨TH⟩, or ⟨TR⟩ tag, or the ⟨/TABLE⟩ tag) should be displayed within a cell of the current table as a header (of a row or column or a subheader of a row or column). This typically involves using a bold or larger font. A table header can be used to describe (to a user) the contents of a row or column.

Additional Attributes

```
ALIGN=[LEFT|RIGHT|CENTER|JUSTIFY|DECIMAL]
```

Specifies the horizontal alignment of the data in the cell. `LEFT` and `RIGHT` align the data against the left or right cell border, respectively. `CENTER` alignment centers the data between the left and right cell borders. `JUSTIFY` alignment spreads the data between the left and right cell borders such that it takes up all horizontal space in the cell. `DECIMAL` alignment aligns data such that the decimal character, as specified by the `DP` attribute, is in the same horizontal position in all cells in the column.

```
AXES="text"
```

text is a comma-separated list of axis names (see the `AXIS` attribute) specifying the row and/or column headers to which the current cell belongs. This information can be used when rendering the document to speech to identify the position of the cell in the table.

```
AXIS="text"
```

text is the header name or an abbreviation of the header data, which could be used when rendering the document to speech to describe the contents of the row or column.

```
COLSPAN=num
```

num specifies how many columns (below and including the current cell) this cell spans. Default is 1 (current cell).

```
DP="char"
```

char specifies the decimal point character for decimal alignment (specified in the `ALIGN` attribute). The default is the period (.). The default decimal point character may be changed by the language context of the text (as specified by the `LANG` attribute of a surrounding element).

```
ROWSPAN=num
```

num specifies how many rows (to the right of and including the current cell) this cell spans. Default is 1 (current cell).

```
VALIGN=[TOP|MIDDLE|BOTTOM|BASELINE]
```

Specifies the vertical alignment of the data in all cells in the row. (This can be overridden for individual cells by the VALIGN attribute in the ⟨TD⟩ or ⟨TH⟩ tags.) TOP and BOTTOM align the data in the cell against the top or bottom cell border, respectively. MIDDLE alignment centers the data in each cell vertically between the top and bottom cell borders. BASELINE specifies that the first line of text in each cell should use the same baseline.

ID, LANG, CLASS, NOWRAP

TR (table row)

Syntax:
⟨tr⟩

Used within the TABLE element to start a new row of table cells.

Additional Attributes

ALIGN=[LEFT|RIGHT|CENTER|JUSTIFY|DECIMAL]

Specifies the horizontal alignment of the data in all cells in the row. (This can be overridden for individual cells by the ALIGN attribute in the ⟨TD⟩ or ⟨TH⟩ tags.) LEFT and RIGHT align the data in each cell against the left or right cell border, respectively. CENTER alignment centers the data in each cell between the left and right cell borders. JUSTIFY alignment spreads the data between the left and right cell borders such that it takes up all horizontal space in the cell. DECIMAL alignment aligns data in each cell such that the decimal character, as specified by the DP attribute, is in the same horizontal position in all cells in the column.

DP="char"

char specifies the decimal point character for decimal alignment (specified in the ALIGN attribute). The default is the period (.). The default decimal point character may be changed by the language context of the text (as specified by the LANG attribute of a surrounding element).

VALIGN=[TOP|MIDDLE|BOTTOM|BASELINE]

Specifies the vertical alignment of the data in all cells in the row. (This can be overridden for individual cells by the VALIGN attribute in the ⟨TD⟩ or ⟨TH⟩ tags.) TOP and BOTTOM align the data in the cell against the top or bottom cell border, respectively. MIDDLE alignment centers the data in each cell vertically between the top and bottom cell borders. BASELINE specifies that the first line of text in each cell should use the same baseline.

```
ID, LANG, CLASS, NOWRAP
```

Math Elements

HTML 3.0 provides a powerful facility for rendering mathematical equations—the MATH element. It is used in conjuction with the other math-specific elements introduced in HTML 3.0, allowing for complex mathematical typesetting.

The elements described in this section, with the exception of SUB and SUP, can only be used in the context of the MATH element. In order to use these elements, you must surround your mathematical expression with the ⟨MATH⟩ and ⟨/MATH⟩ tags. For example:

```
⟨MATH⟩
1 ⟨OVER⟩ 4
⟨/MATH⟩
```

is rendered as the fraction $\frac{1}{4}$.

ABOVE

```
⟨ABOVE⟩content⟨/ABOVE⟩
```

Displays an arrow, line, or symbol above the term or equation defined by *content*.

Additional Attributes

```
SYM=[LINE|EQUALS|CUB|LARR|RARR|HAT|TILDE]
```

Defines the type of arrow, line, or symbol to display above the term or equation in the ABOVE element. Default is LINE. CUB stands for curly bracket (that is, } rotated left 90 degrees and stretched over the entire term or equation); LARR and RARR stand for left and right arrow (respectively); and HAT stands for an open-bottomed triangle (circumflex) placed over the entire term or equation. EQUALS and TILDE display a row of equal signs (=) or a row of tildes (~) above the top of the term or equation.

ARRAY

```
⟨ARRAY⟩
[⟨ROW⟩
  [⟨ITEM⟩content]
]
⟨/ARRAY⟩
```

The ARRAY element defines an array (matrix) of items to be displayed. Each ⟨ROW⟩ tag starts a new row of the matrix. Each ⟨ITEM⟩ tag precedes one item in the row. See ROW, ITEM.

Additional Attributes

```
ALIGN=[TOP|BOTTOM|MIDDLE]
```

Defines the alignment relationship of the entire array to the text preceding or following the ARRAY element. TOP aligns the first line of the array with the previous text baseline or, if there is no previous text baseline, with the subsequent text baseline. BOTTOM aligns the last row of the array with the previous or subsequent text baseline. MIDDLE aligns the middle row of the array with the previous or subsequent text baseline. The default is MIDDLE.

```
COLDEF="text"
```

text defines the alignment pattern for each column of the array, and allows a +, −, or = sign between columns. By default, columns are separated by white space, and items are centered in each column. For each column in the array, either a C (center alignment), L (left alignment), or R (right alignment) may be given to COLDEF. For example:

```
COLDEF="LLLR"
```

specifies that the first three columns of items should be aligned to the left, while the fourth column should be aligned to the right. (This can be overridden for each array item by the ALIGN attribute of the ITEM element.) Placing a +, −, or = between the column alignment characters uses that character as a column separator in each row. For example:

```
COLDEF="C+C+C=C"
```

specifies that in each row, the first and second columns should be separated by a +, the same with the second and third columns, and the third and fourth columns should be separated by an =, producing an array like this:

```
1 + 2 + 3 = 4
a + b + c = d
a + 2 + 3 = f
```

```
LABELS
```

If present, causes the first row and column of the array to be used as the column and row labels, respectively. The text after the first ⟨ITEM⟩ tag in the first row will be ignored, so always start the actual column labels after the second ⟨ITEM⟩ tag (and include a dummy character or word after the first ⟨ITEM⟩ tag).

```
LDELIM="char"
```

char specifies a character to use as the left delimiter (left border) for the array. Common characters are [and {.

```
RDELIM="char"
```

char specifies a character to use as the right delimiter (right border) for the array. Common characters are] and }.

ATOP

```
⟨ATOP⟩
```

Displays the expression occurring to the left of the tag (limited by a ⟨BOX⟩ tag or line break) above the expression occurring to the right of the tag (limited by a ⟨/BOX⟩ tag or line break). This is similar to the OVER element, except it does not draw a horizontal line between the expressions.

BAR

```
⟨BAR⟩content⟨/BAR⟩
```

Displays a bar above the term or equation defined by *content*. Equivalent to ⟨ABOVE SYM=LINE⟩.

BELOW

⟨BELOW⟩*content*⟨/BELOW⟩

Displays an arrow, line, or symbol below the equation defined by *content*. Same functionality and attributes as the ABOVE element, except that the content is displayed below the term or equation instead of above it.

BOX

⟨BOX⟩*content*⟨/BOX⟩

Logically groups the mathematical elements located between the tags. For example:

a + ⟨BOX⟩b⟨OVER⟩c⟨/BOX⟩ + d

would be rendered:

$$a + \frac{b}{c} + d$$

because b, c, and the OVER element are grouped by the BOX element.

NOTE: Within the MATH element, { is a synonym for ⟨BOX⟩ and } is a synonym for ⟨/BOX⟩. In order to display the curly brackets literally, the { and } entities are provided.

Additional Attributes

SIZE=[NORMAL|MEDIUM|LARGE|HUGE]

Changes the display size of the left and/or right border (as specified by the LEFT and RIGHT elements). NORMAL size is the default. MEDIUM, LARGE, and HUGE are each bigger than the previous option. Under normal conditions, the left and right borders will expand to the height of the expression enclosed by the BOX element. If the box has neither a left nor a right border, this attribute does nothing.

BT (bold, upright font)

⟨BT⟩*content*⟨/BT⟩

Displays the expression between the tags in a bold, upright (non-italic) font. By default, in mathematical equations, variables are displayed in italics.

Additional Attributes

CLASS

CHOOSE

⟨CHOOSE⟩

Displays the expression occurring to the left of the tag (limited by a ⟨BOX⟩ tag or line break) above the expression occurring to the right of the tag (limited by a ⟨/BOX⟩ tag or line break), placing round brackets (parentheses) on the left and right sides of the new expression.

DDOT (double dots)

⟨DDOT⟩content⟨/DDOT⟩

Displays a series of double dots above the expression defined by *content*.

DOT (single dots)

⟨DOT⟩*content*⟨/DOT⟩

Displays a series of single dots above the term or equation defined by *content*.

HAT (circumflex)

⟨HAT⟩*content*⟨/HAT⟩

Displays an open-bottomed triangle (circumflex) (^) placed over the term or equation defined by *content*. Equivalent to ⟨ABOVE SYM=HAT⟩.

ITEM (array item)

⟨ITEM⟩*content*

Only used within the content of the ARRAY element. The contents of this element are displayed as an item in the current array.

Additional Attributes

```
ALIGN=[LEFT|RIGHT|CENTER]
```

Specifies the alignment of data within this array item. LEFT and RIGHT align the data against the left or right column border, respectively. CENTER alignment centers the data between the left and right column borders.

```
COLSPAN=num
```

num specifies how many columns (to the right of and including the current column) in the current row the item spans. Default is 1 (current column). The next item will be displayed in the next available column in the row.

```
ROWSPAN=num
```

num specifies how many rows (down from and including the current row) in the current column the item spans. Default is 1 (current row). The next item will be displayed in the next available row in the column.

LEFT

```
⟨LEFT⟩
```

Used only within a BOX element. The character or mathematical entity (see Appendix C) occurring directly before the tag is displayed as the left border on the expression in the BOX element, expanding to match the height of the expression.

MATH

```
⟨MATH⟩content⟨/MATH⟩
```

The content of the MATH element is considered to be part of a single mathematical expression (including equations and chemical equations). Mathematical expressions can be made from a combination of math-specific HTML elements (see the next section) and math entities (see Appendix C).

OVER

⟨OVER⟩

Text occurring before the tag (limited by a BOX element or line break) becomes the numerator of an equation. Text occurring after the tag (limited by a ⟨/BOX⟩ tag or line break) becomes the denominator of an equation. A solid horizontal line the length of the longer term (numerator or denominator) is drawn between the expressions as per a standard division equation.

RIGHT

⟨RIGHT⟩

Used only within a BOX element. The character or mathematical entity occurring directly before the tag is displayed as the right border on the expression within the BOX element, expanding to match the height of the expression.

ROOT

⟨ROOT⟩*num*⟨OF⟩*content*⟨/ROOT⟩

Displays an arbitrary root symbol with a radix of *num* above the term or equation defined by *content*.

ROW (array row)

⟨ROW⟩

Only used within ARRAY content. Specifies the start of a new row of the array.

SQRT (square root)

⟨SQRT⟩*content*⟨/SQRT⟩

Displays a square root symbol above the term or equation defined by *content*.

SUB (subscript)

⟨SUB⟩*content*⟨/SUB⟩

Displays the text defined by *content* subscripted to the last (or next) variable (standard subscript) or character element (for example, displayed under an → (right arrow) or ∑ (sigma symbol)). The text is associated with the nearest variable or character element that isn't separated from the ⟨SUB⟩ tag by white space. This association can be emphasized by surrounding a variable and all its ⟨SUP⟩ and ⟨SUB⟩ text with the BOX element. The underscore (_) is a synonym for ⟨SUB⟩ and ⟨/SUB⟩ within the MATH element.

NOTE: The SUB element can also be used outside of the MATH element.

Additional Attributes

    ALIGN=[LEFT|RIGHT]

By default, *content* is displayed on the same side of the variable or character element as the ⟨SUB⟩*content*⟨/SUB⟩. ALIGN=LEFT displays it on the left of the variable, regardless of which side the tag occurs on. ALIGN=RIGHT displays it on the right side of the variable.

SUP (superscript)

    ⟨SUP⟩*content*⟨/SUP⟩

Displays the text defined by *content* superscripted to the previous (or next) variable (standard superscript) or character element (for example, displayed over an → (right arrow) or ∑ (sigma symbol)). The text is associated with the nearest variable or character element that isn't separated from the ⟨SUP⟩ tag by white space. This association can be emphasized by surrounding a variable and all its ⟨SUP⟩ and ⟨SUB⟩ text with a ⟨BOX⟩ tag. The caret (^) is a synonym for ⟨SUP⟩ and ⟨/SUP⟩ within the MATH element.

NOTE: The SUB element can also be used outside of the MATH element.

Additional Attributes

    ALIGN=[LEFT|RIGHT]

By default, *content* is displayed on the same side of the variable or character element as the ⟨SUP⟩*content*⟨/SUP⟩. ALIGN=LEFT displays it on the left of the variable, regardless of which side the tag occurs on. `ALIGN=RIGHT` displays it on the right side of the variable.

T (upright font)

⟨T⟩*content*⟨/T⟩

Displays the expression between the tags in an upright (nonitalic) font. By default, in mathematical equations, variables are displayed in italics.

Additional Attributes

CLASS

TEXT

⟨TEXT⟩*content*⟨/TEXT⟩

The TEXT element defines *content* as text within an equation or other math object (as opposed to variable names, numbers, or math entities). This is often used in conjuction with the SUB and SUP elements.

TILDE

⟨TILDE⟩*content*⟨/TILDE⟩

Displays a row of tildes (~) above the term or equation defined by *content.* Equivalent to ⟨ABOVE SYM=TILDE⟩.

VEC (vector)

⟨VEC⟩*content*⟨/VEC⟩

Displays a right arrow above the term or equation defined by *content.* Equivalent to ⟨ABOVE SYM=RARR⟩.

Elements by Class

Most elements in this reference are grouped alphabetically. For convenience, the elements are also grouped by class in Table 13.3.

HTML 2.0 elements are listed first, broken down by type. These are followed by Netscape-specific elements. Finally, the new HTML 3.0 elements are listed, again broken down by type.

Table 13.3

Elements by Class

Document Information	HTML HEAD BODY TITLE BASE ISINDEX LINK META	*Head Elements*
Data Elements	BR HR IMG	
Character Formatting Elements	CITE CODE EM KBD SAMP STRONG VAR	*Logical Formatting Elements (HTML 2.0)*
	B I TT	*Physical Formatting Elements (HTML 2.0)*
Hyperlink Elements	A	
Block Structure Elements	ADDRESS BLOCKQUOTE P PRE H1 H2 H3 H4 H5 H6	*Headings*
	DL DIR LI MENU OL UL	*List Elements*
	LH	*List Elements (HTML 3.0)*

continued.

Table 13.3 continued	Form-Based Input Elements	FORM INPUT OPTION SELECT TEXTAREA	
	Netscape Elements	BASEFONT CENTER FONT NOBR WBR	
	HTML 3.0 Elements	ABBREV ACRONYM AU DEL DFN INS LANG PERSON Q	*Logical Formatting Elements*
		BIG S SMALL SUB SUP	*Physical Formatting Elements*
		RANGE SPOT STYLE	*Document Information Elements (HEAD)*
		BANNER DIV TAB	*Block Structure Elements*
		LH	*List Elements*
		CAPTION CREDIT FIG OVERLAY	*Figure Elements*
		BQ CREDIT	*Blockquotes*
		FN	*Footnotes*
		NOTE	*Admonishments*
		CAPTION TABLE TD TH TR	*Table Elements*
		ABOVE ARRAY ATOP	*Math Elements*

continued.

Table 13.3

continued

BAR
BELOW
BOX
BT
CHOOSE
DDOT
DOT
HAT
LEFT
OVER
RIGHT
ROOT
ROW
SQRT
SUB
SUP
T
TEXT
TILDE
VEC

Uniform Resource Locators

A Uniform Resource Locator (URL) is a string that identifies the location of a resource somewhere on the Internet. Work is in progress to define other standard formats to describe resources on the Internet, such as URNs and URCs; see Other URs, later in this appendix.

Syntax

General Syntax

In general, a URL is represented as

```
scheme:scheme_specific_part
```

where `scheme` is the protocol used to refer to the resource (such as http or gopher), and the `scheme_specific_part` is a specific instance of the scheme being used. The scheme and scheme specific part are separated by a colon. For example,

```
mailto:carl@freedonia.org
```

refers to a scheme of type `mailto`, and a scheme specific part of `"carl@freedonia.org,"` which, for a `mailto`-type resource, is interpreted as an Internet mail account.

Generic Scheme Specific Part

In general, URLs that refer to a scheme that directly retrieves information from a server (such as Web or Gopher server) use a scheme specific part in the form

//user:password@host:port/path;params?querystring#fragment

The values for the scheme specific part are described as follows:

user (optional):   a username for those schemes, such as ftp, which allow a username.

password (optional):   if a password is required, it follows the username, separated by a colon.

host: the hostname or its IP address.

port (optional):   a port to connect to. If no port is specified, most schemes default to the standard port for the protocol being used.

path (optional):   a pathname, using the slash (/) as a delimiter.

The slash between the hostname and the path is not part of the path; don't make the assumption that paths begin from the root directory of a host's file structure. While there is limited mapping between the paths of the filesystem of the machine the server is running on and the paths of the server itself, the details of that mapping will vary from server to server. See the upcoming section discussing ftp for details on encoding root directory access.

Generally, paths ending in a slash refer to directories; those not ending in a slash refer to files; see the specific schemes, later, for details on how paths are implemented for each scheme.

You may also use *relative paths* in the construction of URLs. Once a base URL is established (either by the client using the first URL used to access a document tree, or the document itself using the BASE tag for HTML documents (see Chapter 13, HTML reference), you can use relative paths under some schemes (for example, http):

- ./ refers to the same directory as the base reference

- ../ refers to one directory above the base reference

- ../../ refers to two directories above the base reference, and so on.

For example, for a base path of a/b/c/d:

- ./ refers to a/b/c/

- ../e refers to a/b/e

- ../../e refers to a/e

;params (optional):   for those schemes, such as ftp, that allow optional parameters.

querystring (optional):   for those objects that allow an optional query string, such as CGI scripts.

fragment (optional):   for those schemes, such as http, that allow an optional fragment, preceded by a crosshatch (#) symbol. This is not considered part of a URL, and is the responsibility of the client, rather than the server, to interpret.

Reserved Characters

URLs use the ASCII character set, and reserve the characters ";", "/", "?", ":", "@", "=", and "&" for special use. The URL specification also declares the space character, the quote mark, "⟨", "⟩", "#", "%", "{", "}", "|", "\", "^", "~", "[", "]", and "`" as unsafe, because of potential conflicts with delimiters, transcribers, and gateways. Any reserved or unsafe character or character not in the ASCII character set must be escaped using a percent sign and its hexadecimal code. For example, a space is represented as %20. See Table A.1 for a listing of hexadecimal ASCII codes.

Case-Sensitivity

URL scheme specific parts may be case-sensitive; `http://www.freedonia.org/ducks.html` may refer to a different resource than `http://www.freedonia.org/Ducks.html`, although this is not necessarily the case. Because case is only sometimes significant, and since new users and print publications often don't realize URLs can be case-sensitive, it's recommended you name your resources such that case doesn't become an issue. That is, name all your Web documents (and other resources you administer) in all lowercase. This gives you one less thing to worry about, as there will then be no special cases. Do the same for special characters: avoid using filenames that will result in URLs with escaped characters, even if your platform allows, for example, spaces in filenames.

Table A.1
Hexadecimal ASCII
Codes

Hex Value	Character Name	Comments
%00	NUL	
%01	SOH	(Non-displayable control characters)
%02	STX	
%03	ETX	
%04	EOT	
%05	ENQ	
%06	ACK	
%07	BEL	
%08	BS	
%09	HT	
%0A	NL	
%0B	VT	
%0C	NP	
%0D	CR	
%0E	SO	
%0F	SI	
%10	DLE	
%11	DC1	
%12	DC2	
%13	DC3	
%14	DC4	
%15	NAK	
%16	SYN	
%17	ETB	
%18	CAN	
%19	EM	
%1A	SUB	
%1B	ESC	
%1C	FS	
%1D	GS	

Continued.

	Hex Value	Character Name	Comments
Table A.1 continued	%1E	RS	
	%1F	US	
	%20	SP	(space)
	%21	!	(displayable characters)
	%22	"	
	%23	#	
	%24	$	
	%25	%	
	%26	&	
	%27	'	
	%28	(	
	%29	)	
	%2A	*	
	%2B	+	
	%2C	,	
	%2D	-	
	%2E	.	
	%2F	/	
	%30	0	
	%31	1	
	%32	2	
	%33	3	
	%34	4	
	%35	5	
	%36	6	
	%37	7	
	%38	8	
	%39	9	
	%3A	:	
	%3B	;	

Continued.

Table A.1
continued

Hex Value	Character Name	Comments
%3C	〈	
%3D	=	
%3E	〉	
%3F	?	
%40	@	
%41	A	
%42	B	
%43	C	
%44	D	
%45	E	
%46	F	
%47	G	
%48	H	
%49	I	
%4A	J	
%4B	K	
%4C	L	
%4D	M	
%4E	N	
%4F	O	
%50	P	
%51	Q	
%52	R	
%53	S	
%54	T	
%55	U	
%56	V	
%57	W	
%58	X	
%59	Y	

Continued.

Table A.1
continued

Hex Value	Character Name	Comments
%5A	Z	
%5B	[	
%5C	\	
%5D	]	
%5E	^	
%5F	_	
%60	`	
%61	a	
%62	b	
%63	c	
%64	d	
%65	e	
%66	f	
%67	g	
%68	h	
%69	i	
%6A	j	
%6B	k	
%6C	l	
%6D	m	
%6E	n	
%6F	o	
%70	p	
%71	q	
%72	r	
%73	s	
%74	t	
%75	u	
%76	v	
%77	w	

Continued.

Table A.1 continued	**Hex Value**	**Character Name**	**Comments**
	%78	x	
	%79	y	
	%7A	z	
	%7B	{	
	%7C	|	
	%7D	}	
	%7E	~	
	%7F	DEL	

Delimiters

When run in to text, URLs may be optionally preceded by the characters URL: to identify them as such, and may be set off by the angle brackets (⟨ and ⟩). As a result, you might see any of these forms of the same address:

```
http://www.freedonia.org/
URL:http://www.freedonia.org/
⟨http://www.freedonia.org/⟩
⟨URL:http://www.freedonia.org/⟩
```

If a long URL needs to be broken into multiple lines, it's especially important to use angle brackets so that the URL can be easily delimited from other text. The form set off by angle brackets only—the third example here—seems most common; a form that includes the URL: prefix will only become important when there are other URI types in common use (see *Other URs*, later).

Specific URL Schemes

As of this writing, there are seven URL schemes found in common use: file, ftp, gopher, htttp, mailto, news, nntp, and telnet. We'll cover the specifics of each separately.

file

```
file://host/path
```

The file scheme indicates a file available from a particular machine, in which *host* can be either a domain name, the string "localhost," or an empty string, the latter two indicating a file on the machine on which the URL is being interpreted.

Since file doesn't specify a network protocol for files on remote hosts, its use across hosts is limited.

Examples:

```
file://zeppo/www/index.html
```

Refers to the file index.html in the directory www on the machine zeppo.

```
file:///www/index.html
```

Refers to the file index.html in the directory www on the local host.

ftp

```
ftp://user:password@host:port/path;type=typecode
default port is 69
```

The ftp scheme is used to refer to directories and files available via the file transfer protocol (ftp), as either an anonymous or a validated user. URLs referring to a resource available via anonymous ftp are the most common. They contain no username or password, instead, the username "anonymous" and a password consisting of the end user's e-mail address is used. ftp URLs may alternatively contain only a username, in which case the end user should be prompted for a password, or both a username and password. If you're using a password within an ftp URL, keep in mind no attempt is made to hide or protect the password in any way.

Within the ftp path, each successive string followed by a slash (/) is interpreted as a CWD (change working directory) command; a final string not followed by a slash, if present, is interpreted as a RETR (retrieve) command. Note that the slash character is reserved and must be encoded if needed explicitly; if an ftp site's default directory is /pub, and you need to point to the root directory /, you may need to encode a slash to go to the root directory of a Unix-style filesystem. For example, the URL `ftp://ftp.freedonia.org/var/` may or may not be relative to the default directory—that is, it may point to the directory `/var`, or to the directory `/pub/var`. In the latter case, you can use an escaped slash, and form the URL `ftp://ftp.freedonia.org/%2Fvar/`.

The `;type=typecode` portion of the ftp URL is optional. If a type isn't specified, the client attempts to deduce the type from the specified file's extension, if one is present. Typecode can be "d," "a," or "i," in which "d" refers to a directory listing, "a" refers to a text file (ascii), and "i" refers to a binary file (image).

You will occasionally see an HTML file served via ftp. Most Web browsers will display an HTML document retrieved via ftp directly, if it recognizes it as an HTML file either by its file extension or by its content.

Examples:

```
ftp://ftp.hawaii.edu/mirrors/info-mac/
```

Connect to the FTP server of the host ftp.hawaii.edu, and retrieve the directory listing for mirrors/info-mac.

```
ftp://rtfm.mit.edu/pub/usenet-by-group/news.
answers/xanadu-faq
```

Connect to the FTP server of the host rtfm.mit.edu, change to the directory pub/usenet-by-group/news.answers, and retrieve the file xanadu-faq.

```
ftp://ftp.freedonia.org:25713/pub/games/duckshoot.
zip;type=i
```

Connect to the FTP server of the host ftp.freedonia.org on port 25713, and change to the directory pub/games. Then retrieve the file duckshoot.zip as a binary image, since it is a compressed binary executable program.

gopher

```
gopher://host[:port]/[gophertype selector[ %09
search[ %09 gopher+_string]]]
default port is 70
```

A URL specifying a gopher resource is labeled as the scheme gopher.

The optional gophertype code identifies the data type of the resource for the client. The optional selector string points to the gopher resource within the gopher hierarchy, and the optional search and gopher+ string further modifies the resource being referred to.

The most common gophertypes are 0, which refers to a file, 1, which refers to a directory, and 7, which refers to a searchable index database. Gophertypes are sometimes "doubled" within URLs, as in the first example here; in these cases, the selector string begins with a copy of the gophertype character.

Examples:

```
gopher://gopher.tc.umn.edu/11/Information%20About%
20Gopher
```

retrieves the gopher directory "Information About Gopher"

```
gopher://mudhoney.micro.umn.edu/00/Gopher.FAQ
```

retrieves the gopher document "Gopher.FAQ"

```
gopher://mudhoney.micro.umn.edu:4326/7?rice
```

performs a gopher search for rice, using port 4326 of the gopher server mudhoney.micro.umn.edu

http

```
http://host:port/path?querystring#fragment
default port is 80
```

A URL of type http designates a resource available via the hypertext transfer protocol (http). Most HTML and related files are delivered using the http protocol.

Paths ending in a slash refer to a directory, and the file retrieved through the URL should be the default file for that directory. Depending upon the http server being referenced, the file returned may be an on-the-fly generated listing of the directory's contents, a file within the directory labeled as the default file (usually named "index.html"), or an error message indicating that no file was available. Paths not ending in a slash indicate a filename.

An optional querystring may be specified using a question mark (?) followed by a string. Any spaces within the querystring are encoded as the plus character (+); interpretation and processing of the querystring varies according to the host machine.

An optional fragment isn't considered part of the URL, and is not passed on to the server, but instead is interpreted within the client.

Examples:

```
http://www.freedonia.org:6243/
```

Connect to port 6243 of the host www.freedonia.org, and deliver the default document or index for the server.

```
http://www.bugs.org/insects/bees.html
```

Retrieve the document bees.html from the directory insects on the server www.bugs.org.

```
http://www.hotwired.com/cgi-bin/users/search?
wordquery=crypto+clipper
```

Connect to the host www.hotwired.com, and execute a script called search, passing the values for a variable "wordquery" as "crypto" and "clipper".

mailto

```
mailto:mail_account
```

A URL of type mailto specifies an Internet e-mail account. Any percent signs (%) within the address need to be encoded as "%25."

Example:

```
mailto:carl@freedonia.org
```

```
mailto:listserv%25yalevm.bitnet@cunyvm.cuny.edu
```

news

```
news:newsgroup_name
news:message_id
```

URLs of type news point to Usenet resources, and may be in one of two forms. The first type, news:newsgroup_name, refers to an entire newsgroup as a period-deliminited hierarchical name, and will cause a newsreader news-capable browser to show a list of articles available within that newsgroup for reading. A special case of news:* indicates all newsgroups available to the client.

The second type, news: message_id, refers to a specific Usenet message by its unique message ID in the form unique_id@domain_name. Note that Usenet messages date-expire and are sometimes canceled, so any particular message should only be available for a few weeks in a newsgroup with moderate traffic.

Unlike most other schemes, news does not specify a specific news server from which articles should be retrieved. The specific news server used is up to the client, and is often a local server provided for local use only. Despite this, news:message_id URL will point to the same article, regardless of which news server is used, since message IDs are unique for each message posted to Usenet.

Examples:

```
news:comp.infosystems.www.providers
```

refers to the newsgroup "comp.infosystems.www. providers"

```
news:carl-3103952231340001@harpo.freedonia.org
```

refers to a news article with message-ID ⟨carl-3103952231340001@harpo.freedonia.org⟩

nntp

```
nntp://host:port/newsgroup-name/article-number
Port default is 119.
```

A URL of type nntp also refers to a Usenet resource, as an instance of a specific news server. Because of the nature of news (with many local servers, each loosely replicates the contents of the others) news servers are often configured to only allow local access. URLs with a wide audience should use the news scheme instead.

Example:

```
news://news.freedonia.org/comp.infosystems.www.
providers/carl-3103952231340001@harpo.freedonia.org
```

telnet

```
telnet://user:password@host:port/
Port default is 23
```

The telnet scheme refers to an interactive telnet session on a remote host.

```
telnet://chat.hotwired.com:2428
```

refers to an interactive session on port 2428 of the host chat.hotwired.com

```
telnet://whois@rs.internic.net
```

refers to an interactive session on the host rs.internic.net, logging in as the user "whois".

Other URL Schemes

At the time of this writing, two other URL schemes, prospero and wais, are defined, and even more URL schemes are proposed or are in use. These include finger, doc, and mail archive schemes. Of particular interest to some is the proposed mailserver scheme, which allows subject and body text to be specified in a URL that refers to an Internet e-mail account. See the IETF URI Working Group archives, listed in the Bibliography, for the current status of these schemes.

Other URs

You'll occasionally (and perhaps increasingly) see mention of three other UR types: URIs, URNs, and URCs. They are still very much under development, so we can't make any authoritative comments on them.

Universal Resource Identifier (URI)

A Universal Resource Identifier (URI) refers to any address or name that refers to an object. URLs and URNs are instances of URIs.

Uniform Resource Name (URN)

A Uniform Resource Name (URN) is meant to refer to an object with greater persistence than a URL. Unlike a URL, a URN will identify a resource, not its location. A resource referred to by a URN might have multiple instances, might move from one location to another, or might not exist at all.

This is important for services like Veronica, which are offered from several servers and heavily used throughout the Internet; a URN can be resolved to the closest URL for a service. It is also important for documents that are attached to people, rather than institutions. For example, the document "Composing Good HTML," which forms the basis for Chapter 11, will have moved from Willamette University to Carnegie Mellon University by the time this book reaches print. If it had a URN, that change would pose no problem to us, as we could list the URN for the document instead of the potentially changeable URL.

URNs will probably be implemented as a distributed naming system with hierarchical naming authorities, as is the domain name systems (DNS), a distributed database that maps hostnames to IP addresses.

Uniform Resource Characteristics (URC)

Uniform Resource Characteristics (URC) will provide meta-level information about a resource, such as author, owner, content type, or access restrictions.

Appendix B:
Internet Media Types

HTTP uses Internet Media Types to describe the data types that servers pass to clients. An Internet Media Type is meant to describe data such that a browser can properly display or process what it receives. By referring to the Internet Media Type, passed in the Content-type header field, a browser can determine whether it can directly display the data, hand the data off to a helper application, or save the data to disk for later processing. The Content-type header is make up of type and subtype names, and an optional parameter field. The general syntax is

```
Content-Type: type/subtype[;parameter=value]
```

The subtype is required; a type cannot be specified without a subtype.

There are seven standard media types and many subtypes. Table B.1, *Common Internet Media Types*, contains a list of common media types in use on the World Wide Web, based on the configuration files of several http servers and clients. Of particular note is the Application type, which can be extended with an appropriate subtype to describe most proprietary data formats. Unlike MIME (Multipurpose Internet Mail Extensions, upon which Internet Media Types are based), new types and subtypes need not be preceded with an "x-," although they should remain unique, and not conflict with any types or subtypes registered with the IANA (Internet Assigned Numbers Authority). See the Bibliography for resources which list all registered media types.

When Web clients request data from Web servers, they may include an optional Accept header field, which specifies the media types the client will accept. The Accept header also allows parameters that give the user's preference as to the size and quality of the media types listed, if the server has multiple versions of the

477

Content-Type	Description	File Extension
application/excel	Microsoft Excel	.xl
application/mac-binhex40	BinHex	.hqx
application/msword	Microsoft Word	.word, .doc
application/octet-stream	Uninterpreted binary	.bin, .exe
application/pdf	Adobe Acrobat	.pdf
application/postscript	Adobe PostScript	.ps, .eps, .ai
application/gzip	GNU compress	.z, .gz, .tgz
application/compressed	Unix compress	.Z
application/x-gtar	GNU tar	.gtar
application/x-rtf	RTF	.rtf
application/x-stuffit	Alladin Stuffit	.sit
application/x-tar	Unix tar	.tar
application/zip	ZIP	.zip
audio/basic	μ-law	.au, .snd
audio/x-aiff	AIFF	.aiff, .aif
audio/x-pn-realaudio	RealAudio	.ra, .ram
audio/x-wav	Windows WAVE	.wav
image/gif	GIF	.gif
image/jpeg	JPEG	.jpeg, .jpg, .jpe
image/pict	Macintosh PICT	.pict, .pic
image/tiff	TIFF	.tiff, .tif
image/x-xbitmap	X Bitmap	.xbm
text/html	HTML	.html, .htm
text/plain	Text	.txt, .text
video/mpeg	MPEG	.mpeg, .mpg, .mpe
video/quicktime	QuickTime	.mov, .qt
video/x-msvideo	Video for Windows	.avi

same resource. In practice, however, most clients send an Accept header that contains "*/*," which is interpreted as accepting all media types, which is also the defined default behavior if no Accept header is provided.

In order for media types to be processed correctly by both server and client, each needs to be configured to recognize the appropriate media types. Most Web servers provide the Content-type header automatically, based upon a file's extension; for example, an image saved as image.gif would be mapped to the Internet Media Type image/gif through an administrator-configurable media type table, and delivered to the client by the server using the Content-type header "Content-type: image/gif." The client then uses this information to determine how to interpret the data it receives, usually referring to a user-configurable media type table to map the media type to an internal function of the browser or to an external viewer or player. If, for whatever reason, a server doesn't provide a Content-type header, the client may refer to the file extension of the URL used to access the data, or may examine the data in an attempt to determine one. Content-type headers are usually not automatically generated when data is returned by CGI scripts, as the server can't expect to know the type of data being returned: it's the scriptor's responsiblity to return the appropriate Content-Type header. See Chapter 8, *CGI*, for more details.

Appendix C:
Character Entities

Character entities are used to display special and reserved characters within HTML documents. Text within HTML documents defaults to the ISO-Latin-1 character set, which is a superset of ASCII. ISO-Latin-1 (also referred to as ISO 8859/1) is made up of a functional equivalent of the 128-character ASCII character set (ISO 646) and an additional 96 special characters, which, along with each character's entity, is listed in Table C.1. For comparison, Table C.2 represents the 128-character ASCII character set. A character entity, which, in HTML, always begins with an ampersand and ends with a semicolon, is a way of representing these special characters (and the reserved characters ⟨, ⟩, and &) using the ASCII character set.

The ISO-Latin-1 character entities listed in Table C.1 are only necessarily valid for the default ISO-Latin-1 character encoding of HTML; it is possible for servers to specify to clients other character encodings—for example, in order to provide documents in non-Western European languages.

The character entities any HTML author needs to be particularly aware of are the angle brackets (⟨ and ⟩) and ampersand (&), which are reserved characters in HTML and need to be escaped for proper rendering within the text of a document (see Chapter 11, for additional details on using and displaying these reserved characters). It's not a requirement that you use character entities for the special characters within the ISO-Latin-1 character set, if you can enter these characters directly from your keyboard; however, because of different character set mappings, file types, and transfer mechanisms, it's always a good idea to use the following entities instead of the character itself, to guarantee the proper display of these characters across browsers.

Table C.1

ISO-Latin-1 Character Entities

Character	Named Entity	Numeric Entity	Description
		&#00; - &#08;	unused
		&#09;	horizontal tab
		&#10;	line feed
		&#11; - &#31;	unused
		&#32;	space
!		&#33;	exclamation mark
"	&quot;	&#34;	double quotation mark
#		&#35;	number sign
$		&#36;	dollar sign
%		&#37;	percent sign
&	&amp;	&#38;	ampersand
'		&#39;	apostrophe
)		&#40;	left parenthesis
(		&#41;	right parenthesis
*		&#42;	asterisk
+		&#43;	plus sign
,		&#44;	comma
-		&#45;	hyphen
.		&#46;	period
/		&#47;	slash
0 - 9		0 - 9	digits 0 - 9
:		&#58;	colon
;		&#59;	semicolon
<	&lt;	&#60;	less than sign
=		&#61;	equal sign
>	&gt;	&#62;	greater than sign
?		&#63;	question mark
@		&#64;	commercial at
A - Z		A - Z	letters A - Z
[		&#91;	left square bracket
\		&#92;	backslash
]		&#93;	right square bracket
^		&#94;	caret
_		&#95;	horizontal bar (underscore)
`		&#96;	grave accent
a - z		a - z	letters a - z
{		&#123;	left curly brace
|		|	vertical bar
}		&#125;	right curly brace
~		&#126;	tilde
		&#127; - Ÿ	unused
			nonbreaking space
¡		&#161;	inverted exclamation
¢		&#162;	cent sign
£		&#163;	pound sterling
¤		&#164;	general currency sign
¥		&#165;	yen sign

continued.

Table C.1
continued

Character	Named Entity	Numeric Entit	Description
¦		&#166;	broken vertical bar
§		&#167;	section sign
¨		&#168;	umlaut (dieresis)
©	&copy;	&#169;	copyright
ª		&#170;	feminine ordinal
«		&#171;	left angle quote, guillemotleft
¬		&#172;	not sign
-		&#173;	soft hyphen
®	&reg;	&#174;	registered trademark
¯		&#175;	macron accent
°		&#176;	degree sign
±		&#177;	plus or minus
²		&#178;	superscript two
³		&#179;	superscript three
´		&#180;	acute accent
µ		&#181;	micro sign
¶		&#182;	paragraph sign
·		&#183;	middle dot
¸		&#184;	cedilla
¹		&#185;	superscript one
º		&#186;	masculine ordinal
»		&#187;	right angle quote, guillemotright
1/4		&#188;	one-fourth
1/2		&#189;	one-half
3/4		&#190;	three-fourths
¿		&#191;	inverted question mark
À	&Agrave;	&#192;	uppercase A, grave accent
Á	&Aacute;	&#193;	uppercase A, acute accent
Â	&Acirc;	&#194;	uppercase A, circumflex accent
Ã	&Atilde;	&#195;	uppercase A, tilde
Ä	&Auml;	&#196;	uppercase A, dieresis or umlaut mark
Å	&Aring;	&#197;	uppercase A, ring
Æ	&AElig;	&#198;	uppercase AE dipthong (ligature)
Ç	&Ccedil;	&#199;	uppercase C, cedilla
È	&Egrave;	&#200;	uppercase E, grave accent
É	&Eacute;	&#201;	uppercase E, acute accent
Ê	&Ecirc;	&#202;	uppercase E, circumflex accent
Ë	&Euml;	&#203;	uppercase E, dieresis or umlaut mark
Ì	&Igrave;	&#204;	uppercase I, grave accent
Í	&Iacute;	&#205;	uppercase I, acute accent
Î	&Icirc;	&#206;	uppercase I, circumflex accent
Ï	&Iuml;	&#207;	uppercase I, dieresis or umlaut mark

continued.

Table C.1

continued

Character	Named Entity	Numeric Entity	Description
Ð	&ETH;	&#208;	uppercase Eth, Icelandic
Ñ	&Ntilde;	&#209;	uppercase N, tilde
Ò	&Ograve;	&#210;	uppercase O, grave accent
Ó	&Oacute;	&#211;	uppercase O, acute accent
Ô	&Ocirc;	&#212;	uppercase O, circumflex
Õ	&Otilde;	&#213;	uppercase O, tilde
Ö	&Ouml;	&#214;	uppercase O, dieresis or umlaut mark
×		&#215;	multiply sign
Ø	&Oslash;	&#216;	uppercase O, slash
Ù	&Ugrave;	&#217;	uppercase U, grave accent
Ú	&Uacute;	&#218;	uppercase U, acute accent
Û	&Ucirc;	&#219;	uppercase U, circumflex accent
Ü	&Uuml;	&#220;	uppercase U, dieresis or umlaut mark
Ý	&Yacute;	&#221;	uppercase Y, acute accent
Þ	&THORN;	&#222;	uppercase THORN, Icelandic
ß	&szlig;	&#223;	lowercase sharp s, German (sz ligature)
à	&agrave;	&#224;	lowercase a, grave accent
á	&aacute;	&#225;	lowercase a, acute accent
â	&acirc;	&#226;	lowercase a, circumflex accent
ã	&atilde;	&#227;	lowercase a, tilde
ä	&auml;	&#228;	lowercase a, dieresis or umlaut mark
å	&aring;	&#229;	lowercase a, ring
æ	&aelig;	&#230;	lowercase ae dipthong (ligature)
ç	&ccedil;	&#231;	lowercase c, cedilla
è	&egrave;	&#232;	lowercase e, grave accent
é	&eacute;	&#233;	lowercase e, acute accent
ê	&ecirc;	&#234;	lowercase e, circumflex accent
ë	&euml;	&#235;	lowercase e, dieresis or umlaut mark
ì	&igrave;	&#236;	lowercase i, grave accent
í	&iacute;	&#237;	lowercase i, acute accent
î	&icirc;	&#238;	lowercase i, circumflex accent
ï	&iuml;	&#239;	lowercase i, dieresis or umlaut mark
ð	&eth;	&#240;	lowercase eth, Icelandic
ñ	&ntilde;	&#241;	lowercase n, tilde
ò	&ograve;	&#242;	lowercase o, grave accent
ó	&oacute;	&#243;	lowercase o, acute accent
ô	&ocirc;	&#244;	lowercase o, circumflex accent
õ	&otilde;	&#245;	lowercase o, tilde
ö	&ouml;	&#246;	lowercase o, dieresis or umlaut mark
÷		&#247;	division sign
ø	&oslash;	&#248;	lowercase o, slash

continued.

Table C.1
continued

Character	Named Entity	Numeric Entity	Description
ù	&ugrave;	&#249;	lowercase u, grave accent
ú	&uacute;	&#250;	lowercase u, acute accent
û	&ucirc;	&#251;	lowercase u, circumflex accent
ü	&uuml;	&#252;	lowercase u, dieresis or umlaut mark
ý	&yacute;	&#253;	lowercase y, acute accent
þ	&thorn;	&#254;	lowercase thorn, Icelandic
ÿ	&yuml;	&#255;	lowercase y, dieresis or umlaut mark

HTML 3.0 defines a number of additional entities to represent mathematical symbols and other characters. See Table C.2:

Table C.2
Additional HTML 3.0
Character Entities

Character	Named Entity	Description
		en space
		em space
–	&endash;	en dash
—	&emdash;	em dash
…	&ldots;	three dots on the baseline
…	&cdots;	three dots on same level as a minus sign
⋮	&vdots;	three vertical dots
⋱	&ddots;	diagonal dots (top left to bottom right)
⁞	&dotfill;	dots that fill column in an array
		thin space
	&sp;	space
	&quad;	quad space
α	&alpha;	alpha
β	&beta;	beta
γ	&gamma;	gamma
δ	&delta;	delta
ε	&epsilon;	epsilon
	&varepsilon;	var epsilon
ζ	&zeta;	zeta
η	&eta;	eta
υ	&theta;	theta
	&vartheta;	var theta
ι	&iota;	iota
κ	&kappa;	kappa
λ	&lambda;	lambda
μ	&mu;	mu
ν	&nu;	nu
ξ	&xi;	xi

continued.

Table C.2

Additional HTML 3.0
Character Entities
continued

Character	Named Entity	Description
o	&omicron;	omicron
π	π	pi
	&varpi;	var pi
ρ	ρ	rho
	&varrho;	var rho
σ	σ	sigma
	&varsigma;	var sigma
τ	τ	tau
υ	υ	upsilon
φ	φ	phi
	&varphi;	var phi
χ	χ	chi
ψ	ψ	psi
ω	ω	omega

Appendix D:
Java and VRML

Java and VRML are two of the most recent and most exciting additions to the slew of World Wide Web-able document types. Java, developed by Sun Microsystems, is a programming language that can produce either stand-alone applications—programs that run by themselves—or *applets*—programs that run inside an HTML page when displayed on a compatible WWW browser. VRML stands for Virtual Reality Modeling Language. Instead of producing an application, a VRML program defines a three-dimensional world that can be "walked through" using a VRML browser. These two packages are not for the casual Web user or builder—they are, after all, programming languages—but they will be a must-know for serious Web developers in the near future, which in Web-time is about six months.

This appendix is an introduction to the Java and VRML languages, not a full-fledged tutorial on their use. To learn more about either package, visit the Web sites listed after each section.

Java

Java is an object-oriented programming language, modeled after the C++ and Objective C languages, which, among its many features, can be used to create applications that can be run as part of an HTML document (on a Java-compatible browser). The most common of this type of application is one that operates in its own window inside an HTML document, much like an inlined image, except that the contents of the image can change while the document is displayed. Since this is a book about the World Wide Web, not computer programming, this is the aspect of Java we will deal with primarily.

Java's Strengths

Java, as with any programming language, is not for the uninitiated. Some experience with computer programming is necessary, or at least a big help, before jumping into Java. Java's main strengths are:

- **It's object-oriented:** By focusing on the "object" as the main structure of the language, programming is made simpler and more straightforward. If you have a string variable that contains an integer you want to convert to a string, the String class has a built-in method for doing just that:

  ```
  myString = String.valueOf(myInteger);
  ```

  Programming is accomplished by creating *classes* and adding *methods* (procedures) to them. Objects are instantiations of classes, essentially variables that can use the methods of the class to which they belong. For example, valueOf is a method of the String class that converts another type of variable (in our case, an integer) into a string. myString and myInteger are objects because they reference a specific string and integer. A programmer could *subclass* the String class and create a Name class, which might additionally have the methods firstName and lastName (which would return the first and last names of a person, respectively). As a result of subclassing the String class, the Name class would also retain all the methods that the String class had, such as the length method (which returns how many characters long the string is). New programs don't have to do everything from scratch—you can build on what others have done, add your own methods and classes to another project, and go from there.

- **It's portable:** Java programs don't need to be rewritten in order to run on multiple computer types. If a Java interpreter exists for a type of computer, any Java program will run on it. You, as a programmer, don't have to be concerned with platform-dependent details such as creating a new window in Microsoft Windows versus creating a new window on the Macintosh. Your program just tells the Window class to create a new window. This is especially important for World Wide Web applications, because WWW browsers exist for many different computer types—Unix, Mac, PC, Amiga, NeXT, SGI, and so. Java applets are run on the client computer (as opposed to CGI scripts, which are run on the server), which in most computer languages would require a separate executable file for each computer type. A Java program can be compiled on a Unix machine, then run on a Macintosh or PC with a Java interpreter without any code changes, so your Java applets are guaranteed to be viewable by anybody, on any kind of computer with a Java-compatible browser.

- **It's threaded:** Java includes its own thread library, which programmers can use to easily create applications that can run simultaneously. For example, a single HTML page in a Java-compatible browser may be displaying three simultaneous animations, playing a song, *and* allowing the user to draw a picture on the screen. Creating threaded applications and applets using Java is painless, since there is a class (the Thread class) already designed to do the work for you.

This means that Java isn't difficult to use, but it is powerful. If you're already familiar with C++ or Objective C, Java won't seem much different. If you haven't got that experience, learning Java will build a strong foundation for a later move to C, should you deem it necessary.

Why Use Java?

Java is more than "just another programming language." Because of its ability to seamlessly merge with the World Wide Web, it is in a position to become *the* language of choice on the Web. Now that Netscape has incorporated Java in the 2.0 release of its Web browser (discussed in a moment), Java programming is going to become as essential to Web development as CGI scripting is now. Java is truly on the cutting edge of the Web.

Java's importance to Web development is that it gives you the ability to write applications that run *as part of an HTML document.* Normal CGI scripting requires you to write a program on your HTTP server that others access by pointing their Web browsers to your script's URL. CGI scripts are interactive only as compared to the rest of the Web—instead of a static document, you get a document that can change every time it's reloaded. Java applets are downloaded to the client computer along with the rest of an HTML document and run there, not on the server. Java applets run in windows inside an HTML document, where mouse clicks, keyboard typing, and other events can be caught by the applet and used to perform an action. A tic-tac-toe game may allow you to click on an empty square to make your move, and the computer responds instantly with its move, without reloading the entire HTML document. A stock Web site may continuously scroll current stock prices across the top of the page, letting you click on the display to pause the scrolling. An on-line dictionary may let you type in a word and display the definition below your input. Java brings a level of interactability that has not previously been seen on the World Wide Web, and once users get a taste of it, they will only clamor for more.

Using Java

Using Java involves writing one or more class files (thereby creating an applet), compiling them with the Java compiler, then incorporating them into an HTML document. Here is a sample class file, which is itself a complete, though simple, applet that prints the words "Hello World" onto the screen (within the browser window):

```
import browser.Applet;

import awt.Graphics;

class HelloWorld extends Applet {

String myString = "Hello World";

public void init() {

resize (300, 100);
```

```
}

public void paint (Graphics myAppletWindow) {

myAppletWindow.drawString (myString, 50, 50);

}

}
```

The first two lines incorporate two classes that this applet will need. All applets need the `browser.Applet` class, which defines what an applet is and how it communicates with a browser. That way, all you have to worry about is what your applet is going to do. In addition, this applet uses the `awt.Graphics` class, which allows it to display characters (and graphics) into the HTML document of which it is a part. Without this class, the applet would not be able to display to the browser window.

The third line begins the class wrapper. It gives this new class a name (`HelloWorld`) and, by the `extends Applet` part, tells Java that the `HelloWorld` class is a subclass of the `Applet` class. This means that the `HelloWorld` class will be able to do anything that the `Applet` class can do.

The fourth line creates a string object called `myString` with the value of `"Hello World"`. `myString` is essentially a variable, but it has the ability to call the methods associated with the String class (none of which are used in this example).

The fifth line begins the method `init`. This is the first method called when an applet is run, and it needs to prepare everything the applet will use. In this case, the `init` method resizes the applet's window to be 300 pixels wide by 100 pixels tall (line 6), so that it's big enough to contain "Hello World". If the window is too small, part of the words might get chopped off. An applet can only display inside its window—anything printed outside the window's coordinates will not be displayed on the screen.

The eighth line begins the method `paint`. This method is called whenever the applet's window needs to be redisplayed, including when the applet is first run, the browser window is moved or scrolled, the mouse cursor moves over the applet window, and so on. This method already exists in a class other than `Hello-World`, but the `HelloWorld` class is *overriding* the method in order to do something different from the default (which is to clear the window). In this case, whenever the `paint` method is called, the words "Hello World" will be printed in the applet's window, starting at the point 50,50 (the point 0,0 is the upper left-hand corner of the applet's window). Note that, by default, an applet's window does not have any borders around it, so the applet window is indistinguishable from the rest of the HTML page.

To create this applet, type it in using a standard text editor and put the resulting file in a subdirectory called `classes` directly off your root HTML directory. (For example, if your home directory was in `/home/jsmith`, and your HTML directory was `/home/jsmith/public_html`, add the `classes` subdirectory under the `public_html` directory, resulting in a `/home/jsmith/public_html/classes` directory.) The directory must have the same file permissions as your other HTML files.

Next, compile the file using the Java compiler, `javac`. Barring any programming errors, this should result in a new file called `HelloWorld.class`. This file is essentially the executable part of your applet, and is the file that a Java-compatible browser will use to run the applet.

To actually see the applet in action, create a new HTML document in your HTML directory something like this:

```
⟨HTML⟩⟨HEAD⟩⟨TITLE⟩HelloWorld Java demo⟨/TITLE⟩⟨/HEAD⟩⟨BODY⟩

This is a demonstration of a Java applet: ⟨APP CLASS="HelloWorld"⟩

⟨/BODY⟩⟨/HTML⟩
```

and view it through a Java-compatible browser (like HotJava). The resulting page should read: "This is a demonstration of a Java applet: Hello World", similar to Figure D.1. (If "Hello World" doesn't show up, check the file permissions on `HelloWorld.class` and the `classes` subdirectory to make sure they're publicly readable, like your other HTML files.)

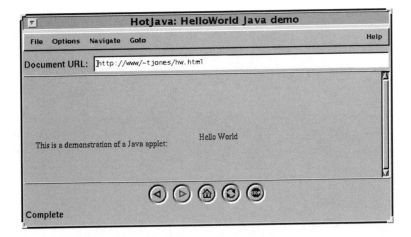

Figure D.1

The HotJava Browser and
the HelloWorld Applet

The ⟨APP⟩ Tag

The ⟨app⟩ tag is new with Java/HotJava, and is the method by
which Java applets are included in an HTML document. It's
generic form is:

```
⟨APP CLASS="classname" ATTRIBUTE1="value1" ATTRIBUTE2="value2"...⟩
```

classname is the name of a compiled Java class file. Applets may
use attributes contained inside the ⟨APP⟩ tag to modify their behavior; for example, the preceding `HelloWorld` applet could be
modified to accept a `TEXT="text"` attribute that would replace
the string "Hello World" with "text" when the applet gets displayed. The applet's display window occurs at the point in the
document where the ⟨APP⟩ tag appears, just like the ⟨IMG⟩ tag. Because the entire applet is introduced using a single tag, browsers
that are not Java friendly will simply ignore the tag and its contents, without disrupting the rest of the page.

HotJava

As of this writing, HotJava, a Web browser written in Java, is the
only Java-compatible browser available, and it runs only on the
Sun Solaris and Microsoft Windows NT operating systems. (Versions for the Macintosh and Windows 95/3.1 are in development.)
However, Netscape Communications Corporation, the company
that distributes the popular Netscape Web browser, has announced

Java compatability into the 2.0 release of its browser. Now, literally hundreds of thousands of Web users will be able to view and use Java applets, and Java programming skills will become much more important than they are currently.

HotJava allows Java applets to be used as described in the Using Java section of this appendix. You do not have to have your own applets in order to use HotJava—there are dozens of existing demo applets available on the Web, which can be found at the Web site listed following the Java section of this appendix.

For More Information on Java and HotJava

Java and HotJava are products of Sun Microsystems, Inc., and links to everything Java that you could ever need are located at its Java Website:

```
http://java.sun.com/
```

This includes: Java language documentation, programming tutorials, code examples, Java and HotJava binaries, and demo applets that will amaze you (and make you forget that you're using the World Wide Web).

VRML

VRML (Virtual Reality Modeling Language) is a language that describes three-dimensional shapes, environments, and relationships for producing virtual reality-style "worlds." A VRML world may be as small as a single 3-D cube, or as large as the imagination can produce—how about a 3-D city that you can access through the Web and navigate on your own computer? VRML allows you to describe shapes (including attributes of those shapes, such as color, size, and position), and link those shapes to other areas of the Web (including other VRML worlds); when coupled with a VRML browser (an application capable of turning the VRML code into a three-dimensional graphical representation), you and your mouse can fly through a virtual scene, which is as close to virtual reality as the general public has gotten so far.

What Is VRML?

VRML is a modeling language, which means the code you write for it doesn't describe how a program should function; it describes how a scene should look. VRML is not a programming language (in its current specification)—areas of VRML code *(nodes)* do not interact except to add to a description of an object or a scene. VRML code does not do anything on its own (much like HTML); it requires a VRML browser to make sense of the VRML code and turn it into a movable 3-D scene.

A VRML file is broken up into nodes, individual objects or groups of objects that remain associated. A node describes an object (such as a cube), a property of an object (such as the color of the cube), or an effect on an object or scene (such as rotating the cube 90 degrees in the Y direction). Here is a node that describes a cube, with faces five units square, centered at (0, 0, 0) in a VRML world:

```
Cube {

width 5

height 5

depth 5

}
```

Object nodes include cubes, spheres, cones, and text. Property nodes include setting font styles, texture mappings, colors, and materials. Effect nodes include setting cameras (initial viewpoints), rotations, transformations, and light sources. By combining these and other node types in a VRML file, you can design a world made up of the shapes and views you programmed that is viewable (and walk-throughable) using a VRML browser.

Why Use VRML?

VRML version 1.0 (the most current VRML level available at this writing) is more than just a modeling language. There are numerous programs and packages available that allow you to create 3-D worlds and navigate through them using a mouse or other input device. The difference with, and the importance of, VRML is twofold:

- **VRML is platform-independent:** VRML uses no set scheme to render the shapes and effects it describes into a graphics format. VRML's job is just to provide the information a program needs to display and move through the virtual world. Consequently, any platform on which a suitable VRML browser has been developed will be able to view the same VRML worlds. (Browsers currently exist for SGI, Windows, Macintosh, Sun, and other various Unix platforms.)

- **VRML can use the Web to add or move between nodes:** Viewable nodes don't have to be located in the same VRML file or even in the same location. The `WWWInline` node reads a VRML file from a URL and displays it as part of the current world. The `WWWAnchor` node loads a new VRML file from a URL and uses it to replace the current world. (For example, if a user selected a door, a new VRML world could be loaded to represent what was on the other side of the door.)

Unfortunately, with VRML 1.0, there isn't much else you can do than create a 3-D world for people to move through. The proposed VRML 2.0 is slated to add much more in the way of simulation, interactability, and connectivity by allowing objects to move, be moved, and for people to be able to interact within the same world. But still, there are valid uses of this language, even in its current state:

- Maps of buildings, campuses, or whole towns or cities, for a real virtual tour or for finding your way around an unfamiliar area.

- Three-dimensional models for product proposals or prototypes.

- Three-dimensional games, especially as an extension to MUD-type worlds.

- Models of architecture, construction, or fabrication, and so on.

Using VRML

As with the Java language described earlier, VRML information is entered directly into a text file. Unlike Java, no compilation is necessary—VRML browsers simply read the text file and render the objects described therein. Here is a small, simple VRML document that describes a cylinder and a sphere:

```
#VRML V1.0 ascii

Separator {

Separator {

Cylinder {

radius 1

height 3

}

}

Separator {

Translation {

translation 10 10 10

}

Sphere {

radius 2

}

}

}
```

When viewed through a VRML browser, the preceding code might look like Figure D.2, a cylinder centered at 0, 0, 0, and a sphere located above, to the right, and behind the cylinder.

The first line of this VRML code is standard (and required) for VRML files. It gives the type and version of the VRML file (so that a VRML browser knows the type of data to expect).

Lines 2 and 3 begin Separation nodes. The first Separation surrounds the entire scene—this is standard practice for VRML. The second Separation is to isolate the cylinder from the sphere. While not as important in this example, it would be necessary if we added property or effect nodes and only wanted them to affect one of the objects. Properties and effects affect all objects after them, unless they are separated by a Separation node.

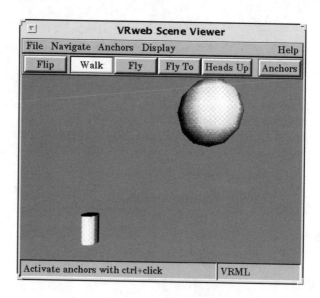

Figure D.2

Viewing a VRML File in the
VRweb VRML Browser

Lines 4 through 7 define a cylinder as having a radius of 1 unit and a height of 2. Since the cylinder has not been explicitly moved to a different location, it will be displayed at the center of the world, at the 3-D coordinates 0, 0, 0. (The cylinder is 2 units tall, so the top of the cylinder will actually be at 0, 1, 0 and the bottom will be at 0, -1, 0.)

Line 9 creates a new Separation node for the sphere. Lines 10 through 12 describe a Translation node, which moves the "current point" in the world (which was previously at the default 0, 0, 0) to 10, 10, 10, or 10 units in each of the positive X, Y, and Z directions. All further object placements within this Separation node will be relative to this point.

Lines 13 through 15 describe a sphere with a radius of 2 units. Because the current point in this world is now at 10, 10, 10, the sphere will be displayed centered around this point; the top of the sphere will actually be at 10, 11, 10, and the bottom at 10, 9, 10.

This is a very simple example of a VRML file, without using any colors, texture mapping, or polygonal shapes, but its purpose isn't to teach you everything there is to know—it's to interest you enough to learn more on your own, by using the Web sites provided at the end of this section.

VRML Browsers

VRML browsers are programs separate from a Web browser that allow you to view and move through a VRML-defined world. Typically, these browsers display the current view of the world in a window on the screen, and by using the mouse, you can move forward, backward, up, down, left, right, or rotate clockwise or counterclockwise or any other direction to view the scene from any angle and from any point within the scene. It is akin to using a flight simulator computer program, where you are allowed to move freely within a simulated 3-D world in basically any direction, getting new views of the world with each move you make.

As of this writing, VRML browsers exist for the Macintosh, Windows, SGI (Silicon Graphics), and various Unix platforms including Sun and LINUX. For an up-to-date list of browsers, check the VRML Repository Web site listed in the next section.

For More Information on VRML

VRML has a lot of users and a lot of proponents on the Internet. It's easy to find references to it on the Web—Yahoo has a section just on VRML—but here are some of the more useful sources around:

- The VRML Repository has links to most anything VRML, including a list of VRML-compliant browsers, VRML documentation, example VRML files, utilities, and more. For learning more about VRML, from how to view it to how to write it yourself, make this your first stop:

  ```
  http://www.sdsc.edu/vrml
  ```

- The VRML Forum at HotWired is the original source for VRML discussion and implementation. You can view the VRML mailing list archives, or subscribe to the list itself, as well as read some of the history of VRML written by the people who made it:

  ```
  http://vrml.wired.com/
  ```

Appendix E:
Connecting to the Internet

We have assumed in this book that you already have a dedicated connection to the Internet. If this is not the case, here are some resources to help you get started.

Types of Connections

Connections to the Internet usually fall into one of two types:

Dial-up connection: Dial-up connections are most often used by individuals. It is not a full-time connection; instead, individuals use a modem to connect to their service providers when they wish to use Internet services (such as reading e-mail or browsing Web documents).

Dedicated connection: Dedicated connections are most often used by companies or organizations. A dedicated connection is a full-time connection, and typically it is a high-speed connection as well. This is necessary for running a server, because the connection must be available so that readers can access your infostructure when they want to (instead of the connection only being available when you wish to access the outside world).

If you intend to run a Web server, you will need a dedicated connection. Needless to say, this is a more expensive proposition than a dial-up connection.

Finding a Dedicated Internet Connection

Internet Service Providers (ISPs) who are willing to sell you a dedicated connection to the Internet are becoming more common. It would be almost impossible to provide a full list here. Instead, we will give pointers to on-line directories of providers, so that you can find one that is close to you. There are several features to look for in a service provider:

- **Connectivity:** How well connected is the provider to the rest of the network? How fast is the slowest connection to the outside world? Your connection is only as fast as the slowest connection between you and your readers.

- **Reliability:** How reliable is the provider? Do they provide full-time technical support for the network, in case there should be any problem? Is there a single point of failure in the network, meaning that if it goes down, your connection goes down?

- **Stability:** How long has the provider been in business? What sort of customer base do they have? Will they still be around in six months?

- **Commercial usability:** Does the provider allow you to use your connection for commercial use? (This is less important now than it has been at any time in the past. Until recently, large parts of the Internet were off limits to commercial use, because of the prohibition on commercial use of the National Science Foundation network. However, this backbone has recently been moved into the commercial sector, making this less of an issue. Still, you should check into the policies of your prospective provider.)

In many regions, you should be able to find more than one provider, so you will be able to shop around to balance the best price versus the best service. Some providers are only local to certain regions; others, such as PSI and Alternet, cover larger regions (the continental United States, in these cases). Yahoo has a list of service providers at:

```
http://www.yahoo.com/Business_and_Economy/
Companies/Internet_Access_Providers/
```

Also, the Cornell help desk maintains a list at:

```
http://helpdesk-www.cit.cornell.edu/IAP/INAccess.
html
```

Dedicated connections usually involve leasing a high-speed telephone line from the telephone company. These telephone lines come in multiple speeds, although the most common are DS0 (which runs at 56 thousand bits per second), T1 (which runs at 1.5 million bits per second), and T3 (which runs at 45 million bits per second). By comparison, most personal connections run at speeds of 14 thousand bits per second (with fast personal connections reaching 28 thousand). While the DS0 speed is the minimum you will need, you'll want to seriously consider the T1 line if you are anticipating that your site will be heavily used. For a T1 line, you can expect to pay thousands of dollars per month.

In addition, if you are not already connected to the Internet, you will need to consider the added organizational costs of creating and supporting a network connection. If all you want to provide is a Web server, this cost may be unjustifiable. On the other hand, if you are also intending to provide Internet connectivity for other members of your organization (such as e-mail and other services), it becomes a more realistic option.

Finally, a lower-cost option (especially if you are planning on running only a server, and on using a personal computer as your platform) is to get a dedicated 14.4 or 28.8 line. This is cheaper, because it uses standard modems and telephone lines. You can expect to pay $100 to $200 a month for these sorts of speeds, and you will not be able to use the connection for much more than a Web server.

Other Ways to Provide Your Infostructure

A less costly alternative to a dedicated line is to use the services of an Internet *presence provider.* These companies provide space on Web servers and e-mail addresses for your organization so that you can have an Internet presence without having to support an Internet connection. Some presence providers will even create a virtual domain for your organization; for example, the NoMI Group might have a domain nomi.com, but no actual Internet connections. Instead, host names such as www.nomi.com are mapped onto the host name of the presence provider's Web server (such as www.presence-provider.com). In this way, it appears that you have a machine on the Internet, without having to maintain one. A list of Internet presence providers is available via Yahoo:

```
http://www.yahoo.com/Business_and_Economy/
Companies/Internet_Presence_Providers/
```

Getting a Personal Connection

We assume in this discussion that you at least have a personal connection to the Internet in order to use these on-line resources. If you do not have such a connection, you can use one of the nation-wide on-line services that provides access to the World Wide Web. These services include America Online (800-827-6364), CompuServe (800-848-8990), and the Microsoft Network (connectivity information is included with Windows 95).

Bibliography

General Resources

The best place to start looking for up-to-date on-line references to Web information is the World Wide Web FAQ:

```
http://sunsite.unc.edu/boutell/faq/www_faq.html
```

The second-best place to look is Yahoo, which maintains a (mostly current) subject-oriented directory of on-line resources:

```
http://www.yahoo.com/
```

Chapter 1

Web Browsers

Arena 0.96, the HTML 3.0 testbed browser, for X Windows.

```
ftp://ftp.w3.org/pub/www/arena/
```

Lynx, the text-based browser, for Unix (version 2.3.7) and MS-DOS (version 0.8).

```
ftp://ukanaix.cc.ukans.edu/pub/WWW/
```

Netscape Navigator 1.1N, for MacOS, Microsoft Windows, and X Windows.

```
ftp://ftp.netscape.com/netscape/
```

Chapter 2

Hypertext

Bush, Vannevar. "As We May Think." *The Atlantic Monthly,* July 1945. The seminal article on hypertext. Also available on-line:

```
http://astrowww.phys.uvic.ca/a200/aswemaythink.html
```

Fraase, Michael. *Macintosh Hypermedia* (volumes I and II). Scott, Foresman, 1990. Don't let the "Macintosh" in the title fool you; volume 1 is one of the best general introductions to hypertext and how it relates to computers anywhere.

Landow, George. *Hypertext: The Convergence of Contemporary Critical Theory and Technology.* Johns Hopkins University Press, 1992. If you're interested in a theoretical, scholarly discussion of hypertext, Landow has written several good books on the subject. This one is a good starting point and provides some useful insight on how to think about nonlinear bodies of information.

Nelson, Theodor. *Computer Lib/Dream Machines.* Microsoft Press, 1987. Xanadu, the brainchild of Ted Nelson, is the earliest hypertext system to go by the name "hypertext," since Nelson coined the term. The "flip-side" of this book, *Dream Machines,* describes Nelson's (still unrealized) notion of Xanadu in some detail. Gives some good ideas about what a good hypertext system *should* be able to do.

File Formats

"Recommended File Formats for WWW Documents," maintained by Ken Jenks, is a good on-line resource for information about multimedia file formats:

```
http://sd-www.jsc.nasa.gov/web_formats.html
```

Chapter 3

HTML Books

Aronson, Larry. *HTML Manual of Style*. Ziff-Davis Press, 1994.

Lemay, Laura. *Teach Yourself Web Publishing with HTML in a Week*. Sams, 1994.

HTML On-line Tutorials

One of the best HTML tutorials—simple, short, and straightforward—is presented on-line by NCSA at

```
http://www.ncsa.uiuc.edu/demoweb/html-primer.html
```

Chapter 4

HTML Editors

Unix

ASHE (A Simple HTML Editor)	`ftp://ftp.cs.rpi.edu/pub/puninj/ASHE/README.html`
City University HTML Editor	`http://web.cs.city.ac.uk/homes/njw/htmltext/htmltext.html`
HoTMetaL Pro 2.0	`http://www.sq.com/products/pst.htm`
HoTMetaL Free	`http://www.sq.com/products/hotmetal/hm-ftp.htm`
HTML-Helper-Mode(for Emacs)	`http://www.santafe.edu/~nelson/tools/`
Phoenix	`http://www.bsd.uchicago.edu/ftp/pub/phoenix/README.html`

Windows

Hot Dog	`http://www.sausage.com/`
HotMetal	`http://www.sq.com/products/hotmetal/hmp-org.htm`
HTML Assistant	`ftp://ftp.cs.dal.ca/htmlasst/htmlafaq.html`
HTML Easy! Pro	`http://www.trytel.com/~milkylin/`
HTML Writer	`http://lal.cs.byu.edu/people/nosack/`
Internet Assistant (for Microsoft Word)	`http://www.microsoft.com/pages/deskapps/word/ia/default.htm`
Live Markup	`http://www.mediatec.com/mediatech/`
WebEdit	`http://wwwnt.thegroup.net/webedit/webedit.htm`
WP Internet Publisher	`http://wp.novell.com/elecpub/intpub.htm`

Macintosh

BBEdit/BBEditLite BBEdit HTML Tools v1.3	`ftp://ftp.std.com/pub/bbedit/` `http://www.york.ac.uk/~ld11/BBEditTools.html`
Carles Bellver's BBEdit HTML Extensions	`ftp://ftp.std.com/pub/bbedit/third-party-extensions/` `HTML_extensions_r10.hqx`
Webtor 0.9.1	`http://www.igd.fhg.de/~neuss/webtor/webtor.html`
HTML.edit 1.7beta4	`http://www.metrics.nttc.edu/tools/htmledit/HTMLEdit.html`

Image and Other Multimedia Tools

Unix

WWWimagesize	`http://www.dcs.ed.ac.uk/home/ark/wwwimagesize/`
MapEdit	`http://sunsite.unc.edu/boutell/mapedit/mapedit.html`
GDIT	`http://www.demon.co.uk:80/3Wiz/gdit/`
GD	`http://siva.cshl.org/gd/gd.html`
GIFtool	`http://www.homepages.com/tools/`

Windows

GIF Construction Set	`http://uunorth.north.net:8000/alchemy/html/gifcon.html`
GIFtool	`http://www.homepages.com/tools/`
GDIT	`http://www.demon.co.uk:80/3Wiz/gdit/`
GD	`http://siva.cshl.org/gd/gd.html`
Lview Pro	`ftp://oak.oakland.edu/SimTel/win3/graphics/lviewp1b.zip`

Macintosh

Transparency 1.0	`ftp://ftp.freedonia.com/utilities/`
WebMap	`http://www.city.net/cnx/software/webmap.html`
GIFConverter	`ftp://ftp.freedonia.com/utilities/`
clip2gif	`ftp://ftp.freedonia.com/utilities/`
Photoshop	`http://www.adobe.com/Apps/Photoshop.html`
Ulaw 1.4b	`ftp://ftp.freedonia.com/utilities/`
FlattenMOOV	`ftp://ftp.freedonia.com/utilities/`
Shutterbug 1.2	`http://goldfish.physics.utoronto.ca/ShutterBug/Sbug.html`

Also of great use is the Transparent/Interlace GIF Resource Page, at

```
http://dragon.jpl.nasa.gov/~adam/transparent.html
```

Chapter 5

Copyright

The Copyright FAQ can be found on-line at

```
ftp://rtfm.mit.edu/pub/usenet/news.answers/law/
Copyright-FAQ/
```

Chapter 6

On-line Information about Servers

Unix

Apache	`ftp://ftp.apache.org/apache/dist/` `http://www.apache.org/apache/`
CERN httpd	`http://www.w3.org/hypertext/WWW/Daemon/Status.html`
GN	`http://hopf.math.nwu.edu:70/`
NCSA httpd	`ftp://ftp.ncsa.uiuc.edu/Web/httpd/Unix/ncsa_httpd` `http://hoohoo.ncsa.uiuc.edu/`
Netscape	`http://home.netscape.com/`
OpenMarket WebServer (and Secure Server)	`http://www.openmarket.com/`
Plexus	`http://www.bsdi.com/server/doc/plexus.html`
Webmasters Starter Kit	`http://wsk.eit.com/wsk/doc/`
WN	`ftp://ftp.acns.nwu.edu/pub/wn/` `http://hopf.math.nwu.edu/`

Windows

HTTPS (EMWAC)	`http://emwac.ed.ac.uk/html/internet_toolchest/https/` `contents.htm`
NetMagic WebServer	`http://www.aristosoft.com/netmagic/company.html`
NetPublisher	`http://netpub.notis.com/`
Netscape	`http://www.netscape.com/`
Purveyor	`http://www.process.com/prodinfo/purvdata.htm`
WebSite	`http://website.ora.com/`
Windows httpd	`http://www.city.net/win-httpd/`

Macintosh

MacHTTP	`http://www.biap.com/` or `http://www.starnine.com/`
WebSTAR	`http://www.starnine.com/`
NetWings	`http://netwings.com/`
Netscape	`http://www.netscape.com/`
CL-HTTP (Common Lisp)	`http://www.ai.mit.edu/projects/iiip/doc/cl-http/home-page.html`
httpd4mac	`http://130.246.18.52/`

Also, Paul Hoffman maintains a list of publicly available server software on-line, listing each server's supported features, at

`http://www.proper.com/www/servers-chart.html`

TCP/IP Packages

Windows

In order to use TCP/IP under Windows, you need a Winsock-compliant stack. Winsock is an API defined by Microsoft for TCP/IP stacks, allowing you to use the same high-level software (such as servers and clients) with interchangable TCP/IP stacks. Many commercial Winsock stacks are available from vendors.

Trumpet Winsock is a shareware/commercial TCP/IP stack available for Windows. It allows a computer running Windows to interface with a network, using a modem connection or network interface. Information on Trumpet Winsock (and other Trumpet products) can be found at

`http://www.trumpet.com.au/`

Other Winsock stacks and applications are listed at The Ultimate Collection of Winsock Software:

`http://GFECnet.gmi.edu/Software/`

Windows 95 and Windows NT come with Winsock-compliant stacks supplied by Microsoft.

Macintosh

MacTCP, the Macintosh TCP/IP stack from Apple, is necessary for running any TCP/IP clients or servers (such as those discussed in this book). MacTCP is available from many mail-order houses and also comes with MacOS 7.5 and later.

A good on-line resource for MacTCP information is "MacTCP And Related Macintosh Software", maintained by Eric Behr:

```
http://www.math.niu.edu/~behr/docs/mactcp.html
```

HTTP Specifications

The IETF HTTP working group archives (including HTTP specifications) are available on-line at

```
http://www.ics.uci.edu/pub/ietf/http/
```

Linux

Linux is a freely available Unix clone for several computer platforms, most notably those based on the Intel 80386 (or later) processor. It provides a cost-effective and remarkably stable Unix environment, allowing you to take advantage of Unix-based Web servers. For more information, check any of the `comp.os.linux.*` newsgroups (especially `comp.os.linux.help` and `comp.os.linux.announce`), and check the Linux Documentation Project (LDP) at

```
http://sunsite.unc.edu/mdw/linux.html
```

LDP has published at least one book in paper form and maintains several others on line in PostScript, HTML, and a variety of other formats. The one that is available in paper format (as well as on-line) is:

Kirch, Olaf. *Linux Network Administrator's Guide.* O'Reilly and Associates, 1994.

Related to this is another book from O'Reilly, which is not part of the LDP:

Welsh, Matt, and Lar Kaufman. *Running Linux.* O'Reilly and Associates, 1995.

Also of interest is the Linux Organization, which provides an unofficial central clearing point for Linux information:

```
http://www.linux.org/
```

Web Robots

Martijn Koster maintains information about Web robots and the robot exclusion mechanism on-line at

```
http://web.nexor.co.uk/mak/doc/robots/robots.html
```

Chapter 7

HTML Verifiers

htmlchek	`http://uts.cc.utexas.edu/~churchh/htmlchek.html`
HTML Check Toolkit	`http://www.halsoft.com/html-tk/`
HTML Validation Service	`http://www.halsoft.com/html-val-svc/`
Weblint	`http://www.khoros.unm.edu/staff/neilb/weblint.html`
Weblint via the Web	`http://www.unipress.com/weblint/`
Webcheck	`http://coney.gsfc.nasa.gov/Mathews/misc/tools.html`

Link Checkers

Link Verifier

Online documentation	`http://wsk.eit.com/wsk/dist/doc/admin/webtest/verify_links.html`
Distribution (in two parts:)	`ftp://ftp.eit.com/pub/wsk/system/webtest/verify_links.tar.Z`
	`ftp://ftp.eit.com/pub/wsk/doc/webtestdoc.tar`
MOMspider	`http://www.ics.uci.edu/WebSoft/MOMspider/`
(libwww-perl also	`http://www.ics.uci.edu/WebSoft/libwww-perl/required)`
WebView (part of WebSite)	`http://website.ora.com/`

Log Analyzers
Unix

Analog	`http://www.statslab.cam.ac.uk/~sret1/analog/`
Getstats	`ftp://ftp.eit.com/pub/web.software/getstats/` `http://www.eit.com/software/getstats/getstats.html`
Getstats graphing tools	`http://www.tcp.chem.tue.nl/stats/script/` `http://infopad.eecs.berkeley.edu/stats/`
Wusage	`ftp://isis.cshl.org/pub/wusage/wusage3.2.tar.Z` `http://siva.cshl.org/wusage.html`
wwwstats	`http://www.ics.uci.edu/pub/websoft/wwwstat`
gwstats (wwwstats graphing tool)	`http://dis.cs.umass.edu/stats/gwstat.html`
WebStat	`http://www.pegasus.esprit.ec.org/people/sijben/statistics/advertisment.html`

Windows

VBStats 3.1	`http://www.city.net/win-httpd/lib/util-support/vbstat31.zip`

Macintosh

WebStat 2.3.4	`http://www.freedonia.com/utilities/`
ServerStat	`http://www.ericse.ohio-state.edu/ss.html`
cron 1.0d16	`http://gargravarr.cc.utexas.edu/cron/cron.html`

Search Engines

Harvest	`http://rd.cs.colorado.edu/harvest/`
Using WAIS with HTML	`http://www.eit.com/software/wwwwais/wwwwais.html`
"How to do a searchable database"	`http://www2.ncsu.edu/bae/people/faculty/walker/hotlist/isindex.html`
Online list of search resources.	`http://www-rlg.stanford.edu/home/jpl/websearch.html`

Chapter 8

Perl

Books

Schwartz, Randal. *Learning Perl*. O'Reilly and Associates, 1993.

Wall, Larry, and Randal L. Schwartz. *Programming Perl*. O'Reilly and Associates, 1991. With this book, you'll be writing Perl programs that actually do something useful, within an hour. Truly necessary for the pursuit of all things Perl.

Tutorials

If you don't want to buy the book, an on-line Perl tutorial can be found at

```
http://agora.leeds.ac.uk/nik/Perl/start.html
```

FTP Sites

You can get the Perl programming language by FTP from many FTP archives on the Internet. The most up-to-date version will always be at Larry Walls's FTP site (since he is the author of Perl):

```
ftp://ftp.netlabs.com/pub/outgoing/perl5.0/
```

Additionally, the University of Florida is home to one of the largest Perl archives anywhere. In this directory you can find Perl for most platforms (Unix, DOS, Mac, Windows NT, and so on):

```
ftp://ftp.cis.ufl.edu/pub/perl/src/
```

MacPerl/MacCGI Extensions

You can get MacPerl by FTP from the University of Florida site noted previously. The MacPerl CGI Extension (PCGI) is available at

```
ftp://err.ethz.ch/pub/neeri/MacPerlBeta/PCGI.sit.
hqx
```

C

Books

Kernighan, Brian W., and Dennis M. Ritchie. *The C Programming Language* (2nd ed.). Prentice-Hall, 1988. The standard reference guide for C; essential.

Tutorials

Vinit Carpenter maintains a list of available C/C++ tutorials (the "Learn C/C++ Today" page) as well as C/C++ book reviews at

```
http://vinny.csd.mu.edu/learn.html
```

Brian Brown has an on-line, in-depth C programming course on the Web at

```
http://www.cit.ac.nz/smac/cprogram/
```

FTP Sites

The GNU C compiler for Unix ("GCC") can be obtained by FTP from

```
ftp://prep.ai.mit.edu/pub/gnu/gcc-2.7.0.tar.gz
```

CGI

Specifications

The CGI 1.1 interface specification can be found on-line at

```
http://hoohoo.ncsa.uiuc.edu/cgi/interface.html
```

This is a very technically oriented description of the inner workings of the CGI interface, especially between CGI and a server.

Tutorials

A quick tutorial on CGI programming (in Unix), as well as other general CGI information, can be found on-line at

```
http://hoohoo.ncsa.uiuc.edu/cgi/overview.html
```

Brian Exelbierd has written an on-line CGI tutorial centered mainly on Perl and forms at

```
http://www.catt.ncsu.edu/users/bex/www/tutor/
index.html
```

CGI Wrappers

CGI-DOS

Information and source for the CGI-DOS CGI interface for Windows HTTPD is available at

```
http://www.achilles.net/~john/cgi-dos/
```

WinCGI

Information and source for the WinCGI CGI interface for Windows HTTPD is available at

```
http://www.city.net/win-httpd/httpddoc/wincgi.htm
```

CGI Libraries

Perl

Information and source for the cgi-lib.pl library can be found at

```
http://www.bio.cam.ac.uk/web/form.html
```

Information and source for CGI.pm, a Perl 5 CGI library, can be found at

```
http://www-genome.wi.mit.edu/ftp/pub/software/
WWW/cgi-docs.html
```

Sample CGI scripts written in Perl are available from NCSA at

```
ftp://ftp.ncsa.uiuc.edu/Web/httpd/UNIX/ncsa_httpd/
cgi/
```

C

The EIT CGI library (for C programs) is available at

```
http://wsk.eit.com/wsk/dist/doc/libcgi/libcgi.html
```

Sample CGI scripts written in C are available from the Shareware CGIs page at

```
http://128.172.69.106:8080/cgi-bin/cgis.html
```

User-supplied CGI Scripts

CGI wrap is a tool that will run a user's CGI scripts with the user ID and permissions of that user. This doesn't prevent them from writing insecure scripts, but it does limit any resulting damage. Any runaway CGI script can do only as much damage as that user can do. CGI-wrap is available at:

```
http://www.umr.edu/~cgiwrap/
```

Chapter 9

Security Books

Two good general-purpose Unix security books are:

Cheswick, William R., and Steven M. Bellovin. *Firewalls and Internet Security: Repelling the Wily Hacker.* Addison-Wesley, 1994.

Garfinkel, Simson, and Gene Spafford. *Practical Unix Security.* O'Reilly and Associates, 1991.

SSL

An overview of SSL and how Netscape uses it is on-line at

```
http://home.netscape.com/newsref/ref/index.html
```

Netscape also provides a more technical description of the protocol itself at

```
http://home.netscape.com/newsref/std/SSL.html
```

S-HTTP

Technical details on S-HTTP can be found on-line at

```
http://www.eit.com/projects/s-http
```

Chapter 10

Announcement Services

comp.infosystems. www.announce charter	`http://www.halcyon.com/grant/charter.html`
Net-Happenings	`http://www.mind.net/NET/`
Submit It!	`http://www.cen.uiuc.edu/~banister/submit-it/`
What's New	`http://www.ncsa.uiuc.edu/SDG/Software/Mosaic/Docs/ whats-new.html`

Indexing Services

Lycos	`http://lycos.cs.cmu.edu/`
Virtual Library	`http://www.w3.org/hypertext/DataSources/bySubject/Overview.html`
W3 Catalog	`http://cuiwww.unige.ch/w3catalog`
WWW Worm	`http://www.cs.colorado.edu/home/mcbryan/WWWW.html`
Yahoo	`http://www.yahoo.com/`

Lists of Mailing Lists and Newsgroups

Dartmouth College's mailing list database	`http://alpha.acast.nova.edu/listserv.html`
Indiana University list of mailing lists	`http://scwww.ucs.indiana.edu/mlarchive/`
NEW-LIST	`LISTSERV@vm1.nodak.edu`
Newsgroups Available at Oxford	`http://www.lib.ox.ac.uk/internet/news/`
PAML	`http://www.neosoft.com/internet/paml/index-index.html`
TILE.NET list of listservs	`http://www.tile.net/tile/listserv/index.html`

University of Illinois
Find-News script

`http://www.cen.uiuc.edu/cgi-bin/find-news`

Chapter 11

HTML Style Guides

Berners-Lee, Tim. "Style Guide for Online Hypertext." This is the original style guide, and mandatory reading:

`http://www.w3.org/hypertext/WWW/Provider/Style/Overview.html`

Ciolek, T. Matthew, Ed. "Quality, Guidelines & Standards for Internet Information Resources." A truly fabulous collection of resources and guidelines for maintaining information services:

`http://coombs.anu.edu.au/SpecialProj/QLTY/QltyHome.html`

————."Catalogue of Potent Truisms." Part of the link cited previously. Pointed out separately here because it's easy to overlook but well worth finding:

`http://coombs.anu.edu.au//SpecialProj/QLTY/QltyTruisms.html`

Lynch, Patrick J. "Yale C/AIM WWW Style Manual":

`http://info.med.yale.edu/caim/StyleManual_Top. HTML`

Richmond, Alan. "A Basic HTML Style Guide":

`http://guinan.gsfc.nasa.gov/Style.html`

Tilton, Eric. "Composing Good HTML." This is the style guide that eventually grew into this book. The style guide itself is still freely available on-line:

`http://www.cs.cmu.edu/~tilt/cgh/`

Chapter 12

Web Style Guides

Berners-Lee, Tim. "Ettiquette for Information Providers." See also the "Style Guide for Online Hypertext" (in the Chapter 11 references):

```
http://www.w3.org/hypertext/WWW/Provider/
Etiquette.html
```

Rees, Gareth. "Gareth's Style Guide." A short collection of handy tips for Webwide elements of style:

```
http://www.cl.cam.ac.uk/users/gdr11/style-
guide.html
```

December, John. "Challenges for Web Information Providers":

```
http://www.rpi.edu/~decemj/cmc/mag/1994/oct/webip.
html
```

Ciolek, T. Matthew, ed. "Top 10 ways to make your WWW service a flop." Collection of useful things to avoid when building your Web:

```
http://coombs.anu.edu.au/SpecialProj/QLTY/
FlopMaker.html
```

Chapter 13

HTML Specifications

The best place to find both evolving and stable HTML specifications is from the World Wide Web Consortium:

```
http://www.w3.org/hypertext/WWW/MarkUp/MarkUp.html
```

Also of interest are the IETF (Internet Engineering Task Force) HTML working group archives:

```
http://www.w3.org/hypertext/WWW/MarkUp/MarkUp.html
```

Appendices

The IETF URI working group archives are available on-line at

```
http://www.ics.uci.edu/pub/ietf/uri/
```

Postel, J. "Media Type Registration Procedure," RFC 1590:

```
http://ds.internic.net/rfc/rfc1590.txt
```

IANA listings:

```
ftp://ftp.isi.edu/in-notes/iana/assignments/media-
types/
```

Borenstein, N., and N. Freed. "MIME (Multipurpose Internet Mail Extensions) Part One: Mechanisms for Specifying and Describing the Format of Internet Message Bodies," RFC 1521:

```
http://ds.internic.net/rfc/rfc1521.txt
```

Also, a good introduction to SGML is available on-line from SoftQuad:

```
http://www.sq.com/sgmlinfo/primbody.html
```

Glossary

access control file (ACF): a mechanism used by NCSA and Windows httpd to enforce an *access policy*—that is, to enforce that users and/or hosts can or cannot access the information on your server.

access policy: who can and cannot access the information on your Web server.

authentication: proving you are who you say you are. This can involve providing a *password* or using a *public-key cryptosystem.*

authentication realm: a set of users and groups of those users. For example, you might create an authentication realm composed of all students at Carnegie-Mellon University, and another realm composed of all students at Willamette University.

basic authentication: a simple means of authenticating users on an *HTTP* server that involves sending a user name and *password* as *clear data.* Supported by most servers.

BinHex: A means of encoding Macintosh programs and data so that they may be safely transmitted over a network.

browser: see *Web browser.*

C: A popular programming language.

clear data: data that has not been encrypted; that is, data that is readable to anyone. Most data sent over the network (including *passwords* entered via telnet, and passwords sent via the *HTTP basic authentication* scheme) are sent as clear data.

client: a program that (typically) runs on a local machine and provides a user interface. It is used in conjunction with a *server*—the client fetches data from the server (at the user's request), and allows the user to use that data. Programs like Netscape, Arena, and Lynx are examples of clients.

CGI: the *Common Gateway Interface*

CGI script: a program run by an HTTP server via the *Common Gateway Interface* in order to produce a dynamic document (see Chapter 8 for more information).

Common Gateway Interface (CGI): a standardized method of calling executable programs for the creation of dynamic documents. CGI allows programs to send information to and receive information from an HTTP server (see Chapter 8 for more details).

crackers: individuals who like to "crack" (break into) computer systems, especially those on the Internet (see Chapter 9 for information about security). Not to be confused with *hackers*.

common logfile format (CLF): a common format defined by NCSA and CERN for logs of accesses made to *HTTP* servers. Servers that support CLF will produce access logs that can be analyzed by most available log analysis programs (see Chapter 7).

compress: to make a file smaller. This is often done to files so that they can be transmitted more quickly over a network. In a Unix-specific sense, this refers to the `compress` command. Files compressed with `compress` will have the file extension `.Z`, and can be uncompressed with the (aptly named) `uncompress` command. Another Unix compression program is *gzip*, which produces somewhat better results. The Mac equivalent is StuffIt, and the MS-DOS equivalent is ZIP.

corpus: a collection of documents. Specifically in a hypertext environment, this refers to a collection of files that are closely related to each other. A user's personal information consisting of several interlinked files might be considered a corpus; a research paper broken up into smaller, more manageable files might also be.

daemon: A background process that takes care of (traditionally) systemwide tasks, such as handling network connections, or performing backup or maintenance tasks. Programs that provide Internet services under Unix are usually run as daemons, and named by using the service protocol's name followed by a d, for daemon—for example, ftpd or httpd. Often pronounced dee-mon, but also as day-mon.

distributed service: A way of providing a resource over a computer network that allows for more than one machine to deliver a service through the use of standard protocols and conventions. The World Wide Web is an example of a distributed service with no central authority.

DOS: in a strict sense, this stands for Disk Operating System, and can refer to almost any *operating system.* In the general sense, this refers to *MS-DOS.*

echo: when what you type is displayed on the screen. This is usually the case. However, when you enter a *password*, it is usually not echoed (that is, not displayed on the screen), so that your password is not displayed to the person looking over your shoulder.

element: the basic building block of HTML. An element consists of a start *tag* and an end tag, and some amount of content in between (see Chapter 13 for an in-depth discussion of elements and tags).

encrypted data: data that has been encoded using some *secret*. It can only be decoded (and thus, can only be read) by others who also know the same secret. See *public-key* and *private-key cryptosystems.*

encryption: a way of encoding data so that only those people who know the right *secret* can decode (and thus, read) the data (see *public-key* and *private-key cryptosystems*).

euphonium: a brass instrument in the tuba family, played in the tenor range. It sounds like a french horn, but has the same range as the trombone (and looks like a tuba reduced by 50 percent).

filename extension: two, three, or four characters at the end of a filename to indicate what format a certain file is in. For example, a filename ending in .sit indicates a file compressed with StuffIt; a filename ending in .html indicates a file in Hypertext Markup Language.

form: forms, or fill-in forms, are the electronic version of paper forms, common on the Web to allow for user input and interaction. Although forms are created using *HTML,* they must be processed using some scripting or programming facility.

GIF: Graphics Interchange Format. A standard defined by CompuServe for sharing graphics data between platforms. GIF supports images with up to 256 colors, as well as images that have transparent backgrounds and *interlacing.* As of 1995, UNISYS (which developed the compression algorithm used in GIF) has required licensing fees for developers using the GIF standard. While this does not directly affect users (there is no fee for viewing GIFs, only for selling software that allows you to view or create GIFs), it may impact the availability of software such as Web browsers that display GIF images. An alternate standard, *PNG,* that uses a free compression algorithm, has been proposed, and may eventually replace GIF in Web browsers.

Graphical User Interface: MacOS, Microsoft Windows, and the X Windows system all provide a graphical user interface to the *operating system,* in which pictures are used instead of words to represent some elements of the OS, such as the filesystem. The Web is often called the GUI of the Internet, although many text-based, command-line-driven browser users exist for which that statement wouldn't be true.

GUI: a *Graphical User Interface*

gumbands: rubber bands.

gunzip: see *gzip*

gzip: a Unix compression program. It often provides better compression than `compress`, the most common Unix compression program. Files compressed by `gzip` have the extension `.gz`, and can be uncompressed by the `gunzip` program. (Note: some old versions of `gzip` used the `.z` extension instead.)

hackers: people who enjoy the intellectual challenge of programming; this is as opposed to *crackers,* who are people who like to break into computer systems.

host: a computer on the Internet that allows users to communicate with other hosts. Not to be confused with *servers,* which specifically serve information to *clients;* every computer on the Internet able to connect to other computers on the Internet as a host, whether it's being used as a client or a server.

HTML: the Hypertext Markup Language. See Chapter 13 for a detailed discussion.

HTTP: the Hypertext Transport Protocol. See Chapter 6 for a detailed discussion.

home page: the phrase often used to refer to the main document in an infostructure. For example, Springfield University might have a home page that lists different services and information available on its server.

infostructure: a collection of organized information (see Chapter 1 for a detailed discussion). This is a play on the word *infrastructure*.

infrastructure: the physical substrate that must be laid down in order to provide a service. The U.S. highway system is one example; the telephone network is another.

interlacing: a means of storing information so that a rough approximation of the data can be displayed fast, and then refined as more information is made available.

Internet Media Types: a standard method of representing document formats on the Web, closely related to *MIME* (see Appendix B).

Java: a programming language developed by Sun Microsystems for downloadable applications (see Appendix D for more information).

JPEG: Joint Photographic Experts Group. In common usage, JPEG refers to the image compression format developed by this group, and to the image format that uses this compression. JPEG supports millions of colors per image, and is best suited for photographic images. It uses a *lossy* compression algorithm, which means that some of the uncompressed data may not be identical to the data that was originally compressed (which is suitable for photographic images). Because of this compression, JPEG images are typically very small.

lossless: a compression algorithm that retains all of the original information. This is the standard, and is desirable for most applications (especially when you are compressing things like text, which are very sensitive to being changed). This is in direct contrast to *lossy*.

lossy: a compression algorithm where data may be discarded in order to make the compressed file even smaller. This is useful in applications such as graphic images, where minor changes in the data are compensated for by the surrounding information. *JPEG* is a good example of lossy compression, and works very well. While data may be lost, it is imperceptible to the human eye. This is in contrast to *lossless* compression.

MacOS: the Macintosh *operating system.*

MS-DOS: Microsoft's *operating system.* It is often used in conjunction with *Windows.*

MIME: *Multipart Internet Mail Extension.*

Multipart Internet Mail Extension (MIME): A standard method of representing document formats on the Internet. (See Appendix B).

NCSA/CERN common logfile format: see *common logfile format.*

nonlossy: same as *lossless.*

OS: operating system. The software that provides basic services for your computer and for the applications you run on it. Unix, MS-DOS, and MacOS are good examples of operating systems.

parsing: the means by which a computer interprets instructions to it. HTML must be parsed by browsers, for example, before it can be displayed.

password: a *secret* known to a user. The user invokes his or her password in order to *authenticate* him- or herself to a computer.

PC: personal computer.

PDF: portable document format (see Chapter 2 for more information).

Perl: a popular programming language.

PNG: Portable Network Graphics. A standard developed in 1995 to replace the *GIF* format. PNG supports graphic images with millions of colors, like *JPEG,* but uses *lossless* compression. See `http://quest.jpl.nasa.gov/Info-ZIP/people/greg/greg_png.html` for more details.

private key cryptosystem: an *encryption* system based on a single, shared *secret.* The secret is used to encrypt a message, and the same secret is used by the receiver to decrypt the message. These systems are typically faster than *public-key cryptosystems*. The question is how to transmit the secret securely over the network.

public-key cryptosystem: an *encryption* system based on two related *secrets*, a public key and a private key. The private key is known only to the owner of the key, while the public key can be widely distributed. Any message encrypted with a public key can only be decrypted with the corresponding private key, and vice versa. Although these systems are typically slower than *private-key cryptosystems*, they have two useful applications. The first is for transmitting the secret used by a private key system—the secret can be encrypted with the recipient's public key, and only decrypted with the corresponding private key. The second is for *authenticating* materials—materials can be encrypted with a private key, and only decrypted with the corresponding public key. In this way, recipients can be assured of a message's source.

recursion: see *recursion*.

redd: to clean up; for example, a harried computer scientist involved in a bizarre rubber band explosion might have to "redd up them gumbands" now decorating her office.

secret: some piece of information used in *encryption*. The secret is either used to encrypt or decrypt a message, and only those people who have the secret are able to read the encrypted data.

server: a program that (typically) runs on a remote machine, and contains useful information. It is used in conjunction with a *client*—when the client requests data from the server, the server provides it. Since the server does not need to provide an interactive user interface, it can serve many more users at once. NCSA httpd, Windows httpd, and MacHTTP are examples of servers.

S-HTTP: Secure *HTTP*. See Chapter 9 for a detailed discussion.

SGML: Standard Generalized Markup Language.

SSL: Secure Sockets Layer. See Chapter 9 for a detailed discussion.

StuffIt: A popular Macintosh *compression* method.

tag: the embedded commands in HTML (see Chapter 13).

tar: a common Unix program for creating tape archives. While the phrase tape archive is no longer accurate, tape archive files (called tar files) are often distributed across the Internet as a way to ship entire software distributions easily.

TCP/IP: Transmission Control Protocol/Internet Protocol

TLA: Three-Letter Acronym.

uncompress: to reverse the effects of compression (see *compress*).

Universal Resource Locator (URL): An address for a piece of information available via the Internet. Used by Web browsers to uniquely identify and locate documents and other information sources (such as images or sound files) on the Internet (see Appendix A).

Unix: a popular *operating system* for workstations and minicomputers.

untar: to extract files from a Unix tape archive (see *tar*).

VRML: Virtual Reality Markup Language. See Appendix D.

W3C: see *World Wide Web Consortium*. Web browser: a *client* program that can access data made available through *HTTP servers* located on the Internet. Usually allows users to follow hyperlinks and display or interpret *HTML*. A browser may also refer to any program that allows you to browse or explore other types of information, such as a VRML browser that interprets and displays *VRML*.

white space: spaces, tabs, or carriages returns. Usually this term implies several spaces and/or tabs in a row. They are referred to collectively as white space because, on the printed page, they are simply blank (or white) space.

Windows: Microsoft's graphical user interface that lies on top of *MS-DOS*. Windows 95 and Windows NT are *operating systems* in their own right.

Winsock: strictly speaking, a standard for *Windows*-based programs to use *TCP/IP* services. In a more general sense, this refers to a program that provides those services (such as Trumpet Winsock) to client and server programs (such as Netscape or Windows httpd).

World Wide Web Consortium: an industry consortium that oversees and facilitates the creation of Web-related standards (such as *HTML* and *HTTP*).

workstation: generally speaking, a powerful computer that sits on a desk.

WYSIWYG: What You See Is What You Get. This model promises that the screen will display your document in a way that is identical (within the bounds of your screen's display capabilities) to any other rendition of your document, be it on paper or on another's screen.

ZIP: a popular *compression* method for *MS-DOS*. Files compressed in the ZIP format will have the file extension `.ZIP`.

Index

533